Sisters in the Brotherhoods

Palgrave Studies in Oral History

Series Editors: Linda Shopes and Bruce M. Stave

Sisters in the Brotherhoods

Working Women Organizing for Equality in New York City

Jane LaTour

*For Dan —
with gratitude
and appreciation —
In solidarity
and
friendship!
Jane LaTour*

palgrave
macmillan

SISTERS IN THE BROTHERHOODS
Copyright © Jane LaTour, 2008.

All rights reserved.

First published in hardcover in 2008 by PALGRAVE MACMILLAN® in the United States—a division of St. Martin's Press LLC, 175 Fifth Avenue, New York, NY 10010.

Where this book is distributed in the UK, Europe and the rest of the world, this is by Palgrave Macmillan, a division of Macmillan Publishers Limited, registered in England, company number 785998, of Houndmills, Basingstoke, Hampshire RG21 6XS.

Palgrave Macmillan is the global academic imprint of the above companies and has companies and representatives throughout the world.

Palgrave® and Macmillan® are registered trademarks in the United States, the United Kingdom, Europe and other countries.

ISBN: 978–0–230–61918–0

Library of Congress Cataloging-in-Publication Data

LaTour, Jane.
    Sisters in the brotherhoods : working women organizing for equality in
  New York City / Jane LaTour.
       p. cm.—(Palgrave studies in oral history)
    Includes bibliographical references and index.
    ISBN 1–4039–6758–X
      1. Women labor leaders—New York (State)—New York—Biography. I. Title.
HD6508.5.L37 2008
331.4′7809227471—dc22   2007052850

A catalogue record for this book is available from the British Library.

Design by Newgen Imaging Systems (P) Ltd., Chennai, India.

First PALGRAVE MACMILLAN paperback edition: August 2009

10 9 8 7 6 5 4 3 2 1

Printed in the United States of America.

Friends, when we come before you to advocate the Cause popularly termed "Women's Rights," we simply ask that woman be not wronged. We ask for her justice & equality—not favor & superiority—the rights and privileges her humanity charters to her equally with man... Create a public sentiment, that shall open wide to woman, the doors of all our mechanic shops, stores, & offices, & bid her go in & work side by side with her brother man, paying to her equal wages for equal services rendered...

—Susan B. Anthony, 1854

Contents

Part Six   Moving Forward

Illustrations

Series Editors' Foreword

It is the personal voice that gives oral history much of its power: narrators are able to speak publicly and for the record about experiences that have been ignored or denied; equally, listeners—or here, readers—get firsthand knowledge of worlds they are unlikely to encounter in their everyday lives. Both are empowered. Certainly this is the case for the women who speak in Jane LaTour's *Sisters in the Brotherhoods: Working Women Organizing for Equality in New York City*. These are gutsy, funny, impassioned women who took seriously the feminist commitment to equality by daring to enter the male bastion of skilled blue-collar work; who rose to the challenges of both hard physical labor on the job and the bruising sexism of male co-workers and union politics; who stuck with it and achieved success as construction workers, stationary engineers, firefighters, communications workers, and transit workers. Moreover, we hope that it is also the case for those who read their stories, as they learn about—and perhaps empathize with—a group of women workers frequently ignored in discussions of women's workplace gains.

Yet on its own the personal voice is necessarily limited; it requires the voice of the historian to give it context and depth, to draw out meaning. Jane LaTour, herself not unfamiliar with blue-collar labor and a dedicated union educator, plays this role, locating these individual stories within the framework of union policy and politics, feminist activism and ideology, and on-the-job social relationships. *Sisters in the Brotherhoods* tells us a good deal about labor history in the second half of the twentieth century. It also articulates a vision of gender equality and blue-collar activism and suggests that change, however difficult and slow and often achieved at great personal cost, is nonetheless possible.

For both the voices it brings forth and the power and meaning of what these voices tell us, we are pleased to include *Sisters in the Brotherhoods* in the series Palgrave Studies in Oral History, designed to bring oral history interviews out of the archives and into the hands of students, educators, scholars, and the reading public. Volumes in the series are deeply grounded in interviews and also present those interviews in ways that aid readers to more fully appreciate their historical significance and cultural meaning. The series also includes work that approaches oral history more theoretically, as a point of departure for an exploration of broad questions of cultural production and representation.

LINDA SHOPES
BRUCE M. STAVE

Preface

Younger people may take it for granted, but one of the most striking urban contrasts between today and 1964—when the word "sex" was included in the Civil Rights Act—is all of the women working in jobs their mothers never could have held. Walk down the street, you run into female letter carriers delivering baskets of mail. Hop on a bus and your driver could well be a woman; venture below in the subway and the underground is full of female transit workers, conducting, cleaning, operating, and repairing the subway cars. Try to beat the fare and you could be arrested by a female police officer. Mostly, these are blue-collar union jobs, in the public sector with good pay scales, health benefits, vacation days, and pensions.

Yet a city walker could venture down many streets and still not find women working in a whole array of blue-collar jobs. Nationally, women in construction work make up less than 2 percent of the industry's total workforce.[1] In New York City, the share of women firefighters is even smaller: only 30 women out of a force of 11,500. The walker would also have to wait a long time to see a woman driving the local telephone company's installation and repair truck, or see a woman working in one of the electrical power utility's "manholes."

Starting in the mid-1970s, unaware of how long and twisting a road they would have to travel, and buoyed by the success of the women's movement in other fields, young women took up the challenge of breaking down gender barriers in traditionally male, blue-collar jobs. They camped out on sidewalks and competed with men for applications to apprenticeship programs. The pioneers who accepted these challenges made history. But they're not *in* history. They're victims of what the historian Nancy MacLean has referred to as a form of "historical amnesia."[2] The lack of attention to the topic led one pioneering tradeswoman to a rueful observation: "I don't know if anyone remembers that there are women doing these jobs."[3]

Many blue-collar arenas remain contested terrain for females. Women still struggle to get training, to get jobs, and to secure a harassment-free workplace. The women working in "nontraditional" skilled blue-collar occupations such as firefighting, law enforcement, maintenance, the mechanical trades, transportation, and construction continue to face daunting obstacles. These obstacles in turn contribute to keeping their numbers low and their lives difficult. Despite the efforts of the pioneering generation, females still enter these jobs one by one and two by two and only against great odds do they remain there.

These oral histories explore the achievements of the women who made history simply by going to work every day. And who by organizing to gain that right for other women created a genuine "right to work" movement. Their embattled presence challenged deeply held notions of gender in the workplace. As the historian David Witwer wrote, "The oral histories provide a stunning account of the vicious and unrelenting opposition that these women met. They go far towards explaining why, despite the passage of time, their numbers remain nominal."[4]

Each woman in *Sisters* has survived the rigors of working in a nontraditional, blue-collar job. Each has experienced the benefits of bigger paychecks and enjoyed the rewards that attract men to these occupations—the pride of building something you can see—or the satisfaction of saving someone's life. Each woman has contributed to the ongoing efforts to preserve and widen this career path for other women. They don't see themselves as superwomen. But each one has been tested and toughened. Their stories form the heart of this book.

The oral history project began as a way to capture the experiences of women who were organizing on their jobs and within their unions. I saw it as a way of providing models for other women in similar situations. I also viewed it as an antidote to the sense of helplessness experienced by women who were isolated and felt overwhelmed—who believed that they couldn't organize to change conditions until their numbers changed. As the director of the Women's Project of the Brooklyn-based Association for Union Democracy, I had contact with many women who *were* organizing. I decided to document these experiences.

My questions focused on the set of circumstances that drew them to the work, how they got their training, their experiences on the job and in their unions, their sources of support, and how they organized to try to change conditions for themselves and others. The first interviews were conducted in 1989 and 1990. What began as a simple idea for a brochure grew into a much larger project. I continued to conduct oral history interviews throughout the 1990s. In 2000, Professor David Witwer invited me to participate on a panel, "The Re-gendering of Labor," at the North American Labor History Conference. That paper—"Live! From New York: Women Construction Workers in Their Own Words"—and its subsequent publication in *Labor History* gave birth to the idea for the book.[5]

As soon as I began work on the manuscript, I realized I would need to conduct additional interviews. This process continued throughout 2006. It could continue indefinitely. But in the interest of brevity, the documentation project remains incomplete. Many voices are missing from the record. My attempt to locate additional participants was given an assist by some of the women in the project. Some attempts were unsuccessful. For their own reasons, some women chose to keep their stories to themselves. I am indebted to the women who led me to others in the interest of filling out the story that *Sisters* attempts to tell.

This is the story of what it was like to go first: to enter jobs that demanded physical and mental courage, both because of the gender-breaking nature of the work and because of the resistance women encountered as they entered this new territory. It is largely about a particular time in a particular place—New York City in the late 1970s and early 1980s. New York City is often idealized as a social democratic city, a bastion of liberalism and progressive thought. Yet the twin features of industry-wide corruption in the construction trades and a long history of racial exclusion within the building trades unions, among others, have acted as formidable, if not unique, Big Apple barriers.

However, construction is not the city's only hostile territory. The uniformed services offer another example of what can only be labeled backward thinking and practice in a city widely celebrated as forward thinking. And the utilities industry is still another resistant sector when it comes to including women in the full-range of benefits including safe, harassment-free worksites. The book concludes with a look at the current situation facing women in nontraditional jobs—the younger women who are taking up where the pioneers left off. *Sisters* remains a work in progress—with new chapters being written every day.

My own compelling interest in nontraditional work began on assembly lines in Philadelphia and later in Newark, New Jersey. For seven years, I experienced the strict division of jobs by gender. Despite changes in the law, tradition held women in place in every factory where I worked, from a printing plant to pharmaceutical and electronic assembly lines. My blue-collar apprenticeship included a couple of years as a building superintendent and apartment renovator/painter. I got used to the frequent comments telling me, "That's a nice job—for a girl!"

I went back to college and served as a teaching assistant for the late Wells Keddie, Labor Studies Professor at Rutgers University. One day, the sociologist John Leggett asked me whether

I knew that thousands of women had worked during World War II in shipyards and were called "Rosie the Riveters." It was 1976 and I had no idea. But soon after, captivated by the topic, I carried out my first oral history project—a paper for Professor Ruth Matthews—interviewing women working at the Ford Motor Company's auto assembly plant in Linden, New Jersey. I went into the factory, toured the continuous-motion assembly production lines, sat in the lunchroom and then in their homes and heard the stories of these working-class women.

A couple of years later, armed with a little more knowledge, I worked at United Parcel Service, UPS, as a sorter on the night shift to supplement my income as a labor educator. I watched the women who came through the huge warehouse in Edison, New Jersey, after they had parked their 18-wheelers in the bays. Evelyn Barnes was one of those women. Short and savvy, she educated me about the life of a "woman on the move" and what it was like to be a trucker for one of the country's premier package carriers. She opened up my eyes to the very small number of women driving the big rigs and shared stories that gave me insights into the difficulties they faced on the road.

As members of the Teamsters, some of us attended the monthly union meetings and sat together. The women truckers, given an opportunity to get out of their baggy brown uniforms, came all dressed up, with make-up, high heels, and sometimes wearing sheer blouses. Still, the men conducting the meetings for Local 177 never got past addressing everyone present as "brothers." We never heard the word "sisters." It seemed strange. Shortly after we started having conversations, we decided that women needed to organize. We prevailed on Mario Perrucci, the head of our local, who would become a Teamster International vice president, to give the union's blessing to our efforts. Evelyn and others put up signs encouraging the women to leave their husbands at home on Sunday in charge of child care and come to the first meeting of the Women's Committee, held right after our regular union meeting. Tremendous effort went into the preparations. When Mario came by to greet the women, his message was that females were facing the same issues as all the other members of Local 177. He failed to see that while the issues were the same—there were *other* issues that especially impacted the women drivers—and affected their retention rates and even their recruitment into these high-paying jobs.

Along with the perspective from the shop floor, teaching in blue-collar academia—the Harry Van Arsdale Jr. Labor Center of Empire State College—gave me additional insights into the lives of women working in nontraditional, blue-collar jobs. As a labor studies professor, it was my job to teach electrical apprentices—who were of course overwhelmingly male. It quickly became apparent that if there was one female in a classroom—or two—they would be completely unwilling to discuss any issue related to gender. Professor Julia Willebrand invited me to present a labor history play to her English class, designed to allow women to get to know each other and to experience a certain level of comfort in the classroom. I later invited her class to sit in on my class—composed of all male students—for a discussion of women and work based on readings from Stud's Terkel's oral history, *Working*.

Shortly after that tumultuous evening, one female apprentice described the young men in my class as "animals." "They just have very different experiences and different expectations," I explained. This book includes stories of men who did act in vile ways toward the women on the job. But it also includes stories of men who went out of their way to teach the women their trades and helped them to gain a solid footing in a foreign environment. Ultimately, my hope is that the book serves as a bridge, not a gauntlet. It represents an ongoing effort to engage others on this topic and to understand the differences and the shared worlds that men and women inhabit at work.

Early on in the process, my friend Elaine Harger taught me how to make a crazy-quilt square. Quilting became my metaphor for putting this book together. It seemed the perfect image for the process—planning a pattern for each chapter—then choosing the proper pieces to stitch together to create the design. Thousands of stitches later, each separate square—a chapter—gets sewn together to make a whole. The stories in *Sisters* seek to convey the messy complexity of the worlds these women inhabited on the job and in their unions. They show the fine line the pioneers had to tread between reacting to the hostility and ostracism they faced and holding on to their hard-earned "insider" status. They show the reluctance on the part of the women to complain for fear of being seen as whiners, alongside their fear of being blacklisted by their unions for registering an official complaint. Loyalty to the union as an institution runs deep within the brotherhoods. Their stories might seem as if they've been exhumed from a time capsule. But together, they contribute to a fuller awareness of a movement that changed lives—the lives of males and females alike.

Although these stories contain many individual triumphs, the point is not to create a mood of triumphalism. The labor historian Nelson Lichtenstein has written that racial and gender equality, a once radical demand, is now "an elemental code of conduct."[6] The oral histories that unfold in these pages demonstrate the deep divide that still exists between rights and reality; between promise and performance.

Much of the history in these pages seems to express the theme in Joni Mitchell's song, "The Circle Game." Round and round these women went, year after year, in their efforts to make their unions, workplaces, and employers responsive to their presence. Yet, finally, there is progress. Despite the fact that time seems to be traveling backward on many fronts—witness recent U.S. Supreme Court cases—progress is being made on the blue-collar frontier, albeit slowly and incrementally. As carpenter Linnea Nelson says, "Now we need to go forward rather than round."[7]

Oral history is one tool to excavate the lives of working women. The prize-winning historian Taylor Branch has observed that cultures preserve in libraries what they're comfortable with. "To get race relations, you have to do interviews," he said.[8] Similarly, interviews are required for bringing out the truth of the civil rights struggle of the blue-collar women pioneers.

I have tried faithfully to stick to the meaning communicated by each participant in this oral history project. I am also aware of the shadow that my long-term role as an advocate for women casts on the construction of my interpretations and conclusions. I have made an effort to bring other voices into the narrative from different sources, including sociologists, historians, and the voices of expert allies who made their own contributions to this history, alongside memoirs and archival documents. In saying this, I do not seek to absolve myself of the inevitable shortcomings in these pages.

One day, while working as an archivist at the Robert F. Wagner Labor Archives at New York University, Yael Goldberg, a young apprentice carpenter, came to use the collection of United Tradeswomen for a research paper at Hunter College. I sat across from her as she examined the fliers, minutes, and programs that together, document the rich history of this grassroots organization founded by and for tradeswomen. She looked at me and asked, "Why don't we know about this?"

The point of sharing this knowledge is to reduce the isolation and invisibility of the women who went first into uncharted, difficult, and ultimately—for the most part—rewarding territory. It's not simply a matter of celebration. Other women need to know about them. Most still remain within narrow occupational limits. Moreover, poverty—what used to be called "the feminization of poverty"—has them and their children in a ferocious grip. They need good jobs that offer benefits, career ladders, and impart real skills. Yet few of the millions inside the lower-class female job ghetto know about those who've escaped, survived, and even prospered—albeit not without paying the inevitable price of all barrier-breakers. *Sisters in the Brotherhoods* is their story.

Abbreviations

Association for Union Democracy (AUD)

Comprehensive Employment and Training Act (CETA)

Coalition of Labor Union Women (CLUW)

Communications Workers of America (CWA)

Department of Labor (DOL)

Division of School Facilities (DSF)

Equal Employment Opportunity Commission (EEOC)

Equal Rights Amendment (ERA)

Health and Hospitals Corporation (HHC)

International Brotherhood of Electrical Workers (IBEW)

International Ladies' Garment Workers Union (ILGWU)

International Union of Operating Engineers (IUOE)

Marine Engineers Benevolent Association (MEBA)

Nontraditional Employment for Women (NEW)

Neural Linguistic Programming (NLP)

National Organization for Women (NOW)

Organized Crime Task Force (OCTF)

Port Authority (PA)

Policewomen's Endowment Association (PEA)

Recruitment Training Program (RTP)

Transport Workers Union (TWU)

Urban Development Corporation (UDC)

United Firefighters Association (UFA)

United Tradeswomen (UT)

United Women Firefighters (UWF)

Women Electricians (WE)

Women in Apprenticeship Program (WAP)

Women in the Trades (WITT)

White Lung Association (WLA)

Women Office Workers (WOW)

Women's Trade Union League (WTUL)

PART ONE

Writing Tradeswomen into History

ONE

Rosie's Daughters

As students of the mysteries of our trade
We uncovered the phasing of our cycles:
           one falling in defeat signaled
          another
                rising in triumph
and so we carried each other
through the sine waves of emotion
re-charging each other's determination
with stored up capacitance for
            derision
            shunning
            loneliness.

                —*Past the Finish Line,* Susan Eisenberg

Strike up a conversation on the topic of women working in nontraditional, blue-collar jobs and often as not, the first association is with World War II's Rosie the Riveter. Between 1940 and 1944, the number of women working not only doubled, but also the percentage of jobs "acceptable" for a woman increased from 29 to 85 percent. The federal government threw open the factory gates to American women with an unprecedented and hearty welcome. What choice was there? The German U-boat campaign and security concerns made immigrants almost impossible to obtain.[1]

As part of the recruitment campaign, Rose Will Monroe from Pulaski County, Kentucky—a widowed mother of two—was picked by the movie idol Walter Pigeon to star in a promotional film. Monroe was the genuine article. She was actually working as a riveter at the giant Ford plant at Willow Run, Michigan.[2] A song, "Rosie the Riveter," and the famous poster had preceded her. Then came an iconic Norman Rockwell cover for the May 29, 1943 *Saturday Evening Post.* It shows a tall, husky Rosie, taking a lunch break, insouciantly eating a ham sandwich. As Rockwell saw her, Rosie is clearly a blue-collar aristocrat, with upswept hair, overalls, and goggles. She casually balances her three-foot rivet gun on one knee and her lunch bucket on the other—all against the background of the American flag. Underneath her feet lies a trampled copy of Hitler's *Mein Kampf.* And appropriately so…America was right to flaunt the contrast between the opportunities available to women in democratic America and the gender rigidities of Nazi Germany—whose idea of women's roles remained confined to the notorious K's—*Kinder, Kirche, Kuche*—raising children, praying to God, and cooking meals for the family.[3]

When Rose Monroe died in 1997, unlike the overwhelming majority of her wartime factory sisters, she'd had a rich blue-collar career—as a taxi driver, a pilot—at one point, she even owned a construction company. She was immediately recognized as a hero, and in her hometown, a section of the Pulaski highway was renamed after her. Moreover, the Kentucky Colonels held a memorial service in her honor. The memorial committee tried to find real-life Rosies to share the honors. But they said they couldn't find any. "It's like the World War II veterans. We're seeing so many of them pass away," Winona Padgett, a club spokeswoman, told the Associated Press. So they held a beauty pageant and fashion show instead. The Colonels apparently never thought of looking for Rosie's present day, blue-collar daughters—and honoring them.[4]

Why not? Why is the whole generation of blue-collar women who were emboldened by the post-1960s civil rights movement to enter male-dominated blue-collar occupations so little recognized, so little mentioned—and when they are—so often maligned? True, their work didn't help defeat Hitler. But the contributions they made to the struggle for equality of opportunity should be recognized for what is: they are part of the honorable tradition of the fight for fairness and inclusion in the American workplace.[5] And shouldn't Rosie's daughters get some credit for swimming against the current? The federal government served as a powerful ally for blue-collar women during World War II. But in the postwar battle for equal job opportunity, it was often appropriate to ask government officials responsible for enforcement of the all-important Title VII, "Which side are you on?"

In the history of the post-Civil Rights Act feminist movement, there were no federal government posters, campaigns, songs, or national magazine covers celebrating women's fight for equality in the blue-collar trades. To move the government forward on affirmative action generally required a lawsuit. In addition, if the court decision proved favorable, there were more suits and appeals to make sure the court order was enforced.

Much of the action by feminist organizations was a kind of war of position of this sort. But without the action of dedicated feminist organizations, both local and national, the small but genuine gains that have been made in the last quarter century would surely not have been maintained.

Perhaps there would be more respect if there were simply greater historical understanding. What's not often understood is the interplay between feminist organizations on the outside and women blue-collar pioneers organizing on the job site. As Alice Kessler-Harris has written, the second wave of feminism eventually earned the opprobrium of being a largely white, middle-class movement.[6] But the early history of that movement was much more variegated and working-class women were a vital part of it. In fact, the big difference between the World War II generation of blue-collar women and their 1970s successors is that the 1940s generation was the product of government policies, while the 1970s generation was feminist-led.[7]

First There Were Feminists

Pioneering 1970s feminists Rosalyn Baxandall and Phyllis Chesler offer first-person testimony to the transformation in women's lives brought about by that movement. It was a "visionary, empowering, unbelievable moment in time," said Chesler. "We opened our doors at the same magical moment, like Norah in Ibsen's play, and said good-by to all that. We found each other on the streets and the cafes, in the demonstrations, on the marches. It was quite unbelievable."[8]

This was the movement that challenged a world where "all the experts were male." Where "sisterhood was powerful"—or could be—where women met in small consciousness-raising or "CR" groups to upend their lives. "We had been destined for lesser lives," said Phyllis Chesler. And then "the world split open."[9]

The women's movement was built by individuals coming together around a common mission. They took action on many fronts—in the media, in the universities, in offices, in government agencies, and in their unions—to transform their worlds. Rosalyn Baxandall refutes the common assertion made by critics that all the action at that point was limited to white, upper middle-class women. She described the momentum to organize that spread throughout offices where women were encamped, doing tasks that included much more than typing.

> Beginning in 1969, women clericals, first in publishing, then in advertising, then in media and finance, then at Barnard, began organizing. There was an umbrella group called Women Office Workers (WOW) and later, that group affiliated with District 65, but they kept their identity as a female caucus. I remember one meeting…in 1969, a conference of clericals, and 300 secretaries came. At this time, male clericals in 1968 made $9,700 a year and females made $6,000 a year…[Female] office workers were objecting to dress codes that decreed no pants, doing the boss's personal favors, like cutting his hair and shopping for his gifts, and generally being patronized and treated like sex objects in underpaid, dead end jobs with no benefits.[10]

Former legal secretary Margie Alpert was a leader in this movement. In the mid-1970s, she was hard at work organizing clericals in the publishing industry for District 65. In 1976, she led a workshop on the essentials of organizing for WOW, just one of many groups across the country set up to promote collective action by women in offices.[11] But what should action aim at?

At the First New York Women's Trade Union Conference in January 1974, Alpert made an argument about male-female pay differentials and the power of a union to boost women's paychecks: "There is no God-given law that says a secretary is making 'good money' when she earns $180 a week while a sanitation worker in New York City is earning entry-level pay at considerably over that. The difference is clear. He's organized in a powerful union. We are hopelessly divided in most offices. Women need unions!"[12] But another argument was looming. Why were all the sanitation workers in New York City men?

As women began to shape their own, more expansive futures, new targets began to emerge. Jobs outside the traditional boundaries of women's work offered another source of employment. Slowly, the appeal of stepping into a blue-collar job with a big paycheck, benefits, and the opportunity to learn a skill began to grow. Yet when women began to apply for these jobs, they faced resistance. It would require a complete failure of imagination to suppose that women could gain entrance to these prized, high-paid, skilled craft jobs, some of them handed down from father to son throughout history, and *not* meet up with resistance.

However, many young women had come to believe in the ideal of "equality in true partnership with men."[13] After all, the law was on their side—theoretically it was illegal to discriminate because of gender. And time was on their side: they were young and bold—bold enough to survive on this new frontier.

Some took it on as a bet; some learned of the opportunity by chance; and some had nursed a dream of doing something different—like Ronnie Sandler. She was one of the women to gain entrée even before the larger push took place in 1978. But she had allies in her effort to earn a living with a hammer in her hands.

Fear on the New Frontier

Ronnie Sandler was one of the tens of thousands of women who entered the blue-collar, skilled jobs because of the Civil Rights Act of 1964 and its Title VII provisions for equal employment.[14] Perhaps Sandler was genetically coded to become a nonconformist and an activist. She grew up hearing stories about her maternal grandmother, Doris Greenburg Strum, who worked with Margaret Sanger, the pioneering advocate for birth control.[15] Like many of the pioneering tradeswomen, she linked her fortunes to both the earlier generation of blue-collar feminists and those of the contemporary women's movement.

Coming of age in northern New England, Ronnie Sandler wasn't interested in taking the traditional home economics class for female high school students. She liked to work with her hands and shop class offered that opportunity. Sent to the assistant principal's office for being obstinate, she got the message: "girls don't take shop."

"Women who are my age...we had choices of being a teacher, a nurse, or a secretary," said Sandler.[16] A college degree did prepare her to teach. But in 1971, she set out on a different course. Sandler became a carpenter. In the mid-seventies, she made history in Michigan. That story had its origins in Detroit:

> When I became a trailblazer and really aware of what I was doing was in 1976, in getting into the United Brotherhood of Carpenters and Joiners of America. I was the first woman to be in any of the trades' unions in the state of Michigan.

On her first attempt to join the union, Sandler got the runaround. The Detroit District Council of Carpenters told her to get a "letter of intent" from a contractor. But she was familiar with this ruse: "Even though I was from New Hampshire where there are not many unions, I knew that the first thing they would ask me on a job site was, 'where's your union card?' *before* I could get a letter of intent to hire. So I sort of gave that up."

Fate intervened in the form of a veteran trade union feminist. "I was in Michigan and I was working on the NOW national conference—it happened to be in Detroit that year—from the office of a woman by the name of Edie Van Horn, who was fairly high up in the UAW," said Sandler. "In the seventies, the UAW controlled Michigan. It was much more powerful than unions are today. Edie was an amazing woman. She had worked on the [auto assembly] line during World War II and had moved through the ranks and she was everybody's idol. She was just this wonderful older woman who was very politically involved in women's issues and [was one of the women who] moved the UAW to back the Equal Rights Amendment and to do a lot of things that were very forward-thinking. When I first met her, I told her I was a carpenter. She said to me, 'You're *my* idol! We've been trying to get a woman into the trades' unions. Would you be interested?'"

Calling the carpenters and dropping the name of a UAW official opened union doors. But, at the time, the $200 initiation fee was out of reach for Sandler. "I happened to be having lunch with Edie that day," she recalled. "Edie, I'll never forget this, she pulled out her wallet and counted out $200. I said, 'I can't take this.' She said, 'If you can't give it to your sisters, who can you give it to?' It was just the most incredible thing that's ever happened to me...So I went down to the District Council, got my card, and got into the union. That was the point I realized: I'm not doing this just for myself. I'm doing this for my sisters. I'm doing this for the women who come behind me."

Sandler's story as a trailblazing tradeswoman segued onto ominously silent job sites. But although at first she was shunned by her fellow carpenters, eventually she went on to a successful career. It zigzagged between the west coast and the east, between working with her tools and designing programs to empower women in the skilled trades.

In addition to the UAW's Edie Van Horn, Sandler turned to other feminists in Michigan for support. Since, once she joined the Carpenters union, her troubles were only beginning. Like the other pioneers who followed her, she had to fight the class war *and* the gender war—every day. "Let me tell you," she recalled. "It was the most difficult thing I've ever done in my life. It was 1976. It was before the Carter regulations. I was on a job of 200. I was the only woman. I knew the guys in my crew, but I didn't know anybody else. There were times that I was scared—physically scared."

Although the work was interesting and she learned a lot on the job, the emotional toll was difficult: "One of the things that happened when I got into the union was, I would come home from these horrible days...and I would talk to my friends, who were guidance counselors or therapists. They would go: 'Oh yes! We understand.' But they had no idea what I was talking about."

I realized that I needed to talk to other women who had the same experience. I spent four months in Detroit, Michigan, trying to find one other woman who worked in the trades. I finally discovered a woman who worked for GM in one of their shops as a tradesperson. That was literally the start of Women in Skilled Trades in Detroit. It didn't start from an activist point of view. It started from a real need for me to be able to talk to somebody else and...really get it...Not be a therapist and tell me: "Yes, yes." But really get it! Oh yeah, absolutely. Those fuckers! You know what happened to me?...That's where *that* really came from.

While working at her trade, Sandler stayed active with the women's movement. She participated in the Michigan Statewide Taskforce on Sexual Harassment. Through this group, she met women from the Office of Women and Work in the Michigan Department of Labor. This networking led to a second initiative.

"One night, Sandy—one of these women from that office—called and asked: 'If you were going to train women to get into the trades, how would you do it?'" recalled Sandler. "I said, 'I'd take all of the excuses I've ever heard about why women can't do it, starting with: They don't want to. They're not strong enough. They don't know anything. And I would answer each of those questions, one by one. I'd do physical conditioning. I'd teach them how to be assertive, because you need to do that on the job. I'd teach them some skills.' We talked for about two and a half hours. About two months later, Sandy called me up. She said, 'Remember that night I asked you about this? Well, I wrote up a proposal and got it funded through CETA (Comprehensive Employment and Training Act). Would you be interested in running the program?'"

"That was the start of the Step-Up Program," said Sandler. It was run out of the Community College in Lansing, Michigan, which did all the apprenticeship programs at the time. The position of director required a journey-level union card and some background in adult education. Ronnie Sandler had the perfect resume.

"Not for Themselves Alone"

Women today enjoy many gains won by the barrier-busting advocates for gender equality. Little girls grow up thinking they might pilot an airplane; or travel into space like astronauts Mae Jemison or Sally Ride, conquer scientific frontiers; play professional basketball on the court at Madison Square Garden; or argue a case before the U.S. Supreme Court. Report on that Court—or the N.B.A.—for *The New York Times*.

To get to this point—women had to organize. The Women's Caucus at *The New York Times* began its collective efforts in 1972. On April 11, 1977, a federal judge signed off on the class-action suit—*Boylan v. The New York Times*—that led to an affirmative action plan for the newspaper.[17] This had major consequences—for women at the *Times*—and beyond. People tend to know about these struggles—much more so than all of the organizing that has taken place by—and on behalf of—women in the blue-collar, skilled jobs.

As women began to compete for "men's jobs" in fields far outside the accepted cultural norms, many recognized early on that, in order to survive, they needed to do more than just show up for work. From the start, this effort—to find a place for females in the nation's steel plants, coal mines, skilled trades, police forces, and fire houses—was conducted on contested terrain. To survive, the women had to organize.[18]

Although the government put forward a very public appeal for women to volunteer for skilled "men's jobs" during World War II, the second generation—despite government support—never benefitted from this kind of a broad public argument put forth on their behalf that would bolster their claim to do this work. The upshot was that from the beginning, women who sought these jobs were regarded as oddities—or—in the words of one carpenter, "like a creature with two heads."[19]

Although Ronnie Sandler was able to gain entrance to the carpenters union in 1976, the real momentum for women to enter the trades took place a couple of years later. A necessary boost came from feminist organizations. In 1976, the NOW Legal Defense and Education Fund, along with a consortium of women's organizations, brought a class action suit against the U.S. Department of Labor for its failure to provide the required affirmative action. In response to organized pressure from the women's movement and the threat of the lawsuit, a settlement was reached. It was in 1978 that President Jimmy Carter issued affirmative action regulations to expand Executive Order 11246.[20]

The new DOL regulations spelled out goals and timetables for hiring women on publicly financed construction sites on a trade-by-trade basis. The initial objective was to have female representation on these sites reach 6.9 percent of the total workforce. The regulations were quite detailed and comprehensive. On paper, they outlined everything from ensuring and maintaining a work environment free of harassment, intimidation, and coercion at all sites and in all facilities, to the percentage of females in each apprenticeship class—20–25 percent of each class.

Women could now apply to the vast number of certified apprenticeship programs overseen by the states. As women took advantage of these opportunities on the blue-collar frontier, they were optimistic. The pioneers expected to be the first in what they thought would be a wave of female applicants. The original goals and timetables for hiring women on federally funded construction sites were set up in such a way to increase over time.

Activists across the country began to gear up. They wrote grants, applied for federal funding under the CETA program (the Comprehensive Employment and Training Act) and set up organizations to prepare women for entrance into the skilled trades. Nontraditional Employment for Women (NEW) was one of the first such groups in California. Soon after the pilot project was successful in getting funding and recruiting women in San Francisco, it became a model for other programs.

Live! From New York

Shortly after NEW was launched in California, the carpenter Mary Garvin set off for New York City, where she set up a similar program. She called it WAP (the Women in Apprenticeship Program). Other organizations in New York City were set up to train women to enter skilled jobs. Joyce Hartwell founded Lady Carpenter and then All-Craft to prepare young women for jobs in the different trades.

All-Craft and WAP—which changed its name to NEW, like the California organization, challenged standard practices in hiring. Both groups, in their early years, participated in collaborative efforts alongside other feminist groups. They lent their names to various efforts—to challenge affirmative action regulations; to litigate against reluctant entities on their own or with others; to demonstrate and in general, to advance women's right to work in these contested jobs. Both organizations brought thousands of women into their programs. Their training provided entrée to a world outside the low-paid female job ghetto. Because of these programs, many women secured brighter futures with fatter paychecks.

Support for women also came from organizations set up to prepare minority males for the skilled trades. The Recruitment Training Program (RTP) in Harlem was one. RTP opened its doors to women after the DOL regulations were enacted in 1978. But there were many others—all offering a way out of the low-wage job ghetto for young women and men. Training organizations took on the task of providing the essential preparation that would allow women—and minorities—to enter and succeed at skilled jobs.[21]

The National Organization for Women (NOW) proved to be an early and staunch ally for tradeswomen. The New York City chapter set up an employment committee and took up the cause of individual women seeking jobs in blue-collar careers who were being denied access, despite changes in the law. In 1979, the first female dockworkers in the city's history received work permits because of a lawsuit NOW-NYC brought against the Waterfront Commission. Although other issues eventually took precedence over the fight for jobs for working-class women, the blue-collar pioneers benefited greatly from NOW's support and expertise.[22]

The Committee for Women in Nontraditional Jobs also sought to bridge the gap between white- and blue-collar feminism. This was the brainchild of Judith Layzer, one of many women who came into city government in the Lindsay administration (1966–1973). Her background in the relatively new field of equal employment opportunity enforcement at the Atomic Energy Commission in Washington led to a job in New York.[23]

In 1969, she was hired by the Bureau of Labor Services to head up EEO compliance in nonconstruction city contracts. Initially, she worked with other feminists as part of a group called Women in City Government. They took on important issues such as health and pension benefits, maternity leave, and insurance coverage for abortion. They lobbied for more women to be appointed to the Lindsay administration.

However, as she worked to increase the percentage of minorities and women in the higher-paying, skilled blue-collar jobs, Layzer came to see that women were being excluded for many reasons. She sought to remedy this and reached out for support from All-Craft's director, Joyce Hartwell. Leaning on Hartwell's expertise, together they set up the Committee for Women in Nontraditional Jobs. The goal was to educate policy-makers in city agencies and private sector employers about the legal requirements to recruit women into the higher-paying, skilled blue-collar jobs. To comply with the city's EEO requirements, contractors seeking business with the city had to demonstrate that they were making a good-faith effort to hire minorities and women.

Starting in 1976, the Committee, a collection of activists from government agencies, elected officials, academia, trade unions, legal experts, women's rights and civil rights organizations, kept the pressure on. Holding meetings, conferences, forums, radio interviews, and challenging employer practices and policies, the Committee put a spotlight on the efforts that were being undertaken to hire a diverse workforce. Through a combination of her official position and her unofficial advocacy, Layzer saw how the EEO game was actually being played. Agencies, contractors, and unions were able to get away with faint-hearted efforts to recruit and hire women and minorities. "We questioned all of this in my office in the olden days," said Layzer. "You know? Because a good faith effort can be serious and it can also be sort of superficial."[24]

The Committee kept up its efforts for 10 years. Over time, they were able to analyze the programs put in place to recruit women, point out any shortcomings, and help to devise specific remedies. For example, after working with the Port Authority of New York-New Jersey, it became clear that there was no mechanism to bring women into skilled blue-collar jobs. There was also no long-range affirmative action plan. The Committee members prodded the Port Authority to put an apprenticeship program in place to recruit women and to add females to the overall plan for fair hiring.

The work of the Committee underscores a crucial point: that a group of informed, highly placed feminists was paying attention to the issue of affirmative action. On behalf of blue-collar, working-class women, they were asking questions, demanding answers, educating employers, and attempting to hold people in high places accountable for their performance.[25]

New York City spawned its own share of grassroots groups supporting women's entrance into the blue-collar jobs. The first group called itself Women In The Trades (WITT). It provided a combination of hands-on training programs—basic auto mechanics or preparation to apply for jobs doing small appliance repair—as well as other, more political activities. WITT set up a speakers' bureau. One speaking engagement took place at a battered women's shelter in Brooklyn, where women expressed an interest in pursuing jobs such as truck driving, tool making, and other areas of nontraditional work.[26]

WITT activists also collaborated with a coalition to address the problem of teenage girls' becoming pregnant and not graduating from high school. Together, they attempted to provide better access to vocational education in nontraditional areas for women. Another activity set up a group of improvisational actors—the WITT's End Players—to act out scenes about sexual harassment described by their audience—"as a way to share your struggles with other women and to strengthen each other."[27]

Other WITT activities lent themselves to educating the broader public about the presence of women in the trades. It might be a story in the *Daily News* featuring a female plumber giving New York City Mayor Ed Koch a lesson on how to save water by doing basic plumbing repairs—or an interview on National Public Radio with Local 3 electrician Melinda Hernandez about sexual harassment. Another radio show aired on the alternative station WBAI called *Career Alternatives*. It featured interviews with young women working in nontraditional jobs.[28]

Some women got together to create a cooperative business to do cabinet-making and carpentry. Their efforts were given a boost in the pages of the WITT Newsletter. Energy and creativity added up to endless possibilities for pushing the envelope of job opportunities for females in an organized, thoughtful way.[29]

The Continuing Fight for Good Jobs

However, within just a few years, a quiet but ominous change occurred, as the bonds with former allies either weakened or disappeared. More and more, women working in nontraditional jobs—the pioneers and the women who came behind them—were out there on their own. Many factors contributed to their growing isolation.

The major thrust for women to enter skilled blue-collar jobs came between 1978 and 1982. By that point, the feminist movement had shifted focus. Although the campaign for the Equal Rights Amendment (ERA) and the fight to keep abortion legal absorbed an immense amount of energy and commitment on the part of activists, it also had other consequences. The combination of the fight for the ERA and legalized abortion energized the right wing of the Republican Party. This in turn fueled an ever-stronger conservative movement.[30] The women's movement was pushed into a defensive posture. In addition, internal struggles developed and diluted the strong focus of the early women's liberation movement. A lot of the oomph went out of organizing on behalf of working-class women.

Attacks on affirmative action gained ground. The argument that America had to revert to the days of gender-blind, color-neutral policies without preference for traditionally excluded groups won an increasing number of converts. Although President Carter could be moved, President Reagan actively opposed affirmative action. The role of the government changed. Over the decades, enforcement efforts were watered down to the point where they became almost nonexistent.[31]

In time, the militancy of NEW and similar organizations set up to train women for entrance to skilled jobs was tamed. This occurred gradually, as the need to secure and hold on to greater amounts of funding to support the training programs took precedence over direct action and legal challenges. The need to develop closer ties to the trade unions also precluded prior, in-your-face strategies. The times changed, tactics changed, and the grassroots character of these organizations changed. The groups survived, serving a critical, supportive, and indispensable role, yet without the wider support and the militant stance they once embraced.[32]

Despite this—just as was the case for Ronnie Sandler—tradeswomen were still able to find allies within the ranks of feminist and trade union organizations and government agencies. In New York City, one source of consistent support came from the office of the

Women's Bureau in the U.S. Department of Labor. In addition, there were other, similar sources of support. Women like Ronnie Eldridge, a City Council member, and EEOC head Eleanor Holmes Norton, throughout their lengthy public careers always kept their ears open and doors ajar to assist women in the blue-collar jobs—from construction worker to civil servant.[33] The Coalition of Labor Union Women (CLUW) was able to offer support to tradeswomen on a haphazard basis.[34] The national CLUW set up a Committee for Women Working in Nontraditional Jobs. The committee members, spread out across the country, were able to press the issue to a greater or lesser degree as they saw fit within their local CLUW chapters.[35]

Legal advocates kept up their support and were especially crucial in the continuing fight to maintain access for women. The NOW Legal Defense and Education Fund (which has now been renamed Legal Momentum), Advocates for Women and Equal Rights Advocates in California, and other public interest organizations sustained the struggle on behalf of women working in nontraditional jobs, in the courtroom and beyond.[36]

Ronnie Sandler was one of the many tradeswomen who continued to make a huge contribution to the advancement of women in nontraditional jobs. Along the way, she learned how to overcome resistance, doubt, and fear on the part of individual women who wanted to try something completely different. Looking back, she recalled the first demonstration program she developed to train women in Vermont for nontraditional, blue-collar jobs:

> When we started Step-Up, the first year was a demonstration project. Then we were trying to expand the funding. I'll never forget [the bureaucrat from the] Department of Employment and Training, who was our major [source of] funding, said to me, "Well, don't you think you'll flood the market...You know, with twenty-five women?" I said, "No. I don't think so."...What we're talking about with women in the trades is economic equity.[37]

Despite the loss of some allies and a push to the margins of public debate about affirmative action for females, women in blue-collar nontraditional jobs were unrelenting in their efforts to organize. Tradeswomen, Inc., the California grassroots group set up in 1979, is still committed to its mission. Throughout its history, the group has served as a North Star for women across the country because of its innovative projects.

Soon after its founding, Tradeswomen, Inc. began to publish the first—and only—national magazine for women in nontraditional jobs. For decades, *Tradeswomen* provided a constant source of information, advice, humor, and first-person accounts by women in a huge range of blue-collar, nontraditional jobs. The message was clear—we're doing this work and you can do it too. In stories and photos, women showed that they could survive and thrive if they were given the chance and if they were willing to take up the challenge.[38]

In 1982, Ronnie Sandler moved to California. She joined Tradeswomen, Inc., paying the $25 to become a member and met other activists:

> I thought: "Oh cool! There is a support group already here." It was very interesting. I stayed with some friends in San Francisco, and one of them worked with Equal Rights Advocates, a public interest law firm that represents tradeswomen. Molly Martin [a pioneering union electrician] was on the board of ERA and was also a founder of and on the board of Tradeswomen, Inc. So I met Molly very early on when I moved to California at an ERA event and we became very good friends. That

was around the time that Tradeswomen was organizing the first national conference in Oakland.[39]

More than 600 women attended that conference, including women from New York City. Sponsored by Tradeswomen, Inc., the organizers celebrated the progress women had made within the past decade. The conference flier projected confidence in a rosy future: "Ten years ago, this couldn't have happened. Now, our time has come."[40]

"Failure is impossible" with the lifelong dedication of committed women, said Susan B. Anthony.[41] Perhaps, since in regard to the outlook for women working in blue-collar, skilled jobs, the story is still an open book.

Out on the blue-collar frontiers, life remains a struggle for women who make up a small percentage of the workforce in these jobs. The barriers—including the opposition within their own unions—have been slow to fall. It's still an anomaly to be a female firefighter, a carpenter, or a mechanic in most parts of the country, including New York City. Their presence on a job is almost like raisins in a scone—sparsely spread out and highly visible.

Yet their stories offer an encapsulated view of their lives, presenting a partial picture of what it was like to walk in their boots, so to speak. They depict the far more complicated world Rosie's daughters inhabit, both on the job and in their unions. And they help to explain why—despite the ability demonstrated by a generation of capable, gutsy women—their numbers are still so small.

United Tradeswomen: Organizing for the Guaranteed Right to Work in Any Job

In 1979, a group of smart, strong-willed women, fiercely independent, but recognizing the need for collective action, forged a new organization in New York City, United Tradeswomen (UT). White and black, Hispanic and Asian, UT was also occupationally diverse: Entenmann bakery truck drivers, bridge painters, utility workers, firefighters, and hundreds of skilled trades' apprentices. It was a group that saw its mission as providing support and advocacy for blue-collar pioneers. For six years, UT touched the lives of most of the women entering the blue-collar, male-dominated jobs in New York City.

UT's mission was straightforward: "That every woman will have the guaranteed right to work in any area of employment that she chooses."[1] Its logo was a hard hat with the woman's symbol. As a grassroots, voluntary organization, its growth depended on the women who poured their creative energies into it and improvised as it grew. They experimented with various ways to get the work done. Potluck dinners and childcare were standard at UT events. They not only charged dues but also baked carrot cakes for sale and held fundraisers to support their organization. They received help from expert allies and advocacy groups and worked together to oppose regulations aimed at weakening affirmative action.

From its inception, UT succeeded in providing a space for women to meet and to talk. The majority of women participating in the organization were experiencing significant hardships at work and meeting up with resistance within their unions. Evan Ruderman was one of the first female electricians in New York City. "We were very isolated on the job. You could go for days without seeing another woman . . . and really be in dire straits just to talk to somebody about something that happened in your work that wouldn't seem trivial," she said.[2] The support they received from UT proved to be one key to their survival.

Over the years, UT held numerous public forums and workshops for members on topics such as sexual harassment, safety and health, affirmative action, and job opportunities in the construction industry. "Early on, we decided to try different things and see what drew women," explained Lois Ross, one of UT's founders.[3] In 1981, the women organized their first picket line. "This was the very first demonstration of women construction workers in the country," said Ross. "It was at the Convention Center." The event scored lots of press coverage as female hard hats rallied in the rain to "demand construction jobs for women."[4]

UT fell apart in 1985 as internal divisions grew and the commitment of the original organizers waned. "We weren't sure what direction to take and that was a tension within the organization," explained Ross. Ruderman described the unraveling of UT in a different way: "I think that each woman began to feel she had to develop her own strategy. I'll just speak for me. I was not conscious of the depth of harassment on the job, of how it was going to the bone, to the heart." Tensions on the job sites and within UT led to its implosion. Its absence left a huge void for women working in nontraditional jobs.

Fifteen years after its demise, UT women gathered to trade stories about their experiences in hopes of setting in motion a similar kind of organization for a new generation of tradeswomen. The stationary engineer Yvone Maitin arrived late. Seeing Lois Ross seated across the room, she asked "Can I give you a hug?"[5] Then Maitin tearfully told the story of how she first came to call UT and spoke to Ross on the telephone. "It was a life saver," she recalled.[6]

Looking back, participants used a common word to describe their experiences. "UT was really fun and we had a good time doing it," said activist Marty Pottenger.[7] "We had so much fun," said the plumber Kay Webster.[8] But beyond the fun, the organization forged enduring bonds among participants.

UT was also the source of sorrow, pain, and regret. Because of its history and promise, its ultimate failure was bitter. But for a time, UT was a vibrant, creative organization, founded by and for working women. It started out with a clear mission. After a while, it got more complicated.

Blue-collar Feminism

For many of the pioneers, taking up the tools of the women's movement was a natural development. The carpenter Irene Soloway clearly saw UT as a product of the women's movement: "It was coming out of feminism in the seventies. It was unquestioned that this was part of feminism. And if it's part of feminism, you do it in a group context. It's not an individualistic type of endeavor."[9]

Looking back, the carpenter Connie Reyes recalled, "Women had more hope. And we had more strength because there *was* a women's movement. There had been the antiwar movement. There had been the civil rights movement. There had been all of this social ferment."[10]

"It was exciting," recalled Pottenger. "We were breaking into the unions. Women were forming women's committees. You know, unions were banning us and men hadn't all figured out how to be allies." The pioneers were operating on optimism and youthful energy, and UT was operating within a climate of activism.

For Pottenger, the political excitement of UT echoed an earlier experience. "I was involved in the women's movement in St. Petersburg, Florida, and I considered that a very great experience," she said. "We had a brilliant and vibrant women's movement and it was not just for the middle-class, white women and all we were doing wasn't getting cushy jobs. I mean, in Florida, we were working on saving women's lives. I really felt grateful for that. And UT was similar. There was a tremendous possibility and tremendous purpose . . . it was very exciting. I felt like UT was an example of that."

Working-class women trying to change conditions for themselves and others held a great appeal for Pottenger. Years later, she used her experiences on construction sites as the basis for a theater piece, "Construction Stories." This led to her play, "City Water Tunnel #3." She credited UT for the path she took in life. "I think it actually explains why I'm here now. I'm sure there were a lot of things I could do, a lot of places I could go. And that is that, working-class women are actively smart—we just did the work and got things done. UT was a group of women who got theirs and were very clear that getting theirs wasn't all they were interested in—they were interested in other women getting theirs."

In their efforts to expand the job frontier for females, UT activists invested energy in trying to work with other like-minded women's organizations. UT got support from the New York chapter of the National Organization for Women (NOW). Some meetings were held at their office before renting a space of their own. As Ross recalled, "We reached out to NOW. I remember that was one of our major groups. They had a Women in Nontraditional [Jobs] group [that held] meetings."[11] As UT activist Cynthia Long described:

> That was the other thing we tried to do more of too—to involve the other feminist women. We let them know what our situations were and tried to draw from them as well. Our organizing in United Tradeswomen went beyond those of us who were actually in the trades. We were also trying to educate other women out there as to what was going on with us and ask them for support.[12]

This was the fertile environment in which UT grew. Growing out of a feminist culture, it developed a blue-collar agenda and traditions of its own. Although other organizations and individuals made contributions to the group and to its programs, UT set its own course.

"Something to Sustain Them"

As the skilled blue-collar jobs opened up for females, the possibilities of learning a craft, getting good money and benefits, and other incentives attracted a wide swath of women. "Women were coming from all different places," observed Ross. "Everyone was real different. People literally sleeping on the streets; people who had drug problems; people who were artists and had BAs in fine arts and really all kinds of women were interested at that point."[13]

The Women in Apprenticeship Program (WAP) began to set up shop in 1978. Lois Ross was the first person hired by its director, the carpenter Mary Garvin. Fresh from studying economics at Rutgers University, Ross was eager to apply academic theories about gender segregation in the workplace within an activist organization. As she described it, "I was just doing counseling and job development and I started thinking. We help them get jobs and then they're out there on their own. They need something to sustain them. I envisioned it from the very beginning as being a political group that would advocate for women in all kinds of ways."

UT was born out of her desire to provide this extra support for the blue-collar pioneers. Tall, thin, and intense, Ross became one of the two unofficial leaders of UT. She poured that passionate intensity into the organization. More than anyone else, Ross was responsible for giving UT life and keeping it going.

WAP provided her with a launching pad for the new organization: "I was really in a unique position. I wasn't a tradeswoman, but I knew virtually every single woman in New

York City who was interested in the trades, 'cause they came through WAP. So I was in a position to talk to each one and to see where people were at. I was identifying people who I thought might be really good leaders for that kind of a group."

Within the small circle of women working in nontraditional jobs in New York City, Consuelo, "Connie" Reyes had the most seniority. "Consuelo was already working in the union *before* WAP," said Ross. As an activist participating in organized protests to get minority men into the skilled construction trades, Reyes finally decided to take a bite of the apple herself. She applied to join the carpenters union. With long dark hair, a brilliant smile, and a charismatic personality, Consuelo Reyes still identifies herself as a socialist and a Puerto Rican nationalist. Her speech is rapid and delivered in complete paragraphs.

> There was me, Irene, Lois Ross, Kathy [Zadoretsky]. I think that was it. We would get together at a coffee shop and I was pushing us: "We need to have an organization of tradeswomen because there's so few of us in each of these trades." . . . It really came from a fundamental belief that I have, which is that women empower women. Men can be wonderful and they can be encouraging and all that, but women empower women. We wanted to help organize a strong political and emotional support system for the women, 'cause we were all very isolated.

Reyes understood that if women were going to survive in the construction industry, they needed to find a way to support each other. As she explained, "The women were in super, super difficult positions . . . They were trying to come into this really hostile industry—hostile to *them*. Their co-workers were hostile. We were in an almost impossible situation. And that's why I thought a woman's organization, made up of all tradeswomen, would give us an advantage, more than we had individually in our trades. Then we could really address the issues of women."

With her history of participating in political groups, Reyes readily appreciated that UT had to move beyond the mission of providing support for individuals having a hard time on the job. It also had to address broader organizational goals. "I felt it was important to continue building the political momentum to get more women into the trades. 'Cause for women to be in the trades and succeed, there's such a wall against that. I felt that, without some political clout, what little gains we had, and we had teeny, tiny gains, would be wiped out."

Irene Soloway became the other unofficial leader of UT. The carrot-topped carpenter with a distinctive high-pitched laugh was one of the creative forces behind much of the organization's activity. "It was a unique group," she said. "Socially, it was a really interesting mix of people. We weren't overtly political, in the sense that we still felt very much on the outside of the construction industry. It felt very scary to us but we created a cultural group that supported ourselves and each other, and we were able to move forward into that industry. I think we did move from the outside to the inside by creating an identity for ourselves, as well as educating ourselves and each other, and trying to educate the union about us. But that was less overt. I think our strong continued presence for each other and ourselves was the main accomplishment of this group."

Typically, women entering the all-male apprenticeship programs, going to work on construction sites, and at the other male-dominated blue-collar occupations encountered their strange and often hostile new worlds one by one. "Most of us were the only women anywhere in a three-mile radius in our jobs," said the plumber Kay Webster.

As an apprentice stationary engineer in Local 30, Yvone Maitin finally reached out to UT. An African-American woman raising a child as a single mother, she was severely stressed by isolation.

When I started working for the Port Authority...around [all] men, it became really clear to me that this was something that was very foreign to me. It was really scary. I didn't know what I was going to do. I felt really alone, isolated. It was scaring the bejesus out of me, I'll tell you. One day, I came home and I was just full up to my eyeballs. I had heard about United Tradeswomen and I had been given Lois's phone number. I called her and I just completely unloaded. I fell apart over the phone. I must have cried: "Oh my God. Do you mind if I cry?" I still remember it. I was just a mess. I needed to talk to someone who would be able to understand. She told me to come on down. It was a lifesaver for me to be around other women who were experiencing the same thing. I didn't feel crazy anymore. It really was strengthening to me. And I did as much as I could to try to help the organization in whatever it was doing.[14]

Evan Ruderman learned about UT after she entered the apprenticeship program of Local 3, International Brotherhood of Electrical Workers. The short, curly-haired Ruderman was articulate, passionate, and willing to lend her great energy to causes that caught her interest.

Her description of UT's origins also centered on the need to connect with other blue-collar women to overcome the isolation on the job. "I think individual women were driven emotionally," said Ruderman. "You had this feeling that you were seeking other women—that was a big driving force."

As one of the pioneers in the electrical workers' union, Ruderman helped to organize a group for the women in Local 3. Then she began to attend the UT meetings. Soon she became one of the leaders of the broader organization. As she saw it, the idea for women from the different unions to form a cross-trades group evolved out of the nature of the problems they were facing.

Some of the unions that were more centralized, like Local 3, we started having our own little group of women electricians. And we did that out of necessity because we were having so many problems on the job. This naturally spilled over into that it's a good idea to bring all the trades together. 'Cause at that time, and even still today, an issue like changing facilities...Let's say there's 500 workers on the job and they're all from different trades. Then, out of that 500, you have three women and they're all from different trades. It didn't make sense to have three different changing facilities for women in the same way that they do for men. So it became a big issue of, "who's going to be responsible to pay for this?"...The men couldn't figure that out. But as women, we sort of had to start working together on jobs across the trades. So it just made perfect sense that we had to organize not just women electricians but we had to organize through the trades, 'cause I was going to run into this problem on every single job, which I did. Bathroom facilities were another [problem].

Kay Webster, an activist living on the Lower East Side, started to participate shortly after UT achieved some visibility. Photos taken in her years as a young apprentice plumber show a face with soft features surrounded by long, dark hair. "UT was the kind of thing that you just knew of after a while," said Webster. "I do think the key thing it provided was just a space where other women who were having similar struggles could get together. You could not feel like it was just *you*."

Webster pointed to another important reason why tradeswomen felt the need to talk to women in similar circumstances: "Often it was hard to talk to other women [about it] because then they would attack the men, who were these working-class guys with whom you might have a fine relationship in some ways, but the sexism was horrific. So it was just nice to be with a group of women who had made these decisions and were fighting those similar battles. You didn't have to explain a lot. Or [have] people saying: 'Why in the world would you want to do this?' And not understanding the art and the beauty of it and the fun of it and just being that powerful and self-determined."

Sexual Harassment of a Different Order

From the start, the women were subjected to a brutal harassment. Sexual harassment had its own distinctive character at work sites where women were the first to perform traditionally male jobs. Today, decades later, sexual harassment is familiar territory. However, not until 1986 did the U.S. Supreme Court hold that sexual harassment could create a hostile work environment and therefore was in violation of Title VII's provisions.[15]

UT women had their own take on these experiences and used words as witty weapons to describe them. For five years, UT published a newsletter that captured the gritty realities they were facing on the job. Stories, poems, essays, and advice to other tradeswomen reflected the intensity of their experiences and the daily need to devise strategies.

Nancy Quick's poem, "Construction Lango" about life on the job, conveys the crude workplace culture. Quick describes the common practice among the men of using language to sexualize everything from tools to basic tasks.

> Do you know how to screw?
> How deep is your hole?
> Is that rod coming thru?
> Nail that piece, baby!
> Put it in there girl!!!
> May I have a nut or two?
> Construction lango…
> That's what I call it,
> We hear it everyday…[16]

The contrast between sexual harassment in female- and male-dominated occupations soon became apparent. The Working Women's Institute in New York City was one of the first organizations to identify and distinguish the two. UT turned to this group as they saw their members trying to come to grips with the problem. The Institute did some of the earliest research on the topic. In an effort to add to their understanding, researchers Suzanne Carothers and Peggy Crull used data gathered from UT members to make this important distinction:

> Harassment of women workers in traditional jobs appears more often as hints and requests for dates, which, when rejected, are followed by work retaliation. Harassment of women workers in male-dominated settings is typically more hostile at the outset. The motive for harassment in the traditional setting appears to be exploitation of role and power differences, whereas in the nontraditional setting the motive seems to be a defense against what male workers take to be an implicit challenge to their gender and work roles.

Sexual harassment in these jobs appears to be a form of retaliation for invading a male sphere and threatening male economic and social status. Women in these positions become objects of harassment ranging from vulgar remarks to outright physical attacks. The sexual behavior they face is more intimidating and abusive than the acts of harassment secretaries are exposed to.[17]

Evan Ruderman understood how harassment could lead to a sense of powerlessness: "It could be individualized. Then you could feel bad about yourself and you could be confused: Is it you? Is it them?"

UT organizers also appreciated the fact that legal rights remained distant and theoretical unless women knew what their rights were and could come up with practical ways to cope with tense, oftentimes threatening situations. The first UT workshop on sexual harassment was an effort to educate women about their rights and to share some coping strategies for the workplace. "We organized the first conference on sexual harassment before it was even being *called* sexual harassment," Reyes recalled.

Casey Wagner of the Working Women's Institute worked with the UT organizers to plan the program held in November 1981. This conference provided additional input to the pioneering research on sexual harassment in nontraditional workplaces.[18]

For Kay Webster, the event was "just a place to come and talk about all that." As she described it, "We got people to come, both experts and the women…And the great thing about it, it gave a voice to the women. We knew what the trouble was and we knew strategies for figuring it out."

"Coffee" and "Cake," Ruffles and Overalls

The new organization needed a name. "United Tradeswomen seemed like a natural," said Irene Soloway. "There was a group called United Construction Workers in Brooklyn, so we borrowed it," recalled Lois Ross. Once they decided on a name, the next step was to publicize the group. To do that, they needed something visually appealing. "Brooke Steel did the logo," explained Soloway. "The logo kind of pulled the whole thing together because we just thought it was so cool." Soon the hard hat with the women's symbol was decorating fliers designed to publicize public forums and membership meetings.

The early meetings were informal. As Lois Ross recalled, "For a while, in the beginning, they were every week…Most of our meetings were in Chrisa Gibson's loft for the first six months or so, until we got an office," said Ross. "Those meetings were very hot and crowded," said Soloway. "We always had beer and Entenmann's 'cause we had an Entenmann's truck driver who was part of our group." "We also had a Bustello truck driver later on, so we used to call them Coffee and Cake," added Ruderman.

This is where the work got done. Over time, participants hammered out how they wanted their organization to develop. Cynthia Long participated in the early UT meetings. She distinguished the degree of difficulty in moving a group like UT forward from that of her own group, which focused on organizing within one union:

> I think that within Women Electricians, it was a lot easier to organize…it was a much easier format because we all belonged to the same union. When we were talking and strategizing, we were dealing with the same structure. We were dealing with

the same individuals. In United Tradeswomen, you're dealing with carpenters, electricians, plumbers; all different trades, different employers. So it was much more difficult to figure out a strategy that would have some kind of positive result.

Clarity on UT's mission was cobbled together over time and in many meetings. Looking back at their mission statement in 1996, Irene Soloway expressed amazement: "Boy, were we idealists," she laughed, while reading aloud the ambitious goals the group set for itself in 1981: "The primary goal of UT—That every woman will have the guaranteed right to work in any building trade or blue-collar job that she chooses." Secondary goals included,

- Increased employment of women in the building trades and other blue-collar trades.
- Improvement of working conditions, and in particular, recognition of the special needs of women.
- Development of working-class women's leadership.
- Building working relationships between the women's and labor movement.
- Developing unity among UT members and between members and their co-workers, families, and communities.
- Recognition of women's caucuses.
- Fair representation in unions: rank-and-file control.[19]

Decisions about the mission, structure, activities, and programs were made by consensus. "In a totally volunteer organization, people just volunteered and then, the ones who volunteer more naturally are more involved. They make more of the decisions," said Ruderman. "This became an issue later on."

Ruderman recalled the momentum and excitement of the early days: "We realized that we really had a growing membership. So that means our name is out there. Women are asking for this. There's a calling for this...a *need*. And we've got to seize the moment—start being visible. That actually carried us tremendously for about two or three years."

Within its first year, UT had its own office on the fifth floor of 316 West 35 Street. In the fall of 1980, the first UT Newsletter carried an invitation for an office warming on Friday evening, September 26. To pay the rent, print and mail organizational leaflets, install a telephone and other expenses, UT developed a dues-paying formula for members. "We were growing at an incredibly rapid rate," Ruderman said. "I mean, unbelievable. And when you begin to have a membership of 500 people on the mailing list...[so] we were trying to establish dues."

The need to be independent and not to seek outside financing or establish an umbilical cord to another group was something that the founding members agreed on in principle. Lois Ross had a strong commitment to maintaining the group's independence. "We had seen some of the women's organizations selling out too, as soon as they got funding, and becoming more 'establishment' and not willing to take the kind of risks and do the kinds of actions and things that might need to be done in a particular situation because you're worried about your funding source," she said. "[We were] almost a little bit paranoid about accepting money from anybody and also proud that we could support our own organization. Women were making good money and hey, we could afford to run the organization without a staff person."

Originally, all were in agreement that the group would sustain itself financially and work together as an all-volunteer organization. "Our final structure was, I think, three hours pay," Ross recalled. "So therefore it was progressive. If you made $5 an hour, you paid $15 a year. If you made $30 an hour, you paid $90 a year. And people paid. They really did. The majority of the people on our mailing list paid three hours of pay and that was a real fair way to do it. That was our [main] source of funding." As Soloway recalled:

We were intent on being grassroots which is like a double-edged sword. Funding was being used for various projects that had more organizational bureaucracy. We were going to be the ones that were *not* funded. We were so intent on not getting funded—our primary identity. If there was anything that was our strength and our weakness, that was it.

UT kept experimenting with structures to accomplish its agenda. "Our activities were very fluid," Soloway explained. "We never actually had a set structure that lasted. We were always changing and tinkering. It also depended on who was around, which was [both] a strength and a weakness."

One early experiment was to set up a coordinating committee. As Ross explained, "We had a coordinating committee where people volunteered. We said: 'Who wants to do the work?'" "The original idea," Soloway said, "was that the committee would do a lot of the work calling meetings and getting the programs together. Then they would get a chance to do what *they* wanted to do."

Soloway described another effort: "We attempted a borough structure because not everybody could get to meetings in Manhattan. There were a lot of single parents and there were a lot of things that people wanted to do. So the borough structure came up as an attempt to have local, like almost chapters that would be easier to get to and more part of your daily life, because, basically, after work, you'd be pretty tired." Starting with Brooklyn, borough meetings spread throughout the city.

Janine Blackwelder was a leader in this effort. "I was the Brooklyn coordinator for a while," she recalled.[20] Her first step was to organize brunches to bring women together. "You are cordially invited to United Tradeswomen's 1st Brooklyn Brunch/Discussion," read the flier, which included a map, a suggested donation of a dollar, and a description of the discussion to be held on a Sunday, from 11:30 a.m. till 2 p.m. "For the first part of the afternoon we will be talking about problems on the job, possible solutions, and sharing funny experiences. Then the discussion will focus on planning activities to build the organization and further its goals."[21]

Blackwelder invited women to participate in the first action for the Brooklyn members: a recruitment table at the Atlantic Antic Street Fair Sunday, September 27, 1981.

The plan is to set up a table displaying UT literature, and photos of ourselves and our friends at work. We will be selling baked goods, food and beverages, and toy hard hats that we can decorate. Try to come to the table to get to know other members and take turns selling. If you wear your hard hat or uniform it will help attract attention to our sale. Bring pictures for the display board. Look for UT's beautiful banner (as seen on Channel's 2 TV)!

Blackwelder added a postscript: "I'm especially hoping to see those of you who work in areas *other* than building construction since most of our construction members are already active in other committees." Although many members of UT were entering the construction trades, others such as "Coffee" and "Cake," were working in jobs outside that industry.

As Ross described:

> Looking at the group as a whole, we were heavily focused on construction. That's where the federal "regs" had some bite. And that's where we, as Nontraditional Employment for Women—as Women in Apprenticeship Program—made a big push for women. The majority of our membership was construction. But there was always another section of women that I worked with on my job—telephone company workers, electronic technicians, public utility workers, Con Ed and truck drivers, maintenance workers...people like that who were always really—I don't know what the word is—their interests were always overshadowed by the construction workers.

As Soloway said: "The construction workers were the most macho and full of themselves. There was a kind of hierarchy. We were the poster girls." Ilene Winkler was one of the "other" women active in UT. "She was a very strong member for a long time," recalled Evan Ruderman. Winkler, a craft technician for the phone company, described her experiences as a member of UT:

> United Tradeswomen for telephone workers, for women who were not in construction, you always felt like you had shown up wearing ruffles, you know, because you weren't macho enough, like everybody else. They *needed* to be. I didn't resent them for it. I think they were right. Their situation was so totally different, they needed it. It was the rest of us that felt kind of funny...It was great, even for me and I wasn't in the horrible kind of situation that they were.[22]

"There was a lot of enthusiasm for our ideas and our projects," said Ruderman. Ideas developed through discussions.

"If somebody had an idea, everybody would say, 'Great idea!' All the ideas were so good," Soloway said.

"As problems started coming up, sexual harassment was a major one, problems with the union, dealing with your union, we started identifying issue areas that were critical to women," Ross explained. "That's really what happened. We started first just doing workshops addressing those particular issues."[23] Topics ranged from the intensely personal, such as how to deal with sexual harassment, to safety on the job, and the politics of union membership.

> When we were in that stage, there was a lot of excitement. We were growing and we were actually doing things. So visibly, when somebody heard about United Tradeswomen, some other woman dragged her to a meeting. Something was happening, you know? And something, for that particular woman, was real.

As UT grew, the group began to develop traditions. "We started all our meetings by each woman standing up and saying what her name was, what trade, and how long she had been in it," Ruderman recalled. "Everybody clapped. It would take us about 45 minutes before we could begin because we had to clap and applaud. That was very affirming for a lot of women to be applauded."

One event early on drew hundreds of participants. "One of our first big workshops was on affirmative action with Esta Bigler, an EEOC official" said Soloway. "At that workshop we had several hundred people. I think about three hundred people. We had it at the Quaker

Church, the Friends Meeting House on Rutherford Place. I think that's when we realized that there's just this amazing groundswell of interest in this. Our workshops were very well organized. We really worked hard to have a structure. We had lots of information and they were well attended. I think that was one of the things we did best."

"Blue-Collar Women Organizing to Survive"

As novices in their unions, the women needed to learn the rules that governed participation. Several of the objectives in UT's overall program indicate the commitment of the founding members to a rank and file, democratic brand of trade unionism. Initially, they embraced their role as sisters in the brotherhoods with a naive belief in the benevolence of their unions. Later they learned about the limits of democracy within their unions. Still they persisted in trying to educate themselves. One way was by holding workshops and public forums on the rights and responsibilities of union membership.

One typical UT panel discussion about the role of blue-collar women in the trades featured Connie Reyes and Ilene Winkler as speakers, along with Vicki Gavin, identified as "an industrial union and political activist since the early 1940s." "Bring your families and interested friends," read the invitational flier. "An inexpensive home-cooked supper will be served, and free childcare will be available."[24] The event was held on a Friday evening, November 14, 1980, at the Friends Meeting House.

The flier depicted a woman in a hard hat hoisting lumber with a slogan on each piece of wood. Topics included sexual harassment; industry-wide racism; inadequate and unsanitary washhouses; unfair job assignments; lack of childcare facilities; discrimination against lesbians; nondemocratic union representation; and revolving-door hiring policies. The ambitious agenda opened up many avenues for discussion and action.

Rosie the Riveter was quickly adopted by the pioneers, eager to embrace any lessons they could take from their predecessors. Janine Blackwelder hosted a program on April 11, 1981, to show the "The Life and Times of Rosie the Riveter." A UT publicity flier described it as a film about "women's work in wartime industry, using clips from 1940s government newsreels as well as recent interviews with five of the real 'Rosies,' who recall what it was like for them to do a 'man's job.' As trade unionists, we want to share with others in the labor movement this opportunity to learn about an episode that is not widely known, and to deepen our understanding and sensitivity to the experience of women and minority workers during World War II. A United Tradeswoman member will lead the question and answer period with our special guest, Ms. Lola Weixel, who worked as a welder on WWII aircraft and is featured in the film."[25]

Blackwelder recalled: "That was a lot of fun. We had people come. One of the ironworkers in Local 580—I bumped into him in the union hall years later, he was a black guy in his thirties maybe—and he was saying, 'Oh, I remember going to that program that you did.' I had forgotten that he had been there."

Reyes attended the screening that Saturday evening. Another carpenter, Frank McMurray, a member of Local 608, was an active dissident within his union. McMurray recalled how he came to attend his first UT event:

I was working with a woman carpenter at the time, and she told me about a meeting which was going to show "Rosie the Riveter". So I decided that would be a good opportunity to go and see what they were up to and to recruit. It was a large hall and

I recall that it was full. I would guess that it was between three hundred and five hundred. The film was shown and there was some discussion by the speakers as to various problems that tradeswomen were having and there was an opportunity to ask questions.

So I got up and said essentially [that] these are tremendous problems—corruption, the hiring hall not being used properly and favoritism—problems for everybody in our union. They certainly affect women even more than they affect everybody else. I'm with Carpenters for a Stronger Union and we're working to change these things. Anybody who's interested in getting involved with that, please come and see me afterward. Out of that three to five hundred people, almost all of them were women, one person came to see me, Connie Reyes. And Connie became a part of CSU pretty much from the very beginning.[26]

This was the start of an uneasy alliance. Although Reyes became active with CSU, she also continued to work with UT. As she saw it, both had a vital function:

CSU was really focused on the Carpenters and on cleaning up the union. That was kind of like the *main* thing and it really wasn't going to address women's issues. And I thought those were important, which was why I did that. I think that's why there really weren't a lot of women in CSU. But women did participate. Irene did. You know? A lot of women did.

The tension between the two choices—working to reform their unions or a self-protective strategy that concentrated on survival—deepened over time for many in UT. While some of the women chose to make common cause with the very small groups of dissident men working to reform their unions, most of the UT activists stuck to the straighter path of trying to survive and find work in an increasingly hostile environment.

Soloway said, "Something that I was always aware of was that we were on the edge between dissidents within our unions and wanting to be accepted and just survive within the union. I think that we were on a thin edge. Most of our membership just wanted to survive in the unions. A small minority wanted to shake the unions and transform them. But because, as an organization with a membership of 300 people, and maybe 25 wanted to shake the unions and 250 didn't necessarily even think about wanting to do that because it was so unusual. Just to be able to get the work and to survive and to have a good time and to keep a job, and all of that. So we were kind of like just on the edge there."

When we were approached by some of the dissident organizations, including CSU, who wanted to work with us, we had an edgy kind of situation, 'cause we didn't have the sort of democratic kind of feeling. This is not something that most of the people in the organization really felt comfortable with. But it was kind of an instinct. Yes, if you're going to stay in the trades and survive, you *need* to reform from within. So that was kind of a running tension within the organization. [It was] kind of an edge that we were just riding.

UT enlisted support from organizations that supplied them with male allies. One major source was groups still trying to integrate the building trades and increase the numbers of minority men. "UT actually got more support from the men's groups, like Jim Haughton's group, Harlem Fight Back," said Ross. "He was very helpful to us. He gave us information. He supported us at our demonstrations. He was probably the best at giving us concrete help. We did try very hard to hook up with some of the men's groups that were out there and having their own problems. They gave us the idea to shape up, in fact. We used to go out on sites at six o'clock in the morning and shape up. They told us, 'If you don't, you're not going to get anywhere.' "

Veteran organizers James Haughton and Gil Banks of Fight Back, who had been active in integration battles in the building trades for more than a decade, began to include women in their own organizing efforts. Haughton recalled when the women first reached out to his organization:

> I saw a lot of black and white and Latino *workers* who wanted to get work, and they were up against the same opposition that the black [male] workers were up against. And so we responded to their call for support. This was because we understood that it was the right thing to do. A lot of these women had families that they were supporting, as it is today. They were the sole breadwinners and they needed work desperately, as desperately as the men because they were supporting their families, the children. So that was obviously a reason to give them whatever support we could possibly muster.[27]

The Fight Back organizers participated in public events organized by UT. An invitational flier for an event on February 6, 1981, featured a drawing of a woman standing at a construction site fence, hard hat tucked under her arm, in front of a sign that reads, "No Women Need Apply." The program featured a film on affirmative action and a panel discussion with four tradeswomen and Gil Banks of Fight Back. The workshop was billed as an opportunity for blue-collar women to learn about the history of equal employment opportunity and the new threats posed to women and minorities by the Reagan administration.

UT also looked to other groups as expert allies willing to share their hard-won knowledge with the women trying to gain a foothold in the trades. Already outsiders, the UT women sought out allies who were suspect to insiders and the subject of intense hostility from the majority of members of the construction trades unions.

One of these joint efforts was a UT workshop on the city's construction industry with participants from two coalition groups, Black Economic Survival, a Brooklyn-based group, and United Tremont Trades from the Bronx. At the time, both were active in other, job-related issues affecting their communities, such as trying to prevent lay-offs in the city's public hospitals.

"We were trying to learn from the black and Latino men's groups. United Tremont Trades was a Latino construction group mostly. [These groups] were in the South Bronx, in the worst section of the South Bronx. They were really willing to help us and were great to us," Ross said.[28]

Although the women were struggling for acceptance in their unions, these collaborative efforts added to their reputation as outsiders—as troublemakers. UT was traveling along two tracks, struggling to become insiders with the guaranteed right to work and to hold a union book, while trying to shake things up alongside other "outsiders."

Pots, Pans, and Protest

Although hundreds of women participated in UT's public programs, a much smaller number kept the group afloat and attended to its broader political agenda. Throughout its abbreviated lifespan, UT tried many strategies to expand employment opportunities for women. They took their message to advocates, to government officials, and the public and sought to put pressure on contractors and developers. The group tried to act as a watchdog for union recruitment drives and to publicize them for members. Moreover, as the backlash against affirmative action escalated, UT devoted attention to the many-pronged attack on women's rights and worked with others to develop a response. As Cynthia Long recalled, "United Tradeswomen was more like a community-activist-type group." But as time went on, UT's ambitious efforts to address every issue and to act on every option left its leadership coming up short on both energy and results.

"We were very action-oriented," said Ross. "We were doing educational work in terms of the workshops. But we also wanted to do actions." UT confronted the contractors about specific practices on the job that targeted women. "We were trying as much as possible to be action-oriented because it was really necessary," said Ross. "It's one thing to provide emotional support. We needed emotional support. We needed information. We needed *action* because, at that point, WAP was really kind of a bureaucracy and their hands were tied partly by being state-funded, whereas United Tradeswomen was totally grassroots-funded. We had no strings attached to anything we did, and we were very free to do a lot of things. So that's what we did."

In May 1981, a protest action took place at an IBM construction site. UT contacted all of the principal parties, including the contractor, subcontractor, and the union, in an effort to hold them accountable. On May 5, Ross wrote to the contractor, Turner Construction, about "the sexist and racist graffiti on the IBM site."

> We feel this is an intolerable situation for *all* workers on the job and is not in keeping with your responsibility to maintain a "harassment free" environment.... We request that the graffiti in question be painted over immediately, or this matter may be brought to public attention.[29]

Copies of the letter went to the union and to the Office of Federal Contract Compliance. On May 6, a letter from the company informed UT that the subcontractors' representatives had been informed by Turner Construction that they would be charged for the expense of removing the obscene graffiti from the walls of the building.

On May 15, Ross wrote to Turner, "We understand that the graffiti at the IBM site has been painted over. United Tradeswomen will continue to monitor the situation and work to develop longer term solutions to the problem of sexual harassment."[30]

Direct action made a difference for the women on those jobs. By responding quickly and demanding accountability from the responsible parties, UT was able to improve job site conditions for some women, without resorting to a strategy that took years to deliver a remedy.

UT also developed a campaign to get women hired onto the huge Jacob K. Javits Convention Center construction project managed by the Urban Development Corporation (UDC) that broke ground in early 1980 on the far west side of Manhattan. "When the Convention Center came up and there was one woman hired out of, I forget how many thousands of jobs, it was just a natural thing," said Ross.

By the time UT members met with the UDC representative on June 8, they had armed themselves with information about the general contractor, the subcontractors, the financing, hiring goals, and the pool of applicants. They had documented the experiences of the women who had shaped for jobs at the site but were never hired. In preparation for their meeting, the women developed a list of talking points. The UDC representative met with 20 UT members and promised to place a minimum of 7 percent females in construction jobs at the site.[31]

But, as Ross said, "After we had gotten three women on the job, two—Gwen Lee and Star Robinson of the Laborers' union—were fired, we thought unfairly. So, we fought to get their jobs back. They were coming to our meetings. We said, 'Okay, we're going to fight for you.' And we did. They were both reinstated because of that demonstration."

On August 5, 1981, UT held the first demonstration by tradeswomen in the country:

On a typically sweltering August day, Star Robinson, a 23-year-old black woman from Harlem, appeared before TV, radio, and newspaper reporters in Times Square. "Breaking into construction has proved even harder than I thought it would be," she told the press. Star is a member of United Trades Women, which called the demonstration to demand more construction jobs for women and to protest blatantly discriminatory practices at one of the largest construction sites in the city— the $375-million convention center. She spoke from experience. Star was one of two black women fired from the site after several days of work for Ferran Concrete Co., a major contractor on the project.[32]

Handouts to passersby described the prevailing climate for females in the industry:

Construction Boom: A Bust for N.Y.C. Women. United Tradeswomen and supporters are here today (in the first demonstration of its kind) to demand construction jobs for women. Most of the city's thousands of construction sites have no women, and only a few have even a handful—mere tokenism. Yet this situation goes on, while increased government attacks on affirmative action are eliminating women's right to earn a decent living at the job of our choice…The jobs are there—these are boom times for builders. A whopping 72 office buildings alone are slated to be built in NYC in the next 3 to 4 years. Women are being left out—especially women of color.

    United Tradeswomen believes that strong, effective enforcement of affirmative action (including goals and timetables) is crucial to achieve anything more than tokenism for women and minority workers. We will continue to monitor the situation for women at the Convention Center site, and we will keep up our fight for women's right to earn a decent living for ourselves and our families at the job of our choice.[33]

James McNamara, a keen observer of civil rights as it played out in the construction industry, witnessed the demonstration. At the time, McNamara was the Assistant Commissioner for the New York State Division of Human Rights. Many of the women who had applied for jobs at the Convention Center had filed discrimination complaints with the state Human Rights agency. "I can remember going up to observe the picket line, a demonstration of the women," McNamara recalled.[34] "It was a revelation to me because I had never seen women actually carrying signs picketing, saying 'We want jobs!' I said: This is great." Subsequently, he made an effort to push the UDC to make good on their goals for hiring women.

Since the start of the Lindsay administration in 1966, McNamara had been developing programs designed to integrate the building trades unions. There was one huge difference between the organizing by males and by females, McNamara said:

Fight Back would shape jobs. They would protest. But a whole [number] of other black groups started out and they would go down in massive numbers. They would come in these broken down school buses and they were violent. So for better or worse, the contractors, if for no other reason, started to take a tighter look at hiring minorities. But you didn't have a parallel situation with the women. Women didn't go down with baseball bats or throw rocks at construction jobs.

Organizing to integrate the building trades had often led to violence and/or the threat of violence. In time, some of the groups involved—the "coalitions"—became rackets of their own. Eventually, some became tools of the mob. However, this history took time to unfold. These organized crime associations were not evident in the late 1970s and early 1980s.[35]

In April 1982, both UT and Nontraditional Employment for Women (NEW) worked together to organize a demonstration at the construction site for AT&T's new corporate head-quarters. Their appeal highlighted the construction boom in the city (the 72 buildings under construction in the next few years) in contrast with the small number of women able to get work in the industry, alongside the Reagan administration's assault on affirmative action. Organizers invited all women to participate: "Even if you don't want a construction job for yourself, come out and support your sisters on May 19. Bring friends and family. There was a similar demo last year that was fun and fruitful. 12 women got jobs at the Convention Center."

The appeal to join the picket line on May 19 advised participants: "Wear a hardhat and apron, and bring a pot or pan and a tool. We want to sound out for the press and TV our demand for jobs...NEW has targeted the AT&T site because it's one of the largest sites, has city taxpayer's money in it, and has been discriminating against women since the project was started three years ago. Frankly, we're tired of begging for construction crumbs. A major goal of the demo is to make women VISIBLE—to hammer it home to the construction industry loud and clear that we're OUT HERE and we have a RIGHT to these jobs."[36] As Ross described:

> The second demonstration was moderately successful. There were a few more women hired...[37] I think our press coverage was not as good for this one com-pared to the first one, for some reason. I think we drew more women in the very first one.[38]

Evan Ruderman was on the picket line that day. "That one was my favorite. That's when we were banging the pots and pans. That was a very good idea."

"I was at all the demos. I helped to *organize* all of them," Reyes recalled. "I don't think there's any choice. You have to bring the message to the street. You have to bring the message to the job site. You have to hand out those leaflets. You have to talk to people."

UT actively opposed initiatives designed to weaken affirmative action. From the first efforts to cut back on Comprehensive Employment and Training Act (CETA) training funds during the Carter years, then on federal contract compliance and finally to eliminate affirma-tive action goals and timetables altogether, UT had many partners in the common struggle. Immediately after the Reagan administration took office, the pace of attack against affir-mative action started to pick up speed. The conservative movement met with a determined resistance throughout the decade of the 1980s.[39]

The point of the activism was to preserve the spirit and intent of Title VII—equal employment opportunity. In effect, this meant that women and minority organizations had to make the case for jobs; for the right to be in the mixture for hiring and training; and to keep the government's enforcement obligation in place. Over time, the need to set specific goals and timetables and to deliver on enforcement all became increasingly contentious.

To make their case and to organize a "determined resistance" against efforts to roll back the "right of women to work in any job of their choice," UT relied on traditional methods. The group used their meetings to communicate the urgency of their message and to get their members active; they publicized information through their newsletters and mailings; they organized public forums and petition drives; they testified at hearings; they documented the placement and retention of women in construction jobs to support their case; they held demonstrations; and they reached out to expert allies and cooperated with other groups.

UT provided a unified voice to speak in behalf of blue-collar, working women. According to Kay Webster, of all the groups that came together to organize for tradeswomen in New York City, "UT was the most comprehensive...I think that they were a force in the city. They hadn't quite turned a corner to become something that people would have to reckon with, but I thought that was right around the corner...That was the beauty of UT. For the longest time, we actually had a core connected group that allowed all of us to stay in, maybe longer than we would have survived otherwise."

At this point, the forces that brought the UT women together were pushing them apart. Aside from burnout amongst the women who had kept the group going, problems accelerated over questions of leadership, race, union corruption, as well as a destructive dynamic that had affected many other feminist organizations—"trashing."[40] Each of these factors now emerged within UT.

Ladies on a Tightrope

United Tradeswomen explored many different avenues in advocating for its members. In addition to the workshops and public forums, UT organized "rap groups, "support groups," and "speak-outs." They discussed racism and other hot-button topics. They worked in coalitions with like-minded groups. But UT had another side and even the group's serious side was typically coupled with fun. In addition to meetings, demonstrations, and workshops, UT organized many "Happy Hours." In the fall of 1984, the group launched a survey project to get an accurate picture of women working in the city's construction industry. UT kicked off the project with a party.

"In principle, UT meetings were *both* political and fun," Ross said. "Our meetings were mostly on Friday nights, so they became big social things," Soloway said. "We'd usually end up going to the bar afterward and they were like marathons. Everybody, mostly, drank a lot." UT women liked to have fun. "We wanted to be able to be very quirky too," said Soloway. "UT was very ground-breaking on a personal level for us. It was very intense. We wanted to be able to be ourselves...UT was a very safe place." For Soloway, this meant being able to express her creativity and sense of humor.

Ruderman recalled one memorable result: "One of my favorite activities was the blue-collar fashion show. That was a great idea."

"I literally woke up one morning and said, 'We have to have a blue-collar fashion show,'" Soloway said. "I think some people thought, 'That's weird.' But then, it just became everybody's idea."

An invitation appeared in the UT Newsletter in 1982: "Did you know that statistics show that women in the blue-collar industries have *strong* party instincts and a definite flair for boogying on down? We are working on creative overtime to put together a dynamite show. Members and friends will be modeling their blue-collar duds and fantasy outfits—everything from thermal underwear to rhinestone hard hats...If you've got an idea you want to try out on us or just want to strut your everyday work threads...Don't be shy. Come in your blue-collar fantasy!" More than 400 people attended. The event raised $1,200, more than a quarter of their $4,000 annual budget.[41]

The following year's fundraiser sought to build on that prior success. "Last year's Blue-Collar Fashion Fantasy established our rep for RAW TALENT and PARTYING FLAIR. The theme for 1983 is Blue-Collar Laffs. We are after a multimedia cabaret style gig focusing on the humorous aspects of our jobs. Sometimes a sense of humor goes further than you can throw a pipe wrench. Come to the UT office to tell some stories from your job, to be used as raw material for our cabaret. Or just come for the wine and cheese."

"Blue-Collar Laffs" turned into "Blue-Collar Follies." A letter invited UT members to get involved in planning for the April event: "Lucky you! Here's a chance to be the conversation piece at your next party—talking about UT's 2nd Annual COMEDY SHOW! Fun/dRaising at its best!! Check out our original comedy skits about life on the job. You're sure to recognize yourself in situations you wouldn't have thought to laugh at before...See your anger subli-mated...Your job fantasies come true...Only at: Blue-Collar Follies."[42]

The final version featured job skits by tradeswomen, an appearance by a clown, and the "Rosie Rockettes." Soloway's flier depicted two scantily clad or appropriately attired ladies—depending on interpretation—doing acrobatics on a high wire. After it was mailed out, the anticipated evening of fun turned sour. The tensions within the organization came to a head around this flier. As Ross recalled:

> People actually accused Irene of being sexist because the flier she had done was a little sexy. They said, "This is obviously sexist. It indicates a sexist leadership in United Tradeswomen." So what we did, in our great equanimity, we decided to let two fliers go out. Let them do a little puritanical flier, which was perfectly fine, but it was much different from Irene's flamboyant one. Instead of saying, "We have a different style," it was like, "This is sexist. She's sexist. It's exploiting women."

As Soloway described, "It was a carnival flier and it had lady tight rope walkers." The second flier featured the same information without the offending graphics. This time, tiny female hard hats in dungarees, with hammers, toolboxes, and tool belts invited UT members to attend the Blue-Collar Follies.

This episode indicated some of the fault lines in the group. United Tradeswomen's dis-integration—its unraveling—happened not like a ball of yarn, unwinding in a linear fashion, but like life, in a mixed-up, messy way, with many things occurring at the same time.

One problem was burnout. Exhaustion heightened emotions and even close friends were turning on each other. Life on the job was taking a physical and emotional toll. "What I feel happened was we were just burning ourselves out energy-wise," said Blackwelder. "We were just running ourselves ragged. I think people kind of dropped out just from exhaustion. [UT] was a wonderful thing, but it died out."

Tensions arose between women who were once close. Soloway directed hostility toward Ruderman, as she recalled: "I remember browbeating her on the street once...We really had a big fight....All this violence is coming out, haranguing people, feeling like they were betraying [each other by]...giving up on the organization. And we were losing people at that point."

Exhaustion resulted not only from the long hours and the physical demands of the job, but also from the intensity of organizing in an environment rife with corruption. Ruderman became a UT casualty. Exhaustion, fear and intimidation, confusion over UT's direction, and the dysfunction inside the group caused her to quit.

As she explained, "Sometimes I do have a deep sense of regret about some things…that we weren't able to continue. But I also have to remember the state, physically and emotionally, that I was in at the time. That's why I personally couldn't contribute and have to assume that other women were probably in the same [condition]."

"I think that each woman began to feel that she had to develop her own strategy. I'll just speak for myself. I really did begin to feel like I've got to figure out some way to survive. I'm coming home with tears every day. I hate the world.…Basically, I was terrified and scared. And that's key."

> UT was going through their problems then. So I withdrew within myself…I didn't have the same energy for United Tradeswomen any more. Unfortunately, if I had been able to bring that to UT, if I had been more confident, less terrified, then maybe that could have been our next emphasis as a group and we could have figured out a job action, like what we did at IBM or do something. So I look back now and one of my regrets is that I didn't have the confidence to say, "Hey, you know. I was walked off the job and threatened. What can we do about that? Or, what does it mean?"

One source of anger was racism. Race was a constant concern of UT women. The heavy double burden women of color bore as they entered the skilled trades was the focus of public programs, discussion groups, columns, stories, and poems in the UT Newsletter.

The carpenter Martha Clanton, a founding member of UT, wrote an article for its newsletter about the struggle to get into the construction trades as a black woman. She described the Catch 22 women faced.

> To get employment in carpentry there is a cycle you must go through. You can't get a job without a union book, and you can't get a union book without a job. There is a tremendous resistance to hiring women and minorities.[43]

But as time went on, what had been viewed as an external issue began to affect the internal dynamics of the group. Early on, members took on the issue as a problem that could be resolved if they confronted it directly. In 1982, UT sent a questionnaire to its members:

> Question #5: What are some ways in which white women in United Tradeswomen can eliminate unaware racism within the organization? Question #6: How does racism affect the building of alliances among workers in the struggle for affirmative action?[44]

Then a group discussion was held. UT members spoke about their individual responses to the effort to discuss racism in a mixed-race group. Most admitted that it felt "scary." The transcript of that discussion was then printed in the UT Newsletter:

> You know, I almost have a headache. Man, this is really hard! I can't tell you.…I feel like we were kind of intellectual but we sort of got in there with the feelings. Let's

keep going. It's really heavy, what we're talking about here. What I want to say is that I didn't feel I could talk this way with the men. I didn't feel this with the black men on my job. Like I couldn't even say, "I'm fucking suffering! Are you?" They would hide that shit so goddamned much, so at least we were able to come here and say something to each other. . . . It is important to have a follow-up because there are a lot of women out there who have a lot to say and this group here is just a grain of sand. You know, UT is a big organization.[45]

In February 1983, Marty Pottenger followed up that discussion with a question: "How would my life be different if racism did not exist?" Her answer: "Really different." As she wrote, "Racism was thoroughly a part of the all-white community I grew up in. It is probably accurate to say that unless racism was being directly interrupted or challenged, it was being taught. What has been less obvious and misleading to me, are the less visible ways racism surrounded and was absorbed by me. No words, no actions were needed to teach it. It was the very absence of contact with people of color." Her attempt to come to grips with the legacy of racism is echoed in other pieces that appeared in the UT Newsletter.[46]

UT continued to struggle with the persistent problem. But ultimately, the anger and divisions created by feelings of racism caused irreparable rifts. This anger bubbled over one evening as UT members got together for another viewing of "Rosie the Riveter." At this event, Miriam Frank was a guest speaker. She talked about the work she did to scout out the original Rosies who eventually appeared in the film. Her reception that night took her by surprise. As she recalled:

There were maybe 15 or 20 women. There were white woman and black women. "Rosie the Riveter" is very, very outspoken about the role of black women in the war industry. . . . It really emphasizes how important these jobs were to black women who, before the war, were mostly working in agriculture and domestic service and now they leapfrogged into manufacturing.

So the lights went on and a quarrel began about racism. I had spoken to many community groups that were racially mixed and there had been arguments. . . . But this one, there was no overview. I had walked into a nest of quarrels, of problems that had been going on in the organization. I had no idea that people really were so angry at each other. It all came out in this conversation. I think for them, it was the ending of their group. It wasn't cohering in the way that it had been.[47]

Years later, Soloway spoke about that night: "Oh, we had a great discussion at Lois's house. People were really dealing with the racism issue there, in terms of that, 'Yes. It's nice to say that we're all in this together, but the fact is that black women are really on the bottom, that they get really, really different types of jobs.' I mean, in the carpenters union, the black women generally went to heavy construction and the white women generally went to inside construction."

So the movie, because it was so affirming of the women and so upbeat, I think it set off a lot of the black women who were there, saying, "You know, we don't feel included in this," even though there were black women in the movie. But Miriam was in shock afterward, 'cause she was expecting a much more positive response to the movie. But I think people (reacted) almost *because* the film was seamless in terms of the unity between black and white women in the shipyards.

Cynthia Long, an Asian-American, shared her impressions of UT regarding race: "I think that [race] was a very difficult issue for people to really get a handle on. I feel that I was often the scapegoat because I would raise the issue of race. I think many people would prefer to just think of me as a white person and I was not going to have that....I would tell people that the way that they spoke was racist....Instead of focusing on the issue that I raised, they would rather break it down to personality."

Although UT activities did focus on issues related to race, Long drew a distinction between that level and a deeper confrontation with the problem. As she explained, "This is the thing: if you talk about racism as an intellectual exercise, it's one thing and there is no bloodletting. But when there are actual individuals who are confronting people, saying 'Okay, you raised the issue of racism so you're at least intellectually aware of it. But I'm here to tell you that the way you say things is offensive to me as a person of color.' They wanted to sweep that stuff under the rug. So I was not going to let them be swept under the rug. I applaud them as an organization for raising the issue and trying to deal with it, but it's a work in progress. It was a struggle and it felt very difficult. It was emotionally exhausting. After a while, I just didn't want to be there....After three years, I felt like, okay. I gave it my best shot and I give myself permission to leave now."

Yvone Maitin also experienced these tensions and shared her thoughts on how this divided UT:

> The women of color felt that they didn't have a real voice in it, that they were not able to be a part of the leadership, that the leadership was primarily white females. It's not an unusual thing. Personally, I enjoyed UT. It was a good experience for me. But I was new and young at that time. I knew that a lot of women of color were complaining about it, that they felt they weren't reached out to. I've heard that over the years, not just with UT, but in other groups. I think it is partly true.
>
> United Tradeswomen, New York Tradeswomen, any of the groups I've been a part of, they are all microcosms of a larger society. They reflect the larger society and there's no way possible that we're not going to see the same kind of contradictions. Working through those contradictions is not simple or easy. They take a lot of work. Most groups, not just UT, don't really want to deal with it because it means crossing from the political to the internal arena. It means dealing with personal contradictions...These are old, long held views. They're a part of this society. So we need to be more patient and more creative in how we're going to confront these things.
>
> I think that the internal contradictions within UT were not only on the side of the white women. It was multidimensional and it was something that everybody needs to take responsibility for their part in it. It really is deep. I think that that was the biggest contradiction. I think that was the thing that made it fall apart because the women of color were not coming. Little by little, they weren't coming. And in the trades, quite frankly, a great majority of the women are women of color.

Another problem was also facing the group: UT was at a crossroads. "We were trying to figure out, what did we want to do? What do we want to become?" Ross said. "We talked about it. Some of the problems were so intense. The problems were so large because of the Mafia connections. People were frightened. And we couldn't decide what we could be. Some of us were trying to be a union democracy organization, a support group, and an action group. There were so many issues to deal with that we really kind of lost our way and weren't sure what we should do next to really be effective. It was at that point, when we were really struggling to identify what we needed to do, that some people came into the organization, and were very disruptive. The organization got bogged down in trying to understand what was going on. We really struggled. We didn't know how to handle it because we had never really had serious dissent in the group."

Tremendous personal rancor began to be directed at the leaders of UT. Although declining to identify the individuals who created the havoc, members vividly recalled their feelings and the results that ensued from the attacks. As Webster described the conflict, it was directed at the two leaders of the group, Ross and Soloway:

> Whenever people attack a leader of an organization like that, a progressive one, it's not that the leader didn't make mistakes. They might have. But it was beside the point. It was like—this is about disrupting and destroying the organization, which it ultimately did, which was a shame. Because Lois and Irene, who were heading it, who did, I think, an incredible job of thinking about the group, both of them were entirely sincere and hard working. And this woman came along who had an agenda and I think probably just had problems with anybody who looked like they were in charge.

Ultimately, Ross summed up the situation as a lost opportunity for exerting leadership. "At that point when we were really struggling to identify what we needed to do most...the organization got bogged down trying to understand what was going on. We really struggled. Some of us really didn't know how to handle it....We were being such democratic women. We *let* them disrupt us....They had a lot of personality problems that they hadn't worked out for themselves....They initiated the attacks and started instigating people....Irene and I were called bureaucrats just because we had been the most committed and done the most work over the years."

Ross felt the personal attacks in a visceral way. Time provided her with a broader perspective: "I've been thinking about this for a while. See this was not just an isolated thing that happened with UT. I read an incredible book called *Between Women* that describes this exact kind of thing happening all across the country. The two women who wrote the book were trying to explain the patterns we develop as women—mistrust of each other, a lack of understanding of leadership, and how to support leadership....But there was so much fear and distrust about anyone getting too much power and this was happening because of our strong democratic tendencies as women and I think, fear of power, because we never had power as women. It made me feel better that we weren't unique....We were still women. We were still demonstrating all the patterns of women; the weakness of women. Men don't have that problem. They have different problems. But, in general, they don't have these kinds of leadership fears."

Every woman took some degree of personal responsibility for the dissolution of the group. Trying to weigh the different problems that drove them apart, they expressed a sense of loss and regret over choices made and actions not taken. But after wrestling for a long time with the question of what could have been done to prevent the break-up of UT, Soloway reached a different conclusion: "It's so interesting. It's difficult to say what we *could* have done. I almost feel like we couldn't have done anything else."

We Still Have a Dream: UT's Legacy

As each woman looked backward in an attempt to assess the legacy of the group they guided for six years, they found some common threads. "What I really liked about UT was that it was a tradeswomen's organization—started, run, and working with the tradeswomen," said Yvone Maitin.[48]

"UT offered a space for women to come and be themselves," Ross said. "After it disappeared, there was a void." When United Tradeswomen collapsed, women working in nontraditional jobs lost a unified voice to speak out on their issues and to push back against the erosion of affirmative action goals. Creating a political voice to bring people together and to organize collective solutions to political problems, rather than individuals acting in isolation, was a major achievement.

As Reyes thought about UT's legacy, she highlighted the support the group provided, as well as its political role: "It played a really big role in women's lives. . . . I'm a feminist, and it gave real emotional support. That was just so important. The other thing it did, for me, it vindicated the fact that you can do political work anywhere. It doesn't matter where you find yourself. Do what you set out to do. . . . I think United Tradeswomen was a miracle. It was amazing what they got accomplished. I would say that the only limitation was the limitation imposed by the larger society. It would have been great if we could have been a mass movement, but part of the issue was that we were tradeswomen and that was again going to limit us as to where we were and who we were."

Reyes pointed to some of the broader contributions of UT's organizing, including the pioneering work on sexual harassment in blue-collar jobs; the connection UT established between the pioneers of the 1970s and the "Rosies;" and the first national conference of tradeswomen in 1983.

This was a highlight, for Reyes: "We participated and helped in organizing a conference of women in nontraditional jobs in California, in San Francisco. One of the things we voted on was for women in the trades to take a stance against nuclear proliferation and nuclear war. We *did* that. I mean, these were politically diverse women. People think it's like a monolith. No. It's not. In fact, I think of all the women I knew in the Carpenters Union, I was the only Socialist. . . . Out of that conference, we took a position against nuclear proliferation."

After UT disintegrated, many members kept its spirit alive. Maitin was active in founding another group, New York Tradeswomen. Former UT members participated in subsequent national conferences of tradeswomen. Maitin attended the 2nd National Tradeswomen's Conference in Chicago in 1989. As she recalled:

> I remember it because it was my first tradeswomen's conference. There were a lot of women there, more than 500, and for me, it felt like *beaucoup* women. . . . All of these things . . . are just very strengthening and reaffirming about who we are as women. Each of these instances and these projects and the things that we put together . . . moves it ahead just a little bit more. That's what it really is all about. It's about making those connections, one step at a time, a little bit more each time. We have to do this.[49]

Irene Soloway saw UT as a part of the political momentum that swept through the city in the 1970s and 1980s—and the groups that acted as catalysts for change:

> Like I was saying all day at the hospital where I work, Lincoln Hospital. "Where are the radicals? Where are they?" I was telling the guys at work, because the hospital [is] so screwed up. It's just so corrupt now. I'm saying "This is the South Bronx, you know? People should be questioning where this money is going? Why are there people waiting nine hours in the waiting room? . . . I don't know where this groundswell is going to come from to fight back against all this."[50]

Kay Webster viewed the support UT provided for women as its chief contribution: "It allowed women to be in the trades, to keep going.... That was the beauty of United Tradeswomen."

UT collapsed in 1985. Support for affirmative action in blue-collar settings was under attack. Although President Reagan's early and unrelenting attempts to whittle away the legal foundations of affirmative action met with mixed results, subsequent efforts succeeded in landing key blows. At the time of its demise, UT's radical vision for "the guaranteed right of every woman to work in the job of her choice" remained a work in progress.

PART TWO

Construction

THREE

Learning to Labor on High Steel

Mike Cherry begins his book, *On High Steel: The Education of an Ironworker* with a note to his readers: "The people in this book are ironworkers. They are the men you see clambering up the columns and walking along the beams that form the skeletons of most tall buildings. They belong to a union called The International Association of Bridge, Structural, and Ornamental Ironworkers. The columns and beams are steel, but the men are called ironworkers."[1] Cherry's book was published in 1974 when all the ironworkers in the City of New York *were* men. They were called the "cowboys of the sky" for their daring feats on steel beams high above the city's streets and rivers.[2]

In 1979, Janine Blackwelder became the first "cowgirl" of the sky in New York City.[3] As a newcomer, standing 5 feet, 7 inches tall, slender, with a heart-shaped face and a pixie haircut, she didn't fit the popular image of an ironworker.

Blackwelder consciously chose a nontraditional job "for the cause" of women's equality. She began her apprenticeship the same year that an agreement between the union, Local 580, and the government—signed after years of litigation—opened up the program to minority males. At the time, Blackwelder was only vaguely conscious of this aspect of the local's history. As a new apprentice, she was paying attention to getting her bearings and learning the ropes.

Once on the job as a "journeyman," she faced the barriers beyond the effort of learning a new trade. In time, her status as an outsider became the foreground. Alongside some of her fellow union members, she participated in efforts to challenge the discriminatory job referral system.

During the dozen years Blackwelder spent in the local, corruption was invisible to her. It was only toward the end of her career that she became aware of these notorious transactions, through the publicity surrounding the trials in federal court.[4]

In 1991, the business agent for her local, Frank Leone, was murdered. She heard the news report on TV where, as she recalled, the camera showed him, "lying on the ground in front of his home with his legs sticking out."[5] The first trial involving Local 580 officials was declared a mistrial. Shortly after, she left New York City.

Three years later, Blackwelder got some perspective on her life as an ironworker. She described some of the costs she bore as a pioneer. Her blunt, straightforward language did not dramatize her achievement in breaking the all-male barrier, learning her trade, and working at it for twelve years.

The Job

Ironworkers perform two types of tasks: structural, where the skeleton of the building is created with steel beams; and ornamental, where the "finishing" jobs at a later stage of construction are done. Dozens of details must come together on any job.[6]

> I was doing ornamental iron work. I was trained in what we call finishing work and ornamental iron work. Finishing work can be something like entranceways and hanging doors and that type of thing, and some of the miscellaneous steel is not seen once it's erected because other things cover it...One of the big items the ornamental ironworker does in New York is put up curtain wall, which is the metal that holds the glass on the skyscrapers.
>
> In most of the country, there's not a separate ornamental local. New York is one of two cities in the country that has an ornamental local....Depending on the type of work it could be me and one other person to a job where the employer I work for has 40–60 ironworkers on a job. It depends on the scale.

Once on the job, Blackwelder's strategy for survival was to try and blend into the scene: "My way of assimilating or integrating—even though I stuck out like a sore thumb from day one—was to try to be kind of the average ironworker in many other ways."

She adopted a self-deprecating style, downplaying the obvious differences between herself and her co-workers. Throughout her career, she experienced varying degrees of hostility, ranging from mild to extreme. She chose to chalk up the insults and harassment to a weakness on the part of the perpetrators. As she recalled: "If someone was really hostile to me, it was 'cause that person was a hostile person anyway. I don't think my presence kicked up anything new in these people. The same guy who hated me, hated blacks, hated Puerto Ricans, hated everybody."[7]

Blackwelder was strong enough to learn her trade; smart enough to survive; determined enough to keep going back every day. The vocabulary of an ironworker came to pepper her speech. She adapted to the culture of the workplace, hung out in bars with her co-workers, attended union meetings, and eventually became a rabble-rouser in the local. For twelve years, she earned her living on high steel. Years later, looking back, she could see what it cost to survive. But throughout her years in the trade, she never identified herself as separate or special because she was a woman. She saw her experiences as representative of those of her fellow ironworkers. As she put it, "I found out through the application process that I was the first woman to come into this particular union. And I think that has some bearing on my experience. But I think my experience over time is similar to other women's as well as men who were before me or who are yet to come."[8]

Breaking Ground

Blackwelder vividly recalled the first time she walked onto a construction site as an apprentice.

> I remember looking for the shanty. I remember the first ironworker I met. I remember the first loud mouth and [one] guy who was very insulting. I remember the first guy who was really nice and kind of took me under his wing. He taught

me things and just allowed me to learn and was willing to work with me. He didn't feel the need to romance me. He didn't feel the need to make me his daughter. We just worked as co-workers. He was actually a foreman and I was an apprentice. But I found myself with a foreman who was a good guy. There were a few who were hostile, but my experience was generally positive pretty much throughout my apprenticeship.

Reactions to her presence at the apprentice school were low-keyed: "There was no fanfare or anything," she said. "The first-year teachers—one guy was kind of old-fashioned and one guy was a little more 'today.' I think it was kind of new to them—funny."

At school and on the job, Blackwelder was in the position of every other apprentice who was struggling to gain skills. The partnership between the journeyman and apprentice was the critical component. Both males and females in the skilled trades encountered situations when some journeyman would resist sharing their knowledge. Some journeymen expressed extreme hostility toward women. Others were willing and excellent tutors. Blackwelder's experiences varied:

Some people you work with, they're not really going to show you anything. You strictly have to watch. They're not teachers and they don't have the skill of being teachers. Some people explain things better than others. You can't necessarily expect that your foreman or the mechanic you're working with is going to break everything down in terms you understand and teach you in the same way instruction is offered in the school. On the other hand, sometimes you'll run into somebody who will share information with you. It's easy and you may learn different types of things than you did just by watching.

You just have to learn that it's not a constant uphill progression. Sometimes you're on a job that is very monotonous and your part is a dummy job. You just try to enjoy the fact that you don't have the pressure and the mind work to do, until the next job, which hopefully, if you're interested in taking more responsibility, somebody will see your skills and give you a more interesting or challenging job. There is no guarantee on any of this.

As time went on, Blackwelder realized she was the beneficiary of knowledge she'd absorbed from her father: "My father used to do whatever fixing around the house that was needed and I used to work with him sometimes. My brothers, for whatever reason, kind of shunned working with their hands. So I was the next one in line and I'd be his little assistant when I was small. As I got a little older, I lost interest. It was only when I was a couple of years in the business that I realized I was more familiar that I thought I was. I came into it thinking that I knew nothing about construction. I realized that a lot of the conversations I had heard over the years—places he had taken me and work we'd done—some of that information came in handy on the job."[9]

Blackwelder chose the job because of her feminist perspective. After she completed her apprenticeship, she stopped encouraging other women to enter the trades, the role that she enthusiastically played during her years as a member of United Tradeswomen. But in the beginning, she was all for the cause.

Once on the job, Janine chose to downplay her feminist motivation for entering the trades: "I think I learned to deny it a lot, when guys would ask me 'Are you trying to prove a point?' I'd say, 'No, I'm here for the money, just like everybody else.' But no. My biggest point probably had to do with the situation with women in the country. I felt that things weren't going to change until blue-collar women had the same experiences and opportunities as men—until working-class women were being paid what working-class men were being paid. The only way you do that is by going after the same job."

The Union and the Search for Work

As someone who identified with the left, and, in her words, "the noble proletariat," Janine looked on union membership as a valuable part of the craft experience:

> I had at that time and still do have a very positive attitude about unions. In fact, I'm kind of an idealist in a way. This comes from reading, learning a little about the history of this country, seeing how in other countries the establishment of labor unions generally means an opening up of democracy in a country…I feel unions are important.

Local 580's jurisdiction includes the five boroughs of New York City, Westchester, Suffolk, and Nassau counties. During Blackwelder's years in the trade, general membership meetings were typically held in Manhattan on the fourth Thursday of every month at the Marc Ballroom, on the west side of Union Square.[10]

> I would go and I would listen and see that my ideals of democracy were not reflected in those meetings. They were not especially well attended…In the actual formal meetings, the officials are listened to by some people. It's difficult to keep order in the meetings, to keep people quiet. We have a sergeant-at-arms to walk around and tell everybody to shut up and some do and some don't. When people speak, they're not always respected. I mean, this is certainly not the floor of the British Parliament or something. Anything can happen. You can be called out of order, booed down. To the extent that Robert's Rules of Order are used, you often find they're used just to shut up an opinion that somebody doesn't feel comfortable hearing. So I've told people that I feel that some of us have seen more democracy at a Girl Scout meeting than in the union meeting.[11]

After three years of apprenticeship, Blackwelder graduated at the head of her class. She was one of the two top students to receive a ring from the local as a symbol of this achievement.[12]

She began to look for work as a journeyperson, and soon discovered that she was on her own: "It gets more difficult sometimes when you become a mechanic and then you have to be more competitive and kind of fend for yourself, more than as an apprentice."

In the construction industry, apprenticeship programs are often the training ground for the industry's key workers and foremen, and consequently, the demands of the programs are far more rigorous than what the typical journeyperson requires.[13] Under ordinary circumstances, as tops in her class, Janine might have been looking forward to a career with additional responsibilities, advancement, and some of the other benefits of the trade, including a hefty paycheck. In fact, this wasn't her experience:

> As far as me being recognized for my skill or being tried out in different circumstances to take more leadership, that opportunity was not open to me.…I know that there are men with the same amount of skill who have made three times my

yearly income, and consistently, year after year. Sometimes I've felt like, after the first few years, that I had finally graduated from some kind of lower economic class to finally being able to identify with the middle class. It shouldn't have been that way. It should have been more lucrative, I think.

Looking for work is the central fact of life for most construction workers. Jobs are of different durations but they all end sooner or later. Then the search for the next job starts. This is a constantly recurring reality in the trades. For newcomers, but especially for those seen as "outsiders" in the trades, meaning minorities and women, looking for the next paycheck is complicated by the two systems that govern the search for employment—the formal rules and regulations and the informal connections.

A huge body of research seeks to explain how discrimination works inside the construction industry. The work of sociologists Thomas Bailey and Roger Waldinger provides a clear blueprint describing how minorities are excluded. In their essay, "The Continuing Significance of Race: Racial Conflict and Racial Discrimination in Construction," they pointed to one critical factor: "Despite the high degree of formal regulations and requirements in the industry, it is the *informal* system that also governs the construction industry which works against black workers seeking entrance. For blacks, the continued informality of the union sector has been particularly consequential, because it prevents groups not already integrated into networks within the industry from firmly establishing themselves in construction work."[14]

As Blackwelder said, this reality governed the search for work for certain categories of Local 580 members:

> The thing about our local is, and one thing that I feel that us as a group, minorities and women, may not understand, especially coming into the local, is that you're really seen as a free agent or an independent contractor or a freelancer in some respects, even though you're a union member. In our local, you have the right to solicit your own work. You can solicit that work through communication with the employer, with a foreman you've worked for, with an old friend. You can shape the jobs, which means show up on the job site looking for somebody in charge and saying, "I need a job. Are there any openings?" You can talk to the general contractor.
>
> So with us, we have to try everything to stay steadily employed. If you don't have anybody guiding you along, and most people don't, you have to try and get a job from your contacts, meaning union or employer. You have to shape the [hiring] hall, which means sitting down in this room in the early morning and seeing if you're next to go out on a job. You need to shape the sites themselves. And when you're really desperate, you start doing the work of the business agent and even find out where the work is going on because you feel like somebody's not doing enough or you'd be working. So it can be all-consuming.
>
> As you get further into it, you realize that because certain people are steady with the company or because of their experience or because of who they know, they might have some of these lighter jobs sewed up, or some of the more lucrative jobs sewed up. And when you're unemployed and hustling to get the next job, you're in a position that you'll take anything that comes along.

Once on the job, kinship is just one of the powerful connections prevalent within the industry. "In Local 580, oftentimes I was replaced by somebody's brother," Blackwelder recalled.[15] In discussing the job situation, words such as "cronyism," and "inside circle" continuously crop up in her speech. This was the case when she described a big project she worked on in Lower Manhattan:

> I was on some jobs that were longer jobs. But when they reduced to a small gang just to finish up the job, I still hadn't gotten into the inner circle. This job I was on, the Shearson Lehman building, where I was good friends with the general foreman...unfortunately he had given the hiring and firing power to his second in command, and it was that guy who laid me off as the job was winding down...What was left to do was some of the finishing work inside. We had put up the outside skin of the building and now there was some of the decorative stuff and closing off, which I was clearly good at. But his buddy wanted to keep people who were his cronies. So I never got into the inner circle where I would really work or stay the longest—being one of the people to stay throughout the whole job.

One plum job landed in her lap through happenstance. This was to be her sole experience in running a job, that is, acting as the person in charge: "I only ran this one job. That was kind of by default, because this other guy was supposed to run the job, but he didn't like what the boss offered him. Maybe he asked for too many extras or something. So he got in his station wagon and drove away. The boss told me that he was going to make me the foreman. Basically, because I would do what I was told and he wouldn't have to give me all these extras."

Throughout her years in Local 580, the hiring hall operated by the union continued to function with separate tracks for certain members. When Blackwelder described the system in 1990, she still held out some hope that things might improve:

> One thing that exists and hopefully this is going to change in the next 10 years, is that there's a kind of back door and a front door when it comes to shaping the hall. A lot of the people who feel kind of left out are sitting in the back room, and it's usually mostly black men, one or two women, and one or two white guys who seem to be being punished for one thing or another. I don't believe that the extent or frequency of your employment necessarily reflects that you're a good or a bad worker. I think both things are true: that if you're a good worker, chances are you will stay more steadily employed. But I also know that there are good workers who are sitting down at our union hall waiting to go out on a job, and the reason why they're not working has a lot to do with their nonfavored status among some of the bigots in the local.[16]

The Consent Agreement

In 1979, Local 580 was in the first year of a court-supervised agreement between the union and the government to integrate the Ornamental and Architectural Iron Workers in New York City. When Blackwelder began her apprenticeship program, little more than a year had elapsed since the union had signed off on the agreement with the Justice Department. The apprentices were aware of the agreement. At the time, she had only a vague understanding of its terms:

> The union was under a consent judgment to hire minority workers, meaning I guess, black and Hispanic and other ethnic men. I don't remember in that consent judgment anything that mentioned women.

The consent judgment included specific provisions for the recruitment, selection, admission, and training of minorities in the apprenticeship program, as well as job referrals for the new apprentices. The affirmative action plan was designed to increase the minority membership to 24 percent of the total membership within five years.[17]

The government's case, *Equal Employment Opportunity Commission vs. Local 580*, began in 1971, when the U.S. Department of Justice filed a complaint charging Local 580 and its apprenticeship program violated the Civil Rights Act of 1964. The complaint charged that the union and its training program were "engaged in a pattern and practice of resistance to the full enjoyment by nonwhites of rights secured to them by law." In 1974, the EEOC was substituted as a plaintiff for the Department of Justice when the consent judgment was being negotiated.

On July 21, 1978, the consent judgment went into effect. Under it, Local 580 was required to increase its nonwhite participation, to validate its selection criteria, to maintain records, and to report all employment data to the EEOC and to adopt a nondiscriminatory referral system.[18]

Twelve years elapsed between the time that Blackwelder joined the local, 1979, and the year she left, 1991. During that time, Local 580 was under the supervision of the court. Every facet of its operations was prescribed by the terms of the consent agreement. Yet the "back door" and the "front door" continued to operate in the hiring hall and in many other aspects of union life. In all those years, the local never complied with the terms of the agreement. "All that was going to happen *after* I stopped working with Local 580," said Blackwelder, in reference to an agreement to put in place a fair system of job referrals.

Local 580 resisted through dilatory maneuvers. The local spent copious amounts of time and the members' money in and out of court and paying fines after being found in contempt. Mounds of court documents describe the stratagems the union used to push off the day when it would comply. All of this occurred very, very slowly, typically taking years for each scenario to reach a resolution. That would then turn out to be no resolution at all.

On September 11, 1987, a court proceeding was held to discuss remedial measures. A Special Master was installed, appointed to oversee all aspects of the case and to supervise the defendants' compliance. "The cost of the Special Master shall be charged upon and apportioned among the defendants as the court may direct, subject to the Special Master's recommendation. The charge will be due on a quarterly basis."[19]

On June 18, 1991, there was another court proceeding. A settlement conference reached an agreement on a new formula for hiring and a new referral system for jobs. The new system relied on the installation of a telephone referral system and on journeymen's being referred to jobs "on the basis of consecutive days on the referral list."[20]

This was the referral system that led Blackwelder to express some hope for fair hiring in Local 580's future. Yet three years later, this referral system was still not in place. "Local 580 is in the process of putting in a computerized system for hiring. The government [is] going to monitor it," she said, in 1994.[21]

The telephone system proved illusory. Despite oral promises by union officials, installation stayed in a holding pattern. In 1997, it was sighted at the union hall, still in boxes. Union democracy watchdog Herman Benson, founder of the Association for Union Democracy, summed up the situation: "Tales of racial discrimination, favoritism, blacklisting, and links to organized crime are not unfamiliar in the New York City construction industry. What distinguishes Local 580, however, is discrimination right under the nose of the federal government. The ongoing consent judgment, the contempt ruling which cost the union $5 million, the hiring hall rules imposed under the judgment, and even oversight by a Special Master appointed by the EEOC, have apparently done little to end job discrimination."[22]

As Benson reported, "26 years after the original complaint, this 1,300-member local has between 300 and 400 minority members. Justice at last? Think again. Once again, in 1996, some members have brought renewed charges of discrimination to the EEOC. They say that few of those African-American, West Indian, and Latino workers can get work regularly out of the union hiring hall, that many receive so few referrals that they don't come close to working the 1,000 hours a year to qualify for insurance benefits."[23]

What was the role for the union member in all of this? The main role was to offer testimony in court, which then led to retaliation. Other than that, the system relies on attorneys and other assorted law enforcement personnel. Robert Fitch, author of *Solidarity for Sale*, offers an apt critique: "It's just a jobs program for lawyers and bureaucrats. If they ever solved the problem, they'd be off the gravy train."[24]

Over the years, affirmative action has moved from substance to a shadow play, away from goals and timetables, effective evaluation, enforcement, or any substantive remedies regarding contract compliance.[25] "Affirmative action," though still capable of igniting heated debates, became a useless tool for the most part. In Fitch's words, "Affirmative action has joined 40 acres and a mule in the catalog of empty promises made by the white man."[26]

A lone woman—or a minority male—showing up for work at a site where federal dollars are being poured has this truth brought home to her. The actual experience of trying to get hired onto a construction project remains a world apart from the laws and regulations that are on the books. By and large, minimal efforts are made by contractors to comply with the first "goal" established in 1978—to bring the rate of female participation up to 6.9 percent on federally funded construction projects. "Affirmative action" requirements remain remote, arcane, and almost totally unenforced. Blackwelder's experiences underscore this point. She shared some observations based on her twelve years in the trade:

> At different times throughout these years, I think there's been some pressure put on certain jobs to have a representation of women there. I don't really know to what extent that's been done. I haven't felt that it's been any kind of feather in my cap that I'm a woman—that that means I'm going to be more steadily employed than a man or anything like that—because if I've been hired or kept on a job because I am a woman, it's been kept from me.[27]

In very few instances did the federal regulations kick in to get her hired:

> I think [on] one or two jobs, I was given that impression that I was there because they want to show a woman. My contractor wanted to have a woman on his payroll. But either because of their funding or their subsidies or their tax breaks, I don't really know. I'm not well versed in that. Frankly, when you get on the job, you're so busy finding out what to do and who to take orders from and where's the bathroom and all this other business that you don't spend time even investigating who the owner of the building is, much less the financiers.

In time, she saw that minority men and women in the trades had much in common. The similarities became evident. She described some of the parallel situations.

> It certainly is uncomfortable to stick your neck out too far because you're always the new person, as a minority or a woman. I also say minority in the sense that I feel some

of the experiences and some of the psychological stuff that goes on with me, I know that there are some black guys or other ethnic groups who might experience similar things. Like just this morning, this guy said that he's going to take a job with the city. It's less pay but it's better for his head. And he's clearly talking about the oppression that he feels as a black guy in this local...I can relate to that feeling.

After spending some time as a journey-level worker, her idealistic nature prevailed. In an effort to have "more of a say on the job" and to bring some "democracy" to union affairs, she got active with a group organized by other outsiders in Local 580.

"Don't Knock His Jock Off"

Blackwelder was always a person who took action on the job when she saw something that didn't seem fair. To a journeyperson, the inequities were glaringly apparent. After time spent trying to buck the system, she got involved in challenging it. This was not the standard way of doing business in Local 580. She described the culture of conformity in the union: "There's an expression: 'Don't knock his jock off.' If you want to challenge someone, do it in a bar, not in public or at a union meeting."[28] Despite this common wisdom, her frustration led her to make common cause with some of her fellow ironworkers who were challenging the unfair practices of the hiring hall. The group, which called itself "Alters," was made up of black and Latino men and black and white women:

> It was a rank-and-file group with a particular mission—to work with elected officials and other members to open up opportunities in a more even-handed way, for a fair distribution of the fruits of the business. We saw ourselves as outside the network that got the good jobs, the shop steward jobs, the foremanships; all the things that might make a bigger salary.[29]

To organize meetings, the group relied on word of mouth contacts and mailings. As Blackwelder learned, "There were no burning issues. It wasn't about making the union more democratic...The issue was getting work."[30] In addition to talking in bars, the group held meetings, made up T-shirts, and was active in trying to elect their candidates to union positions.

> We had discussions with the candidates about work distribution. We had an effect in the 1990 election. We pledged to vote as a bloc to back one individual for business agent (B.A.) and he was the B.A. who got the most votes. It's one reason why one B.A. is no longer in office. The first black official was elected in a less important category. The first Puerto Rican got in also. There was some resentment that we existed.[31]

However, after the local election, Alters fizzled out. The attempt to change the grip the union had on their ability to earn a living proved disappointing. As Blackwelder explained, although Alters saw itself as "a loose group of individuals working to enlarge the rights of minorities, for some, it was a means to stay employed." As an example, she said "the head of Alters got a job pretty readily and stayed employed." The "opportunistic motivation" of some proved only one disappointment. The newly elected officials continued in the tradition of rewarding their friends. "It was all a cronyism kind of thing," Blackwelder said.[32]

Although women did participate in Alters, they were few in comparison with males. This reflected their numbers in Local 580. As Blackwelder recalled, "The number of women in the local went up and down." In 1996, according to public testimony provided by the union, 16 women held books in Local 580.[33]

Overall, she recognized the limitations she faced. As she put it, "I didn't see myself as a leader of union democracy. I didn't think there was an opportunity there for me."[34]

The Windows Corruption Case

While the tortuous discrimination case wound its way through court, new public tribulations arose in 1991. A highly sensational chapter in the history of the mob and Local 580 unfolded under the short title "The windows case." From 1978 to 1990, four of the city's five crime families created a cartel of window-replacement companies that dominated the public sector of the industry. While Local 580 controlled the supply of the window-replacement workers, the Lucchese crime family controlled Local 580.[35]

As the high-profile case began to unfold in the federal courthouse, union members became aware of its impact on the life of the union. Occasionally, Janine ignored the conventional wisdom to keep silent at meetings and avoid public challenges to the union officials. She recalled one episode:

> The B.A. was spending a lot of time in court, partly to defend himself and the union against allegations that they were continuing discrimination against minorities, even after the [consent] judgment. But he also...was indicted with a bunch of gangsters in this case involving these nonunion companies getting jobs installing windows. I think it might have been a big [public] housing project or something having to do with the government. So supposedly, this business agent, Thomas McGowan, was taking payments for ignoring the fact that these jobs were being done nonunion. And somehow involved in this were these Mafia-type guys. I guess they owned the companies that were involved.
>
> Actually, with the idea that he was spending a lot of time in court, I stood up and asked him to give up working on the territory of Brooklyn and Queens, because there was work coming up there, and it needed a lot of attention. I pointed out that he was spending a lot of time in court...He stood up and said that the best way for him to get through this period of time would be to stay busy and he was doing a good job out there. Of course, his buddies in the audience clapped very loudly in support of him...to show me that I shouldn't have opened my mouth.[36]

Within a short time, two Local 580 officials were killed. The business agent John Morrissey, a defendant in the case, was gunned down right before the trial began. Then Frank Leone, Blackwelder's B.A., was slain in front of his home. Morrissey was later identified as a member of the Lucchese crime family. Some Local 580 members speculated that Frank Leone was also killed "possibly because he was honest and wanted to see the local cleaned up."[37]

Subsequent racketeering trials showed the scheme lined the pockets of "corrupt union officials, Housing Authority officials, and Cosa Nostra bosses." The pay off for each window, $1 to $2, was imposed "on most public and some private window replacement contracts in New York City."[38]

Lucchese captain Peter Chioda testified on September 12, 1991, about some of his official mob duties: "I handled some of the unions that were under their control." He added that he carried cash payments from Local 580 to top leaders of the Lucchese family.[39]

In November 1991, after Blackwelder's neighbor was murdered, she made the decision to leave town:

> I had wanted to leave New York for some time. The final departure was expedited, I think, a little bit by the fact that this guy in the adjoining building in the co-op in Brooklyn…was brutally bludgeoned to death in his apartment. So here, I had my business agent murdered, the next door neighbor murdered, and it was like, let's get the hell out of the city…I didn't feel safe in my apartment. I didn't feel safe on the job.

Last Exit—the Bronx

For most of the last year she lived in New York City, she worked on a permit out of Structural Ironworkers Local 40. She was hired to work on a Coast Guard drawbridge on the Bruckner Expressway in the South Bronx. As she described:

> When I took the job as a structural ironworker, it wasn't so much to get away from Local 580, but that the work was winding down, and I was able to get that job because that was one of the rare situations where the state of New York was coming by and enforcing that there be some women on the job.
>
> When I went to work for the Structural Ironworkers on that bridge, I was making really good money with them. They had an extra annuity fund, so, in addition to the $23.50 [per hour] or whatever it was we were making, there was another $10 or $20 in annuity funds and vacation. That was the best money I made. I think I made $40,000 or $45,000 that year, and maybe the best I had made with Local 580 was $39,000.

This was her last job as an ironworker. Before leaving town, she got a withdrawal card from the union: "They have an expression: 'putting it on the shelf,' taking a withdrawal," said Blackwelder. "What that means is, for some sum of money, $200 or $300, if I wanted to go back to work, I could."

After leaving New York, she cast a backward glance. Her emotions changed over time. At first, she recalled some of the pleasurable memories. Over time, other feelings surfaced. As she recalled:

> It was interesting. I really thought much less about the difficult times. Maybe this is a natural process of how one's memory takes care of the pain from the past. When I thought back, I'd think about being up on a roof somewhere and seeing a pretty

sunset. I'd think about having some laughs with this one or that one. For the most part, I thought about the good times.

As far as what I've accomplished for my life, I have very mixed feelings...I think, having toughed it out in New York, both as a woman and as an ironworker, has that built character? Does that make me feel strong, like I can accomplish this—I can conquer that? It hasn't had that effect. So I'm not sure what I've accomplished.

A few years later, Blackwelder looked back from her home in Chesterfield, Massachusetts. "I did accomplish a lot," she said. "Just to survive in that situation, I accomplished a lot. I guess I've broken ground [so] that it'll be easier for other women to do the same."

Let me think about pioneers. They were blazing new ground. They faced difficult odds. They met up with people who were friendly with them or not. In that sense, I knew that it was going to be a different experience for myself and the people I would be working with. I had already had some experience of working in a nontraditional job.[40] But the fact is that there were women around the job, even though they didn't have my particular skill, they were there.

What I really didn't consider coming into building construction is what it would feel like to be surrounded completely by men and almost never find another woman on any job site I was on. I didn't think about it. Actually that's something that did affect me. Just to be surrounded by men. You know, I don't know what to say about it. There's too *much* to say about it.[41]

FOUR

When Worlds Collide: The First Women in Electricians' Local 3

Blood Brothers

Bloodbrothers is a searing novel about the De Cocos, a family closely tied to Local 3 of the International Brotherhood of Electrical Workers. Tommy, the patriarch, has high hopes that his 17-year-old son, "Stony," will follow him into the union. Marie is his long-suffering, stay-at-home wife. Albert, the eight-year-old, suffers from brutal family tensions. The author, Richard Price, depicts Local 3 as a harsh world. The scenes involving men take place on the job, at the bar, and at home. The women, a sorry lot, are all mothers, daughters, aunts, girlfriends, waitresses, or whores. Understandable, perhaps, since Price's novel appeared in 1976—two years before the advent of the first women electricians in Local 3.[1]

What's also missing from *Bloodbrothers* is a sense of what was special about the electrical trade as practiced by members of Local 3, why fathers were so eager to have their sons follow them, what made Local 3 perhaps the most desirable niche in the construction field.

The journalist Murray Kempton, writing in 1957, summed up the benefits the union bestowed on its members: "In this city of indifferent workmanship, Local 3 of the International Brotherhood of Electrical Workers is the nearest approximation we have to an intact survivor of the great craft guilds of the Middle Ages. The 6,000 of its 33,000 members who are master electricians...are products of the five-year apprenticeship system—an extensive night-school drilling process. Their 'A' cards of membership, the apex of Local 3's social pyramid, are in many cases hereditary. They are among the most successful and secure workers in town. The custodian of all these great treasures is Harry Van Arsdale."[2]

Van Arsdale, the charismatic business manager of Local 3, spent his three-decade tenure building up wages and benefits, including the first employer-funded pension plan for construction workers in the nation. He secured a five-hour day, cooperative housing for the members, complete with childcare and a fully staffed nursery, and control of the jobs to the point where union electricians in New York City were regarded as "the aristocracy of labor."[3]

The higher wages, shorter workday, and generous benefits made gaining entrance to the union's apprenticeship program a highly sought plum. Traditionally, the route to Local 3 was paved by family connections. Like the fictional Tommy De Coco, fathers all over the city looked forward to the day when their male progeny would follow them. In *Bloodbrothers*, the senior De Coco daydreams about that day: "Stony. Oh Stony. A son-and-a-half. Thomas Jr. Fuckin' A. He thought about Stony coming in with the electricians. Tommy could swing him in easy. Maybe they could even work the same job."[4]

In addition to this patrimony, the worlds of Local 3 electricians were circumscribed by other expectations. The craft union constituted a tight fraternity. Rituals of male bonding initiated each generation. Stony De Coco is the recipient of the initiation his first day on the job, with his father at his side. He then gets to feel the high of initiating the next new-comer: "After ten seconds of painful silence, Stony stepped forward, his heart pounding. 'Hey, kid?' Sensing all eyes on him, he put a hand on Phillip's sweaty shoulder. A charge of power and excitement ran through him like alcohol...He felt a sense of brotherhood that morning. It was mean, yeah, but...He didn't know if he felt like a jerk or a man. But he knew he felt good."[5]

For generations, Local 3 maintained the basic father-son fraternity through the ritual of sponsorship.[6] Each apprentice had to be sponsored by a member in good standing. In the 1930s and once again, in the 1950s, a small number of minority men were admitted into the union.[7] Still, the racial barriers were largely intact until 1962. In that year, Van Arsdale paved the way for the carefully constructed entrance of minority males into Local 3.[8]

Though carried out as a fait accompli, the decision to open Local 3's doors to a group of 1,000 minority males was not popular or uncontested. These men bore the brunt of a great deal of hostility from their fellows. Fierce boom and bust cycles of employment and unemployment in the industry continued to generate a proprietary sense of entitlement over the slots available in the union's apprenticeship program. The eventual absorption of these "outsiders" in the sanctioned union activities of Local 3 was a well-oiled process that slowly absorbed most of the militant minority members into the brotherhood of the electrical work-ers. In time, they were able to establish both a sense of racial solidarity and an acceptance within their union, albeit always with the knowledge on everyone's part that they were the newcomers. They were still seen as interlopers, though tolerable. In 1977 and 1978, as a lengthy recession began to lift, more black and minority males were admitted into the Local 3 apprenticeship program.[9]

Thanks to Harry Van Arsdale Jr., Local 3 became a powerhouse within the New York City labor movement. While a reputation for corruption clung to the union when he first joined, he earned a reputation for cleaning up the local.[10] Somehow, in the sewer of the surrounding corruption that permeated the building trades' unions and the construction industry, the public perception was always that Local 3 stood above it all. On many counts, Van Arsdale Jr. put Local 3 into place as the best of all the building trades unions in New York City. Yet even within the craft union most renowned for its progressive record, women electricians would be hard put to find a welcoming hand.

In 1978, women won the right to enter the electricians union. All across the country, locals of the International Brotherhood of Electrical Workers got a taste of feminism within their ranks.[11] In New York City, the experiment started slowly. Over time, the numbers of females in the huge local crept upward. These first women faced numerous challenges. They sought to establish solidarity to support them. They persevered. In time, they earned "journeymen" status. This presented a new set of obstacles.

Going First: The Few, the Proud, the Brave

But you don't understand. Women are for *after* work.[12]

—Local 3 Journeyman

Sixteen years after the entry of black men, the International Brotherhood of Electrical Workers (IBEW) opened its doors to women. The first females to enter the construction division of Local 3 were few. They were ready to take advantage of the opportunity to apply to the apprenticeship program, to pick up tools, to learn a trade, and to enter the foreign terrain of work sites. Their stories convey the courage and determination it took to succeed on this new frontier. By design of the union, the numbers of women enrolled in the first few classes were minuscule. Full of a sense of excitement, they soon collided with the sense of entitlement of their co-workers to what had always been "men's work"—the ticket to a decent standard of living for their families.[13]

This sense of entitlement was shaken when women showed up on the work sites. Their presence violated the male perception of propriety—women were wives, daughters, mothers, lovers, and whores—not future electricians. Evan Ruderman, a member of the second class of Local 3 women, viewed the integration of males and females on the job site as one of the chief contributions of affirmative action. As she put it:

> ... [I]t put people together in a day-to-day work environment that had never had to deal with each other before. I worked with men who had no other interaction with women in their lives except their wives...their mothers...and their daughters, if they had them. Then the ones who were single were just always on the hunt. But I think, for a huge percentage of men that I worked with, it was quite an astounding thing to actually work with a...female. I think that we—in such a minority that we were—still had quite a big effect.[14]

Despite their hostile reception, each of the five women in these stories was able to carve out a successful career. They were Cynthia Long, an Asian-American; Evan Ruderman, a Jewish high school drop-out; Brunilda Hernandez, a Puerto Rican New Yorker with a smattering of college; Joi Beard, an African-American from Louisville, Kentucky; and Laura Kelber, Jewish and highly educated. Each woman chose to participate in efforts to improve conditions for the women who followed them into the IBEW.

Long entered the local in 1978. She is short and round and communicates in a straight-up style. Photos from her years as an apprentice show her with long dark hair flowing past her shoulders. Now her hair is close-cropped, her hips more padded. Her laugh is frequent like punctuation marks for her narrative:

> I was born in a car on the way to the hospital on September 2, 1955, in Toronto, Canada. My father was [a] second-generation immigrant from China and my mother was an immigrant to Canada from China.... When I was growing up, my Dad was a mechanical engineer. My mother was a stay-at-home mom until I was in the sixth grade, when she went to school to become a computer programmer.[15]

In 1965, the family moved to New York City. After high school, Long recalled, "I went to the State University of New York at Buffalo on my Regents scholarship for two years before

I dropped out…One of the reasons I dropped out is that I couldn't declare a major because everything fascinated me."

She then found employment in a traditional field for females—office work. "I worked as a clerical worker for Simplicity patterns," she said. "Then as a clerical worker at Marsh & McLennan, which is a large insurance brokerage firm. So I already knew about low-paid work and I didn't find *any* of these jobs particularly satisfying."

During her short college career, women's studies gave her some exposure to feminism. This helped to widen her career horizons and she was open to new opportunities. "My primary motivation had to do with wanting to get a good-paying job [so] that I could support myself and hopefully, it would mean a career," she said. "So I was just trying to explore other types of work, and becoming a construction electrician fell into my radar at the time."

She took advantage of two CETA-funded training programs. "I went through All-Craft.…It was strictly an all-women program. Then, after I finished that program, I got into another CETA-funded program at Apex Technical School in air-conditioning and refrigeration…Of all the trades they exposed me to, the one that I was most interested in was electrical, but there was no direct entry into electrical. So I figured I would give it a try." Then she said she met the director of the Women in Apprenticeship Program, Mary Garvin, who talked about becoming an apprentice and learning a trade.

> When Mary talked about the different trades,…I asked what the requirements were.…Basically, it sounded like, as long as you had been just normally physically active, of average strength and ability, that you could do it.

Primed to apply for one of the highly coveted slots in the Local 3 program, her day finally arrived. "Somebody in Queens called Mary and said, 'They're starting the line,'" she recalled. "So we packed up our sleeping bags…and sat on the line, and slept [out]…five nights to pick up the applications on a Monday morning."

As Long explained, the demand for applications was especially high in 1978: "Mostly that was because they had not opened up the books; that is, they had not taken in any new apprentices in approximately three years. So because of that, we anticipated that there would be a big group of people wanting the applications…We didn't want to take a chance on being shut out of the process, so we camped on the streets of Flushing to do this." Long began her apprenticeship in August 1978 and completed the program in May 1982. At the time, age limits for the electricians' program were strict and narrow. Only 18- to 21-year-olds were accepted.[16]

Brunilda "Bruni" Hernandez was in the second class of women to enter Local 3. She grew up on the Lower East Side of New York City. "I was born at Gouverneur Hospital on Henry Street on March 14, 1959," she said. "My parents are from Puerto Rico. My Mom came over to the mainland when she was 14-years-old and my Dad came over…when he was 18. When we were youngsters, my Dad worked in a Tootsie Roll factory, which was cool because he used to bring Tootsie Rolls home…and my Mom worked in the garment district in the factories. She was a seamstress. She's a very pro-union worker. When the Tootsie Roll Company moved, he lost his job. After that he worked somewhere on the Bowery unloading trucks for a packaging company."[17]

> I finished high school in 1977 and the first semester I entered college I went to Marymount in Manhattan. I just did one semester and then in the spring of 1978,

I wasn't in school. I was looking for work...at that point my mom and I were in a struggle—a mom-daughter kind of thing. I left the house and moved in with Evan [Ruderman].

The two friends lived in an apartment on Houston Street, across from Katz's Delicatessen. Both were eager to explore new employment opportunities. Ruderman was a native of New York City and a high school dropout. She had also attended the All-Craft program. While going through that short training program, she put her name on a list of women applying to be hired onto the Brooklyn docks.[18] When a pioneering slot with the International Longshoremen's Association didn't come through, she cast about for something else. She worked as a nonunion electrician for a year.

As Hernandez described, "We found this recruitment and training program for young adults. They would train people for interviewing and looking for work. R. T. P. was located on 125th Street in Harlem. So we went there...and the gentleman who was training us said, 'IBEW Local 3 has opened up to women. Why don't you two try to go into the electrical union?' I had never thought of being in construction or anything like that. I used to like looking through the peepholes in the construction [sites], but that was as far as I got close to even thinking about it.... So Evan and I said, 'Okay.' We got trained in manual dexterity and math and all that. Then we went and stood in line."

I think they had 500 spots they wanted to fill with apprentices, but I think there were 1,500 applications or something like that. So Evan and I were number 300 and 301. The way they used to do it, they would line up all these young people outside to go in and get the applications...We all camped out overnight. It poured that night. And so Evan and I were there and the next morning we got up and got the application.

"We had to go for an interview. [I think] they had four or five men in a round table interviewing: 'Why do you want to be an electrician, you being a woman?' 'Do you have the strength?' 'Do you think that you can do it?'...Things like that...We had to go through the interview, take a test, and then we got a notice that we were accepted." Both Ruderman and Hernandez began their apprenticeship in 1979.

Joi Beard was born into a blue-collar family in Kentucky in 1958. Her father worked in a foundry for International Harvester and was a union member until he became a supervisor for the company. Her mother stayed home to raise Joi, her three sisters, and two brothers, until the youngest daughter went to school. Of average height, Joi's lithe frame is a container of compact energy. In 1979, she entered the Local 369 IBEW apprenticeship program in Louisville. She described her serendipitous introduction.

"Truthfully, I just happened to be looking for something else to do," she said. "So I was at the State Building and on the directory they had 'Apprenticeship and Training.' The person in there was telling me: 'It's in construction and there are the different trades.' I had no clue of *any* of these trades. He said, 'What was your best subject?' And I told him math. He said, 'Since your best subject in school was math, you should consider going into the electrical trade.'"[19]

He advised her about the application process and recommended that she seek some assistance from the Urban League. She followed his advice on both counts: "Once I found out about the apprenticeship program, I was application 701, and they were only taking 50 in. Then I went to the

Urban League and we went through the mock interviews. The Urban League provided me with pre-apprenticeship training and information."[20]

"Back then, only two women were in the trade down there and in my class there were five of us—total. Really, I was a last-minute type of thing... Two African-American men dropped out, so they had to pick up two more people of color or some type of minority, one way or the other. So they were able to pick me up and then they picked up another white guy because I filled two minority spots."[21]

Laura Kelber entered Local 3 in 1981. Born in Brooklyn in 1957, she was the middle of three daughters of left-wing parents. Both her mother and father were labor journalists who were blacklisted during the McCarthy period. Her father then joined the International Typographers Union and worked as a linotype operator for the *New York Post*. Her mother worked part-time as an editor for a medical publication. She was greatly influenced by her mother, Miriam "Mim" Kelber, whom she described as "an ardent feminist. She was very retiring, personally, but she was a tremendous inspiration. [For her], feminism was not about a woman getting ahead, or getting elected. It was about, how is this going to affect women?"[22]

After graduating from Yale University in 1979 with a degree in political philosophy, Laura went looking for work. "I majored in philosophy. So, what else was I going to do but be a construction worker," she said with a small, rueful chuckle. "I was thinking I should try and become a railway conductor, 'cause then I could travel around. My mother had a friend, Joyce Hartwell, and she invited me to join the All-Craft program that was training women to get into construction. It was on St. Mark's Place in this great building. It was her organization and it was really a great idea. It got a lot of women into the trades. It was an introduction to electrical, plumbing, carpentry, and cabinet making, just a basic introduction."

"But then they actually helped us apply to jobs. I applied to the Cement Masons Apprentice [program] and I got in and that was my first job in the trades... It was just working on the street out in Jamaica, Queens. They were redoing the little islands in the middle of the street. So it was easy enough... It wasn't [a] heavy-duty construction site. I did that during the summer. I got an incredible tan and people said, 'Where'd you get that tan?' I said, 'Jamaica.'"

Of all the trades she was exposed to at All-Craft, Laura was most interested in electrical work.

"At that point, my father was good friends with Harry Van Arsdale," she said; "so he knew a lot of people at Local 3 and he asked me if I wanted him to put in a few words for me. But I didn't. I wanted to just apply with the other women." In her modest fashion, Laura didn't mention that her father was the former director of the Educational and Cultural Fund of the Electrical Industry.[23] She went through the application process and stood on the line with all of the others.

"You had to wait in line for a couple of days," Kelber said. "I didn't know anyone. There were women but I didn't even know who they were. I waited in line in the summer of '80 and I got called into the apprentice program... I started the school before I started work actually, in February of '81 and I started work in March."

Once accepted into the apprenticeship program, she began classroom instruction. Hernandez described how the system worked in 1979: "There are 4 years of apprenticeship and 18 months of a mid-mechanic kind of journeyman. And each time you move up, you have to take a test, and then you become a journeyman wireman. The electrical union, in cooperation with the labor studies program of Empire State College, would accept the apprentices from the union to get an Associate's degree in labor studies. So we had to go to school two nights a week... We would be studying [electrical] theory. We would be studying unions. We would be studying electrical formulas and anything that had to do with electricity and [with] the labor movement...I liked my instructors. I didn't have any problems in class at all. I think we did two-and-a-half hours a night."

In Louisville, Beard was part of the same system. Her experience was also very positive: "The program was really good. We had *very* good instructors. You would think that they were truly teachers. I think they were all workers in the trade, but they taught at night, because we went to school one night a week for four hours. The apprenticeship program is a little bit different in other cities than it was there. Back then, it was four years, now it's five."

The five women in her class made common cause. "We basically stuck together," she said. "We did our homework together and stuff like that and we all made it through."

On the Job

The main purpose of any electrical circuit is to convert electrical energy into some other kind of useful energy, such as heat, light, or motion.[24]

For the women, the beginning of their careers in construction stands out in stark relief. As Long put it, "The first job usually is fresh in your memory. It's like the first lover. You remember that very well."

Beard recalled her first job, working for a small contractor in Louisville: "Once I got in [to the apprentice program], I was working within two weeks...The first year, it just so happens, my first contractor was Link Electric, [owned by] a little old German guy with his Mercedes Benz. It was a small shop. I worked with this guy, and I remember us going out on the job, because he was a service-call guy. So I was riding in the truck with him every day to a different job. He had at least 25 years of experience."

He quizzed her on their field trips together, asked her to identify terms such as "empty, flexible conduits," and schooled her in the lore of her trade. "As time went on, when things got slow, we would work in the shop and I was able to learn the material," Beard said. "But back then, you were a more hands-on apprentice." While she worked for a small contractor, the electrical apprentices in New York City worked on large construction projects.

"As an apprentice, it's different because you're somewhat protected," said Cynthia Long. "For me, most of my work was in private industry when I was an apprentice." On her first job, at New York University Hospital, she had a good experience: "The foreman was a gentleman by the name of Don Lang, who will come back into my life later on. He was the general foreman of the job. I was so naïve, not understanding the structure—anything! I found him and...I thought he was the owner of the company. He laughed and said, 'No. I'm not the owner. I'm the general foreman.' I think he understood—'cause he was a really decent guy—the difficulty. So he had me work with a journeyman who wasn't going to be a ball buster. And the guy said, 'Okay. Have you ever spliced before?' The wires had already been pulled and now it was splicing out."

"Splicing is done to make a connection," Long explained. "You connect the wires so that they complete the circuit." Her journeyman set her the task of splicing out the room: "I just went around, I stripped the wires, I spliced them together, and left them open so he could check on them before I put the wire nuts on them. I must have done it okay, 'cause we just closed them up....This was a big job. There were lots of guys on the job, and so it was on the following days that difficulties began, because they only had the men's locker room, which they called the shanty—the men's shanty. And there was no place for me."

"Don, being a good guy, what he did is he took a corner and had the carpenter build me a little shanty that was the size of a telephone booth, so there was some place for me to sit, to change my shoes, change my clothes, and leave my clothes there, and that it would be locked...so they couldn't violate that space and it was a separate space for me. I think it took a week or two for them to build that little shanty for me."

Hernandez made her maiden voyage on a major construction project in 1979. "I will never forget my first job," she recalled. "It was at City College and they were doing their first wing. You come in with your nice brand new, shiny toolbox with all your tools and you're given your little pink slip and you're showing up for work. I get all these stares from these guys just sitting around. It was really nerve-wracking. I was so nervous. It's a *huge* building. Pretty much, the first six months were getting to know how things work around male-dominated construction and [being] a single woman on the job with all these guys around. It was hard."

She maintained a low profile and put up with the comments of her co-workers. Remarks such as "What are you doing here?" "Why are you here?" "Why aren't you home? You're taking the place of a man. You're taking the place of a husband," became part of her daily routine. Eventually she adopted a more assertive style: "For the first six months, I went in and I was nice and timid. [But] every day, you become a little more like, 'Oh my God, I really have to stand up for myself because most of these guys don't want me here.' I mean, that's what I was thinking, from the comments. After that, it was like—I'm going to be here. This is what I want to do. I want to learn this trade and I'm going to do it. Whatever it takes, I'm here, and you'll have to deal with it."

Each apprentice was on a steep learning curve. "You were learning a lot and you really did have to learn," said Hernandez. "With electricity, one of the guys told me: 'You really need to respect it. It can kill you.'" Like every other electrician, she had to overcome the fear of working with high voltage. As she explained with a laugh, "You just make sure the circuit is off and that you're putting the right wires where they go. Nothing is going to blow if you really pay attention. I've had several times where I got a nice little shock, and its like: 'Whoops! That one's on.' Or 'Whoops! Those wires need to be crossed.'"

Journeymen electricians were convinced that the women coming into the trade were only there to prove an ideological point. In her study of gender relations in Local 3, Francine Moccio, director of Cornell's Institute for Women and Work, wrote: "Through the eyes of male unionists, women's entrance into the local construction division was seen as a kind of ruse."[25]

That the first applicants to the union were recruited by feminist organizations such as WAP and All-Craft only added to the suspicion over their entrance. But the women showed that they could master the work. Although Hernandez hadn't grown up dreaming about becoming an electrician, she quickly found that craftwork held great appeal for her. Early on, she knew that she loved the work. "I liked it right away," she said. "It was working with your hands. It was using your brain as you were doing these formulas and you were figuring out how electricity worked and how to hook up panels...just how it all worked."

Hernandez was determined to learn as well as stand her ground. Six months into the job, she was paired with a journeyman who harbored a deep resentment.

"I had this mechanic who was a bastard," she said. "I mean—he really did not want women in the trades. And the thing with being the first women on the job, there were no changing facilities. There were no toilets or bathrooms or anything like that prepared for women coming into the trade. So every job that you went on, you had to make sure that there was a toilet and there was a changing facility and that was a struggle. On this job, the toilets were enclosed in plywood and they were lined up. So what they did was, they just slapped plywood up in the middle and that was my toilet. Plus that was my changing facility. I didn't have a trailer or a room. That was it. That was my little home, a toilet closet."

"This guy was a drunk and I was kind of afraid. But he was my mechanic. So after lunch, he would be drunk. You could smell it. He would get more abusive. Italian guys—and this was my experience then, it might have changed—they are really verbally abusive. There was this one Thursday that I had to go to school. What he did, this was his joke, he took the 12-inch cinder blocks, they're the big ones, and put them in front of the door to my changing facility. So I threw all the cinder blocks down, got in, changed, and just went my way and didn't ever confront it. I sort of knew who it was."

"Friday comes. Three o'clock, you're out of there. Well, he did the same thing. And Friday, he really gets plastered. So he covers the front of the doors. It's time to go. This was the first time I ever let my anger get the best of me. I was so angry I knocked it down. We used to have these gang boxes where we have all the tools and stuff. I took a two-by-four and I put it under the gang box and flipped the whole thing over, and it rolled over and the tools got all mixed up. There was a lot of oil on his tools. He was so particular. So he threatened me. We were in a circle. All the guys circled us. He was cursing me: 'You son-of-a-bitch. Who the hell you think you are? You don't belong here.' I was so scared. Like, how stupid can I be to just let this man get the best of me? He was two inches from my face with his finger, [saying]: 'You this; You that.'"

"Well I mean—I was what? 19 maybe? I was skinny, five-foot-five, and I'm like: 'Oh my God. I'm going to be killed.' I was so scared. It was that bad. It got that close. And there was this guy who was Jamaican—Hector. I will never forget him. He said, 'Don't worry, Bruni. I had your back.' He had pulled a knife and he had it down by his leg. And he said: 'If that son-of-a-bitch touched you, I was going to get him.'"

"That was it. From that moment on, we never talked to each other. He was not my mechanic any more. After that, people on that job just left me alone. I got good mechanics and they were teaching me.... I was just learning a lot. As an apprentice, you're on the job for at least a year, maybe more. And they have to switch you 'cause they have to show you different types of work and move you around... So after my year, I got the pink slip. You're out of there and [you] wait for the next job. After that, I went to Battery Park City. I was the only woman at City College. At Battery Park, it ended up Evan was working there and Laura."

Building Battery Park City

For a time, the three women worked as apprentices at the giant complex in Lower Manhattan. They donned their oversize rain gear to go for coffee. They got to share their own shanty. When Kelber showed up for her first day of work as an electrical apprentice, she was, in her own words, "painfully shy." As she recalled, "It was the first three buildings going up at Battery Park City, the Gateway Plaza, the apartment building, and I didn't know what to expect. I had absolutely no conception of what it was going to be like. It was a *huge* construction site. I showed up at the front gate and I had a little pink slip [with] the name of the company I was supposed to report to. Some guy at the gate kind of leered at me. He said, 'I'll drive you over there.' It was a huge, muddy site. So he took me to a trailer. It was a company—National States—and there actually were some other women working there, including Evan and Bruni."

The foreman was talking to some other guy: "Well, where should we put the girl?" They said "Oh, put her in the mill," which was a huge shed where they had pre-fabbed all the pipe that was then going to be put in on the decks on the buildings...Three buildings were going up at once, so it was a huge amount of pipe that had to be cut to certain lengths and that's what they did in the mill. It was like a little factory. I walked into the mill and the head guy there came right up to me and the first thing he said to me was "Are you Jewish?" So I said, "Yeah." He pointed to a sign that said, "Jewish Mill." He said, "We're all Jewish here. They put all the Jews here." There was one black guy working there. I kind of looked at him. He pulled out a little Star of David hanging around his neck.

There was a lot of heavy ethnic racism as well. You know, on any job, they wanted to know your last name to figure out who you were. A lot of jobs were very segregated. Blacks, Hispanic, Italian, Irish, Jewish, and the work got divided out accordingly. You had the blacks in the boiler room...and the Irish got the fire alarm system, which was the high prestige job.

Like the other women, she experienced taunts from her co-workers: "They were sexist and constantly making comments, like 'I'm getting out of shape. I should do some push-ups. Hey Laura, get underneath me!'...that kind of stuff."

But she also had positive experiences at that site. "There were a couple of guys in particular who I have very fond memories of working with," she said. "One of them was this guy, John. He and I worked together it seems like maybe half a year, just as journeyman and apprentice, going from job to job, and he taught me an awful lot."

Twice a week, she traveled uptown after work to the apprentice school on 18th Street for classroom instruction. Once there, she was also on her own. "I was the only woman in my class," Kelber said. "Most of the women were the only ones in their class. And I quickly met other women in the bathroom. That's where we hung out and that's where I met Cynthia....[She] said, 'We're having a meeting. You should come.' Cynthia and I really hit it off and became very good friends. We both were really into organizing. We really pushed the organizing—meeting women, signing them up, getting their addresses, and doing mailings—figuring out what we should do at meetings."

Piss, Porn, and Put-Downs

> It's hard to say that some woman was unable to maintain a job because she complained about photographs or some individual relieving himself in full view, which has been traditional in New York City. I don't think it's fair to describe that as sexual harassment. I don't think it endangers the individual's chances of being a success on the job. I would say pornography is common in our industry.[26]
> —Thomas Van Arsdale, April 26, 1990

In the nineteenth century, Mother Jones called herself a "hell-raiser." She traveled the country defending the rights of miners. She encouraged them to stand together. They called her "the Miner's Angel." She provided a beacon of hope for workers who were being ground under the heel of mine owners. "Don't mourn, organize," she famously exhorted the miners. Mother Jones was fearless in standing up to the coal companies' goons.[27] But she never took up the miner's tools. She never went to work to earn her keep as a coal miner. Had she tried to do so, the miners might have coined other epithets for her.

Long knew something about women like Mother Jones and other female organizers from the women's studies courses in college. In New York City, she'd been active with a group called Asian Women United. These experiences underpinned her role in creating a support group for the women entering Local 3. By the time she met up with Kelber at the apprentice school, this group, Women Electricians (WE) had been meeting for three years. Early on, Long recognized the need for some form of organization.

> At this point in time, it was kind of a radical idea. Even though other women had done it in the past and had been able to work together—it was kind of a difficult thing for us... to get to that point of putting aside ourselves individually to work together.[28]

Three other women entered Local 3 with Long in 1978. In 1981, approximately 30 women entered the apprentice program over the year. The first few classes of women all knew each other. But as more women came in, the strength that could have been derived from their greater numbers was diluted when they were distributed into separate classrooms.

Each woman was absorbing the shocks of pioneering on her own. "I think that the stress affected me physically, and I know it did other women," said Ruderman. Their interest in organizing was fueled by isolation, and the desire to create support for each other.

As women entered the trades, new issues arose: Changing facilities and bathrooms for the women, sexual harassment, pornography. The newly sex-integrated construction sites produced conflicts, and the women looked to their union for assistance. Local 3 had done nothing to prepare its members prior to the women's entrance. In fact, it took years and several lawsuits for Local 3 to begin to educate its members about gender-related issues. Contractors also did nothing.[29]

The problems that came up on one job were going to reappear on every job—from shanties to sexual harassment. If women were going to stay in the industry and make a career out of the electrical trade, they realized that they would have to make both the union and the contractors responsive. Sticking together for mutual support and organizing was one obvious solution. Women Electricians began its existence informally. As apprentices in Local 3, they were required to attend the monthly union meetings.

"Union meetings were really the only time we would see each other," said Long. "So we would try to sit together and then go out and get something to eat. From that we started to realize that, to really work in a conscious, cohesive sort of way, we needed to be in a different space."

The big question was how to go about organizing. A strong culture of conformity pervades Local 3 and the other construction craft unions. "Don't rock the boat" is the unwritten rule. Dissidents who have tried to expand the democratic rights of members have oftentimes paid a high price in the IBEW.[30] Yet the women made the choice to organize on their own and remain autonomous.

Like the rest of the building trades unions, the structure of Local 3 is designed to ensure that decision making starts and stops at the top. Independent activity by rank-and-file union members is rare. The entire framework discourages all such independent activism. In Local 3, activity by the members is carried out within officially sanctioned "clubs" organized along ethnic, religious, and political lines. These social clubs provide a way for union leaders to maintain control of rank-and-file activity.[31]

"We were so intent on not being aligned with the established union leadership that we actually stayed way out on a limb, maybe a little bit to our detriment, in retrospect," said Ruderman.[32]

Long has had many years to reflect on the work of WE inside Local 3. She explained the decision to organize as an independent group rather than to seek affiliation as an internal club with official sanction.

> I was part of the dissenting group that didn't want to become a club of Local 3, because I really felt that, once we became a club, they would just co-opt our energy and have us do all these other things that really were going to take energy away from what we needed to do.
>
> Look, there are like 10,000 electricians in the A-Division [construction division]. If they can't get enough guys out of the 10,000 to focus on leafleting or whatever, oh well. But I knew that, of those 10,000, only the women—and a handful of the women who were in the industry—were going to care enough to organize and spend energy to try to change things. I felt that I didn't have enough energy to spread around, that I needed to retain that independence from the union to move our agenda.[33]

That agenda was simple, as Kelber described: "The purpose was just to be a clearing-house for women. We weren't going to make the women like each other or be pals with each other." WE started as a means to share information, to educate each other about their new industry, and a place to find a sympathetic ear for "gripe sessions." But early on, it stepped up to fill the vacuum left by the union's failure to address the conditions women were facing on the job. WE activists began to educate themselves and their union about the issues, the law, and their responsibilities toward the female members.[34]

The women began by taking small steps of solidarity. From the beginning, WE adopted a democratic style of decision making that didn't put particular figures forward as the "leadership." Cynthia described the concept of consensus decision making, which was common to feminist organizations:

> Back in those days, I was still in the framework of, "We're all leaders." As a strategy, we discussed that as a group. Also I felt that it was important that if we're going to take a stand or something, we *all* have to take a stand. If we write a letter, it's not just one signature on this letter, it better be all of us or none of us, because if we go out and just put our own name, they're going to pick us off, one by one, and get rid of us.

During their early days as apprentices, the strange and complicated structure of the construction industry, the personnel and protocol at the job sites, in the union and the Joint Management-Labor Industry Board were all critical parts of the same puzzle that the women needed to piece together. As Long recalled:

> At the time, we were struggling to understand the structure and who it was we should be addressing things to, 'cause, when something happens on the job, one of the steps you take is, you address the personnel on the job who have control over these things. And some of the women couldn't quite grasp who that was. So it usually started with a specific incident and then we would respond to that by writing letters to the foremen or the GC [General Contractor], or whoever, on that particular job.
>
> Whether it's the leadership in the union, the leadership of the contractors—the Electrical Contractors Association, or the Joint Industry Board, 'cause those were

the three entities that had jurisdiction over different aspects of our livelihood, of our *life* at the time. So a lot of it was trying to learn for ourselves and sharing that information with each other, so that you could go out and cope with things.

The first women in Local 3 shared a similar way of looking at the world: "I had the background in women's studies," said Long. "Beth Goldman [first class of female apprentices] also had a background in women's studies, Evan Ruderman had an activist sort of background from her parents, and Laura Kelber was a Red Diaper baby. Again, she was someone who felt that we had to work together as a group for the benefit of all of us. I think that there were so many of us of a similar sort of feminist sensibility, so that it was kind of easy."

As more women entered the union and worked on jobs throughout the five boroughs of New York City, contacting each other became more of a chore. Communication grew more difficult. Involving others became time-consuming. "Organizing becomes knowing who this person is and what it takes to get her to a meeting," said Kelber. "Does she want free sandwiches? Does she want childcare? I always thought we should organize something to go out to Chippendales to hoot at the men. I thought that would attract a lot of the sort of party girl types who we were having trouble getting. Then a lot of the gay women were really mad at me—furious! So it was very hard to get everyone on the same page. I still think we did a lot in terms of collecting lots of personalities at one time or another. They were aware of us and aware of each other, so that was the good part."

As Kelber described it, mutual support among the women was far from the promised land of the "sisterhood" she had expected: "The reality was that it wasn't always easy to work with other women. I was surprised sometimes at the lack of support. It varied from person to person. Not all the women were feminists and I think that the men probably played women off against each other too. So I had good experiences working with other women where we really supported each other, and then bad experiences where they were hostile. . . . It was a very mixed and difficult group of women. It wasn't like walking into the sunset where everybody bonds. They were a cranky bunch."

Long also viewed the expectation of a pervasive feminist consciousness as a fault line running throughout the history of WE. "Just because we're women doesn't mean we're feminists," she said. "Just because we're women, doesn't mean that we're going to be cognizant and sympathetic of other women's perspective."

Differences of class, race, sexual orientation, and sensibility pervaded the ranks of the Local 3 women. WE made attempts to bridge the gaps. "It was an extremely mixed-race group," Kelber recalled. "Then there are the women who sort of prostituted themselves on the job. You had a huge range. But women were having a tough time on the job and *that's* when they tended to come to meetings. We tried to be there and sometimes, it worked out well. Sometimes they were just angry and wanted to vent. We really tried to at least keep in touch with most of the women. I think that, because of this group, it did help women meet each other and they did have somewhere to go."

Despite differences, the activists made a good-faith effort to reach out to everyone who fit the description—"woman electrician"—in an attempt to be inclusive. As Long recalled, the failure to interest all of the Local 3 women in the organization wasn't due to a lack of trying: "Those of us who did come together as WE, it was always our goal to be open to anybody who wanted to participate. If somebody needed help, we would try to help. We deliberately planned a structure that was designed to be as open as possible and there wouldn't be issues that would be considered taboo."

One constant issue was harassment. Typically, it took place in one-on-one situations. WE sought to overcome the isolation of individual acts of gross sexual harassment. The activists chose not to remain silent about the atrocious conditions women were facing.

Sometimes, the sexist behavior had a direct impact on job performance. Occasionally, the situation would get serious enough for a union steward to intervene. Hernandez described an episode that escalated to this point. "Pornography was a way to harass the women on the job," she said. "I really had a bad experience with that [at] Hunter College. There was this one guy who really, *really* could not stand women. I think he hated women period. But he did not like that women were coming into the trades to work. At one point, he told the shop steward—the shop steward is the person who is supposed to be our [advocate], right?—He told him: 'I don't like her. I don't like any women working in this job and I will not work with women.' So we didn't work together."[35]

On Mondays, we were supposed to have a safety meeting, which was one of the good things that happened with the union on jobs. And the unfortunate part is the safety meetings were in the men's locker room. So we would have to go to the men's locker room, which, there was always some kind of *Penthouse* or *Hustler* or some kind of magazine around. And it was fine. Everyone was around and it was turned over or hidden or whatever. But this one guy had it in for me. So he would plaster these naked pictures of women. I would tell the shop steward: "I'm not going to that meeting. I'm not going to expose myself to that....It's obvious that they have a problem with me coming, so I'm not going to do it." So I would refuse to go to the meeting and when you were an apprentice, you were supposed to sweep up. We did all this crap work, sweep the shanties, and sometimes, I would refuse. I just didn't want to expose myself. Other times, I would just blow it off and look away.

But this guy would plaster the walls with these pictures. So the shop steward said, "You need to take those pictures down, 'cause we can't have that." A lot of the guys didn't like it, but they refused to do anything about it. So he ripped them down, but then he just kept doing it. Then one day, there were naked pictures on *all* the walls of this shanty and the ceiling, and I don't know if he did it by himself. But all four walls and the ceiling were plastered with this. They weren't going to tolerate that, which was nice. The shop steward was really for a good working environment. So eventually he was sent to another job...There were always pictures and words and drawings. Every job was different and you had to deal with it.

Rather than having to depend on individual union representatives who might or might not chose to act, the women sought the cooperation of their union to put some sort of policy in place. In the first year of their apprenticeship, they met with the director of the Local 3 apprenticeship program, Lafayette "Buddy" Jackson, about job-related problems. His response was to let them know that, as "pioneers," they would have to face up to the conditions as individuals. His basic message was that the women were out there and that they were on their own.

Kelber understood that pornography went beyond men's entertaining themselves at their worksites. "It is a huge issue," she explained. "It's not like—there was some pornography on the wall and I'm offended. They tended to use it very aggressively and make a point...to sort of tell you: 'You're not welcome here. You're in our territory.' You walk in the locker [room] and the guys start reading out loud from a porno magazine. So it was an issue that we wanted it off the job."

We wrote a letter to Tommy [Van Arsdale, Local 3 Business Manager], and he actually answered us. In written form, he said that this is a personal matter for the membership and he can't interfere with the personal lives of the membership. The whole concept of a hostile work environment, and clearly, that's what it created, it's part of the *definition* of sexual harassment.

Not getting a remedy from the union, Kelber and the other women prepared handouts on sexual harassment and distributed them. "We wrote stuff up for the women about what to do and that you have a right to a pornography-free environment—a harassment-free environment," she recalled. "I know it certainly emboldened me to know that, I'm working with these guys and I can say: 'It's against the law.'"

All of the activists had to educate themselves before they could educate others. Out of all the women, Long, the daughter of conservative Republicans, had to travel the greatest distance to become a trade unionist. Once in the union, she began to seek out the knowledge she needed to become an informed activist. She enrolled in the Cornell program for trade union women. "We were just like sponges," she recalled. "I was going to school at Cornell and specifically focusing on sex discrimination and sexual harassment."

She soon became an articulate spokesperson for union democracy issues. "What we were organizing for was the duty of fair representation," she said. "If you have a rule about *men* having a changing shanty, then the extension of that is, if you have women, you should have a changing shanty for women. So it's not about acceptance or recognition, it's about fair is fair. We never tried to bypass the [internal union] process."

As individual union members, you ought to be able to challenge the system. Whatever my need is...I should be able to raise it. The union, since they *are* the union, since I'm paying you my dues, then it is your duty to fairly represent me. If you don't know what's going on, it's my job to educate you. But if I make that effort and you just pooh-pooh it and say: "This is not important," then you have failed to represent me...And here I am, paying you my union dues.

On one occasion, WE was able to make common cause with the male electrical apprentices when the leadership sought to extend the number of years required to obtain the A-card. Although a fierce reaction set in and even led to a broad "Bill of Rights" being drawn up by the apprentices, the fires of dissent were quickly doused and the men retreated. Acquiescence and loyalty to the leadership was rapidly restored.[36]

But the activists in WE viewed their efforts to make the union and the contractors confront issues of sexual harassment, pornography, and other, generic work place conditions as essential. Especially in regard to sexual harassment, Long saw it as critically important for women to speak out and resist, rather than remaining mute and internalizing the abuse:

Those were the most heinous things that we felt we had to speak up about, because there was nobody who was going to come to our defense about it. So if we didn't raise the issue, if we didn't frame the issue and suggest to them how it ought to be dealt with, it wasn't coming from the leadership.

For different reasons, not all Local 3 women chose to make common cause with WE—some chose not to rock the boat they were traveling in, seeing that as the safer course. Not every woman regarded pornography and other entrenched workplace practices as something that had to be challenged.

Male co-workers were quick to label the activists as lesbians. Standing up and confronting conditions was interpreted as antithetical to proper "female," that is, passive, behavior. The "L" word was always an issue. As soon as the women showed up on construction sites, the word "lesbian" was leveled as an epithet and accusation. The argument went, they must be lesbians, because no "real," that is heterosexual, woman, would want to do this work. The presumption was used against all types of women, from the very feminine to the very butch, since every woman working in the trades presented a threat to the common deeply held beliefs about gender-specific jobs and women's proper "place".[37]

Dyke-baiting was one factor that played into individual women's decision about getting active with WE. Some men took to warning newcomers to stay away from the "lesbian" activists. Sometimes, the threat of being identified with an unpopular group worked. Sometimes it failed.

The topic of sexual identity was more of a hot button item in the late 1970s and throughout the 1980s than it is today. "That was another big issue," said Ruderman. "The issue of homosexuality in 1978 was not where it is now [1996]. Women were not willing to come out at that point on the job, not that many. And women were just being accused, right and left, of being gay." As Kelber described:

> A lot of the women were gay, and a lot of them were wildly homophobic. I remember once, one of the women was talking about homophobia, and then this other woman in the room said, "Are there *gay* people in this group?" I think it was pretty impossible to have any serious discussions about that.

Differences of opinion existed within WE about how to handle the issue of homosexuality. Even the use of the word "lesbian" in printed materials was disputed. Long described this:

> Looking back on it now, I think that back then, when we were in our twenties, we were struggling with our identities and our own belief systems.... We would invite all women to come and participate. We would hear through the grapevine that women did not come because the men had talked them out of coming, saying: "Don't associate yourselves' with that bunch of lesbians." So it was immaterial whether any of us really were lesbians or not. It was enough to scare the women to not participate. People made their own decisions. They made their own choices.... The way that I see it is that there were women who chose not to participate and chose not to be active and involved because it's also a time-consuming process.

Journeywomen Stories

On The Day I Finally Cried At Work

I'd had twenty years of stiff upper-lipping.

Pulling myself up by the bootstraps.

Twenty years of keeping it all together.

Of never letting them see me sweat.

Twenty years singing as I worked.

The day before, I had worked and sang.

Looking forward to a week of wages.

Then he punched me. At the union meeting.

Everything went dark and hazy.
I could barely find my way home. I threw up all night.
My head and neck hurt.
The next morning at work I still felt sick.
When my tool partner asked, "Where's your smile?"
I couldn't take it any more.
And against every rule I'd ever made...
I finally cried at work.[38]

—Ana M. Medina, Local 332, IBEW, San Jose, CA

Cynthia Long: Advocate for Tradeswomen

Women Electricians was at its most cohesive when the members of the group were in their apprenticeship years. After that, the women began to go their separate ways. "I guess that the need and the desire to stay together kind of evaporated," Long said. However, more women were entering the union because of a class action suit against Local 3 that ended the narrow age limits for the apprenticeship program. The final result actually benefited males and females throughout New York State in all apprenticeship programs as age requirements were broadened. As their presence increased in the local, WE continued to get new recruits.[39]

WE maintained a small, vibrant presence within the local. "After we became journeywomen, some of the most important stuff did happen," Long said. One of the important events was a women's conference in 1986 held at Bayberry Land, the union retreat on Long Island. "Unionism and Feminism" brought all the women in the construction division together, including members with travelers' cards who were then working in New York City.[40] "I was proud that we were able to have the first women electricians' conference," Long said.

"When we first approached the chairman of the Joint Industry Board, his perception was that we wanted to get together to trade recipes. So we said, 'Okay. We'll take that.'" She recalled the event:

> We organized it and [the union] paid for a bus to come pick us up outside of the Port Authority. I think that it was a very successful conference for us. But it takes a lot of organizing, a lot of effort, and energy. We also included women who were travelers from out-of-town. Joi Beard and many of the women who were working at the convention center, we invited them all. We opened it up to any women electricians— apprentices, women from out-of-town, everybody was invited. I think that part of our legacy from that is that Donna Hammond, who was from Portland, Oregon, went back to Portland, and she became very active and moved up in the [union] hierarchy in Portland.

Despite the willingness of the Local 3 leadership to go along with the agenda for the conference, they were unwilling to do any follow-up. In fact, they pointed women toward another sanctioned women's club, the Amber Light Society, which had been in existence since 1954 for all the female members in the other divisions, but distinctly outside the A-Division for the construction craft workers. This official women's club exhibited a pronounced passivity on gender issues. Yet the Local 3 leadership placed its imprimatur on the group as the proper vehicle for the female members. The trailblazing women refused to accept it.

At one point, Cynthia's life in the trades curved back to where it began, with Don Lang, the general contractor on her very first job. "At the time, I had a back injury and I didn't think

I would ever work in the industry again," she said. "So I went to Hunter College to find myself a new career. While I was there, a young woman came up to me and said, 'Are you *the* Cynthia Long?'…I said, 'My name is Cynthia Long but I don't know about *the* Cynthia Long.' She said, 'My Dad is Don Lang.' I instantly remembered him. She told me that he also had gone back to school, and he wrote about my first day on the job."

> At that time, he was working for Olympia & York. So he said, "If you're not doing anything, I have a position open as my assistant." I went and interviewed and he hired me. I worked for Olympia & York for about two and a-half years although I had that back injury.
>
> The good thing was I had this additional perspective from working for the general contractor as a superintendent. When I would see pornography in the gang box, I would talk to the foreman and say, "You've got to take that down." I tried to use my position to make change that way. Maybe it had some effect. I know that other women who are project managers, they have that power. They can do that. It's just a matter of: Do we do that? Are we willing to? But I think that's what changes the culture. That's what changes the offensive pornography.

Long has experienced many highs and lows in her career. Mentoring her electrical apprentices has been one of the highs. "Nowadays, there are more women coming into the industry, so that it's not unusual to have a female apprentice," she said. "So for me, it's a lot of fun because I just talk to them and I tell them things and I try to instruct them. But this is the same thing that I do with male apprentices as well. I try to share with them as much information as I can. But it's been a lot of fun when I've had the women apprentices."

Looking at her own career, Long considers herself fortunate:

> I still recommend being a construction worker. It can be a very fulfilling type of work. I think that the women who will do well are women who are somewhat independent, who are willing to work hard. They can make good money. They can support their families. You're in a unionized work environment. And the best thing of all is that in this trade, you get to be creative. Whether you're working as a carpenter, or an electrician, or a sheet metal worker, you're working with different materials. If you have that desire to be creative and deal with physical things, being a construction worker is a wonderful thing.
>
> I am so glad that I was born when I was so that it was possible for me to do this. I don't think I could have fit into any of those pigeonholes for women. It would have been really difficult. So for me, this was a good fit because I was able to be the person that I am, be who I want to be, and make a good living.

Evan Ruderman: Rank-and-File Activist

Throughout her short life, Ruderman never encountered a situation she didn't jump into with both feet to try and improve. "Evan was my best friend," Hernandez recalled. "We were friends since we were 17 and we were two weeks apart in birthdays—[born] the same year. Evan was always involved in something that was good for the community. She was involved in the Latino struggle; in the women's struggles. She was always there like a pillar. Encouraging others: 'Even though we're going through this and it's painful and frustrating, we need to do it so that other women coming after us will have a better experience.' It was that kind of attitude. For the little, short woman that she was, Evan had a lot of power and she was there to do the things that needed to be done."

One of the things that Ruderman thought had to be done was to speak up about conditions on the job. This got her into a lot of tight spaces. As she described it, right from the start, her life as a journeywoman was fraught with threatening situations:

> After five and a half years, when I got my A-card, it was such an incredible achievement to me. The first day of the first job that I went to, where I was now making equal pay, was a *nightmare*. My partner refused to work with me. It was like, are we going back to square one? Are we starting over again? An incredible thing started happening all over again. My first A-job was the [Javits] Convention Center. I was working 7 days a week-12 hours a day, on a job that also had a lot of other weird stuff going on. The FBI was all over the job. I had a partner that, every day, [it] was not just one fight but many fights. I would leave to go get material and he'd urinate right where I was working, practically on my tools. Or I'd lay my ruler down when I was measuring pipe, turn around, cut it, turn back around, my ruler was gone. It really built up.[41]

Corruption added to the stress: "We were seeing—just speaking for myself—corruption at every level in our unions. Personally, on the job, I experienced intimidation. We saw things happen that I would definitely link to underworld mob influences, and I felt like I'm in way over my head with these guys. I began to become very guarded, 'cause I didn't really know—If I'm talking to my shop steward, who is he really? I know for myself, I got to the point where I really couldn't trust anybody except for the other who came in at the same time I did and I knew who were just as scared and intimidated and perplexed and suffering as much as I was."

Despite Ruderman's feeling that the stakes for activists were escalating, her path involved taking personal risks. As she described, "On the job by this time, things were getting to the point where I was seen as a very serious agitator. I was accused of being a Communist, I was red-baited because I was a worker who had some consciousness…who was standing up and saying, 'You can't do this.' I got up when there was a job with asbestos and I had the White Lung Society come to the job and do a presentation and talk about OSHA. Two days later, I was off that job."

"Different things were happening. My life was threatened on the job. Physical things started to happen and I saw that you can be killed in construction. And it didn't really matter if you were big time or small time. The guy who's the general foreman of the electricians at the Convention Center, which was one of the biggest jobs at the time, was shot seven times and left in the company van. Who did he cross and what did he do? Local 3 put out a reward. They never really found [out] and they never will."

Ruderman faced other perils. "I had an incident in which I was physically locked in the women's changing shanty on a Friday night and I couldn't get out," she said. "The only way I got out was two, two and a half hours later, screaming and yelling at the top of my lungs for all that time, and a security guard whose job was to make the rounds heard me. [He] had to get a bolt cutter and cut the thing. When I came to work on Monday morning—furious—nobody knew anything. How did this happen? Then I was walked off the job by a shop steward and severely threatened. Stuff was happening. Me personally, I began to see that, if I'm going to continue to organize and fight, I'm going to be more serious. Otherwise, it's just like putting your head out for decapitation. So I withdrew into myself. I didn't even share some of the worst things that were happening to me with the other women."

"We had a situation with [another female electrician] which is still a mystery to this day. She was attacked on the job. Now she tried to say it was an accident, but it was clearly not an accident. It was very, very serious. She could have died. Both her arms were sliced and she was left on the 21st floor, bleeding. She had to make her own way down. Now what was that all about? It could have been about many, many things. I'm just saying that the environment itself, even for men, is very rough. It's like, you can joke around and play around and then, all of a sudden, somebody pulls the trigger and it's not funny any more. So that's what was happening to us. You know, we were palsy-walsy with the guys on the job, at the coffee break, and in the union meetings. Then, all of a sudden, something would come out of left field at you on the job and nobody would be there. It was very, very bad."

As a pioneer, Ruderman experienced the full brunt of the hostility directed toward the women who dared to go first. "It's just mind-boggling to me that we felt at this time, that, if you had the ovaries to be a woman and could *dare* to work in a man's trade, that this is what you were going to have to eat," she recalled. "So eat it, swallow it and stay alive, and keep your mouth shut, leave, or get hurt."

> I was not conscious of the depth of the harassment on the job...of how it was really going to the bone, to the heart. That's key, because it always perplexed me how—in the face of such blatant sexual harassment daily—we never went to court. We never followed legal channels. We followed channels to get women in, to fight for bathroom and changing facilities, but we never did a class action sexual harassment suit. Why? We met with a couple of women lawyers, we as Women Electricians did, and we talked about it a little. We were scared of being blacklisted. We were scared of the fact that we had really put ourselves out there. I think that most of us who now had been in the trades for four or five years, who had been active and really hung our necks out, we were beginning to suffer from the effects of that. I'd go to a job and they'd have already made calls about me before I got there. So it was really difficult to try to establish the fact that I'm not really this person that you've been told I am.
>
> What I felt like was, I dreamed and wished that there was a militant rank-and-file organization in Local 3 that was already established that I could go to and be a part of.

Ruderman took an early retirement. Afterward, she felt able to take even greater risks as an activist: "A big difference is that personally, I had to retire from Local 3," she said. "I'm still a member and I still get my benefits from them, but I'm no longer on the job, and it makes a big difference. I'm willing to take risks that I had reached the point where I wasn't before. Also, I feel that I have inside knowledge and experience that I can use, even in diplomacy."

Though employment opportunity for women was far from equal, she believed it was a still a worthy goal: "I think that there really is importance to integrating the work force on all levels. If you have to do it by force-fed means, then absolutely, you have to do it. [The absence of] affirmative action is a great loss to everybody, not just to those who benefit in the pocket."

Laura Kelber: Pregnant Electrician

Laura Kelber is the proud mother of three. Should you dial up her home telephone and get the family message machine, you'll hear a greeting that includes the names of Mom, Dad, the three kids, *and* the dog. Shy, soft-spoken Kelber paved the way for other female electricians.

Her crusade on behalf of a woman's right to be pregnant on the job took place after the pioneers became journeywomen. Long described the price Kelber paid for her lack of complaisance:

> Laura took the Joint Industry Board to court about pregnancy disability, pregnancy leave, light duty, and those kinds of issues. Because of her bravery, those things did have to change. All the women who came in after benefited from her self-sacrifice. Sadly, she had two miscarriages, which was her motivating reason for taking them to court. She paid a big price, 'cause, aside from the miscarriages, she's no longer working in our industry. I would say that that had to do directly with the fact that she took them to court. They didn't make it easy for her when she came back to work. There's a good reason that she had this lawsuit. It has to do with the fact that, when you're pregnant, you can't be chopping for eight hours a day.

Long explained "chopping," a task that is typically relegated to the lower-paid labor and is also a very "macho" kind of job:[42]

> Usually, you have a chopping gun that has a lot of vibration to it. It's a hard physical job, a lousy job to do. It's the kind of job that you assign apprentices to because they get paid the least and you want this job done, and there's incentive for them to get it done quickly so then they can go on to other things and learn the trade. But when Laura told them she was pregnant, it seemed like they would automatically hand her the chopping gun and say, "Meet your new partner." So it felt to me that they were trying to harass her out of the industry. When she filed the lawsuit, she was standing up for herself. Because of the lawsuit, the lawyers at the Joint Industry Board had a realization that they had to change the policy. They had to change so that there would not be any future litigation. But again, she paid a tremendous price and we lost a great trade union electrician when Laura left the industry.

Repeatedly, decent instincts vanished when some men took it as a personal affront when a pregnant woman showed up on the job. Pregnancy crystallized the issues surrounding women working in nontraditional blue-collar jobs. Some found it incongruous; others found it offensive. Time-honored protective practices in the construction industry, such as "covering" for sick co-workers, "set-asides" for men age 55 and older, and light duty for disabled electricians, disappeared when it came to pregnancy.[43]

Culpability was shared by all three entities—the contractors, through their Employers' Association; the Joint Industry Board, the agency responsible for distributing jobs; and Local 3, in charge of representing members. Initially, as Kelber began to experience the crazy-quilt policies that shortchanged pregnant members, she made an effort to address through her union the issues of disability, light duty, and medical benefits.

In a friendly, detailed letter to Thomas Van Arsdale, Local 3 business manager, she wrote: "Dear Brother Van Arsdale: I am an 'A' journeywoman and have been a member of Local 3, IBEW since March, 1981. On March 12, 1988, I gave birth to a baby boy who will hopefully become the fourth generation in his family to be a union member."[44]

Laura suggested that together, the union and members, with her own voluntary efforts, could put in place a policy that wouldn't discriminate against pregnant women. Sadly, this was not to be the case. Throughout three successful pregnancies and two miscarriages, Kelber got to fully experience the animus directed against a pregnant electrician.

In her letter, Laura recounted an episode involving a union steward: "I was surprised when I was transferred off a job because the foreman had told me he liked my work and intended to keep me as long as I was able to work. I later found out that the shop steward had convinced him to transfer me to a job with worse working conditions and without proper bathroom facilities. This steward did not think a pregnant woman should work, and he hoped the harder conditions would force me to quit. They did not, but they made my life more uncomfortable."[45]

Kelber described how she earned the appellation of "Lawsuit Laura:"

I was working at an indoor location at the World Financial Center, a kind of very light, easy job, when I became pregnant. It would have been a good job to be pregnant on because there was no heavy lifting. It was indoors in an occupied building. There were clean bathrooms. And when I told them I was pregnant, very soon after they sent me to a [new] construction job. It was a surprise. It wasn't like they had a transfer coming up. I was sent to this freezing cold [site] close to North Moore Street. There was some heavy lifting. There were no clean bathrooms. It was the worst type of job. I was going to stick it out as long as I could because if you left too early, you only got 26 weeks of disability. I was near the end of my third month and I had a miscarriage.

In fact, before I was transferred to that construction job, there was a guy who had multiple sclerosis. He could only sit. He could barely work and the foreman kept putting his arm around him, saying, "I'm going to take care of you. Don't worry." Then they took me from that job and put me, pregnant, on the construction job. That was for Forest Electric. So I sued them. It ended up with a settlement. They were going to give me a little money, but I said what I wanted was a pregnancy clause...a commitment that pregnant women are entitled to light duty jobs.[46]

Working for another company, Kelber became pregnant with her third child. "Again, I told them I was pregnant," she said. "What did they do? They fired me immediately. They fired me that same day. So I went to the union and said, 'I got fired for being pregnant and I want to be put on a light duty job. Where did they send me? They sent me to the Coney Island train yards. There's live track. It's heavy work." The foreman there said that the jobs dispatcher for the JIB "must have had it in for you if he sent you here," Kelber said.

An exchange with a union representative ensued. "He gave me the run-around," said Kelber. "He ended up saying, 'So do you know if you're going to have a boy or a girl? If you have a boy, he could become an electrician.'"

To ensure a safe birth, Kelber went on disability. Through a loophole, she lost her medical benefits. After her daughter was born, Laura brought a lawsuit against the Joint Industry Board. Although she lost in court, she won on appeal. Her husband, an attorney, had permission from his firm to work on the case pro bono. Kelber described her experiences:

We lost the trial. It was a horrible, horrible experience. The judge had ruled that Tommy Van Arsdale did not have to testify. My husband got it overturned on the basis that it [his testimony] was relevant. This decision was actually featured on the front page of the *New York Law Journal* because it was a big deal. A civil rights activist lawyer called us up and said: "That's a great decision, because you're holding the head person liable." It was a great victory.

On July 1, 1994, the appellate case was featured in the *Law Journal* as "The Decision of the Day." Before it went to a second trial, one at which Thomas Van Arsdale would be required to testify, the JIB agreed to a settlement.

Soon after her experience in court, Kelber decided to leave Local 3. Although she never officially withdrew, she did stop working as an electrician:

> After the lawsuit, I started feeling like there's no future for me there because I was now a troublemaker...."Lawsuit Laura." The first job I went to after the lawsuit, they sent me out to Kennedy Airport. Someone told me that when I walked on the job, a foreman for one of the other companies—and there were several electrical companies on the job—ran into the locker [room] and said, "Stay away from her. She's got lawsuits up the yin-yang. You know? You say hello to her, she'll sue you."
>
> But I remember, I was working with this one guy, and I sort of confessed to him that I actually had a lawsuit against the Local and he looked at me and he said, "Let's put away our tools." He said, "Let's find someplace to hide. Okay. Tell me everything." He was thrilled that someone had [done this] because so many guys hated the way they were treated by the hiring hall. This was a conservative guy and he was thrilled that someone had sued the Joint Board.

As Laura spent her last days as a Local 3 electrician, it saddened her to see such general deterioration. "What disturbed me the most about the union right around the time that I left, was that Tommy has really run it into the ground," said Laura. "He's dismantled so many of the things his father did to make it a great union."

Not everyone is a Norma Rae. Not everyone is willing to stand up for what they believe is right. But in assessing the situation of all workers today, male and female, union and nonunion, Laura is cautiously optimistic: "These things go in cycles and what's happening now will create the seeds of another wave of people willing—demanding—rights and getting them."

Joi Beard—Cutting through the Glass Ceiling

The Louisville electrician completed her apprenticeship program in 1984. The next year, she followed her future husband and other Louisville electricians to New York City where work was then plentiful. Her first job was at the Javits Convention Center. She had the approval of her home local and Local 3 to work as a traveler in the city. "We were working for L.K. Comstock," she recalled. "We had to install 45,000 feet of pipe for air-conditioning controls. From May until October, we were on the roof doing pipe work."[47]

While she was the only female on that crew, other women were working at the Javits Center. "That was a great job because at the peak, we had nine women electricians working there," she said.

Beard moved from being an electrician to set up her own company. Long spoke with pride about this:

> She became an electrical inspector for the city of New York. She and I both attended classes at the Mechanics Institute. Joi was very successful. I believe she's the only woman who worked as an electrician to become an electrical contractor. She was the first black woman. She's had a lot of firsts. She's currently a Local 3 contractor, which is I think a really big deal.

Beard named her company Derby Electric. She laughed: "I'm from Louisville—home of the Kentucky Derby!" Her road from journeywoman to electrical contractor did begin at the Mechanics Institute in midtown Manhattan. "I was studying engineering drafting," she said. "You wouldn't believe how much you learn from that school and back then, it was only $50 a year. But you had to be in the trades to get into the school. One of the teachers, Mr. Peter Amos, told me 'You should join the Electrical Inspectors Association.' He brought me the paperwork and I joined the organization."

In 1991, she took the test for city inspector and passed. "Every day, it was something different," she recalled. "I would be on union jobs, nonunion jobs, big jobs, small jobs. It was just a great thing." She incorporated her business on July 7, 1995, and got her contractor's license on September 26.

In addition to Derby Electric, Beard has a long list of other activities, many related to supporting women in construction. Teaching at the Local 3 apprenticeship program is close to her heart. She sees it as one more way to break down stereotypes.

I've been doing it almost 10 years. I started right about the same time I started the business. I love teaching. I teach the first year—first half—as soon as they come in. I really would not teach any other year because this way, when they come in, they already know they're going to see women on the job. They teach sexual harassment the first year. Some people may blow through it. I spend a whole night on it. And of course, I bring it up all the time.

I tell them about my experience. There are still misconceptions, so I try to get rid of most of them. I tell them: "I can work circles around you." It goes back to being a woman, being a person of color. I've got to do twice as much to get half the credit. So I keep that in mind. It's in the forefront for me because that's how it was back then. And to a degree, it's still that way. Don't ever think we got it made. It ain't like that!

Brunilda Hernandez: 10 Years and Out

Even before her graduation, Bruni Hernandez recalled that conditions for women were improving:

I started my apprenticeship in 1979. I think by the time I was entering my fourth or fifth year, it was getting a little better. Men were more responsive and willing to work with you. You still had the few guys who really didn't want you on the job. But more and more, they were accepting the fact that women were coming into the trades. Even before I got my journeyman card, I was being respected a little more. Once you pass your apprenticeship and you're going into mid-mechanic, people are like: "Okay. This person probably knows something." They would give you more elbow room to work.[48]

Her description makes electrical work sound like an abstract art form: "What I like about running pipe was—when the pipe was going to be exposed—it was a concentric pipe run," she said. "You really had to use your knowledge of formulas and math and angles and 90 degree turns and elbows and offsets...If you're looking at an industrial plant, when you look at the pipes, you see they're all going nicely where there's nothing that's bumping out. And when you look at it, it's kind of like a river.... I love that because it was like we were looking at a painting. When you run a nice line of pipe, people look up, they're like: 'Oh yeah. She knows what she's doing.' They leave you alone. It's like: 'Okay. That's good workmanship.'"

In 1989, after 10 years in the trade, Hernandez left to pursue her dream of a career in medicine. "I did not want to retire in construction," she said, "because construction can be very dragging on your physical being, mentally and physically, and sometimes spiritually. And I did not want to be an old lady in the trades."

She looked back at her years as a craftsperson with satisfaction: "I really got to enjoy being an electrician. Once I decided that I wasn't going to be in it any more, it was something I could take with me. I will always be able to do it. And I thought that was an asset. And like I said, it's so neat to wire up a room. Everything is in. You go to the panel and turn that switch on and—there's *light*! You did that. It's amazing. It's like a miracle."

She also takes satisfaction from her role as a Local 3 pioneer. "I feel really good that I was part of the first group of five women," she recalled. "It was a scary thing to do. It was something unheard of and especially in the electrical union. But I feel very fortunate and honored to have been in that group. A lot of them did a lot for the women who came in after them."

The first women to go into the electrical union showed the IBEW that women could become electrical workers in more ways than one. Now they've become union organizers and shop stewards and leaders within the union. So there's many different ways.

After a few years of medical school, Hernandez switched to nursing. As a county public health nurse in Virginia, she provides maternal and children's health care in a clinical setting. Having gone from a mostly all-male to a mostly all-female environment, she discussed the two cultures: "The difference is in nurturing support—sisterly support. You can cry on each other's shoulders if you have to. The male environment was that you needed to pull yourself up. Suck it up. You need to be strong. Men pay a big price for that. It's unfortunate. I saw guys who I worked with that I really liked who were old beyond their age. They were just hunched over. They were tired. Their hands—everything—hurt. They were always complaining and a lot of them were miserable. They would retire and in two years they would die."

Hernandez views keeping the doors open for other women as critical: "I think women should be welcomed more. It's unfortunate that it's only 2 percent [women in construction jobs]. I think women should get into the high-paying jobs, especially as an electrician. It needs to be open, and it needs to be fair. People need to say 'Okay, we'll hire you. Let's see what you can do.' Not every woman can do it. Not every woman can be a nurse. Not every woman can be an electrician. There should be a way to let people decide for themselves. Just give them the opportunity to show it. It's that opportunity that needs to be opened and in a lot of places, it's not."

"No taxation without representation" was a rallying cry of American colonists that set this country on the road to independence. Local 3 women paid dues to an organization that was hard put to respond to their legitimate requests for representation. Local 3 placed its female members in the A-Division in a classic Catch-22 situation: while the union didn't represent them on issues that mattered, they also didn't want the women to organize on their own.

The trailblazing women in the A-Division refused to accept the status of victim. They refused to be passive. Although branded as "anti-union" for their independent, unsanctioned, and therefore uncontrolled activity, they chose to take matters into their own hands. Pro-union to the core, they formed their own support group.

WE helped many Local 3 females to survive and go on to lucrative, satisfying careers. Another change that they ensured was the entrance of the daughters of electricians into Local 3. The father-to-daughter model became possible because the generation of pioneers persevered. Although the group, Women Electricians, didn't provide them with a voice or power within their union, it did give them a voice in their own affairs and some small degree of power over their own destinies.[49]

FIVE

"Ticket to Ride"

As women set out to enter the skilled trades in the late 1970s, Kay Webster first made an ultimately unsuccessful effort to take up plumbing via the union Route. Although she never went through the apprenticeship program, she learned the trade "by the seat of her pants" and worked at the craft for 14 years without benefit of a union book. Webster was able to stay employed doing residential jobs during boom and bust cycles. She also taught plumbing in a couple of programs and was able to pass on her knowledge of the trade to other women.[1]

Elaine Ward saw a journeyman's card as "a ticket to ride"—a passport to a trade that would enable her to earn a good living and to travel at the same time.[2] As an applicant to the apprenticeship program in 1985, she couldn't foresee the hardships she would undergo trying to find work as a member of Manhattan-based Plumbers Local 2. The combination of being blacklisted by union officials for testifying before the New York City Commission on Human Rights and a severe recession in the city's construction industry forced Ward to take to the road in October 1992 to survive.

On June 6, 1994, a photo of Ward at work on a stadium project in downtown St. Louis ran on the front page of the *St. Louis Post-Dispatch*. By that time, a well-publicized corruption scandal in New York City—the first in a series involving the plumbers—had shown the elected leaders had sold out their members. Blacklisting of members was just one way that union officials violated their obligations.[3]

After years of traveling, Ward returned to New York City, earned a master plumbing license, and set up shop as an independent contractor. This is a strategy that appeals to ever-greater numbers of tradeswomen, as the doors to employment and advancement remain stuck shut.[4] The stories of Ward and Webster trace the tenacity it takes for women to acquire a skilled trade. Ward made determined efforts to try and get her union to work for her. When that failed, she had the courage to take up the role of a traveler in her trade. Webster's efforts eased the way a bit for other women seeking to enter the plumbers' union, the United Association of Plumbers and Pipefitters. After that, she was able to survive and thrive. Both women became proficient plumbers, but on two different tracks—union and nonunion.

"You Have to Be a Pest"

Looking backward, Ward could only wonder, with a little laugh, if, given prior knowledge, she would have chosen to enter the plumbers' union: "I guess if somebody showed me a video…beforehand, before I ever knew anything, that I was going to get into this trade, and said to me, 'Doesn't this look like something you'd want to join and be a part of?' I don't think so. There's just so much pettiness. It's such a shame."

Elaine has soft features, curly hair—black and later, gray—and a fair skin. But her personality distinguishes her. She never tried to use her attractiveness to her advantage. Although most females of her generation grew up learning to use smiles and other stratagems to dilute strong messages, this wasn't her style. A straightforward delivery was her trademark. Her willingness to head right into a subject, sometimes to her detriment, and a single-mindedness that could be obsessive became her hallmarks.

From the beginning, she showed determination to succeed. With a background in ceramics, a bachelor's degree in fine arts, and a history of juggling low-wage, part-time jobs, Elaine pondered her future. Realizing that she needed training in a well-paid trade that could provide her with a satisfying career, she sought to hop on board the union express in 1985. When a female carpenter told her that the plumbers' union was giving out applications for its apprenticeship program, Ward made her decision.

After delivering pizzas in the evening, one of her three part-time jobs, Ward drove into New York City and stood in line nine hours to get the application. The only other woman she recalled seeing was there to get an application for her grandson.

"The line was three blocks long when I got there…I got application number 357. They were only giving out 500. There were police barricades up…I remember guys were catcalling the working women who were walking on the street…I didn't drink anything or eat anything that morning…because I didn't want to have to pee."

She then went to Nontraditional Employment for Women (NEW) to get help preparing for the tests and interview: "A lot of it was geared toward spatial relations," Ward recalled. "The preparation I received was very good so that when I went into the test, I was not nervous at all. I went to the interview, dressed conservatively. I remember I had a pants suit on and no makeup, and I was only asked three questions: Did I know the starting wage? Was I afraid of heights and high places, and was I married?"

The plumbers' program held two attractions for her: "One was that every six months we got a raise automatically. And at the end of four years, if we went to school and did what was required of us, we would automatically be given this wonderful hourly rate of pay, which, at the time, was more than $20 an hour. The other thing was—I do remember thinking that the locals are all around the country—and card-holding union members with their dues paid up can travel. That was a hot button for me, the idea of working and traveling."

From the beginning, Ward's experience differed from the rest of her apprenticeship class. As she explained:

> It was really unfair from the get go. All the rest of the people in my class were guys and they were all working…Plumbing contractors hired out of Local 2 and the other apprentices were getting paid for the day and were already on the clock to get their benefits, because you had to have six months of work time in before the

contractors would start paying into your benefits. So the first thing was that I wasn't getting paid for the days I went to school. I started working in June and so my benefits didn't start until December...A lot of them were the sons of members. I went to the apprentice school for about three and a half months before I was put to work on a plumbing job.

Elaine's practical education about the plumbers' union began with a private lesson, when the director of the apprenticeship school offered her some advice: "I remember going to see Pete Marzec one time and he said to me, 'Well, the union's not exactly open arms to women. You have to be a pest. You have to call every day.'" She took his advice to heart.

She started calling the union hall regularly and finally she got word to report for work. Her first job was on June 16, 1986, at First Avenue and 38th Street. The first journeyman she was paired with was five years her junior. "He had been a journeyman for a couple of years already and he had been a foreman for a while," she said. "Sometime, you can find good out of almost anything. He liked to brag about how much he knew. The good thing was—I got to learn a lot of stuff from him because he did know a lot about the trade and he liked to tell other people what he knew."

She sought to prove herself: "When I started working, I just tried really hard to do everything I was told...When a delivery came, if there were two boxes, I'd grab the one that was heavier. I'd have to be there on time. I'd have to show up for everything."

Throughout her apprenticeship, Ward made every effort to absorb all that she could about the trade, the industry, and the union. "I survived by stubborn persisting and a strong-willed state of mind. I had a beeline for the end of the road, which was the journeyman's card....I thought if I did everything I was supposed to do and then some, that would put me in the right light in the eyes of the men."

She enrolled in Mechanics Institute courses: "I wanted to do it to learn, but I also thought that the by-product would be that the union officials and my co-workers would recognize that I was somebody who's serious about being in this business and that I deserved to be treated and acknowledged in that way."

I went for three years at night and in addition to my apprenticeship, I got a design certificate. I learned about the plumbing code, about blueprint reading and design situations. Plus my apprenticeship school gave me some courses that I attended at night.

Being the only female in the shop classes was intimidating: "The instructors were very good and knowledgeable. I was the only female so most of the time I was not that comfortable with myself because I wasn't used to being in a classroom with only men."

Walking into the crowded monthly union meetings as a woman was also daunting but she did it anyway. She embraced this as another important part of her education as an apprentice. As she recalled,

Occasionally, I would see one or two other women at the union meeting, but oftentimes not. I was an unfamiliar face and I was female. I was stared at for that reason. A lot of them would stand in the back. It was social time for a lot of the guys. They were pretty chaotic.

Ward's response was one of the strengths of her personality and contributed to her ability to survive in a strange and oftentimes hostile environment. As she explained, her reaction was to face the fear:

> It's easy to feel fear...Intimidation is when one person wants to control another person in a negative way by making them feel bad about themselves. If I had those feelings, I never let them stop me....One of the things I learned was that what was fearful and intimidating became familiar. And I learned that I could ignore it...I was learning not to take those things personally.

In the future, as she went out on the road seeking employment on huge industrial projects, her ability to walk onto a work site populated by hundreds of men with her fear under control was an asset firmly in place.

Learning about the mechanics of her union took some time:

> The fellows who were in the position of supposedly being the sentries to control the meetings did not do anything to keep the people who were being a nuisance from doing whatever they did. The supposed leaders did not seem to be in control. So it just really boggled my mind.

She struggled to find something positive about her union experience. As she described it: "I would walk around the city and think about all the plumbers in the last 35 or 40 years. The huge amounts of plumbing and piping that are in all these buildings were mostly installed when they were new by these union plumbers."

In the spring of 1990, Elaine completed her apprenticeship. Of the 60 people completing the 4-year program, she said 45 showed up for graduation.

> The union put on a big dinner for us at this place in the Bronx. We were allowed to invite one person. Most of the guys brought their girlfriends or wives. I asked Melinda Hernandez [another tradeswoman] to come with me. She gave me a [red] tool box as a little gift. I bought new clothes, a nice pair of pants, and a fancy blouse and these nice boots. We had the dinner and they called out our names, and they gave us our certificates.
>
> Three women were taken into the apprenticeship program when I got my application in 1985. But on March 1, 1990, at our dinner, I was the only female graduating.

"The Hands of a Plumber"

As women entered the plumbers' union one by one and two by two, each woman had to devise her own strategies for survival. There was no way to compare notes, connecting to each other, or learning from others' experience. In fact, the women's very presence remained almost on the level of folklore. James McNamara, at the time the assistant commissioner for the New York State Division of Human Rights, was in charge of minority recruitment when the first woman became a member of the union.

He recalled the fanfare and how the union bosses fought to take credit for the historic development:

> It was such an unusual event. There was a woman plumber, a Chinese woman...I get a call. We're going to have a ceremony at City Hall because the plumbers' apprenticeship program is graduating their first woman apprentice.... The Employers Association, who really put together this event, [has] a character named George Waylon. The head of the local gets into an argument with Waylon, to the effect that, when we take the pictures, he says, "Remember, this girl belongs to me." So they're all proud of it. I remember the *Post* ran the story.[5]

Kay Webster was the second woman to try for a union card. Years later, she vaguely recalled another woman before her. "There had been a woman prior to me, a Chinese woman who they kept talking about, and I never met...She left after a few years. I don't know why."

Webster's own story began in Buffalo. Born in 1953, she was the daughter of a carpenter.

> My father did the layout of buildings, ...and in Buffalo, that's no joke because the weather is so cold! My mom was for a long time a housewife and mother and then moved into working for the Post Office.

After moving to New York City, Webster worked as a waitress:

> The money wasn't very good and after a while, I thought, if I'm going to take harassment, I might as well get better paid. So I actually went to trade school, to All-Craft, for a bit of time. I was doing some carpentry, building walls. I could hang doors, and I could get some work doing demolition and basic carpentry. But...oddly, there were a lot of women carpenters, and so I decided to take up plumbing.

She landed a job with a contractor doing freelance plumbing jobs on the Lower East Side. "I was working on galvanized pipes that would fall apart if you breathed wrong," she said.[6] Making "very little money" and working jobs that were "rough, rough, rough," she decided to try the union route. As she explained, there were two ways into the plumbers' union: one was the typical path through the apprenticeship program, and the other was as a trainee in a program created specifically to get around the exclusion of minorities, and later, women, in the construction trades. Her first try was as a trainee.

Mayor Lindsay started it, she said, "and it wasn't doing what it was supposed to do.... You could be training forever and not ever be admitted [to the union].... It wound up being a catch-all, to sort of keep people of color and/or women nonapprentices."

Webster attended one class a week at the plumbers' union. "There was always an atmosphere of heavy tension in the room," said Webster. "We walk into the class...The classroom portion was very hostile." She described one memorable classroom experience:

> I walked into the room one day and there was a picture of a woman spread-eagled on the board with a plumbing term written to point to her crotch. Basically it meant, "from a putrid source." So I walked up to the board and tore it down and

threw it in the garbage can and sat down. But I was very shaken up. It felt scary being there, even though I think some of the guys had no ill intention...I went to the bathroom, we had to use the teacher's bathroom, there was no women's room there, and threw up. Then I just had to look myself in the mirror and say, "Go back and do it for your mom." She had to do this when she was in the postal union. She was the only woman on the line and she had to have that job. We needed the money. So I just steeled myself and said, "You're going to go back in there." Eventually, they were supposed to put us on a job, and of course they never did. The funny part was the excuse was always, there weren't any women's toilets, which I thought was funny for the plumbers union to say.

Still, Webster applied to the apprenticeship program, although she had reservations:

At that time, they had links to organized crime. I won't say any more. I heard about it and then I stood in line, got my application, took the test...and I had the interview. I remember distinctly one of the things the guy said in the interview: "These are not the hands of a plumber." Meanwhile, I was working nonunion doing a lot of plumbing every day, so I thought that was interesting.

When I got my test scores, they said I tested low. So I went after that. I had to write to the state to get my score and they said, "No, you tested high. Where you had trouble was in the interview." So I wound up filing charges and the result of that was I was offered a second-year apprenticeship.

Instead of passively accepting the actions of the officials who had conducted the interview, Webster sought a remedy before the city's Human Rights Commission. "My main point," she said, "was to get those discriminatory interviews knocked out."

She reached an agreement through the Commission that resulted in a change in the interview process. The simple, streamlined interview that Ward went through was the result of the charges Webster filed. This small but significant step marked a milestone for Webster. She felt she'd fulfilled her commitment to breaking down barriers. Years later, she explained her decision: "I wanted it changed. I felt like that's something I could leave with in good conscience. But it was still true that a lot of the guys of color couldn't get into those unions; a lot of the women couldn't get in those unions."

After that, Webster was subtly threatened for having the temerity to challenge the process. As she described:

I never went to the apprenticeship thing. I was warned by some of the guys there. "Don't come back here." Not in an unfriendly way. They just said, "They're talking about you...about not being on a site with these guys." By that time, I was already on the nonunion job. We were doing this project of 143 units. It was a big job and I was the manager. Why am I going to go to the second-year apprenticeship and work under these hideous conditions when I actually have a group of guys who I'm working with that are actually pretty good, and I'm earning enough money.

Although Webster sought to become a union member, it didn't work out. As she recalled: "I had wanted to go the union route for a lot of reasons and I always recommended it...I did a stint teaching plumbing at All-Craft and I always told them: 'You don't want to learn the way I had to…just by the seat of my pants.' It was nerve-wracking to be a woman out there…I said: You want protection. You want to build a pension. You want to have the insurance. You want somebody to train you so you really know. That's the reason."

Blacklisted

For Ward, reaching her goal of a journeyman's card and getting her first big payday bonanza gave her a boost:

> The great part of it was that I went from making $11.80 to $26.91 an hour. I remember a guy who I knew was on my side…we kidded around and we used to go to the bank on Thursdays to cash our checks. The first time I got to cash a full journeyman's check, we were working on Sixth Avenue. He said to me, "Your smile is all the way from here to Broadway." I really thought I had it made, that's where I was at.

But the reality was to be different,

> I thought that after a certain period of time, they would all get used to me being around…they would have seen that I wanted to work and…that eventually, the harassment and/or hostility would decrease. But it increased. As I got closer to the big bucks, my interpretation is that, then I was due for more hostility *because* I was succeeding. I believe that everything along the lines of the intimidation I experienced was an attempt to really test my ability to persevere. But I also believe that a lot of the intention of the guys who dished it out was to discourage "the woman" and set it up so that they could keep it a boys' club. I decided that I was not going to keep my mouth shut anymore.

Soon after her graduation in the Bronx, Ward attended the tenth-year reunion of United Tradeswomen, held in a church basement on the Lower East Side.

> It was such a big deal. I guess the bottom line is: How do we survive? As time went by in my apprenticeship, I wanted to keep educating myself as far as the things that weren't right about my experience, and if I could do something to change those things. Also, I wanted to be a good union person and I really wanted to be involved in what the union was about…I did go to conferences and workshops. I was interested in organizing. I was interested in women trying to help each other. And I was interested in getting to know the women in my union.[7]
>
> At this point she began to work with others to challenge some of the practices she saw: "At the end of my apprenticeship, I became active with women who were trying to make changes in construction. I became involved with women in other trades who also experienced similar things that I experienced, because I went through a lot of things that were unpleasant and seemed to be definitely related to the hostility toward women being in a trade and nothing to do with our ability to do the work."

Less than three weeks after earning her journeyman's card, Ward testified at public hearings on the construction trades. On March 13, 1990, she sat at a microphone before the Human Rights Commissioners describing conditions she had experienced:

> I have managed to survive the harassment. My experience has been like it has been for other women in the construction trades, that the work is not the problem. The women who do it are smart enough, physically able, and determined. However there's a determination on the part of the men to consistently keep women off the jobs and to create situations where women will eliminate themselves. Harassment is mental, emotional, and physical...I received continuous teasing, taunting. This is my livelihood, and yet, day by day I'm being told in various ways that I am not supposed to be there.
>
> The reason women drop out of this business is not because of the work itself, but because of the harassment. The harassment is a symptom of a greater problem, which is that there are not enough women on the jobs. As long as I'm one woman alone on a job—and I must say that...99.9 percent of the time I have been the only woman on almost every job I have worked on. Right now, I'm in a 40-story building, and I'm the only woman on that job. The harassment works. Eventually, the women are timid enough, exhausted enough, and tired of paying for shrinks to keep their sanity. They quit.[8]

Besides harassment, women and minorities had to deal with a perpetual ploy to keep them off the job:

> I shaped so many jobs...I would go up to the foreman and I'd introduce myself. I'd show my union card and I'd say I was looking for work...The foremen would tell me I'd have to go to the superintendent, or the boss, or the contractor, as far as getting hired...Then they would tell me that I'd have to go to the union hall. So they could play this cat-and-mouse game where I would be sent back and forth and in the meantime, I would never be hired.

Ward explored every avenue open to her. She kept shaping jobs; she took notes and kept records; she sent certified letters to contractors and to her business agents; she filed grievances with her union—much to their surprise; she filed discrimination charges with the New York City Commission on Human Rights, with the state's Division of Human Rights, and with the federal Equal Employment Opportunity Commission(EEOC). Sometimes her persistence paid off, and she would get put on a job. A couple of her charges resulted in financial settlements that were concluded years later. She even succeeded in obtaining the benefits owed to her on a job. This story illustrates how her guts, determination, and unwillingness to play it safe ultimately worked against her.

Nonpayment of benefits is one common scheme used by corrupt union officials and collaborating contractors. What was uncommon was Ward's appeal to collective action to challenge the practice.

> In 1990, by pressuring the EEO officer for Turner Construction, I got the guy to put me on the job up at Columbia University—it was the Science and Engineering building for a contractor called High Tech Mechanical. At the time I was hired on the job, the benefits were not paid. It was October and the [union] elections were coming up,

and one of the business agents came to the job and gave everybody lip service that the job was going to be shut down if the benefits weren't being paid. Then, right before Thanksgiving, they got their checks. We used to get vacation checks twice a year...October 22nd I got hired and when I got laid off on February 22nd 1991, still—none of the benefits had been paid for that time. I remember talking to some guys on the job and saying "Hey, let's do this collectively instead of individually." One young guy said, "Oh, I only care about what's in my envelope." ...But his first, immediate response was, when I asked him to go in on this was: "If I'm out of work six months, I'll lose my house." In other words, he was so brainwashed with the thinking that, if he said anything, he was going to be laid off, he didn't even say that part to me. That was already a given. It blew me away, because these are grown men...and they had been so indoctrinated by whatever propaganda...that was in front of them that they were not even willing to call the hall—that didn't even mean that anything was going to get done! It was a pretty pathetic situation.

I called the hall a bunch of times and was given the runaround. I went to the foreman on the job, [who] at that time was the cousin of the president of the local, and he said to me, "Honey, you have two choices. You can go to work every day or you can go down to the union hall and tell them you don't want to work." In other words, if I wanted to keep working, I'd better shut up, which was part of the indoctrination that had all these guys scared.

Anyway, there's a clause in our collective bargaining agreement that says the delinquent employer has to pay on a terminated employee. So I said to myself, 'I'm going to be laid off anyway.' As soon as that happens, I'll force the issue...The accountant for the contractor gave me lip service...The woman at the Industry Board—I finally had to threaten that I was going to file a grievance and take it as far as I needed to get satisfaction...For the four months I was working there, that was almost $2000 that they owed me...I got my benefits paid. But the other guys *still* didn't have their benefits paid.

The upshot was that she did find herself out of work. It became harder and harder to get hired onto a job precisely because she opened her mouth and didn't back down. Shaping up at job sites where federal guidelines applied, she was rarely hired, despite the fact that no other women were on the job. Clearly, the contractors were not in compliance with the guideline requiring 6.9 percent women on jobs using federal funds. As she described, she adopted a very conscious strategy for seeking work:

There were a lot of jobs in New York City in the early 1990s that were federally funded. I targeted these jobs. I also went to the EEO officers. I started going to the general contractors before the jobs were even in the ground. I'd go to the EEO officer and get my name put on the list. I was the very first tradeswoman for that job down at the courthouse. Eventually I got work there. But in 1991, I worked a total of five months. And in 1992, I worked in New York City not at all.

By not accepting the rules of the game as it was supposed to be played—by challenging the system, she wound up blacklisted.

James McNamara has a long, distinguished record in construction trades oversight, going back to 1966. Eventually he carried two briefs: discrimination and corruption. He lent his expertise to countless efforts to eliminate both plagues from the construction trades. He summed up why women who challenged the system were kept off job sites that clearly came under the 6.9 percent guidelines.

> Elaine Ward brought some complaints...So although she is a qualified plumber, she's a troublemaker. I told the employer: "Why don't you just put her to work. She can do the job." She was vocal. So now, word gets around: This particular person is a troublemaker. Now, that's blacklisting, 'cause she can do the job.

As doggedly as Ward went after the contractors and her union representatives, she pursued the enforcement agencies with the same determination. She found the contradiction between what was supposed to happen and the reality of what did happen too galling. "I was extremely persistent and I made a lot of waves because I was very unhappy with the lack of enforcement," she said.

She learned that her union was not going to put her to work. As she explained, "The more persistent I was, the more they made it clear that they were not going to do too much to help me and that it didn't matter what the laws were. It didn't matter if jobs were supposed to have women on them."

In October 1992, Elaine tried another route—she took to the road. "What was really terrific was that, for the first time, I did not need my officials in Local 2," she said. "I had found out they were useless."

"Booming Out"

> When there are no bridges to be built, they will build skyscrapers, or highways, or power dams, or anything that promises a challenge—and overtime. They will go anywhere; will drive a thousand miles all day and night to be part of a new building boom. They find boom towns irresistible. That is why they are called "the boomers."[9]
>
> —Gay Talese

A chance encounter with an ironworker led to Ward's maiden voyage as a boomer. He spotted her with her hard hat, construction boots, and Carhartt jacket, and struck up a conversation. From him, she learned about a job in Erie, Pennsylvania, at a paper mill where the union contractors were hiring travelers. She picked up the phone and called the business agent at the plumbers' local in Erie:

> The business agent said: "It's only four tens"—meaning four days for ten hours. I had been out of work for so long I was really desperate to go to work. He asked me when I could be there. I said, "5:30 the next morning." So he said, "All right you can come." So, I got myself a job.

Five years later, Ward wrote about her experiences for the dissident publication *Hard Hat News*:

> For those who cannot imagine leaving the security of the familiar, working out of town will be unimaginable. For me, it's been an education. In the last 5 years, I have

worked out of 21 U.A. halls in 15 states I'd never seen. I've learned what I know from working with union sisters and brothers all around the country...As a traveler, I am an outsider to the immediate politics and social order of the membership, but by my presence I create an impression that will forever be associated with my home local and my home town. And because I am female, I have the added responsibility of representing my gender. When I leave that job, that union hall, and that town, I also leave forever an image of a woman construction worker, and, for the union brothers, a union sister.[10]

The open road proved a great teacher. Not only did Elaine learn to navigate the world of travelers, to locate jobs through union hall referrals, but she also learned a range of new skills doing pipe fitting and gained mastery of her trade. She also had amazing adventures.

After arriving in Erie, on Amtrak with her sleeping bag and work boots, she headed for the 24-hour coffeehouse. "A guy came in and sat down next to me and I started talking to him. He was going to the same place I was, so I got a ride. Then, the first 15 minutes I was there, I found out more about what was going on in the country in the construction business than I had the whole time I was in Local 2. I soon discovered that there was this little network...when you go on a job and there are travelers or boomers, as they're called, and this cuts across trade lines, but in this case, it was plumbers and pipe fitters...We're in the same International. There are people from all over the country who've been traveling around. The information that they have, you can't get in a book....I learned that I could get jobs on my own. I still had to be dispatched out of the union hall, but I could make direct contact with the business agents around the country."

Her first job in Erie led to a second. "I was able to get an apartment and I stayed there for about three and a half months," she said. "That was the beginning of my being able to work out of town. I started practicing calling the business agents around the country and saying, 'Hi. My name is Elaine Ward and I'm a UA traveler.'"

She soon learned that it was better if she didn't say she was a plumber. As she explained:

Most of the out-of-town work for travelers in our organization is for pipe fitters—it's industrial work...Most of the plants around the country—the car plants, the steel mills, the paper mills, the power houses—most of those are all jobs where, when they have shut downs or when they're doing new construction—they hired pipe fitters, not plumbers. But in most cases, the plumbers and pipe fitters are part of the same local.

She traveled to Topeka, Kansas, and from there to St. Louis. Eventually, Ward worked in Oregon, Ohio, Minnesota, Colorado, Idaho, Georgia, and Virginia. She learned to get "friendly" with the system that offered her a living and the chance to use her skills. "Who cared how many miles" she had to go, she said, when there was a job with a paycheck at the end of each trip.

A lot of these jobs were bigger than any job sites I'd ever been on in New York City—the amount of construction workers was much bigger...I had to be willing to go among a lot of the guys that I'd never met before, from all over the country, guys with a lot more experience than I had.

If she had problems on the job, she attempted to deal with them directly. "But if I couldn't mediate the situation or get satisfaction through the foreman, or if there was no shop steward, through the superintendent, and I couldn't find any way to work it out myself, then I could leave the job," she said. "That's a plus about traveling. I think one of the reasons I experienced good treatment was because, as a traveler, I'm going to a place that's busy, and when I'm in a place that's busy, people aren't as threatened by somebody else. They have their job. So I'm not taking anything from somebody else, I'm there because there's a need for more than they have. And the flip side is—if I don't like being there, I can leave."

Overall, she met up with positive reactions. As she described: "It was also my experience, in places where the history of the state and the people originally being farmers, the people themselves are much more connected to women working. On farms, men and women work. So that, when a woman comes on the job, it isn't like: 'Oh, what's *she* doing?' It's like: 'Oh, there's a woman who's working in this trade.'"

> I did encounter some forms of chauvinism in different ways, but not as much as in New York City. The other thing is that the wages aren't as high as in other places...In New York City, some of the chauvinism has to do specifically with this really, really conservative notion that women are supposed to be home...That the men are only seen as being good men if they are the provider. In New York City, my experience on the job was that the wages are so high that, that's a threat. Women aren't supposed to be making that kind of money.

As a traveler, she found acceptance and some sense of solidarity, that was sadly lacking in New York City. As she recalled, "There are so many guys who have traveled. There's some locals, they call them suitcase locals, with no work in their area, and the local exists primarily to send the guys around the country...And it's a given that they're going to do what they need to do to take care of their families...And everybody has to help each other. And that's what I did not get here, when I was in New York City...One of the most important parts of the union is for people to help each other...All the greed and corruption and everything else aside, that's the biggest downfall of the union—that what's being passed along is not that we are here to help each other."

Down the Drain

The first affirmative action regulations aimed at women working in construction were meant to be, "A key to open doors that had been unfairly locked. But the existence of a key did not by itself open doors," Susan Eisenberg wrote in *We'll Call You If We Need You*.[11] The initial regulations, established in 1978, included goals and timetables, as well as detailed provisions about procedures to ensure equity.[12] Despite this, the pursuit of plum union jobs by women has proved quite difficult. Filing complaints with the bureaucracies charged with oversight of equal employment opportunity is slow and usually costly.

James McNamara can trace the enforcement mechanisms through the arc of his 25 year career. According to his assessment, the scenarios play out over and over in the same predictable way, while the trend is always toward a weakening of enforcement.

> The EEOC, to their credit, in the 1970s went to federal court in the Southern District of New York and charged half a dozen building trades unions with violating

Title VII of the Civil Rights Act in discriminating against minorities and in some cases, they had an impact. The problem that I saw was...that the follow-up or policing was nonexistent or weak.

They appointed a private practice attorney, a decent old gentleman named George Moskowitz. Complaints come in that the hiring hall is being ignored. I was working with the Organized Crime Task Force (OCTF) at that point and the OCTF had court orders allowing them to wiretap conversations involving some of the Local 46 representatives. One of them I distinctly remember. This white guy would call the B.A. at his home. He says "You know, I need a job. Do I have to go to the union office up at Third Avenue and sign in?" The answer is "No. That's just for the Niggers." He says, "Don't worry. I'll take care of you."

We supported a complaint to the EEOC: Your court order—your consent decree—is not being enforced. They didn't even know, until I told them, that the man they assigned to monitor it had died. George Moskowitz died a year or so before. So when you talk about the EEOC, yes. They've done some things, but the follow-up is weak.

Despite her blacklisting, Elaine Ward remains a strong union proponent in principle. But she has witnessed the erosion of union standards and working conditions. She articulates the insidious way cynicism creeps in and standards are undermined.

As the collective bargaining agreement has not been enforced, conditions start to slide, and contractors are allowed to do things that are against the bargaining agreement, and people go along with the idea of turning their head the other way. Then, all of a sudden, a lot of people are out of work, and they're looking around, and they're saying, "What's going on here?" Now they're upset and at this point, they're too scared to open their mouths...So you have a situation in which kind of the whole purpose of the union has sort of fallen apart. Even if they open their mouths, they won't get any satisfaction because there's been an agreement between the [union] officials and the contractors that they don't have to play by the rules any more. We'll make up our own rules and do whatever we want. This didn't happen all of a sudden. It's just that people became aware of it and start crying about it in a moment of their need. But by then, it's too late because so much has been lost. I'm really sounding negative, but I foresee it as a really long haul.

Ward is slightly more positive on the topic of women working in the trades. She sees her own struggles as having advanced the cause for the other women in her union—her four-month fight for the first shanty for a female construction worker at 52 Duane Street—her crusades within the union to bring about an awareness of sexual harassment—and also by her example. But change takes time and is incremental, as she pointed out:

Making contractors and unions be more receptive to women, I think that's only going to come from women being willing to go on the job and stay on the job and do their job and speak up for their rights and put up with the backlash and stick with it. Prove, time and time again, that they can do the job and they're capable and that they're decent human beings and that they have a right to earn their livelihood. We live in a society that wants everything instant, from the fast food to the button you push for the TV. But that's not the way human beings change. That's not the way human beings become receptive. I don't foresee the chauvinistic thing going through a mass, overnight change. I don't see that happening.

Postscript on the Women Plumbers

In Webster's home on the Lower East Side, a new generation is growing up and getting a different perspective on gender and work. Her young son Lee gets to see his mom at work, building a new room for him. "My son sees me and he thinks all women do construction work," she said. "I'm the one who does construction. Dad does other things, you know? Dad cooks. It has to start that early."

> I did very well with plumbing and it suited me. I still like it. I still do the work. I do the plumbing in my own house. I fix my mom's stuff. I don't earn my living at it [any more] but I love it. I love knowing that I can do that.

Webster observed that there are factors that make the learning curve that much steeper for women.

> There's such an internalized message of incapacity...There's a built-in thing in our heads that says we can't do it. That was one of the joys of teaching. It's like, "Yeah. You can. Take that saw." And then watching a woman finally be at home with a tool....Boys grow up from the time they're seven with that stuff. It's not inherent. But there's an internalized message in here, and then there's an institutionalized message out there.

In December 2006, Ward, the sole proprietor of Isis Plumbing, was the subject of a profile in *The New York Times*. "When Elaine Ward became an apprentice in 1986, the only female plumber most Americans had ever seen was Josephine the Plumber, a character in 1960s and 1970s commercials for Comet cleanser," wrote the reporter Joseph P. Fried. "Today, Ms. Ward remains anomalous. She is still one of a handful of women who work as plumbers in New York City; one of an even smaller number of women who own plumbing businesses in the city; and, according to the Buildings Department, one of very few women licensed by the city as master plumber."[13]

Only 50 women—1 percent—are members of Plumbers' Local 1. But the percentage of women in the apprenticeship program is increasing. And Ward, who started up Isis Plumbing in 2001, offered an upbeat assessment: "Things are changing a little, but a little goes a long way."[14]

PART THREE

The Agencies

SIX

"Sticking to the Union"

As a perceptive, politically aware person, Yvone Maitin provides an answer to an important question: despite the horrific treatment that many women working in nontraditional blue-collar jobs have experienced from their unions, why is it that so many continue to hold a very pro-union position?

Going to work in an all-male environment presented Maitin, a stationary engineer, with a daily challenge. Yet she succeeded in moving from ostracism to acceptance. Early on, she worked with—forced—her union to win a favorable resolution to a grievance. Then she served as a shop steward. As a member of Local 30, International Union of Operating Engineers (IUOE), she's traveled along two tracks. At some points, she's assumed a role as an active participant. At others, she's limited herself to observation, albeit from the perspective of a critical rank-and-file member who understands the role of democracy within a union. At all times, despite the significant limitations of her local, she has held to a firm belief in the critical importance of and potential power of unions.[1]

Maitin is small in stature, but her five foot frame contains a large and powerful spirit. Her coffee-colored skin is set off by curly gray hair. Frequent outbursts of laughter puncture any sense of self-importance, both her own and that of others. She is quick to locate the absurdities of any situation. Throughout more than 24 years as a tradeswoman, her sense of humor has stood her in good stead. In 1983, at age 33, Maitin entered the apprenticeship program of Local 30. The single mother of a 12-year-old son, she found the strength and determination to work full-time, attend school, and travel between two boroughs. Early on, she got involved with tradeswomen's groups and contributed her organizing savvy to their efforts.

From a young age, Maitin was a political person. She brings a definite class perspective to every aspect of her life. As she described, she was initiated into political awareness as a child:

When I was a very young girl, my mother used to go on "Ban the Bomb" marches... She was a young woman with five small children who were beginning to see these things in the world. So I went with her. She always dragged us around. Wherever she went, we went and that was the beginning of my knowing [about politics]. Even at that age, I really appreciated being told the truth about reality so that I could be more prepared. I must have been six years old.[2]

Connections between theory and reality come easily to her. "It's always so funny to me when I hear people saying, 'Oh, I don't get involved in political stuff. I'm not political,'" she said. "Whenever I hear them saying that, I always say 'You can't get away from it. If there's water, it's political...Is it polluted...Non-polluted? What kind of pesticides are they using? Is it full of lead and mercury? It's all political'. You can't get away from [it in] this world."[3]

Her Union is a powerful, albeit corruptible labor institution in New York City. One reason is that the highly paid positions at the helm of the huge cranes that dot the skyline are held by its members. In 2005, shadows fell over two of its locals, Local 14 and Local 15, when high-ranking officials were charged with taking bribes from contractors. Five Local 14 officials, including the local's general manager, pleaded guilty in federal court.[4]

Corruption and union leaders on the take in the construction industry are a familiar story in the Big Apple. Yet there are other forms of corruption that weaken the union. In May 2005, a rank-and-file group in the Laborers' union used a Web site to point out the connection between corruption and the lack of democracy within the Operating Engineers. After Thomas McGuire—a top official at Local 15 from 1975 until his indictment—received "a mere slap on the wrist" for his illegal actions, they wrote:

> Rumor has it that Thomas P. McGuire Operating Engineers Union Local 15 has received 3 years probation and $3,500 fine. This is the sweetest deal in history. One cannot calculate what his behavior cost the regular members of Local 15 in the forms of employment. The International union in Washington, D.C., that McGuire was part of, has not had a contested election in more than 50 years and not one dissenting vote by any member of the executive board. The corruption goes unchecked and the union does not have any small element of democracy on the national level, as well as Locals 14, 15.[5]

Operating Engineers Local 30 has its own sad history. But over the years, there has been a very active insiders-outsiders ballgame going on. Year in and year out, small groups of insurgents seek to challenge their entrenched leadership. The leaders then pass constitutional bylaws aimed at limiting the ability of their challengers to communicate with the membership. Periodically, the union officials throw other, punitive obstacles into the path of these active members who are seeking to attain elected union office and might possibly—if given the opportunity—act to broaden democracy within the local. But fundamental reforms remain far outside the sight-range of most of the 2,800 dues-paying members of Local 30.[6]

Maitin's own story is colored by an additional circumstance. This theme run like a current throughout her career—regret that she never acquired the proper training in her apprenticeship so that she could master her trade. This is a common problem for tradeswomen, one that was especially pronounced for the pioneers. In her case, responsibility is shared between her employer's and her union's neglect.

In 2002, after 19 years of employment for the Port Authority (PA) of New York-New Jersey and jobs at the airports, port and bus terminals it maintains, Maitin summed up the situation.

> As women in nontraditional work, a few critical things still remain out of our reach We are still not well represented, ergo the term nontraditional. This alone allows for discrimination. We are undertrained and have to fight hard for every bit

of information we need, to get the training we deserve just as human beings. This is part of the reason the guys still challenge my right to the job…I stand on that right because I am clear that I have struggled hard and paid dues, twice more than what any man has had to pay. They also often have not been trained properly, but they have the privilege of being men. It is quite obvious I am not a man and they don't let me forget that. This is good 'cause it keeps me sharp. I have no illusions, which is something many of them suffer from. I know whose side I'm on. I am also a woman of color…This field of work is still held predominantly by white men.[7]

"Steam Heat"

While Maitin was growing up in Chelsea, a steady stream of ships berthed at the North River piers close to her home. They transported cargoes from and to distant points. Early on, she succumbed to the lure of the vibrant blue-collar life on the waterfront.

> I had always, from when I was very young, been very much interested in what was happening in the background of things. I lived near the docks in Manhattan and trains were going through there and trucks and all kinds of things. That was always very exciting to me. I was sort of a tomboy, whatever that means. But I would go with the boys to the docks and we would investigate…That was always something very interesting to me, very intriguing.[8]

Maitin grew up in a project, Elliott Houses, on West 26th Street. "I had an interesting and somewhat scary childhood," she said. "My mother was not a very nice person. My Dad used drugs. I went to parochial school. I was a very shy young girl and teenager. I moved around a lot once I left Chelsea. I went to junior high school in Puerto Rico. I lived with my grandparents there. Then I left and moved out to San Diego, California, with my parents again and I went to high school and my first year of college out there. When I returned to New York, I returned with a little boy who was two weeks old."[9]

She was able to support herself and her son by going to work for the Board of Education in a traditional job for women—meaning routine clerical labor at low pay. After 11 years, she learned about a training program for women at the New York City Technical College. "It was called Building Maintenance and Repairs, and it was a six-month program," she recalled. "Then when we finished, they asked us each individually what we would like to do. I said I would like to do something with my hands and with my brain. So they put me in contact with the union people. I went out to Local 30's union hall in Richmond Hill, Queens, and they sent me on an interview to a couple of places. I got accepted into the job that I'm doing now."[10]

Her new job, working for the PA of New York-New Jersey, got her an instant raise. "I left my job making $11,000 a year and started making $16,000 at this one," she said. "…Like any woman in her right mind, there was no question which job was winning out, especially since I was a single parent and had to pay the rent alone."[11]

The PA is a vast quasi-public agency set up in 1921 to plan, develop, and operate port terminals, transportation, and other facilities of commerce that involve the two states. It operates interstate tunnels and bridges, a regional system of airports and heliports, marine terminals, and other transport facilities. The World Trade Center was once a part of the PA's mission to promote the foreign commerce in the harbor. In addition to maintaining its own police force and professionals on its payroll, it employs all manner of blue-collar personnel.

Maitin's first job as an apprentice in 1983 was at La Guardia Airport. Setting out for work on her first day, she was all geared up for something new.

> I came into work and I had just had my brand-new, short-short hair cut, and I had been preparing for this kind of work by doing weight-lifting and a lot of running—a lot of exercise to get ready for the job, and I was really surprised to find that it required the minimum of physical activity. I was so happy to have gotten this job. I walked in and I remember seeing the men. I walked right up to them. I was such a silly girl! It's so funny when I think about it...I told them my name and asked, "What's your name?" I went up to one guy in particular and he just stared back at me and didn't even put out his hand. I just stood there. All of a sudden, it was like the reality just came and smacked me right in the face. This is what it's really going to be about. And that was my first day at work.

As an apprentice, Maitin was working in a supervised capacity in the airport's huge heating plant.

> We had 2 very big boilers, 40 million BTUs is what they call them. They're like one and a half stories high. 40 million BTUs, 350 degrees under pressure, so if anything were to puncture any one of those pipes, the steam would come out. You wouldn't see the condensation, so you have to be very careful 'cause steam at that pressure could slice your head off. People think that you can see it. But you don't see it until it starts cooling off and condensing...On that particular job, it was going all over into different areas of the airport. It would generate the heat to keep the space warm. Part of this heat would be to heat water and that would be the secondary job of the steam. Then they also had industrial air conditioners. They're very big machines and they have what they call the cooling tower that works with the air conditioner. That was a whole separate building next to the heating plants that move the water throughout the system.
>
> Her supervisors were in charge of the plant, overseeing its operation and maintenance and the mechanics working there. Two men were in charge of supervising Maitin. "I had one immediate supervisor and then he had a supervisor," she said. "Their office looked down into the plant so they could see everything you're doing."

Her immediate supervisor's supervisor was into controlling and "micromanaging" others. His managerial methods had a lasting negative impact on Maitin's chosen career, as she explained,

> A lot of the guys didn't particularly care for him, the white men as well. This fellow was white. He just had a lot of issues that had absolutely nothing to do with me. But he was willing to visit that on whoever gave him the opportunity, whoever he thought would be an easy target. I was an easy target only in that I was a project provisional apprentice, and I couldn't really say much to him. I couldn't really do much. But in my own way I fought him and kept him from crossing the line with me up to a certain point. He never yelled at me. He tried to humiliate me in front of other people but not too often. But he was just a nasty, snide kind of guy. The biggest thing that he did to me was to keep me for those three years from getting truly trained, because I could have been.

My boss would often give me a work order to work with a mechanic and to do work that had to do with the field I was about to be involved in. Every day, I mean literally *every* day, he would come down and he would take that work order, put it to the side, and say "No, no." He would have myself and the other female apprentice cleaning, mopping, sweeping, and dusting for three years.[12]

After the first six months, she was joined by a second female apprentice, Margaret McMann. "We had a good working relationship, and she took some of the weight off of me—some of the pressure and focus off of me," Maitin said.

Together they did the mopping, dusting, sweeping, and painting that they were assigned. In this way, they were kept away from the machinery and away from the practical, hands-on training that was the purpose of their apprenticeship. Throughout her three years as apprenticed labor, she rarely worked with the mechanics and when she did, it was sporadic. Seeking remedy from the union was futile. She recalled:

When we complained to the union, they said to us, "Well, you know how the guys are. This was really a man's job for such a long time. They're having a hard time accepting you. Don't worry about it."[13]

This attitude perpetually frustrated Maitin. She was close to the machinery, but denied the opportunity to work on it. "I found it very exciting to be there and to finally get a chance," she said "... and I think the hard part for me that was most disappointing was getting there to see it and then being held back from being able to really learn and get my hands on it."

From 7 a.m. to 3 p.m., Maitin worked in the heating plant. Then, usually twice a week, sometimes more often, she headed off to the classroom part of Local 30's apprenticeship program at the union hall. There, from 6 to 9 p.m., she struggled to learn alongside her fellow apprentices. Although she started off with five other women in her program, by the end there were only two.

Stationary Engineers, Local 30, is part of the IUOE. To explain how this came about, Maitin referred to a book that's perennially popular with kids:

The reason why operating engineers and stationary engineers are part of the same union is because the operating engineers operated the big cranes with those big buckets and those vehicles were fired up by a small boiler in it...like the children's story about the steam engine, "Mike Mulligan."

As boys and girls learn from the story of *Mike Mulligan and His Steam Shovel*, the machine is displaced by changes in technology and Mike Mulligan sets out to find a place where his steam shovel, Mary Anne, can show how fast she can work to dig a hole. In fact, back in the early days of its existence, the Operating Engineer's Union was called the Union of Steam Engineers: it was chartered by this name by the A.F.L in 1896. Technological change played a big part in the hybrid nature of Local 30's jurisdiction. Mechanical refrigeration became one addition to the requirements for the stationary engineers.[14] Since schools were not offering courses in this new specialty, the union put together the books to teach the technical principles.

When [Local 30] moved out to Richmond Hill, Queens, they took on their own apprenticeship. But in my opinion, they were ill-equipped...It was a really terrible apprenticeship. It was primarily geared toward people who had already been in the trades for many years to prepare them to take their license exams—the refrigeration license and the watch engineer and stationary engineers test.[15]

There was virtually no shop. I think we had shop a couple of days in one class and that was it. So it was very difficult, not just for myself, and not just for the women, [but] probably for the men, to transfer what you learned theoretically to what your reality is, because a lot of times what you learned in theory is not in actuality what you do in practice.[16]

As Maitin described the program, she was regretful. "This is going to be difficult for me because I'm making a very big indictment of my union. Number one—they made out the books—I don't know where they got their information. They were an added expense to all of the expenses that we had when we had to buy them. There must have been about five or six books, really, really thick volumes, and no indexes...As a matter of fact, one of our teachers said that those books were virtually useless." He said, "If you don't have an index in a book, when you want to look up information, then you have to go through the entire volumes of books to see what the hell you're looking for." That's not very encouraging.

We had one teacher who would always tell us to ask questions. This was actually my very first teacher when I went to the apprenticeship school. He was a very learned man. You could tell that he knew his stuff. He was very pleasant on a personal level...Then I saw that any time anyone would ask him a question that he felt was challenging him—he would go berserk, yelling at these guys. It was incredible! These guys would say "Well what about this? How about that? How come I don't understand this?" And he would go off. And virtually the whole class went quiet.

For three years, the trek from her home in the Bronx, to work at La Guardia Airport, to school in Richmond Hill, Queens, and home again, involved a big commitment of time, in addition to its other stressful features. Maitin described the route she traveled between the boroughs:

I've always been a very physical person, so it didn't bother me. I was young and full of energy and had the stamina to be able to do that without it being a major problem. The worst part was when it was time for me to go home. Quite frankly, what would happen is that it would be nine o'clock at night. So what I would have to do is...try to hustle to get somebody to give me a ride back. There were times when one fellow gave me a ride back...He dropped me off on the highway and told me, "Okay. You can walk from here." I walked off the highway in the dark. He dropped me off on the 138th Street exit on the Major Deegan highway...So I would hustle quite often to try to get somebody to give me a ride...Getting on the train wasn't an easy way home. It was on the M train, all the way out there in Jamaica, and it would mean getting off the M to the F to the D to...get up in the Bronx.[17]

But the most difficult aspect for Yvone was being separated for so many hours from her teenage son. As she explained,

When I got into the trade, my son was 12 going on 13. So he needed some supervision, but he was also able to be alone. It was very difficult. I felt a lot of guilt because I would be gone before he was ready to go to school. A lot of the time, I wouldn't get home until he was in bed. So that was really very hard for me. But I needed to make a living. I needed to be able to pay the bills. So I just kept going. It was just sheer will. There were a lot of things that my son could do by himself. I think, emotionally, it was very difficult for both of us.[18]

While she struggled throughout her apprenticeship, she encountered some men who were willing to share their knowledge with her. "In my apprenticeship, there was one fellow, [and] I think this is one of the big saving graces for me in school," she said. "To this day, he is still my friend. He was an older West Indian man who was not afraid in terms of his skill. He was not afraid of the women and women doing their jobs and learning. He understood a lot about oppression. So if I didn't know something, if I was unsure about something, he didn't act like I *should* know it. He would just tell me or show me. We kept in contact a lot by phone." In addition to this friend, Neville Holloway, there were others. Toward the end of Maitin's apprenticeship, she worked with an able and helpful mechanic at La Guardia. As she described it, they had a mutual antagonist:

> He was being most willing to share his experiences because he was also being dumped on. He had had a problem with the union. They were blackballing him, giving him a hard time. So they put him to work where I was and my terrible, terrible boss gave *him* a hard way. This guy happened to be in the trade for a very long time. He was an engineer, not just a mechanic, and he was good at what he did. He was the most willing person to help me and the other woman to learn something about what we were doing.

While Maitin tried to make the trade her own, she never quite accomplished her goal. Over the years, she encountered others who were also shortchanged by the program. She described the experience of one man who felt similarly:

> One of the guys I work with...went through the same apprenticeship that I went through and he's totally mortified. This guy is a professional carpenter and [then] came to work for the Port Authority. He was pushed and prodded by his father to join a different trade, and so he joined the apprenticeship. He went through the same exact apprenticeship with the same people that I went through, with no shop. He finished the apprenticeship and was totally mortified because he felt totally unprepared to do his job. He took the test and was able to pass it, but he feels like a moron as a mechanic.[19]
>   "I said, 'Well sometimes, when I have problems, I have a friend who is a stationary engineer. I'll call him. Do you have anybody to call like that?' He's a man. He doesn't feel that he has the right to call another man and tell him: 'Listen. I don't know my trade. Can you be my partner? Can I call you if I have a problem?' But we made a connection and he is a real fighter. He's got a fiery kind of personality, and I said to him, 'You know, I have come to learn, in my years of being in the trades, that there are some struggles that I will fight, and there are other struggles that I'll just duck and get out of the way and let it pass me by, because I can't take them all on.'"

The Grievance

The first struggle that Maitin fought with the help of the union took place when she and her fellow female apprentice, Margaret McMann, were left off the list of the apprentices scheduled to take the test to become a mechanic. This action earned Maitin the enduring enmity of her supervisor at La Guardia. Years later, this came back to haunt her at the hands of his son, a shop steward at another PA facility.

Although the apprenticeship system has many unpleasant aspects, one of the positive features is that it has a finite term. As they enter into the system, each person is aware of the length of their servitude. As Maitin viewed it, the apprenticeship system had many oppressive aspects:

> I don't think it was personal that they [her co-workers] were not being friendly... You have to look at the history of apprentices and also at the conditions of production workers and people who do construction and maintenance, 'cause I'm in the maintenance trade, and the alienation that we have from our jobs. Then, when you have a boss like the one that I had, nobody wants to be there. I wasn't the only one. I'm sure the guys didn't want to be there either.[20]

As Maitin's three years of apprenticeship drew to a close in 1986, the qualifying test for the mechanic's license was the last step. That was when she learned that, inexplicably, she and her female colleague were not on the list. They reached out to the union to file a grievance. Local 30's callous refrain—"Don't worry"—turned into an imbroglio. The supervisor who was overseeing the three apprentices working at the La Guardia facility held a huge amount of power. Maitin described how he exercised it:

> He was extremely abusive. At this point, what he had done was he tried to keep us from being able to go on to the next level and become full-fledged mechanics... At any moment, he could just say "Well, they're not working out." He could do whatever he wanted. We'd lose our jobs. So he had a tremendous amount of power over us at that point... The way he did it was, there were three apprentices. Two of us were women and one was a male and he had the least amount of time. We both had three years and according to our contract...we were entitled to take the test. We had to finish our apprenticeship, which we had. We had to have our refrigeration license, which both of us had, and we had to have three years of experience, which both of us had. The fellow had half of that and didn't have any of the licenses. Well, we all applied. He was accepted to take the test and the day before the test, I found out...that he was going for the test and we hadn't even been notified...There was a letter in our files that said that we were not allowed to take the test because we were not prepared...The sexism that was happening was just so blatant....It was only at that point that any issue was made that we had not been properly trained.

Both Maitin and McMann filed a grievance against the supervisor. With union backing, the resolution of their grievance resulted in a number of remedies for the women. "This put the union on their P's and Q's to do what they were supposed to be doing," Maitin said. As she recalled:

> So in my files there is actually a letter that says, number one, that we had not been trained properly, number two, that we were going to be allowed to take the test, and number three, that there had been overtime that was given out to male apprentices that was not given out to us. So we were entitled to 53 hours of overtime we could get either in comp time or the money.

In a sadly ironic twist, Maitin's test-taking put her on the top of the list. As she described:

> What was so funny was that a whole bunch of people who had been apprentices in different facilities took the test. I knew this one particular fellow who had just finished getting off a ship where he was doing this exact same work. He took the test and came out last on the list. I came out over him...This fellow had a tremendous amount of experience in this field. He came out at the bottom of the list and I came out at the top of the list.

The lack of training became a perpetual problem. On her second job for the PA, her co-workers raised the issue. But Yvone was adamant that she had paid her dues and meant to stand her ground:

> When I got to my next job, they were trying to tell me that I would lose my job...And I told them: "I'm not going anywhere. I've worked hard. I've earned my place here and I have a family to take care of. I'm not leaving this job, so forget about it."...The reason why we won this whole suit with my supervisor...was that I fought for that, not so much the union. But the union was there for show. I'm sure they thought that they did it. But let me tell you—I made a list of questions that I wanted to ask about what was going on. When we had the meeting with the top people at my job...I got my chance to speak. I pulled the list out of my pocket and asked very pointed questions...One of the things was around this overtime. In three years, I made maybe 40 hours overtime. In a year and a half, he [the male apprentice] made 150 hours. They said the reason was that he wasn't going to school. I said, "Well, I only go to school on Tuesday and Thursday. So I'd like to know if, for a year and a half, the overtime fell on every Tuesday and Thursday...Let's get the paperwork...So I felt that the reason we were able to win was because I asked very specific questions...They were forced to recognize that, if they did not take me seriously, this would go a lot further than it was going...It was a good experience but it was horrible. It made me really angry to have to go through that."

This stage of her life came to a close. But she recalled a conversation with a co-worker.

> He criticized me for being angry about the pressure I was feeling. He said, "I went to school and did all of my work without any problems, so what's the deal Yvone?" I told him: "You had a wife to cook, clean, and take care of the kids and make your lunch and wash your clothes and make sure the kids didn't disturb you while you were studying. I have to do that all by myself. If I had a wife I wouldn't feel guilty either and school and work would be a cinch. I'd be able to concentrate my extra energy on getting you guys off my back!" He responded: "Oh, I hadn't thought of that."[21]

"42nd Street"

The La Guardia facility felt closed off and oppressive to Maitin, and she wanted a change. While one site felt constricted, the second job site offered more variety. She started off her life as a full-fledged mechanic at a new location—the P.A. bus terminal. The huge facility occupies the whole block on 42nd Street, stretching from 8th to 9th Avenue on the west side of Manhattan. She described the differences between the two sites:

> I was working with a much larger group. I wasn't working in a heating plant. I was at a transportation facility and the equipment was all over the building. I was working in midtown Manhattan…I knew it would be a lot better for me working there because I knew I would feel better being able to leave the building and walk into the general community, whereas at the airport I felt very isolated…It gave me more a sense of being where people were at as opposed to this ghetto kind of environment, which I found the airport to be.[22]

In addition, the personnel, the attitudes, and the issues changed as well. For starters, the P.A. facility on 42nd Street was a much more diverse group of employees:

> [When] I was working at the airport, I was working around primarily white men and at this facility I was working around primarily black men. By no means does that translate into not having to deal with shit, by no means. But what it did do, it changed the whole dynamic for me. Number one, I wasn't dealing so intensely with the racism in the same kind of way. These men understood oppression themselves. The white men, by no means do I think that they don't understand oppression. They are oppressed as workers. But they have this other privilege that they can lean on, whereas these black and Latino—mostly black men—didn't have that privilege. So that was like a relief to not have to deal with that so blatantly…Then the other thing was that it was a much larger crew. I worked with people from different trades.
> Most of the black men that I worked around were not mechanics, in terms of a specific trade. They were maintenance men. Also, there were a lot more women…I don't necessarily mean in the trades, but in the area—in the building that I worked in…So it was much, much less stressful.

Her move in 1986 to 42nd Street opened up another vista. Fresh from the experience of fighting her grievance with the union, she learned that the 42nd Street facility had no shop steward. Maitin decided to step into the breach.

> I approached the union about it…In our union, the shop stewards are appointed…So they wanted to appoint me but I told them no. Let's have an election and I will take responsibility for making that happen…I did not want to get appointed because it would make my position weak…I put up notices all over…"We're going to hold nominations and they should nominate whoever they wanted." I put down what the stipulations were to be able to be nominated: that you had to be a full-fledged, dues-paying union member…Lo and behold, the day came for the election and nobody nominated anybody—[just] myself and another woman. That was it. So I called up the union and I told them to appoint us…They sent a letter to our bosses and we became the shop stewards.

At this point, a fellow union member expressed interest in the position of steward. Maitin told him, "Well it's too late." She was the steward now. Her rationale for taking on the position was twofold—she was eager for a new learning experience—and thought that someone had to stand up to management. As she explained:

> I could see the injustices that were happening. I felt like somebody's got to be standing here for me…Somebody's got to be saying: "No. This is not going to be the way it is. You can't just do whatever you feel like whenever you want to." So I said, well, let me be the person.

Local 30 provided the shop stewards with a short course to prepare them for their new role. "I think it lasted one or two days for a couple of hours," Maitin said. "To me, it felt like a real farce because what I see about this is that the [union leadership] is not really wanting to encourage people to take over…It's like they want to be the imperial force for ever and ever…and keep it amongst them and away from the [members]. If they don't know, then they don't become powerful and they don't begin to challenge what 'we're' [the union is] saying."

Yet Maitin's overall perspective about trade unions was positive. It was informed by her experiences with United Tradeswomen. She brought this broader awareness to her job as a steward:

> I was very good. I think the thing that made me good is that I believed in what I was doing. I believe in unions and I believe that we have rights. For me, the biggest force in terms of taking a stand and in understanding this was actually my experience with the women in United Tradeswomen. The other women and the things they were talking about and beginning to understand something about unions and what they were supposed to be about and what they were supposed to be doing. I actually did not learn most of that from my union. I learned it from being around United Tradeswomen and listening to other women's stories…about what was the responsibility of the union. That's how I learned it. I really believe it. I still believe in it, even though I think that they're a horrible organization. I still, very strongly, believe in the union and in union principles. But it was a very empowering experience to be a shop steward.

Shortly after being appointed as stewards, the other female steward left the 42nd Street facility and went to work at Maitin's former location, La Guardia airport. The shop steward there was someone who took full advantage of his "empowering" position and had put it to use—albeit on his own behalf. Yvone described his behavior:

> The steward there was a man who was the most horrendous, horrific person you ever met. This guy had 500 hours of overtime, while the other workers had 150. This guy was in the boss's office every day. But he also had heavy connections in the union. No one argued with him. No one disputed him. No one questioned him. The guys didn't like it. They thought it was unfair, but they wouldn't say a word.

At 42nd Street, Maitin's co-workers accepted her in an official capacity and brought their grievances to her for help in their resolution. "Once I became shop steward, it seemed like a lot of the fellows started showing initiative," she said. "They said, 'Oh, we have somebody to protect our rights now.' So they would come to me if they had a problem."

She found the whole experience "very, very interesting." She learned that sometimes, the men were willing to complain, but unwilling to stand up for themselves. "They would not want to take a stand, so I would end up standing there by myself," she recalled. Sometimes, the men didn't want to put their grievances down on paper, or would share their stories selectively. Oftentimes, she found herself lodged in the familiar place of a union steward—between a rock and a hard place. She described one of these no-win situations:

> This one fellow had a record like Swiss cheese. He would hardly ever come to work. He wouldn't call and when he came in, he would come in late. This was a record that had been accumulating over a period of three years. The guy had 15 years working for this company, but in the last 3 years he was doing very badly. I'm looking at the records, and I can't argue with the records. The facts say you're not coming in...you're not making a full week any week...I particularly liked this person, so I would ask him "What's going on?" In retrospect, I think the problem was probably drugs. One day, I finally had to tell him "Listen! If you were working any place else than here, you'd be in the street. You'd have lost your job a long time ago." We got into a big argument. The fellows knew what this guy's record was about and still, they insisted that it was my fault.

Looking to the union for backup as the grievances moved to the next level of the disciplinary process yielded more frustration. Maitin would call on her union officials to show up to represent their members, oftentimes to no avail:

> The union's contention was—you don't come to union meetings so we're not going to come to you—that became like a Catch-22. A vicious cycle, because the fellows would say "Well. They don't come to us so why should we go to them?"...I felt it was incumbent upon the union to take that first step. That's why they're the organizers. That's why they're the people who get paid the union dues, because they're supposed to come out there on the sites and encourage the people to want to be union members.

Despite the fact that she declined to continue in this role, Maitin was enthusiastic about the value of the two years she spent as a steward:

> On a certain level, it's very much like my experience being in the trades—difficult, but something I wouldn't change for anything...It's been a really great learning experience. I chose not to represent the workers as a shop steward for a couple of reasons...primarily because I felt it was a lot of babysitting. The guys liked to complain a lot but really didn't want to take a stand. I'd take a stand for them. Then they would back off. They wanted me to do the work.[23]

42nd Street Postscript

Years later, Maitin was once again working at 42nd Street. Her shop steward turned out to be the son of the supervisor at the La Guardia facility who stood in the way of her getting training in the trade. The father couldn't forgive the fact that she bested him through her union grievance. He transmitted this resentment to his son. She described the hateful events as they played out within the first and second generation:

I think he was never able to forgive me. It's very interesting that he focused it on me because there were two of us, myself and the other apprentice...She was white. I think there was a racial element, but I think also the other thing was that he was never really able to get to me. There was always a part of me that was reserved. So when he lost control...he focused on my being the enemy in that situation.

Then...I was working in the 42nd Street bus terminal and his son was my shop steward. I needed to get some information that I wasn't going to be able to get except to go to my shop steward to get it...I had a feeling that he held resentment toward me the whole time that I was there, before I ever talked to him about anything. It was just the way that he would either ignore me or the tone of his voice whenever he would speak to me, which wasn't very often. When I approached him, he made it very, very clear and told me that he was going to pick up where his father left off. He drew a swastika on the table and told me that described him and that he was a mean son-of-a-bitch. He just rattled on. It was just him and I alone in the room. I was just standing there looking at him as he's drawing this and talking to me, totally stunned. It was like: This is not happening. He's not going there. But he really was. He was going there. When he left, I talked to a friend and my friend said, "It's really serious, Yvone. You need to go to the police." First I went to the union, and the union suggested that I go to the police. I filed a police report.[24]

She didn't succeed in getting what she had started out trying to get, which was a transfer to a facility closer to her home. Though her union representative had made a commitment to act on her behalf, the transfer never materialized. Yet Maitin wasn't discouraged. As she explained:

I think this is a really important thing for us, as women, to understand. I could have felt defeated because I didn't get exactly what I wanted. But in the end, actually, I won. The reason I won was because he was very much like his father. He was a real racist pig, and he was a shop steward. A lot of people told me that when he talked to people of color who worked at 42nd Street, cleaning staff and other people—they said that he treated them like they were nothing, in a really racist, nasty kind of way, subtle, but very clear to them. And after this whole thing, he changed...One of the things that had happened was that he was embarrassed and ashamed to tell his wife what had happened. Eventually, he got so uptight because the Port Authority detectives wanted to investigate and he got really, really nervous.

My point being this: I didn't win what I wanted, but I won because his attitude toward everybody changed. He knew that he was on notice. People knew what he was doing because I went around and told everybody. The second thing I won was that he left me alone. He didn't bother me...I think it's really important to recognize as women that you have to be able to be flexible and recognize that a victory doesn't always come in the package that you want it...I was able to get him off my back and off everybody's back and I was very happy with the outcome.

"A Bridge over Troubled Waters"

In 1988, Maitin transferred to work as a stationary engineer mechanic at the George Washington Bridge. For the next four years, she worked on a rotating schedule. For the most part, she took the midnight shift. "I relieved the person [who was] there before me," she said. "So the only contact I had with my co-workers was in the few minutes that we reported to each other what's going on; what's happening and what's not happening." As she explained, this move was a calculated choice because it gave her a way to overcome a common problem she faced on the job: co-workers withholding the technical information—the data they had but wouldn't share with her—that put her in a frustrating as well as dangerous position:

> I made this decision to go into this place and to do this kind of work and to work these hours very consciously. I knew that, because I work alone, if there was any information that had to be given, I was going to get it. There was no way they were going to be able to avoid giving me the information because I'm on by myself...However, it's like everything else in life. You get something and you give something up. That has been so in this job.
>
> By the time I left the 42nd Street bus terminal, I was really, really ready to leave because I could see that I wasn't going to get the information. There were all kinds of reasons why. Many of them stemmed from my apprenticeship. A lot of the guys there resented that I was a mechanic. I didn't have the knowledge they thought I should have, and I was getting the same pay as they were. And under most circumstances, I might have agreed with them. However, I knew that I had fought really hard to get this job; to stay in this job; to get where I was at. So I felt justified and I didn't have a problem with them if they challenged me on my work. But it was very stressful when I was asked to do something and I didn't know how to do it. And I wasn't going to get the information that I needed. So I figured if I went to work at a place where I was working alone, whatever information they gave me, they *had* to give me.[25]

Maitin did find a few tradesmen at the 42nd Street facility who were willing to share their skills with her. She recalled two of the men who weren't afraid to share:

> There was one guy who subsequently lost his job because he got hooked on crack, but had been working for the Port Authority for many years and he was very good at what he did. He was not in my trade, he was a steamfitter, and he did befriend me. When I needed some information, he never held it back. He was right there...helping me to think things through as a tradesperson and I really appreciated that about him.
>
> There was another worker who was Italian. He gave me a really hard time at first, and we had a big blowup, a confrontation. After that he was really quite friendly and forthcoming with information—if we were alone. If we were around the other guys, especially other mechanics, then he wasn't quite so forthcoming. But if I caught him and we were working alone, he would give me information. No problem. He also was an excellent mechanic.

These men stood out because—in all her years in the trades—they were exceptional.

There are a few men I have worked with that their ego is not so invested and they're willing to allow you to share. But I have to say that...I can count on one hand how many mechanics I've worked around who weren't feeding their ego at my expense. That really is a shame. It needs to change.[26]

By going to work alone at night on the New York side of the George Washington Bridge, Maitin had settled on a new strategy. While one of her sister stationary engineers on the New Jersey side of the bridge had a very stressful workplace existence, being forced to do the cleaning and putting up with a workplace plastered with pornography, Maitin found a way to reduce the troubling dimensions of her job:

It was a compromise. I did that for my own mental and emotional well-being because I had been through all these years of all this crap. I just said, I'm not doing this any more. I was thinking, at one point, of leaving the trade...And I realized: This is what I want to do. I really enjoy doing this. I can keep this job...I still feel somewhat resentful [but] I'm not filled with this kind of remorse that's tearing me apart. I guess I'm sad more than resentful, that I have a trade and I don't feel it really belongs to me. I feel like it's a shame. That shouldn't happen to anybody...It's not as stressful as any other place that I've been in. I've given up the opportunity to really know my trade because I've decided I don't want to spend the next 15 or 20 years fighting these guys about every freaking little thing.[27]

In addition, she turned herself into a silent agitator to eliminate yet another source of insult. "What I've done now is that I refuse to have pornographic material on the job. They did it for awhile. Every time I would find it, I'd throw it away. They'd come in the next day and they don't know who threw it out. It was gone. So they don't bring it. Nobody brings it to the job."

She now began to limit her union activism. As she explained to a co-worker, there were things she would now "duck and get out of the way as they passed her by." Then there were other issues she was still willing to take a stand on:

The issues that I will fight for are bread and butter issues. If it's going to mean my job, if it's going to be my pay, and if it's going to have something to do with my life, if it's dangerous for me, then I will stand there and I will fight with you. I've made that decision being in this job.

"Solidarity Forever"

In summing up her story, Maitin sees herself as a pro-union person who has made a choice to embrace other issues. In 2005, she chuckled as she explained her decision to get away from her role as a union activist:

The reason I'm not involved in the union is because, number one, I work a rotating shift and that makes things a little bit difficult for me. Number two, because I work around men all day—eight hours a day, sometimes longer, sometimes eight days in a row—and when I get finished, I've had it. That's why I've got a female dog and a female cat. I like you guys but enough is enough. I've had enough testosterone. I made a decision. So I try to get involved with women in nontraditional work.[28]

But she still looks at every trade union issue through her political prism. She sees serious limitations within the union.

> In my opinion, and it's also part of my experience as a shop steward, there were many times when I asked the union to, "Come on down. Please talk to the members." And the union representative's position was, "Well, they don't come to meetings. Why should I come to them?" I was furious about that. It made me livid to hear him say that. Because the fact is that we pay your salary. And that nice little car and that nice little house that you live in because we pay the union dues. So to some degree, you have a responsibility to come down here.[29]

Despite the serious shortcomings, Maitin still holds union membership as an important value:

> I'm glad that I belong to a union. I definitely believe in unions. I know that if I wasn't in a union, the guy next to me would be getting paid more money than I am and I may not have the job and he might get benefits that I don't get...So in that way, I am absolutely glad that I am in a union. But I am totally disillusioned with unions, because their agenda is making sure that they have a job, not that we have our rights taken care of. Their political agenda is just like the rest of the politicians....There's not a whole lot of hope for there being any major change in this job, partly because of the union, and what stands they've taken, but also partly because there's so much of our work [that] is contracted out.

Experience has reinforced her lack of faith in the union as an institution. Instances of blind obedience in which the members defer their own opinions to support those of their leadership, as well as inaction on the part of the leadership to address critical questions have led her to see the union as a limited vehicle for change. Major issues confronting the workers in her industry, such as contracting out and collective bargaining agreements that whittle away the rights of future generations go unchallenged.

She views the broader national political situation, the movement to the right, and its impact on labor—weakening its position and diminishing its ranks—as daunting. "It seems like one of the biggest obstacles that I have seen in my lifetime," she said. "Crazy as the Sixties were, it was crazy enough to get it all moving and changing. There were so many things going on. It was scary but it was also very exciting and many things were happening."

> It goes across the board. It doesn't matter what color you are. It doesn't matter what sex you are. It doesn't even really matter what class you're coming from. Just across the board, people are moving in that direction—toward political apathy.

The ongoing effort since 1983, when she entered her trade, to eliminate affirmative action is part of this national movement toward a conservative ideology. "I think one of the saddest things to me is that affirmative action is being dismantled," she said. "There are not too many women coming into the trades now. And there was a time when you were constantly seeing a new flow of faces of women coming in. It's not that way any more."

Now she concentrates her political efforts on tradeswomen's issues. "I prefer working with women who have already been in the trades for an extended period of time and want to do something to affect this new situation," she said, "To talk about it on a deeper level—what we've learned—where we're going."

I don't think it's okay to not fight for...women to get jobs in the trades, to get into the union, and to get jobs...It's not okay to me that they don't have minority contractors—women and people of color. To me, that's not all right. It's not okay that we get 10 percent of whatever's available out there.

The fallout from the affirmative action wars has generated a lot of anger. But in Maitin's opinion, men's anger is misplaced:

White working-class men are angry and fighting us for these jobs. My understanding about this is very different from the men whom I talk with. Because I believe that these men who are angry about these things, what they are fighting for is absolutely correct. They are absolutely right. Everything that they are angry about, they are entitled and correct to be angry about that...They're angry because they don't have jobs. They don't have medical care. They're angry because their kids can't eat. Their marriages are falling apart, because everything that was supposed to be is not happening. Well they're right to be angry about that. But where they're wrong is that, instead of looking at where the real problem is, they're fighting us for our measly 10 percent...It's a class issue and it turns into a sexist and racist argument...My feeling about racism and sexism, and particularly racism, is that racism is really an issue of economics. That's the bottom line.

For Maitin, the struggle to open up blue-collar jobs to women is still a burning issue. "We have to do this," she said. "It really is important for women to get into the trades."[30] To underscore this point, she shared a story:

One time, I was at home, and this fellow knocked on my door...He was trying to get me to donate money for something...He asked me what kind of work I did and I told him: "I'm a mechanic." He said, "Wow! That's great." And I said to him, "No, that's not. Great would be that you would not have to say that it was great because then we would be normal in these jobs and it wouldn't have to be great. That would be really and truly great." And he said, "I didn't think about that."

She sees a "thread of solidarity" running through all of the different attempts to organize tradeswomen. She has participated in numerous organizing efforts, including United Tradeswomen, New York Tradeswomen, and her most recent effort, Sisters in the Trades. At one point, tradeswomen working with Legal Momentum [formerly NOW Legal Defense & Education Fund] approached the Women's Committee of the New York City Council to try to get some financial support for an upcoming conference. As Maitin described, there were many other women represented in the City Council chamber joining forces to secure money for their cause: domestic-violence:

There were women there for battered women—women in jail and young women, teenaged women, all living in poverty—all these women from all these different organizations pulling together asking for money for their organization. I turned to one of the women and I said to her, "You know what? We need to make a connection here because you want to know something? These sisters—these women—need these jobs...If she had a job making enough money she'd kick [her batterer] to the curb."

When we put together the conference, what I would like to see is if we can get these women and groups to come. It really is important for all of us to see that there's a connection here between us. There's a connection between the seamstress who doesn't get paid enough money...All of this is connected.

It was very interesting to me. You find these things—these little jewels—in places where you least expect it. One of the most important things is crossing those lines and making those connections, because by doing that, it's like weaving a basket. You make it stronger. We need to be able to support each other and to see those connections, where they cross. We need to see our similarities and not focus on our differences.

SEVEN

Uncivil Service at the Board of Education

Ann Jochems spent a number of years pounding nails on historic preservation projects. This was just one of the ways she went about gaining the skills of her craft. Once she had five years of experience, she applied for a city civil service job. She became the first, and for many years, the only, female carpenter to work for the Board of Education (BOE) in New York City.

Run by political appointees, the BOE was an infamous labyrinthine bureaucracy with a high tolerance for minor and major league corruption. Jochems was employed by the Division of School Facilities (DSF), which was charged with maintaining existing schools. It was a sweet job, since the wages for civil service craft jobs in New York City are tied to the prevailing rate for building trades jobs in the private sector. The actual demands of the high-paying skilled trades jobs were far from onerous, and the culture that ruled the workplace was dedicated to keeping it that way.

Jochems was never included in the sweet life that held sway at the BOE. From the start, abuse of an extraordinary nature was heaped upon her. She felt the sting of daily isolation on the job and experienced years of sexual harassment at the hands of her co-workers. Although she won promotions and came out near the top of every competitive civil service test, going to work every day was a grueling ordeal. She took courses at Cornell's labor studies program and even served a stint as a shop steward for the carpenters' union. She took part in numerous organizing efforts on behalf of tradeswomen, won a Mayor's scholarship, and earned a Master's degree. Throughout her years at the BOE, Jochems battled an alcohol addiction, greatly aggravated by the circumstances she faced on the job. Attending AA meetings helped maintain her sobriety.

Jochems's journey crossed that of another pioneer at the BOE. In February 1989, Susan D'Alessandro became the first female to win one of the coveted, skilled, and high-paid positions as a boiler plant tender for the school system. She too quickly came up against the culture of corruption. From the beginning, D'Alessandro represented a threat to the business as usual ethos. Like Ann, she won the enmity of her male co-workers, who were determined to oust her, and succeeded. Four years later, after going through great travails, including a lengthy trial, she was vindicated. The BOE was ordered to reinstate the small, plucky, and fiercely principled woman.

While working together at the agency, Jochems and D'Alessandro made common cause to persuade management to address workplace conditions for tradeswomen. They tried to move management toward implementing a plan for affirmative action at the BOE. These endeavors never generated more than a feeble response from the employer.

After 16 years on the job, Jochems was fired. For two years, her case played out in the system. Back at the Division of School Facilities, the men who perpetrated years of illegal sexual harassment against her paid no price for their actions. Jochems always admitted her culpability. She had taken advantage of a practice that was common at the BOE and extended her lunch hour to attend AA meetings. But termination was excessive, especially when measured against penalties levied against other employees whose violations far exceeded her own. She left her job convinced that the system had been stacked against her. Meanwhile, the entrenched culture of corruption and other uncivil practices at the agency continued with impunity.

Fertile Ground

Affirmative action usually begins with individual acts of independence. Ann Jochems's quiet determination to be herself, unfettered by others' perceptions or by past practices regarding the "proper" place for a woman, began at an early age.

As she came of age in Wichita, Kansas, far from the metropolitan hotbeds of activism, the cause of feminism reached out to her. Jochems seized the message that females could create their own destiny and step outside traditional boundaries,

> It sort of evolved out of the overall vision of just wanting to change the world that manifested in this particular way of being drawn to nontraditional work after I graduated from college. The traditional men's jobs paid more and I gravitated toward that kind of work... then getting more skills and wanting to be self-sufficient; getting caught up in sort of the back-to-the-land; [the idea that] each of us should enable ourselves... to do anything, *especially* as women and feminists. Then I helped friends build a house and I got interested in it that way.[1]

Jochems's circuitous road from Kansas to New York City was a rocky one. In 2003, she wrote, "My personal approach to becoming a tradeswoman was from an academic perspective. College-educated and a lesbian feminist, I took on vocational sex-role stereotyping pretty much by myself. I met great resistance along the way. While I benefited from affirmative action, going it alone brought enormous emotional costs."[2]

After graduating from the University of Kansas with a bachelor of arts degree, Jochems began to cobble together the skills of her trade. She worked at odd jobs and applied to different programs. She attended a pre-apprenticeship training program in masonry; a vocational education program in carpentry supported by federal funding from the Comprehensive Employment and Training Act (CETA). She then applied to a union apprenticeship program in Kansas City:

> I wasn't successful. Even though I passed the first test and got interviewed... it was like a charade because they didn't really take me seriously. I never felt like they honestly ever considered accepting me and they didn't.

Her next step was a four-month program for carpentry and building maintenance at Kansas City Vocational Technical School. She was the only woman in the class, though all of the students suffered from the limitations of poor instruction:

> The teacher was horrible and didn't really impart the skills very well. I just read the books and sort of muscled it out...and tried stuff. I'll never forget, the first table saw lesson was really ridiculous. When I look back on it, I just cringe that I still have my fingers.

While attending school, she worked as a handywoman doing building maintenance for a "slumlord:"

> It was another woman and myself...This guy had inherited 80 old Victorian houses from his mother and they were in total disrepair...He didn't want to put any money into them but he had to do something...Like he had to change locks when he kicked people out and patch the holes and not let the roof leak. It was from plumbing to electrical.

In 1981, she moved to upstate New York, near Syracuse, and continued her quest to improve her skills:

> I got jobs, but they were all nonunion. They lasted like two or three months. I was just scraping things together and then I'd get laid off. I'd just walk down to construction sites. One of them was building a metal truck stop and one of them was residential. And the other one was restoring old houses again...It got really exhausting...always being the only woman. Then I got into this other program. It was a CETA-thing where I went every day for nine months to this carpentry and building trades program in Onondaga Madison BOCES. That [program] had a pretty good teacher.
>
> I love school. School was great because there's not the pressure to produce and there's sort of the freedom to find your way through it. In a way, I think it's more advantageous than the apprenticeship program...It gives you more creative license to explore more interesting ways of doing things without a boss and without your job being on the line.

Her most satisfying educational experience took place after she enrolled in a yearlong program for woodworking at a community college and had the opportunity to study with a supportive teacher:

> I fell in love with woodworking and decided that that's what I'd like to do. I read about this woman in a magazine and decided I'd like to learn from her. Maybe that would be different. I went there and it was the best thing I ever did for myself....This professor, Liz Bradbury, had her Master's in woodworking, and she was truly an artisan and a technician.[3]

After getting an associate's degree in woodworking, Jochems applied to an apprenticeship program with the National Trust for Historic Preservation. The first historic property she worked on was Lyndhurst, in Tarrytown, New York:

> Lyndhurst is a spectacular place, but now, not only am I working with all men, but living with them too. So now it's a 24 hour thing...I don't even get to go home at night. I felt like I wasn't given the same opportunities...Some of the people were sent to do the work at Gracie Mansion. Some were sent to do the work on some spectacular homes in the area, the good jobs. I felt I was never given the good jobs. At one point, I was sent to paint a house in Ossining...That's a whole lot different than [working on] reproduction moldings at Gracie Mansion.
>
> It paid so horribly and the area was so expensive to live, that as soon as I had an opportunity to go as a restorative craftsperson at Central Park, I did that. It was terribly creative...Rustic architecture was what it was and it was fascinating.[4]

Working for the Central Park Conservancy, she got to do the carpentry she loved, for a low wage. She was the only woman on the job – at first. "I personally recruited several. There was a woman's bookstore at the time, and so every time I heard they were hiring, I just went and put the ad up myself and did get two other women hired. And that was great."

> [The] job was really great. But it was nonunion and sometimes you would be working side by side with union people. That was sort of annoying because the truth of the matter was that we really worked harder and got paid less. We also didn't have job security.
>
> Here I was doing the more interesting kind of work in Central Park for no money and then you had city workers who were making bench slats for *huge* money. And that's how I became a city worker. Money won out. That's what really inspired me to take the test to be a city carpenter.[5]

Only a handful of tradeswomen have worked for the BOE or any of the other, numerous city agencies in these coveted civil service skilled trades positions that pay the prevailing wage rates. Jochems earned her position as a pioneer in 1985:

> When I came [to New York City] I took several city civil service tests [that were] advertised...and rated high and got interviewed and got the job. In a way...I feel like it was one of the luckiest breaks of my life that they inadvertently hired me, because it's highly competitive, now especially. There are probably a thousand people that want the job, even though it's far from perfect. That's what got me in the union at journey-level status, having amassed all my education and eking out my job experience on my own, because it's a hefty requirement.[6]

"Trapped in a Time Warp"

On her way to a career as a carpenter, a trade she loved and excelled at, Ann Jochems had to jump many hurdles. She found a way to learn her trade, despite the doors that shut in her face. She acquired the requisite five years of work experience that kept many women from applying for civil service positions. She scored high on the civil service test and secured a top spot on the job placement list for city carpenter. She also avoided being rejected through the "one-in-three rule" that let the agencies doing the hiring select one out of the three top candidates. Now she was ready to take her place as the first female carpenter for the New York City BOE. In doing this, she faced a whole new set of obstacles.

Given that Ann was the first woman to enter the previously all-male craft of carpentry at the DSF, it might seem obvious that management would do something to prepare the work force. This didn't happen until much later. "It wasn't until the 90's that they recognized that this might be a problem, [that] if you put one woman in with a hundred men, things might not go smoothly," Jochems observed, wryly.[7]

In lieu of that, another option would have been to monitor the workplace situation of the new employee. Yet all of Jochems's efforts to alert management to the sexual harassment she was encountering went without response.

Jochems went from a position as a field mechanic (1985–1991) to that of carpenter supervisor (1991–2002). She then started the demanding certification process to teach carpentry in the vocational high schools. She ranked #3 when she took the competitive citywide test, consisting of both a hands-on mastery of skills and a written component. At the end of her career, Jochems was poised to move up again in what would have been a "giant step forward" when she ranked #22 on the promotion roster for the supervisor of mechanics position. But, while the doors of opportunity opened for her, they led to a chamber of horrors.

Jochems summed up her initial reception on the job in one word: "Horrendous." She described some of the responses she encountered after her entrance into the ranks of the DSF carpenters:

> I felt that they just did everything to get rid of me…With very few exceptions, I felt like most of them just wished I wasn't there…As a field mechanic, I went from school to school doing maintenance and repairs. I was the only one who didn't have a partner. They would always give me the least skilled work and the heaviest schlepping and very little woodwork, which is what I liked. I asked them to put me in the shop and they wouldn't. Anything they sensed that I wanted, they did the exact opposite. They generally went out of their way to make my life miserable. They transferred me to a point that was very far away from my home. They normally try to accommodate you and let you work close to your home. Just the exclusion, being told about everything after it happened, and never, never really being included, always getting the bad jobs.[8]

Early on, Jochems's supervisors found her wanting. In their evaluations of her job performance, they rated her as "incompetent," "insubordinate," and possessed of a "bad attitude." The discriminatory practices leveled at her took place with their complicity. The time it took her to travel to and from work clocked out at between three and four hours on a daily basis. Decisions about job assignments and the distribution of overtime were made at the discretion of supervision. In the trades, overtime is an important consideration that can add thousands of dollars to annual income. This was routinely denied to Jochems.

Throughout her career at the BOE, Jochems felt that her work was sabotaged and that she was constantly under a microscope. To deal with this pressure, she developed a habit of over-compensating, constantly trying to prove that she could "cut the mustard." Without acceptance or support, she was very hard on herself.[9]

She remained a stranger to those who spent years working with her. There was something about her that "rubbed many of her more culturally conservative colleagues the wrong way."[10]

That was the fact that Jochems was a lesbian, and a proud one at that. That fact seemed to fuel the campaign to make her uncomfortable and caused her co-workers to shun her.

As Jochems described it, "coming out" on the job was never in question:

> I always did identify myself as a lesbian. It's funny, even now, I hear people say that it's best not to say anything. It's so integral to who I am. And it's so contrary to the dominant culture in the trades, in maintenance work, in blue-collar work, in the carpenters union. It's like the antithesis of their value system and who they are and all that. But, most people are just normal, decent people. For 70 percent, it doesn't matter. It's just labels. But it's the few, the very few that cause the problem. So it dominates you. That's what makes all the havoc in the world. I insisted on saying who I was out loud, which gave them fodder. At the BOE, the very first week, I was already out to everyone.

Miriam Frank has been writing about the issue of lesbians in the building trades for many years.[11] "Homophobia in the building trades—you could either write an encyclopedia about it or you might as well say nothing—there's so much to say," she said.[12] She told one story that encapsulated a commonly held perception about women working in nontraditional jobs. One Saturday morning during a roundtable discussion at Cornell about working women, a professor of economics summed up the situation of women as she viewed it: "Let me tell you about those women in the trades: They're lesbians and they're loners."

> That lesbians and loners thing just really tickled me. But I think that there's something to be said for that. There were a lot of lesbians, and because they couldn't say they were lesbians, they were loners. If you are being silent about who you are and it's an important part of your life, you're not going to make connections. On the other hand, there were lesbians who were very social.

Frank recalled the first time she spoke on the topic in New York City: "Once we had [organized] the Lesbian and Gay Network in New York City, Barbara Trees asked me to do a session on homophobia in the building trades." This event was the first gathering sponsored by New York Tradeswomen, a support and advocacy group founded by carpenters Barbara Trees and Lisa Narducci. It took place on October 19, 1990, at District 65's union hall on Astor Place. The talk given by Miriam Frank was entitled: "Homophobia and Women in the Construction Industry: An Overview of Gay Rights."[13] As Frank recalled:

> At this meeting, there were many women who came and said, "I'm not out at work." Many of the women who were at that meeting said nothing, because they didn't want to be recognized. It was one of these really intense things. The subject was how *much* they couldn't be out. "This one knows, but that one doesn't." "I'm out to my partner but not very much." Or—"I refer to my lover as 'he.'" It was all about being in the closet....They talked about rough stuff—They talked about dread. One woman did talk about having come out and being terrorized on the work site.
>
> It's a nonissue because no one brings it up as an issue. It's an aspect of the terror that women go through in trying to enter the trades and trying to work with men and in trying to go up against all the things that go on...It's very complicated because all the sexual harassment has to do with: are they dykes or *not* dykes.
>
> I think it's very clear...that dyke- baiting is essential in the harassment that women go through when they enter the job. I think it's less loaded than it used to be, but that doesn't mean it isn't really powerful and profoundly loaded.

As Jochems explained, "It's predominantly a white [male], blue-collar place, so there was resistance to the *other*. First there was resistance to minority men. Then, if there was a woman, it was like: Whoa! [There was] worse resistance to her. Then, if there was a lesbian, or a woman of color, or a lesbian woman of color…There was a progression that led away from the 'norm.'"

The further out one was from that norm, the more resistance it generated. Jochems was the source of uncomfortable feelings that resulted in specific, hateful actions directed at her—an outsider—female and lesbian. But as she described, the experiences of all the outsiders bore certain resemblances:

> There are two black men that I like pretty well. Basically, we've been through almost identical experiences. There are more minority men than there are women, but I'd say it's 95 percent white men and 4.5 percent minority men, and .5 or less women. So I think it's a little easier for minority men. I do know one minority woman who's an electrician's helper. There are three other women. They're all white. That one minority woman has the double burden: black and female.[14]

Jochems recalled an incident in which another woman was the recipient of this "resistance:" "They're just so hostile to a woman in the workplace. There was a plumber's helper, and I feel that they just chased her out of there. She quit. Who quits a $35,000 a year job?"[15]

In 1988, when Jochems took the civil service test for carpenter supervisor, she ranked at #23 on the civil service list.[16] As she described it:

> When the Supervisor's [civil service] test came up, I did really well on that. I should have sued them when they started calling from the list for the job, just for affirmative action, just because I was the only woman on the list in the whole city—citywide and in my agency. But I decided to be patient. Then they made me an acting supervisor. But it's incredible. If my boss stuck out his foot, he could have kicked me.[17]

After languishing in that position sitting at a desk, without being given any responsibilities, Jochems was finally promoted in 1991. At that point, she began to direct a team of skilled mechanics in the alteration, repair, and maintenance of 75 schools in 3 districts, located in Brooklyn and Queens. Fortunately, she was able to develop positive relationships with the men whom she supervised. She described her crew in 1994:

> The people who work for me and I get along pretty well. I actually think I have the best crew, but I feel like the reason that happened is 'cause they didn't know how good those people were when they were assigned to me.[18]
>
> But the people that are my peers are the ones where I feel the greatest conflict. It's the same old battle again. I feel like I often get the short end of the stick, the tools and the resources available there. I'm just not a full-fledged team player. I feel like I have less information than everyone else, like I'm working blind a lot.

One of Jochems's first actions when she was promoted was to rid the carpenters' shop of pornography. This won her a great deal of enduring enmity:

> I think it's just a power struggle. I don't think they ever forgave me for fighting to have the pornography removed from the carpenters' shop. The pornography thing was a big issue with me…But the most flagrant displays are gone now and I guess

that's a small victory. The backlash from that is that there are those who just know you as the ogre that didn't want it. It's hard to have affable relationships with them when that's how they are.

I won the battle but lost the war...The hostility toward me was what eventually led to my demise. I believe that. I built my demise by trying to make a habitable workplace for myself. I can't believe the hatred that ensued just from wanting the dirty pictures down. On the surface, it improved, but it manifested itself in other ways, with pockets of hatred and sabotage directed at me throughout my tenure there, which, I believe, ultimately led to my ouster.[19]

In 2002, the veteran labor journalist Jack Schierenbeck wrote a profile of Ann Jochems that described in stunning detail the "pockets of hatred" she coped with on the job. He wrote:

"From the beginning, they've made her life a living hell," says a former male co-worker, who didn't want his name used. It didn't matter that she knew her stuff. She was a woman and that was enough for them to abuse her. They do that to women, especially anyone who stands up and speaks out about what's right. They become a target.

Target is the right word. What else would you call it when, early on in her Board career, a supervisor ordered her to make a dangerous cut of a 12-foot board with a table saw, knowing full well that safety called for the cut to be done by two people?

What else would you call it when a well-built male co-worker intentionally drove his shoulder into the 5-foot-7, 135-pound Jochems, almost dislocating her shoulder? Or when workers in a BOE van deliberately gunned the engine and swerved up onto the sidewalk? Just missing her, they drove off laughing. Pretty funny, huh?

Sexual harassment? Walls of sexually explicit photos were just the titillating tip of a pervasive and pernicious male-locker-room gestalt. Add to it a constant stream of crude comments about women in general—"those [female genitalia] in the coffee truck" to more personal stuff—"Too bad you don't have any [breasts]"—to lurid speculation about her personal life. Even cruder was the conversation piece in the carpenters' shop: a giant carved penis placed in the middle of the coffee table that, Jochems heard, was dedicated to her.

As painful as all of this abuse was, it was the sheer isolation of the job that hurt Jochems the most. "Carpentry is, for the most part, a partner trade. But for years I had to work alone," she says in a voice cracking with emotion. She recalls how on school holidays, while all the other carpenters worked together, she was left alone all day in an empty school building. "They treated me like a leper," she says.[20]

In 1991, Anita Hill placed sexual harassment on the national agenda. Up to that point, the tortuous experiences of many women in the workplace had largely escaped attention. Hill had left her job at the Equal Employment Opportunity Commission (EEOC) in 1983. The harassment she alleged was well in her past. The irony that this harassment was directed at Hill, an attorney, working for the EEOC—the agency charged with enforcing the law on sexual harassment—at the hands of the head of that agency, only underscored the complex reality of the nature of sexual harassment.

Until that point, the fact that sexual harassment in the workplace is no laughing matter but a serious violation of the law had escaped the attention of many people. But Hill's riveting testimony about the behavior of her boss, Clarence Thomas, before a *very* condescending

Judicial Committee of the U.S. Senate, had a great deal to do with changing that reality. As the committee considered Clarence Thomas's suitability for a position on the U.S. Supreme Court, the national audience got a tutorial from Professor Hill on the painful topic of sexual harassment. Anita Hill became an inspiration to women all across the country.[21]

A scene in the movie, *North Country*, about the class action suit of the first female miners employed by Eveleth Mines, shows "Josie Wales," the fictional stand-in for lead plaintiff Lois Jenson, standing transfixed before the televised testimony of Professor Hill. The glaring national spotlight on sexual harassment resonated deeply for women such as Lois Jenson, Ann Jochems, and all of the other women who had endured similar crude and humiliating incidents in isolation as just another part of going to work every day.

After years on the job, Ann Jochems was still subject to the outrageous misconduct of her co-workers. "It still feels sort of like being trapped in a time warp where it's just an all-male environment and there hasn't been any positive change," she said in 1994.[22] It was only going to get worse.

Jochems was never vindicated in her complaints against her employer. Instead, she became the object of an investigation into her own behavior. Afterward, she moved on, absorbing the psychological scars she carried as a pioneer. On the other hand, the outcome for Susan D'Alessandro, who surreptitiously carried a tape recorder, was different.

On the QT at the BOE: Proving a Pattern of Disparate Treatment

Aside from the hostile reception she received at the BOE, the other remarkable feature of life on the job for Ann Jochems was the degree of systemic corruption. She first described this aspect of the job in 1990:

> I can't estimate the corruption aspect of it...just the scam that they have going is really, really horrible....Nobody ever talks about the corruption...which has gone on from the beginning of time and has been a huge cover-up [in] itself...in a big way that you can hardly imagine. I've never seen anything like it.[23]

Looking back in 2004, Jochems recalled that, throughout the trades, "production was so low, it was practically at a standstill...I can't imagine that any place had *less* accountability."[24]

Like Ann, Susan D'Alessandro had to jump through many hoops before she got her job at the BOE. She was highly credentialed by the time she arrived at the position of plant manager. She'd spent three years in a boiler room to get the "steam time" needed for her stationary engineer's license. She'd mastered the heating and refrigeration trade and acquired other licenses along the way. Now she was about to break through another barrier.

As Jochems described, D'Alessandro's entrance provoked a strong reaction:

> I think that her experience was similar to mine, although she was a greater threat than I was at the time because she had reached a higher title. She had a high-pressure license and I think she was the only woman in the city to have that license. So—Danger! Danger! She became a target and [was put] under the microscope.

D'Alessandro's new job as a district plant manager put her in a position of authority over a notorious group of entrenched employees—the custodians. Members of Local 891, International Union of Operating Engineers (IUOE), New York City school custodians operate as semi-independent contractors, controlling their own big budgets, with purchasing and hiring authority. While reaping huge salaries, the custodians continued to win notoriety for legendary feats of do-nothingism, oftentimes not even being present on the premises at the times when their custodial duties were supposedly carried out.[25]

In February 1989, when D'Alessandro went to work for the DSF, she was placed in charge of supervising 30 school custodians. The first female to enter this closed world, she immediately found herself pitted against a system rife with corruption. Just to perform her administrative job in any sort of conscientious manner put her at odds with the powerful custodians, their union, and her supervisors, most of them former officials of Local 891.

Stop number one on a tour of the schools in her district started off with a bang. At Grover Cleveland High School in Ridgewood, Queens, she encountered the first of the many recalcitrant custodians lodged in the system under her supervision. Her efforts to get him to do his job earned D'Alessandro a quick trip to the Bronx—her first transfer. And so it went. Her next transfer landed her in Brooklyn.[26]

As D'Alessandro set about trying to get the custodians to do their jobs—to post signs, to scrape up the gum off the floors, to clean-up the crumbling, filthy interiors—a disciplinary file was being built up against her. After she testified at a public hearing on race and gender discrimination, her file grew fat.

A member of IUOE Local 30, D'Alessandro was an activist at heart. "She was a big-hearted woman who liked helping others," said Ann Jochems. Jochems and D'Alessandro cooperated in an effort to improve the situation for tradeswomen at the DSF. Starting in February 1990, they attempted a number of different strategies. As Jochems recalled:

> It was exciting at first. We met a couple of times with management. It was really three members of management and us two. We made this agenda and set out all these elaborate goals. My wheels were spinning: how can we include more people—and their wheels were spinning—we have to cut this thing off. We had two meetings and then that was it. They said they were going to do a survey of all the women and all the minority men employed in the Division of School Facilities about their experiences with harassment. They gave a rough draft to those of us at the meeting but they never distributed it. Then they said they were going to give everybody a copy of the EEO policy in the next paycheck. They created a tradeswomen's liaison and she was going to set up private appointments with everyone for this survey. They never did it.[27]

In hindsight, according to D'Alessandro's attorney, her efforts to discuss discrimination in the workplace landed her in even *hotter* water. "This was one point that was brought out in the case," said Robert Felix.[28] It only got worse, as he described:

> Ultimately, she was shunned. Her co-workers wouldn't eat lunch with her. It became difficult to work in that environment. She was written up for things that others were not—for the way she filled out paperwork—for not having her cell phone with her. They made so many claims against her.

On March 12, 1990, D'Alessandro testified at the public hearings sponsored by the New York City Commission on Human Rights and the Division of Labor Services to investigate the extent of discrimination in the city's construction trades. As she pointed out:

Almost all women in nontraditional employment work as lone representatives of their gender on a given job site, in a gang or crew. We are, by that circumstance, ostracized before the fact. We continue to lose significant numbers among us because women are becoming distressed and burned out before they achieve the skills necessary to assure stability and market them.[29]

The bulk of her testimony astutely recommended practical remedies involving financial penalties for noncompliance. D'Alessandro concluded her presentation with a poignant appeal:

Were someone to pose the question as to whether things were improving, I would pass on a quote from a recent conversation that was held between one of the two women at Local 30 and her business representative. He said to her, "We seem to be losing a lot of women lately and I have no idea why." I would like to leave you with that thought and with the hope that these hearings will address that statement.[30]

The Dinkins administration didn't comply with this request. On the contrary, it held out until the last possible moment before releasing its report on the hearings. "Building Barriers: Discrimination in New York City's Construction Trades," the massive document containing graphic testimony about every aspect of life in the trades and recommendations from hundreds of experts, languished for years on the shelves of the Human Rights Commission until December 1993. This ensured that no fall-out would accrue to the Democrats from their close associates in the contractors' associations and the construction trades unions. On releasing the report to the public, the Dinkins administration called on the *next* administration to follow through on its findings. The next mayor, Rudolph Giuliani, took office in January 1994. The report, with all of its damning details, was dead on arrival.

Women such as Susan D'Alessandro and many others put their hard-won careers on the line. The hearings did have repercussions. Despite denials that this bore any relationship to her testimony, D'Alessandro's job performance was rated "inadequate." Her supervisor filed the first of 15 disciplinary memorandums within 48 hours of her appearance at the hearings.[31]

D'Alessandro was fired on March 15, 1991. As Jochems recalled,

I remember her last day on the job. I was with her the day she got fired. I remember helping her carry boxes out to her car and she was pretty low. I'd say she was pretty depressed.[32]

New York Magazine called the DSF, "An all-American symbol of corruption, mismanagement, and sloth." Susan D'Alessandro and Ann Jochems both worked for the DSF under division head Amy Linden. Linden, appointed in 1988 to run the system, was described as "a financier who knows more about bonds than boiler rooms." The closed and complacent system that D'Alessandro walked into didn't welcome her presence. Her persistent attempts to get custodians to do their jobs—civil servants earning in excess of $83,000 a year and enjoying many expensive perks—earned her the enmity of just about everyone in the system.[33]

However, *before* March 15, 1991, when D'Alessandro was fired, Hugh Bovich, her Brooklyn boss, shared a valuable piece of information. "Bovich told her that a lot of people were out to get her," said attorney Robert Felix. This nugget of "news" led D'Alessandro to begin taping the conversations, disciplinary hearings, meetings and her other encounters at the DSF. Unlike Linda Tripp's wiretapping experience of Monica Lewinsky, the information D'Alessandro recorded was admissible in court in New York State.

Robert Felix represented D'Alessandro in the legal case she filed against her employer. "It was a gender discrimination case," he said, "not a sexual harassment case. We were able to prove disparate treatment—that she was treated differently than the others—the other men in her position. She was the only woman employed as a plant manager. She was also the only one who was fired!"

Many heads tumbled as a result of the case D'Alessandro initiated against her employer. In effect, she put the system on trial. "In a lot of ways, her case was about tying in a lot of people," Felix recalled:

> It was about how the custodial engineers operated; about how people got certain positions and favors. It was clear that she was doing the right thing but that she didn't have the assistance of the males. Susan brought a case against 12 people. She was 12 for 12. Every one of them resigned; retired; or left...Bovich went back to being a custodian.
>
> Susan had an ability to know a lot of things about the other plant managers—all male. Information that they didn't have credentials; or nepotism; or favoritism; or that they didn't have to go for training; or licenses; or that they had outside businesses. Susan was *great* in her testimony and in her cross-examination. She handled herself extremely well. She was great on follow-through and she had a lot of people who were helpful to her.
>
> Brenda Bishop [Director, Women's Project, Association for Union Democracy] testified for her. She basically talked about what it was like for other women in nontraditional jobs. Susan had a psychologist testify. He was good. He tied in how consumed she had become with her case and had no [other] life. He emphasized the stress involved. District Superintendent James Mazza testified for her, to show that this was a very dedicated person who was interested in getting things right and anybody who said otherwise was way off base....Many people testified that she was top notch and that [for her], the safety of the children in the schools was paramount.

Ann Jochems also testified in D'Alessandro's defense. "We brought Ann in and the BOE argued that, whatever happened to Ann was independent of Susan's case," said Felix. "Ann did a very good job [speaking] about what [had] happened to her. She did very well in her testimony."

Jochems described how she was able to put some inside information to good use on D'Alessandro's behalf:

> I had lunch one day with...the director of human resources, which is a pretty powerful position. She said all the stuff that I think [also] helped Susan D'Alessandro win her case. She told me "off the record" this and "off the record" that...I testified for Susan and I repeated a lot of the stuff that she said off the record [in order] to get it on the record.

Robert Felix described the trial and the verdict:

> Susan's case was brought before the New York City Commission on Human Rights. There were 20 days of hearings before an Administrative Law Judge. It started in March 1994 and finished at the end of the summer. Then there were posthearing briefs. The decision was rendered in 1995. Toward the end of '95, she was reinstated...She received some back pay in the range of $80,000 and $20 to $25,000 for emotional distress. The employer also had to pay the attorney's fees.

"Covering Rough Ground"

Susan D'Alessandro did return to her job as a plant manager at the DSF. But, as Jochems recalled, she did so as a different person. The feisty, very vocal, and always up-for-the-good-fight girl was gone. As Jochems recalled,

> She went back to work and she seemed really changed by it...She was very, very quiet. She got totally changed. She won the battle but lost the war also. Well, she won big, but it wasn't the same.

New York Magazine's feature story on Susan's case and the corruption at the DSF came out during the trial. "Swept Away" described the flagrant abuses that had gone on for years. Subsequent stories about corruption among the custodians continued to hit the mainstream media in the years after Susan opened up the cesspool for inspection.

Robert Felix described Susan as, "a very persistent and particular person." As he recalled,

> Susan was memorable. Her case involved massive work. She knew she could win if it was presented right and she was single-minded about gathering the information. Susan's position was that she had the same skills and tools as the men and they didn't let her do the job.

The question of her sexual orientation was never raised. "It didn't come up, not from Susan—she never brought it up," Felix said. However, in her attorney's expert opinion, "It was a factor."

"She was another one that called it like she saw it and didn't collude. *And* she was a big dyke!" said Ann Jochems. "Basically, that's what drove them crazy!" In 1996, D'Alessandro was diagnosed with cancer. She died in early January 2001.[34]

That year, the New York City Department of Citywide Administrative Services established new promotion rosters for Supervisor of Mechanics jobs at city agencies. Ann Jochems ranked #22 on the BOE list.

> This is the highest [Section] 220 [prevailing rate] title in city service. So it's like the pinnacle of one's career. Hundreds and hundreds of people took the test, and most didn't even pass. I would have been supervising a hundred or more

people—men—and there was a huge pay increase. I think it was about $83,000, plus overtime.

Things got very tense around that time. So after it was pretty much certain that I had passed, there was just a lot of intangible stuff happening. There would just be a lot of hostility and then, shortly after that, I became increasingly isolated among my peers and supervisors. Then I found out that I was under surveillance by the office of the Special Investigator for Schools.

The official charge against Jochems was "theft of services." She admitted her culpability, but argued that there were other circumstances to consider in her case:

My behavior wasn't 100 percent pure because I was extending my lunch hour to attend these AA meetings. But I feel that my mistake was that I had forgotten to work twice as hard as the men. I don't think I was doing anything anybody else wasn't doing. But that was no excuse—certainly not in the mind of the Administrative Law Judge who recommended termination.

It took two years for the case to wind its way through the City's Office of Administrative Trials and Hearings. Throughout the whole process, Jochems remained convinced that her co-workers had "dropped a dime" on her and were instrumental in bringing her to the attention of the Schools' Investigator:

I felt that it was a witch hunt and that I was targeted. They started laying for me...I was put under a microscope. I think it was their worst nightmare to think that I might get this promotion.

She felt remorse over allowing herself to get sucked into the corrupt workplace culture rampant at the BOE,

Everyone did it and got away with it, everyone. It was a problem. But you pick your battles. I felt offended by the sexism, racism, and misogyny. I *did* go against the things that bothered me. But I didn't go against the things that benefited me.[35]

Michael Power represented Jochems on behalf of the carpenters union in the case that was brought against her. His official title was assistant to the president for Civil Service Affairs. He had served as the business agent for all carpenters working in city agencies since May 1994. As he described her situation:

I sat through the trial. First of all, she was charged with theft of services, which can result in termination if found guilty. She was, in my mind, guilty of some things because during lunchtime she did go to meetings. She was photographed and all of that kind of stuff. And she was caught a number of times sitting in her truck and reading the newspaper. Now I believe that, even though she was my member, she was guilty of some of the charges. But in my mind, none of these charges were worthy of termination. There were many other things they could have done. I actually brought to the court many, many instances of carpenters who had similar or even more egregious types of charges and were not terminated. I was involved in them and I know directly that I was able to negotiate a different kind of settlement...I really thought that she would not be terminated.[36]

Although gender wasn't factored into the case by the Administrative Law Judge, it certainly was a factor for Jochems. After the judge delivered his verdict, Mike Power was of the same opinion:

That was the only conclusion I could come up with. My conclusion was that she was being discriminated against because she was a woman. I also believe that she was discriminated against because of sexual orientation. I really believe that a lot of people at the time, [made the decision] to get rid of this woman and they made a concentrated effort...I still believe that today.

A newspaper story about Jochems's fight to hold onto her job included a quote from Mike Power: "They wanted her out."[37] Power said:

"They" was the Board of Ed. The management at the Board of Ed, I believe, made a decision that they were going to terminate her long before this trial and before the evidence was presented that she was *out*. I picked that up from conversations I had, because I tried to negotiate all kinds of different scenarios for her. I actually had her agree to step down as a supervisor and they could have done that. I had her agree that she would take a 30-day suspension and keep her job. She was reluctant in the beginning, but I told her, because I got a good sense of what was going on. I said: "Ann, they're after your job and they're going to get you. So let's negotiate something. It is for you, as long as you keep this job"...She was of an age—she was in her fifties at this particular point in time—she was very fragile. And for her to go back out into construction just was not going to happen. So, we tried everything to save her job.

Clearly troubled by the circumstances of the termination, Power shared some aspects of the unequal justice that was meted out in Jochems's case, based on his many years of experience in representing civil service carpenters:

What really upset me, and still upsets me somewhat today when I think about it, was that, in almost every case that I was involved in with the Board of Ed, I was able to negotiate something or other outside of termination. There was one particular case where I represented two carpenters who were assigned to a shop in Queens, who were sent to Brooklyn to work. These two carpenters, who lived in Bayside, Queens, were leaving the Flatbush area in Brooklyn and going to Bayside High School and punching out there at 3:30, which meant that they were [taking] at least an hour every day. And they were doing this for a long, long time and finally got caught. Now I was able to negotiate on that. They were being terminated too, because that was a big time theft of services. I was able to negotiate that they would voluntarily take a 30-day leave of absence. And both of them saved their jobs. I always had the sense that it could be worked out. In Ann's case, I never had that feeling that there was any leeway. Every time I brought something up, it was "No, no, no, no, no. We can't do that. No, no, no, no, no." It was unbelievable. It really was.

In Jochems's case, management's responsibility to monitor and defuse a workplace situation that constituted sexual harassment of an employee and a hostile work environment was sadly lacking, in her case, for 16 long years. "Everybody in management has an obligation to the workers to arrest the problem before it becomes a major problem. The Board of Ed could have done so many things," Power said.

In needlepoint, a pattern emerges, an image or a favorite saying on one side, while on the other, the many threads hang loose. In real life, situations more often resemble the back side of a needlepoint project than the neat, clearly delineated front. The story of tradeswomen working as civil servants still has many loose threads.

A breakdown of the number of skilled tradespersons employed by the DSF from 2003 to 2006 indicates the number by trade, title and gender. However, surprisingly, the DSF does not track these employees by race. In 2003, there were five tradeswomen: one carpenter, one electrician, one machinist, one plumber, and one steamfitter helper. During Fiscal Years 2004 and 2005, there were four tradeswomen. Fiscal Year 2006 saw an improvement: six tradeswomen—two electricians, one carpenter, one machinist, one plumber, and one steamfitter.[38]

As Susan D'Alessandro described in her public testimony, women who work in the nontraditional blue-collar jobs in city agencies work alone. They work in isolation. Still pioneers, more than four decades after Title VII provided women with the right of "equal employment opportunity," they are often targets, as Jochems and D'Alessandro were, for sexual harassment and gender discrimination. One by one and two by two, they take up their high-paid skilled positions in city agencies, still operating on the frontiers of gender equality.

1. Ironworker Janine Blackwelder. All photographs © Gary Schoichet

2. Plumber Elaine Ward

3. Stationary Engineer Yvone Maitin

4. Elevator Mechanic Margarita Suarez

5. Carpenter Irene Soloway

6. Electrician Laura Kelber

7. Electrician Joi Beard

8. Firefighter JoAnn Jacobs

9. Carpenter Veronica Session

10. Electrician Brunilda Hernandez

11. Teamster/Transit Union Official Eileen Sullivan

Double Vision: Breaking Down Doors at the FDNY

In 1982, even before Probationary Firefighter Brenda Berkman's arrival at her first assignment, firefighters had already formed opinions about her. "It was impossible for me to keep a low profile," she said. "Everybody knew my name. I had been getting death threats. I had to get an unlisted number...My picture had been in the paper. Everyone knew that I was a lawyer. So that gave them another reason to dislike me. They thought I was Jewish, so that was another reason—another unacceptable group—plus I wasn't from New York."[1]

As the lead named plaintiff in the class action lawsuit—*Berkman v. Koch*—that opened up the doors of the firehouses to women, her career was constantly shadowed by the perceptions about her created in those early days. Throughout her 24 years in the department, Brenda Berkman was a "lighting rod" for all of the emotions that swirled around the subject of female firefighters in New York City. As far along in her career as 1993, the New York City Fire Department (FDNY) was still issuing orders about Berkman: That no photos could be taken of her—either on or off duty—inside or outside of a firehouse.[2] After being promoted to lieutenant in 1995, her superior officer paid her a visit at Ladder 12. As she recalled:

> The Captain was not particularly happy to have me come there...A lot of it just had to do with reputation versus reality. The saying in the Fire Department being: "Telephone, telegraph, tell a firefighter." There's this very speedy and often inaccurate network of rumors that get spread about people. Not just about me, but *definitely* about me...The main thing that has improved our relationship is just getting to know one another. He realized that a lot of the rumors about me were inaccurate—that I'm a hard worker; that I'm conscientious and I'm trying to do the best that I can—that I'm not looking to cause problems in the firehouse; that I don't have a thin skin. I have a good sense of humor. So these sorts of things allayed a lot of the initial concerns he had about me coming there.[3]

In 2004, Berkman found it "hysterical"—her word for funny—that there were still men who wouldn't take a seat next to her at union meetings. Even then, Steve Cassidy, the head of the United Firefighters Association (UFA), the union that fought so hard to keep the women out, couldn't interact with her. "Every time I see [Steve] Cassidy, he won't talk to me. He won't look at me," she said. "As far as I know, he's never met with the women firefighters' organization [United Women Firefighters]."[4]

JoAnn Jacobs is short, soft-spoken, sports-minded, and smart. When she showed up at her first firehouse assignment in 1982, the fact that she is African-American might not have worked against her. "They didn't work with black women, so [I was] a totally unknown quantity," she said.[5] Very few firefighters had even worked with black men. Also, Jacobs didn't conform to their expectations: "I think, them not having any firsthand experience, they probably thought that I carried a knife, based on how the media portrays minorities...So here I come and I didn't fit any of their stereotypes."

Despite the common knowledge of the extreme difficulties faced by the first females in the Fire Department, Jacobs's story was not to be one of rude, crude, and hostile treatment. "They at least gave me a fair shot and a lot of the other women too—they gave them a chance also," Jacobs said.

As the individual who forced the issue of gender discrimination within the Fire Department, Brenda Berkman became a bugaboo—a source of aversion and fear—and extreme and uncensored harassment was directed toward her as well as toward many, though not all, of the women coming into the job. The issue of gender ignited a fire storm within the FDNY. No other arena has generated the same level of controversy.

Despite the passage of decades, the topic is still controversial. By now, both Jacobs and Berkman and many of the pioneers have retired after successful careers. Yet the Fire Commissioner as well as the City of New York still struggle to find a way to integrate African-Americans into the department—in numbers that correspond to their presence within New York City's population—just less than 25 percent.[6] Announcements for plans to increase their representation continue to make the front-page of the city's civil service newspaper; "Letters to the Editor" on the topic are a staple item; and lawsuits continue to unfold.[7]

JoAnn Jacobs and Brenda Berkman share a number of similarities—some small and some large. Both women were born in 1951. Both are the daughters of soldiers. Both are conscious of the place that race holds in American history as well as in the everyday world of ordinary citizens. Race is a part of Jacobs's everyday experiences as an African-American woman in America. The word "community" is a constant part of her vocabulary. Brenda Berkman finds a source of inspiration in the heroes of the civil rights movement of the 1950s and 1960s. Both women are ever-mindful of the way that divisions can creep into conversation and act to push people apart and divide them. Consequently, each woman is extremely conscious of how she chooses to speak about the women within the brotherhood of the Fire Department. Each woman is well-aware of the importance of serving as a role model for the next generation of young girls and of keeping the doors open for other women to follow in their footsteps. But despite all these similarities, their experiences within the Fire Department were very different. While Jacobs eventually found acceptance and tolerance, Berkman faced a threatening level of hostility.

Their stories represent the two sides of the FDNY—the one that is honored for its courageous and selfless sacrifices on behalf of their fellow citizens—and the other—where sickening levels of hatred and hostility directed at women who dared to go first were given the green light. They illuminate the strategies the pioneers devised for survival, acceptance, and eventual success within the FDNY; the sources of support they found for their efforts and those they created; how divisions developed amongst the women and once planted, bore bitter fruit; the all too frequent failure of leadership on many levels within the department itself;

and the irresponsible actions of their unions against the women who came to love doing their job—the one they all describe as—"the best job in the world."

"One of the Last Bastions"

Maureen McFadden is a passionate advocate for women in nontraditional jobs. She has lent her expertise to the ongoing debates over recruitment and retention strategies, test standards, and gender discrimination. As the Vice President of communications for Legal Momentum (formerly known as the NOW Legal Defense and Education Fund), she made a tremendous contribution to gender equality. McFadden was the first non-firefighter to serve on the board of Women in the Fire Service, a national organization. She offers a fresh perspective on the issues of race and gender in the FDNY. In 2005, calling the department, "one of the last bastions" of gender discrimination,[8] she placed its record regarding the hiring of women and minorities within a broader context:

> The Fire Department has one of the worst urban records in the country. It's not the worst, but it's close to the worst, and it's been that way for a long time. It's now 91 percent white male. The massive hiring that went on after 9/11 was a missed opportunity, since there were so many vacancies. Had diversity been a priority, I think a lot of the problems in the Fire Department could have been solved. "But there seems to be no political will in New York to make the change from the top, which has made some cities very successful in terms of hiring."

In New York City, despite the small and diminishing number of females— 45 in 1982; 35 in 1993; 24 in 2003; and 30 in 2007—in the FDNY, their individual accomplishments add up to an outstanding record of achievement. "Women in the FDNY have been promoted," she said. "They were first responders. And by rights, the amount of discrimination that some of these women went through, the belittling, should have shaken them to the core. You wonder that they could function at all. But they've risen to the top. So that really speaks to something. Plus, there's not a woman firefighter who doesn't say, 'I love my job.'"

For other, more successful urban models, McFadden points to the Miami/Dade and Minneapolis Departments: "[There] it comes from the top and so the Chief and the Mayor are in agreement that something had to give, but that hasn't happened in New York." San Francisco offers another example of progress, as McFadden described,

> I think San Francisco has 20 percent women and it has a woman Fire Chief. They have done something right...Attention was paid, a wrong was righted, and we don't see the city of San Francisco burning down, 'cause women are doing this job. Clearly they can do this job. The time to ask, Can women do this job is so long over!

How the City by the Bay got to this point is illuminating. For 25 years, the San Francisco Fire Department operated under court action and 10 years of a court-ordered consent decree, monitoring the department's testing, hiring, and promotion policies. The consent decree was lifted in December 1998. At the time, the department was headed by its first African-American Fire Chief, who had been a plaintiff in the litigation that resulted in the issuance of the decade-long consent decree. In 1987, when the consent decree was imposed, the uniformed force numbered 1,500. Out of that total, there were approximately 70 African-American males; 35 Asian Americans; and 80 Hispanics; there were no women. In 1998, the uniformed force was 40 percent minority and 10.4 percent female. Whites made up 60.1 percent; blacks 11.1 percent; Hispanics and Asians 12.6 percent each; and Filipinos 3.32 percent. One year before lifting the consent decree, Federal Judge Marilyn Hall Patel ordered the city to meet its goals of minority and female hiring and to create a cadet and officer candidate training program.[9]

Stepping Off the Beaten Path—JoAnn Jacobs

JoAnn Jacobs, like her mother, was born in Brooklyn, while her father was an immigrant from Barbados. "My father was in the Korean War and he was actually overseas when I was born," she explained. "I was the second child of four. My father was an electrician, and he was injured in a fire when they were working at Idlewild Airport. He was in a manhole that caught on fire and died of his injuries. At the time, I was five and a half years old. My mother, who was a housewife, had to go out and get a job in order to keep us in Catholic school and maintain the house that they had bought. So that's what she did. I remember her working in the meat department of the A&P, and then the job she retired from, which was with the State Department of Labor. She worked as a secretary/receptionist for 28 years."

After graduating from the all-girls Bishop MacDonald Catholic High School and York College, Jacobs used her newly minted degree in sociology to secure a job as a social worker in 1973:

> I got a job in a children's shelter...It was an institution that housed children between the ages of 7 and 17 who had been abused or neglected and there were disciplinary problems as well. I did that for seven years. I worked as a pseudo-mother from 10:30 at night and got off at 8:30 in the morning. The reason I stayed working at nights was so that I could play tennis during the day and on the weekend.

Then she made a career-switch that set her on a blue-collar pioneering path by going to work for the airlines. As she recalled:

> I had a friend who worked for Northwest Airlines as a ticket agent and he knew that I enjoyed doing outdoor stuff, between the tennis and the hiking and that kind of thing. So he thought that the [job of] baggage handler would be right up my alley, so to speak. He picked up the application for me and I remember spending the evening with him and his wife filling out the application to make sure that I answered the questions in the correct way because I was going to be the first woman to apply for the job...I was hired by Northwestern Airlines at JFK [Airport] to be what was called an Equipment Service employee.

She became a member of the union and immediately got a big boost in pay. "It was the International Association of Machinists and it tripled my salary," she said. "I remember I was about to get a raise to $9,000 with the shelter and the airline job was paying $21,000. The only hitch was that I had to get my driver's license...So I did that because at the end of that process, there was a nice big check for me."

At the airport, Jacobs was able to establish a rapport with the men after a period of having to prove herself. "It was difficult, mainly because the men couldn't understand why a woman would want that job, and they didn't feel that I was strong enough." She laid out the economic facts for them: "Hey, look. I have a college degree and you have a high school education and you are earning three times what I was earning. I showed them that, yeah, I had to lift the luggage in a different way, but I could do the job. I asked them, when they went on trips, didn't their wives carry the bags? Or do they carry them all?" This combination—ability to do the work and the economics of the situation—succeeded in convincing them that she had a right to the job.

She joined a workforce that was made up of 90 percent white males. Once there, she encountered some resistance from an unexpected source:

It was interesting because the few black men that I worked with, initially I expected that they would be really supportive, but they weren't. They weren't antagonistic, but they were more or less neutral. After getting to know them, I understood that they were in a precarious position themselves. They were a minority as well, even though they were men, and they wanted to protect their positions within the union and within the area that they were working. Once they saw that I was able to do the job, they started to come around and were a little friendlier. By the time I left, there really wasn't a problem.

Four years later, Jacobs was still the only female handling baggage for the airline. But this situation changed within a short time. "It's interesting, now women are all over," she said. "They are doing that work in every city you fly into. So that's good to see because you get travel benefits. You get union benefits and health benefits. It was an enjoyable job and I'm really happy to see that women have blossomed."

Even before Jacobs was enticed by the recruitment fliers for the Fire Department, she had applied to the Police Department. "I had taken the test for the New York City Police Department [because] I had a leaning even earlier toward blue-collar civil service work, mainly because of the benefits and the salary and also because the Police Department was saying that it was a way to do something that was worthwhile," she said. "But it was interesting because of the physical. It was the first time I'd had to take a physical that meant lifting things and using my body in a particular way. At the test site...they also had a sanitation physical going on and it was interesting to see what the men had to do. At that time, women hadn't been allowed to take that test, so it was interesting to see the rigors that they had to go through in order to be sanitation men."

A hiring freeze put the Police Department job on hold. "It was disappointing," Jacobs said. "But in the four years that I spent with the airlines, I was enjoying myself." Then she learned about the possibility of going to work as a firefighter through the Vulcan Society, the fraternal organization founded by and for African-Americans: "I did find out about it and I applied. I found out that the Vulcan Society (Many fraternal organizations in the FDNY are organized on the basis of ethnicity.) was training people for the physical and I went to a couple of their training sessions...By then, I was much stronger than I had been four years before. So I really didn't pick up on any kind of negative reaction as far as being a woman. If anything, they were a little more solicitous until they saw, well okay, you can do that!" The Fire Department allowed all the candidates to go to the test site and run through the test so you got an idea of what it entailed. At that stage, department personnel didn't yet have their antennae up against the women. Jacobs recalled the treatment she received at the training site:

> What I found was that the men who were proctoring the practice were real
> encouraging; very encouraging. They actually told me I could come back and do it
> again. So I think I did it once or twice more at the Armory in Brooklyn where they
> were going to give the test and ran through it. That was my preparation, other than
> running and doing push-ups and that kind of thing on my own.

Jacobs took the written test for firefighter in 1977. She took the physical test in 1978 and
continued to work for the airline. "I was sent a letter and told that there was going to be a class
action suit and [asked] did I want to be a participant," she recalled. "Of course I did! Then
we were hired in 1982."[10]

From Pipsqueak Protestor to Pioneer—Brenda Berkman

Brenda Berkman enlisted in the fight for gender equality at an early age. As a child growing
up in Minneapolis, she had a precocious awareness of gender preference in favor of boys. Her
love of playing baseball was struck down when her mother received a call asking whether
the "B. Berkman" on the Little League application was a boy or a girl. Sadly, she learned
that girls were not allowed to play Little League ball. "I have a very vivid memory of what
happened," she recalled. "This was crushing to me, because I was at least as good as most of
the boys through junior high and high school—all through lack of opportunities for girls in
athletics."[11]

But there were other barriers in place, including academic opportunities. "It was just
incredibly frustrating to me that girls did not have the same opportunities as boys," she said.
"I had a very strong sense as a little kid that it was a lot more fun being a boy! That there were
a lot more opportunities for boys than there were for girls. And I wasn't particularly interested
in the stereotypical roles that were presented to me as my future as a girl and a woman."

During college and graduate school, Berkman studied history and created her own oral
history projects. At St. Olaf's College in Minnesota, her senior thesis was based on interviews
about Norwegian-American women. "People were just starting to get into the idea that maybe
history should look a little deeper than [at] just the surface, great man approach to studying
the past. I interviewed the sons and daughters of these women, and in one case, a woman
who had actually come over. That was considered fairly oddball at the time...Then when I
went to Indiana, there were several women professors...I did an oral history of the women's
movement in Bloomington, Indiana. It had been fairly active. By the time I got there in '73, it
had pretty much petered out...So I interviewed the people who had been active in the movement...It was very interesting and I did my own little project."

Finding a satisfying career was the next step. Teaching history at the college level was
one option but opportunities were limited due to a glut of historians on the market. Then law
school became an option. At this point, Berkman moved to New York City and entered into
the milieu of an activist attorney.

> I worked for a summer in my future father-in-law's firm...He ran his own shop and
> he was very much a change agent. He had been involved with defending blacks in
> the South who were accused of crimes against whites and various kinds of civil rights
> actions. He had been involved in the very early stages of the Lawyers' Guild...He

got more conservative as he got older, but he was still fairly liberal. One of the groups that he was representing was women police officers who had been laid off during the fiscal crisis and I did some work on that case. He dragged me around to meetings and I met these women cops and I found this stuff all very interesting. He was encouraging me and my husband was encouraging me to go to law school. I applied and got into NYU. One of the reasons I wanted to go to NYU was because they had a good clinical program and it seemed to me a much more liberal environment than other law schools I looked at. It had a very high percentage of women. So I thought, this could be for me. But little did I know what a conservative discipline the law is…and so I went to law school. I hated it, basically.

As a young attorney practicing labor law at her father-in-law's firm, Berkman continued to cast about for a more exciting career. She began calling the Civil Service Commission to find out when tests were being given for the Police and Fire Departments. As she explained, "I really wasn't all that interested in Police, because I couldn't see myself pointing a gun at somebody. My ex-father-in-law also represented the Uniformed Fire Officers Association for 30 years and so I met all these Fire officers. This seemed to be the perfect opportunity for me to do something really interesting. It was active. It was sort of a heroic type of activity where you were helping people at the risk of your own life. Every day was different when you went to work. You never knew what you were going to encounter. You were very much respected by the public. The Fire Service has one of the highest approval ratings of any occupation, certainly much higher than lawyers. And the public loves firefighters and why shouldn't they? After all, there are very few people who come to your door and risk their lives—run into the burning building to save your cat or your wheelchair. They don't ask what color you are, how much money do you have; can you pay your bills; do you have insurance? They don't ask any of those things. They just go in and they do their job to the best of their abilities and then they leave. There's nobody really that's not happy to see a firefighter. Also, it had good pension benefits. At that time, it had a halfway decent starting salary and it had career opportunities. So I thought: This is great! So I kept calling and calling. But they weren't giving the test."

Berkman's next door neighbor alerted her to the fact that the department was accepting applications. "They were heavily involved in recruiting African-Americans at that point, because there had been a whole series of litigations about the Fire Department's failure to hire people of color—men of color," she said. "They were required at that point by law to open up to women, but that wasn't really their orientation."

In 1977, 500 women showed up to take the written test for firefighter. Of that number, the great majority passed. The department then changed the physical agility test from a pass/fail system of grading they had been using before the women applied to a rank-ordered test. They also changed a number of the events. The department offered all candidates the opportunity to take practice exams at the Fire Academy. The media came out to cover the women. As Berkman recalled:

You had all these people in the department and in the union and the media saying, "This is such a hard test, no woman is ever going to pass it." And they were right. Because of all the adverse publicity, only about 90 women showed up for the physical portion of the test. And of that number, everybody failed, including me. Now I thought this was very odd because I had been training very hard for this exam and I was in great shape. I was a marathon runner. I was a cross-country skier. I had gone up into the woods and I was chopping wood and I was lifting weights and I was doing push-ups and pull-ups and sit-ups—all this stuff to get into shape. I was in tremendous shape, and yet I couldn't pass this exam. I thought: This is crazy. You mean to tell me that not a single woman in the entire city of New York is fit to be a firefighter?

The physical test became the core of the dispute that—in the first round—turned into four years of litigation. Berkman sought the counsel of Professor Laura Sager at NYU Law School's Women's Rights Clinic.

I said, "I don't think this case is going to take any time at all." And [Laura Sager] said, "I think you have a good case here. I'll represent you." Almost 20 years later, the case was sort of winding down. After about a year of doing it herself, she went out and found Debevoise & Plimpton and they agreed to come on as cocounsel. Plimpton is one of the premier law firms in the country and the amount of resources that they were able to bring to bear on the case made it doable.

Attempts were made to settle the case. Congresswoman Bella Abzug accompanied the attorneys and Berkman to meetings with the city and the Civil Service Commission. "We made this argument," Berkman said. "Just come up with another test and give it to these women—a test that's job related and doesn't discriminate. Well, that was out of the question. So I filed my EEOC complaint and got my right to sue letter. We ended up in federal court before Judge Sifton...I think it's really to the credit of the attorneys that through very patient and hard work, and just being right, they turned Judge Sifton around, from being very unsympathetic to the case to eventually ruling in our favor."

The outcome of the court case made history: As Berkman described it:

Judge Sifton ordered the city to develop a new test, which they did by taking a group of incumbent firefighters and having them perform job simulation types of tasks and seeing what kind of pace was required to perform them. Then they gave the same test to us—the women. This was always a big bone of contention. Guys who had failed the test wanted to take the new test but they had never been part of the lawsuit. The judge ruled that they didn't have any basis...So they were barred. Then it became the women's test. It was always: "They're lowering standards 'cause things have changed.' Well, the test has been changed throughout the history of hiring, but because it was changed for women, well, now they were lowering standards...The test was *based* on male incumbent performance. They didn't bring any women firefighters in and say: 'Look, this is how women perform the job."

The judge ordered a pretraining program and a pretty high percentage of women went out, on their own time, week nights and weekends and we practiced running through this test. The interesting thing was, as people practiced, they got to the point where they could pass it. And they did. We passed it in much higher numbers than the department had anticipated. They thought that maybe 10 or 12 women were going to pass this test. Then it turned out that 50-some women passed the test. They were like: "The test must be much too easy! Look at all these women who passed it." Well, the point was that almost all these kinds of job simulation tests like they were giving at that point, women improved tremendously if they were just given a little opportunity to practice the test. It's been shown that they improve at a higher rate than men do, because women come to this with less familiarity with how to perform these kinds of all-out, beat-to-completion types of things than men do, usually by reason of athletic involvement. The judge ordered the city to set aside 45 slots. It turned out that there were 45 women who wanted to go in. So they put us all in this one class.

Taking the Heat

Randall's Island, situated in the middle of the East River, is the site of the Fire Department's Training Academy. This is where New York City's probationary firefighters take part in a six-week training course to prepare them for their new jobs. The "probies" are then assigned to firehouses where they receive additional on-the-job training. This is the normal course of events in the FDNY. But the abnormal superceded the normal when women came into the department. Berkman explained:

> With men, traditionally, it's been [the case] that once you pass the test...when you go into the academy, it's assumed that you can be trained to do the job. Well, that wasn't the case with the women. Right from the get-go, it was like: "We lowered the standards. Well, we have to see if they can, in fact, be trained to do the job." So they developed all kinds of additional hurdles for us in the Fire Academy. They made a concerted effort to get rid of us—to get us to quit. Things went on out there that really put peoples' health and safety into jeopardy. As a matter of fact, one woman was severely hurt in a training accident. It was purely a matter of negligence on the part of the instructors. It's amazing nobody was killed. Some of us got very sick. I had the worst case of carbon monoxide poisoning I've ever had since I've been on the job.

"It was like a whole new set of obstacles. The men were completely ignored. They might as well not have been there. Everything was focused on the women. The women were under a microscope. Every day, the rules changed. When we went in there, it was 'Okay, all you have to do is perform these various tasks and you'll get out of here.' Now, all of a sudden, they decided that, if the instructor thinks you're not quite up to snuff, he's going to issue you a deficiency slip. But you can get rid of the deficiency slips by repeating the tasks...Then it became, 'Well. If you have X number of deficiency slips, you're not going to graduate on time. You're going to have to stay over for an additional training period.' Then it became, These people are going to have to repeat the whole training period."

Years later, JoAnn Jacobs looked back on this experience:

> It was very stressful. I had taken a three-month leave of absence from the airline job in order to do the Fire Department and to see if I liked it at the end. So in the Fire Academy, I felt that I had a leg up because I'd been doing physical labor for the past four years. I was still playing tennis. But actually, I got most of my physical labor from the airline job. You're lifting mail freight and baggage every day. Actually, it was much more demanding than the Fire Department was because you don't have a fire every day, and you definitely have flights going in and out that you have to load.

Jacobs described some of the obstacles created by those in charge at the academy that placed an extra burden on the women:

> The department found ways to hold [the women] back. They initiated something called deficiency slips, which was a way of measuring or grading performance in doing various aspects of the job: raising ladders, directing a hose line, hooking up a hose to the hydrant, demolishing buildings, tying ropes. Everything that we learned we were graded on and if one of the instructors felt that we were deficient, we would get a deficiency slip. It was pretty arbitrary who got one and who didn't. You were never really sure why they were doing that, except that at the end of the day or during your lunch period, you had to go and work on whatever it was that you had gotten a deficiency in. It wasn't until we were supposed to graduate, when they were getting down to the fourth or fifth week, we found out that they were going to use the deficiencies to hold you back. And again, we weren't sure how many would count.

To get out to Randall's Island, Jacobs carpooled with a male probationary firefighter and another woman. As she described:

> He'd been in the job a year and he had a knee injury, so he was just coming back. But he was a real firefighter. The woman was Cecilia Salters, now Cecilia Cox, so we had that camaraderie…I didn't see Cecilia during the day because she was in another squad. She would cry going home at night. She was trying to raise a daughter on her own and I remember her talking about how she went to charm school and what is she doing? The typical feminine—"what the hell am I doing here?"—type of attitude. Troy, the firefighter, we would try to cheer her up. All three of us were black and we lived in the same neighborhood. It was kind of funny that years later, Cecilia was the first woman who transferred to a truck company—the macho of the machos—she had gone full-circle, which was good to see.

Jacobs's strategy for survival at the academy was to seek shelter from all of the attention. "We were like goldfish in a bowl," she said. "I would guess [that] in the six weeks we were in the Academy, every Fire Company in the department came to Randall's Island for something: to pick up a hose, a fire extinguisher, whatever. But the looks that were directed toward us were not pleasant. I absented myself at the times when you really would be in close contact with active duty firefighters during lunch in the cafeteria. So I would sit in my locker room with my sandwich and do my homework."

For Brenda Berkman, there *was* no escape. "The women…relied on me to deal with the administration. If they had a problem with the Training Academy, then I was expected to go and talk to the head of the Training Academy about the problems and see if we could resolve them. But it was very difficult for me. I was on probation myself. I had no idea what was going on. I had no experience with the Fire Department. Nobody was telling us: Well, this isn't the way it's usually done."

As the date of graduation approached, it became clear that many of the women would be held back for additional training. "They didn't let a lot of the women out who should have been graduated and I think it was because of the media attention that we would have gotten," observed Jacobs. According to her, this calculated decision had lasting, negative consequences. "It really hurt in terms of the perception that women couldn't do the job…There *were* some women I would have been terrified to go to a fire with. But there were also some men—after watching them in the Fire Academy—I would have been terrified to go to fires with!"

But, as Jacobs knew from her own experience, the selection process was completely arbitrary:

One of the instructors came to me and said, "You got a deficiency for scaling ladders." I said, "Well, no one corrected me. I thought I was doing it okay." He said, "Who were you working with?" I said, "I was working with Lois and no one said anything to her." He said, "I'll look into it." And he came back and said, "Okay. I took care of it...No one could remember why they gave it to you so it was torn up." I found out at the graduation ceremony that...one of the captain's I'd had an incidental conversation with in the very beginning...found out that I'd worked for the airlines and that's what he had done before going into the Fire Department. So when they went to him and said, Listen. Someone gave Jacobs this deficiency, he remembered me as having worked with the airlines loading luggage and he gave me the benefit of the doubt and tore up the deficiency...I had gotten two or three others and that was the one that would have broken the camel's back and I would have been left back. So it was that arbitrary.

Lois Mungay was one of those left back. She wound up spending 20 years in one of the busiest companies in Brooklyn. So how is it that the two of us had worked together through our six weeks in the Fire Academy—how as it that I got out and she didn't?

As fire trucks go speeding through the streets, most New Yorkers don't distinguish between the different types of trucks and the separate functions they perform. Berkman described the division of labor:

The two firefighting groups are primarily engines, which are the pumpers who put the water on the fire, and the ladder company—which are the tools—they do ventilation and forcible entry and searches. They play around with a lot more tools. They have the "jaws of life" as civilians call it. They have the axes and the hooks and the saws. They're doing the stuff with the equipment. It's the engine's primary responsibility to just get in there and put some water on the fire.

Like Jacobs, she viewed the decision to hold some of the women back as yet another piece of the calculated puzzle improvised by the department to impede their progress. "During our probationary period, they kept changing the rules on evaluation," she said. "Women started getting very acceptable—very decent evaluations. They sent us all to the engine, so the department went: All these women are going to be tenured...Something's wrong here...The department looked at our evaluations and they thought: Oh my God, these women can do engine work, but I bet they can't do truck work; they can't do ladder work. So we'll send them all to the trucks for 30 days."

Although initially, all the women were brought together at the Fire Academy, as they were sent out into the firehouses, each woman went alone. JoAnn Jacobs offered her explanation of how this happened:

I know that some women were assigned to companies where discipline was lacking—to put it nicely—and the hope was that we wouldn't last. I don't even think it was that devious. I think they didn't think we would last anyway. They didn't really target particular firehouses, so I'm retracting what I just said. I think that they threw us in there. They split us up. They threw us out to the wolves and based on what the union was saying and the men were saying, they didn't think we would last. And I think they were surprised by the fact that [we did].

Trouble at the Top

JoAnn Jacob's first assignment was fortuitous. "I was lucky because the captain in my firehouse ran a tight ship, even before I got there," she said. Engine Company 324 in Corona, Queens, was a short commute from her home. Under the leadership provided by Captain George Donnelly, life in the firehouse was regulated and well-run. Jacobs described the scenario she encountered within the context of the department:

> We had a lot of captains and officers that decided, "Okay. Well, the girls come in and we'll straighten out the whole house. So the woman was blamed for the complete change around. But in this case, this captain was a by-the-book guy well before I got there. And what that did was give me breathing room. It scared the men enough that they actually got to know me. He even had one man transferred. He transferred him before I got there because he was saying that he wouldn't work with me, and this, that and the other. . . . Believe me, if my captain felt that I was incapable of doing the job, I would have gotten bad evaluations, and I didn't. He was fair—he and the other officers and senior men in the company as well."

Unfortunately, this type of leadership was not the model for those in the top positions of command. In the midst of the generalized mayhem that greeted the entrance of women to the FDNY, both the department and the unions fanned the flames of resentment and resistance. It's not surprising that an organization based on fraternal bonds of brotherhood that had endured for more than a century would find it difficult to adapt to a new, equalitarian era. But the opportunity to set the tone for compliance and to provide a fair playing field for the females had to start at the top and this was not the case. As Jacobs pointed out, individually, many officers and firefighters did "give women a fair shot." But a template for fair treatment was never put into place. Likewise, the union representing rank-and-file firefighters set itself on a course of opposition. As Berkman recalled:

> The union was out there every day, looking not to protect us, but to see if there was some way they could assist in getting rid of us. The union had come in on the side of the city [in the litigation]. When we won, they took an appeal. They were the only party that took an appeal to the 2nd Circuit, where they lost. But the union had been fighting us from the get-go. The president of the union, Nick Mancuso, was like: "Well. We can't have these people on the job" . . . [they were] taking this very negative attitude toward us. So the union was no good at all.

As Jacobs, Berkman, and nine of the other women who were allowed to graduate in the first class were celebrating their first big milestone in the FDNY, the UFA was present to throw a pail of cold water on them. Jacobs described the events:

> I was aware of the role of the union at the swearing-in ceremony, when [they] showed up with banners: "Don't let a girl do a man's job." Their wives picketed in

the street in front of Ella McNair's firehouse. [There were] newspaper articles and bumper stickers. In my firehouse, there were bumper stickers. But at the swearing-in ceremony, there was a huge contingent from the union making it known that they didn't want women—girls—in the job. And once the lawsuit was settled, the union persisted in continuing it on their behalf, [even though] the city had given in.

On March 12, 1986, Judge Sifton issued a ruling in the ongoing litigation directing the department to rescore the 1983 exam given for firefighters. The unions were still united in opposition. Thousands of firefighters organized by the UFA rallied outside the courthouse. Prominent amongst the picket signs was one large board held aloft that read "Preserve the Merit System." The next day, New York's "hometown paper," the *Daily News*, reported the story from the aggrieved union members' point of view: "Brooklyn's Cadman Plaza became a battle zone yesterday [March 12, 1986] as 4,000 firefighters stopped traffic. The union members were protesting a federal judge's order calling for lower hiring standards in the city Fire Dept. Uniformed Firefighters Assn. head Nick Mancuso led the noon rally at federal Court. He labeled Judge Sifton's decision—restructuring hiring standards—a 'kamikaze attack on New York City's civil service system.'"[12] *Fire Lines*, the UFA newspaper, pronounced their demonstration, "a huge success." UFA President Mancuso was quoted in the story that spread from the front-page inside with a full page of photos. "Mancuso, during the firefighters rally on March 12, vowed to fight the ruling all the way to the U.S. Supreme Court if necessary and he urged the city to do likewise."[13]

The Uniformed Fire Officers Association and the UFA then joined forces—hiring a pollster to conduct a survey of New Yorkers to demonstrate that the public stood on the side of the unions—in opposition to women in the department. Both unions made common cause with Fire Commissioner Joseph Spinnato in their adamant claims that, "It was impossible to deal with the firehouse battle of the sexes on a department-wide basis."[14] *The Chief-Leader* editorialized in 1986 about the phenomenon of women firefighters: "The department did a lousy job of dealing with the bad [attitude] most firemen had. Result: A sorry history of sexist insults, harassment, even violence."[15] As the "sorry history" unfolded in the firehouses, the unions did nothing to represent their female members in the face of the attacks.

Years later, Brenda Berkman spoke at a conference of labor union activists sponsored by the Association for Union Democracy. She said, in part:

I have to fess up a little bit, that I am a former union attorney. Prior to becoming a firefighter, I worked at a union [law] office that was regional attorney for [the] Civil Service Employees Association here. I come from a family of union attorneys. My late father-in-law had represented the Fire Officers union for 30 years until they fired him when I came on the job, as a *result* of my coming on the job...The unions refused to stand up and resist the harassment that was occurring against women firefighters. In fact, the union delegate...was one of the prime instigators of the harassment that was going on in my firehouse. It causes me some pain to see that the UFA's offices are named after him. There were a large number of physical assaults that occurred on women firefighters by male firefighters. And whenever that occurred, the union defended the male firefighters and did not help the women firefighters. In fact, in one particularly egregious assault, where a woman was cut by a knife by a male firefighter, when the man was suspended, the union found him a job.

We were unable really to attend the union meetings. By we—I mean women firefighters—because if we [did], we were harassed unceasingly; verbally harassed. And the union leadership did nothing to defend our right to attend union meetings or protect us from that harassment...This whole history was particularly painful to me because I considered myself to be extremely pro union and I did not really understand how this could be occurring in a movement that I felt was supposed to be there to represent me and protect me from bad conditions...We were paying dues during all this, but in fact, our unions were acting in opposition to our being on the job.

As a result, many women in the Fire Services, not just in New York City, formed advocacy groups outside the Fire Service, and that included my formation of the United Women Firefighters here in New York City and also the formation of the national group, Women in the Fire Service. Once we formed these advocacy groups, we were treated by the unions, including the International Association of Fire Fighters, as rival labor organizations. That was not our intention at all.[16]

Sisterhood, Brotherhood, and the Bonds of Solidarity

Even as women entered the FDNY—before they built organizations of their own for internal support—they found some sources of solidarity. One group that extended itself to the women was the Vulcan Society. Turn east off Eighth Avenue onto Harlem's famed 125th Street and a bright green sign proclaims that it's named in honor of Battalion Captain Wesley Williams. The Vulcan Society was the brainchild of Williams. The mission of the fraternal organization was "survival with dignity." All too few passersby know of the legendary firefighter's contributions. In a predictable chapter of city history, when African-American males were finally able to join the Fire Department, they met up with a mighty resistance. Wesley Williams, who placed number 13 on the civil service list for appointment, joined the department on January 10, 1919. He began his career in Lower Manhattan at Engine Company 55. The captain of the company retired on the spot as of that day so as to avoid the stigma of being the captain of a company where the black fireman was to perform duty. Every man in Engine Company 55 then submitted a request for transfer. In 1940, Wesley Williams founded the Vulcan Society.[17]

Berkman described how the history of African-American firefighters affected their response to the women:

> The first group that we really networked with was the African-American group, the Vulcans. The Vulcans were the only men that stood up for us when we first came on the job. I'm not saying every African-American man, but as an organization, they stood up for us. Their president testified on our behalf at the trial. We had some striking parallels between our situation and what I had read about the first African-Americans to come on the job. As a matter of fact, the founder of the Vulcans, Wesley Williams, who ultimately became a Battalion Chief, and was the first African-American to be promoted on the job, wrote the story of his career and the whole thing about being ostracized. They actually had Jim Crow beds for them, some of the blacks had to carry their own silverware around with them, 'cause the guys refused to eat off the same utensils. They were always given the shit assignments, long after their seniority wouldn't have warranted it anymore. We had exactly the same kind of situation. So they were very supportive of us.[18]

JoAnn Jacobs, destined to be the first African-American woman in the FDNY, learned about the Vulcans and their help in preparing the women to take the physical test as soon as she set her sights on going into the department. She took advantage of this and benefited from their support in other ways. As she recalled, "Another way of getting support was that the Vulcan Society assigned each [African-American] woman a mentor who was an officer. Mine was Captain Duran."

But early on, the women—in particular Brenda Berkman—realized that they needed to organize amongst themselves for survival. "Based on my experience with the women in the Police Department and the organization they founded, the Policewomen's Endowment Association (PEA), I decided that we had to have our own organization," she said. "So I convinced the other women that we should form a fraternal organization, like the Emerald Society or the Vulcans, or the Hispanic Society, we should have a women's organization. I went to the PEA and got a copy of what they had written up and their constitution and bylaws, and I changed a few things to make it more Fire Department-related, and we formed an organization. We took it to the department and said, 'Listen. You recognize these other organizations. You have to recognize us.' They hemmed and they hawed for a while, but eventually, they recognized us. We had an election and boom! There was our organization. I was the president and that was the deal."

As Jacobs pointed out, "I think that Brenda was the only one who was politically aware and dealing with things on that basis." But JoAnn did pitch in and participate in the activities of the United Women Firefighters (UWF). She described its origins:

> It started up in the Fire Academy. It didn't actually start up. Brenda started it. She realized that we would need an organization for moral support and in terms of technical support...Not just, how do you deal with harassment. But that turned out to be one of the major benefits of having the organization. The women felt from the very beginning that there was someone they could go to and talk to and we could hash [it] around and figure out how to solve problems.

Divisions soon began to develop within the small group of women. One source was located in the interplay that went on in the firehouses. Jacobs described how being on the receiving end of a compliment from her fellow firefighters was in actuality a backhanded denigration of other women:

> The thing I picked up on, and I'm kind of sorry I did because it was really nice being patted on the back, but...because I'd gotten out in that small group, the whole job now knew about these 11 women, not 30 or 40, so I stood out. I realized early on [that] I was getting patted on the back. "Well, you have a good attitude." Then I realized, if you're saying that I have a good attitude that means the rest of them don't. So I was able to catch on to that pretty early on so that I didn't disrespect the women that I had worked with.

As Berkman was aware, some of the women chose to make what she termed "their own accommodations." She described the strategy as it played out for some of the female firefighters:

> All these women came to the job from very different backgrounds...from somebody like me, who had a law degree, to a couple of people with graduate degrees, and

some who were teachers, people who were students, or housewives, or secretaries, who were basically in the pink-collar ghetto; people who had grown up in New York and people who had not grown up in New York. The great majority of us had never had any experience with a male-dominated profession and we're all thrown together...and expected to just meld and get along. There were too many things working against us. I think it's amazing that any of us are still talking to each other. Some of us have become very close. People who didn't know each other, we're like family now. Other people don't want anything to do with certain people. I was like that for a long time. People would not want to have anything to do with me, even when I was president of the organization. It was like: "Oh, she's a troublemaker. Stay away from her."

[Then there are] those who have sort of gone into a little hidey-hole out in the field. They don't feel any need for the group and they've sort of made their own way. They made their own accommodations. Now I look at some of those people, and I see that their accommodations involve drug and alcohol abuse. They involve getting divorced. They involve taking a desk job and never being in the firehouse. Those to me are sort of sad ways of coping with all the things that have gone on. But that's the way they've chosen.

Bringing the disparate group of women together was always a challenge. As Berkman said:

The organization has always had problems getting the women to work together as a group, 'cause we have been so isolated. I think all the psychological warfare that was waged on these women—to tell them every day that they went into work—that they weren't as good as the men that they worked with. They weren't capable of doing the job. They didn't deserve to be on the job, and on and on. It really had a very telling effect. Then there were divisions between the black and white women. A lot of the black women felt that the white women were racist and didn't stick up for them. And to some degree, they were correct. So there were all these divisions between the different groups.

Another source of division developed over time between the women who were being seriously harassed on the job and others who were able to escape that experience. JoAnn Jacobs was one of the later. She described how this division affected participation within the UWF:

Unfortunately, what I found to be the case...was that—for these women, and I'm speaking specifically about myself, that I was not having the horrific problems that the other women were—we really didn't get a hearing. It was very difficult to go into one of the United Women Firefighter meetings and talk about the fact that you were having success, or what were your tactics; what were you doing that was working, because those women were having problems. Their needs came first and so that's what was talked about at the meetings. That persisted, even outside of United Women Firefighters. Everyone always wants to hear all the horror stories. But I feel that that negates the hard work that I put forward to make things work in my situation. I think that happened for a lot of women who were *not* having problems. They stopped coming to meetings and they insulated themselves in the firehouse because, well, at least there they were being listened to and they were having a good experience. I think a lot of women who were mixing well and were successful in their firehouses stopped [going to UWF] meetings.

Despite these and many other divisions, both Berkman and Jacobs continued to support the organization. Jacobs served as president in 1987–1988. She also lent a considerable amount of time and energy to running the training program for women attempting to enter the department in later years. Berkman continued to provide innumerable forms of assistance to the group. As she pointed out, "The group has worked best for the people who needed it most."

The power of organizations such as UWF is that, *despite* deep divisions, personal grudges, and other sources of internal conflict, women have been able to come up with an agenda and then channel the desire, determination, and drive to keep moving it forward—together. Although the bonds of solidarity were stretched taut at times, they endured and provided an institution that still is able to offer young women welcome assistance as they set out on a career within the FDNY. While Brenda Berkman served as a sort of glue to keep UWF together, other women have come on board to do the same. As she observed, "I think that happens with a lot of women pioneers—certainly with the women in the Fire Service—that they developed this extreme emotional commitment to trying to change what's going on."

Can-Do Career Women in the FDNY

In 1979, when Australian actress Judy Davis played the lead in the movie, *My Brilliant Career*, the fate of the women destined to become the first female firefighters in New York City was still being decided in court. But the question raised by Davis's character in her debut as a star was eternal: how does the heroine maintain her independence as a person? The choices for women have expanded but the perpetual problem remains.

Both Brenda Berkman and JoAnn Jacobs served out their careers within the FDNY and each experienced a high degree of success. Each woman made choices suited to her own sense of self and personal goals. For Jacobs, planning for her career within the FDNY began immediately. In 2004, she recalled how she laid out her plans early on:

> I had written a letter to a friend while I was in Probie School—I'd outlined my whole life—that actually turned out! I was going to study. I was going to buy a house. I was going to retire in 20 years. That was my goal because that's how I looked at the Fire Department. With the airlines, I would have had to work 30 years and be 55 [to retire]. With the Fire Department, 20 years, no matter what my age, and I can retire. I just watched my mother work all those years supporting us, and there didn't seem to be an end in sight. She eventually retired because she had emphysema and she died two years after. That was in 1985. [But] I didn't know that in 1982. [So] I had written [my plan] down in this long letter.

Jacobs stayed with the same company for almost the complete duration of her years as a firefighter. As she explained, "I liked that firehouse. It wasn't that busy. A lot of the men, and one in particular, would say, 'Well, if you want to be a firefighter, why don't you go to a busy company?' And I said, 'Why don't *you* go to a busy company?' He'd been [there] for

15, 20 years, and so I'd tease him. I said, 'What are you doing here?' He was a big guy. It was great...I was doing a job and I took a lot of pride in what I did, but it wasn't who I was. It brought me a lot of respect. I loved wearing my uniform, especially as a black woman. I'd walk down the street in my uniform and [feel] really special. Otherwise, they think you're a nanny—because of the perceptions in this city and this society. I really loved wearing the uniform. I felt that it was a higher calling in terms of letting young girls, especially, see me in uniform. So I would go to schools in a neighborhood and do fire safety talks. I did it on my own time."

She also did recruiting as tests were scheduled by the department. Finally, in 1990, the Fire Department hired firefighters to be official recruiters. Jacobs was asked to be a part of this effort:

> They took us out of the firehouse, put us in an office, and said, "There's going to be a test in a year. We want you to recruit." There was me, Eileen Gregan, a black firefighter who was the president of the Vulcans at the time—Al Washington—and a Hispanic firefighter. We were the first firefighters ever paid by the FDNY to do recruitment...We did it on our own, figuring out what to do and how to do it. Do you go to a four-year college or do you go to a community college? Do you go to a high school or a job fair? Before that, the department would give you a bunch of fliers and you'd stand outside the marathon office where people were going to pick up their numbers, or you'd go to where the women lifeguards were getting ready to be in a competition. That's well and good, but it's not really focused in the way that it needed to be. So we were in the first Fire Department Recruitment Unit. We did that for a year and then we were unceremoniously kicked out. They just disbanded it, and then they kept reinventing the wheel every year. Every time there's a test, then recruiting became a plum job. All of a sudden, you had all these white firefighters doing it. But some of my proudest moments were in that recruitment unit because early on, I figured that that's what I wanted to do. I wanted to at least replace myself.

Her next step was to study for the Fire Marshal test:

> I thought about which job would prepare me for my 20 year retirement. The fact was that the fire tests—the lieutenant's exam, the captain's exam—there was so much material to study. Crates and crates of books, that you never really had a sense of what to study and whether you were going to do well and I didn't want to spend five years studying for a test. I'd much rather go to law school...So I decided to study for Fire Marshal because that would prepare me for a career after the Fire Department. I would have a gun. I'd have police credentials. I could do something else. The Vulcan Society had a study group, and I went to that study group for a solid year.

As Jacobs prepared for the test, her co-workers extended a helping hand to her. "I'd carry index cards around with me. The guys would let me stay on the rig when we went to do building inspections. I just devoted my life to that for a year. And I was number 127 on the (civil service) list, which was very good, except that it took them four years to promote me—promote anyone!"

She got a gun and a gold badge, along with her promotion in 1992. But she also experienced a couple of unexpected setbacks:

> The other thing was I didn't realize that you lose a lot of respect as a fire marshal because you are no longer going in fighting fires. And they didn't wear uniforms. I like my uniform! These guys wanted to get into suits and jackets and ties. So I lost my uniform privileges...I was the second woman promoted to Fire Marshal.

In 1996, she received the City of New York Sloan Public Service Award for her outstanding work with the Juvenile Fire Setter Program.[19] Even before she started to work with this program, she had offered to volunteer, but was turned down. Finally, after a year as a fire marshal, she was assigned to the detail. The job called on many of her strengths—her commitment to her community; her pride in being a role model within that community; and her training as a professional social worker:

> This unit was started in the late 70s because a fire captain was killed in a fire that was set by a nine-year-old boy. You could arrest him and what would that do? So they started this unit. It was based on one that was operating in Rochester...It was just great...We were building up a rapport with firefighters that knew this unit was something good.
>
> I enjoyed what I was doing. What was really special for me was that, again, the majority of the people that you saw were black and Hispanic. So you knock on the door of this family whose child had played with matches or started a fire and you say, "Fire Marshal." They'd open the door and there's this black woman standing there. It was a real pleasure to work with that unit...It really challenged you...We needed to get in and do an evaluation of the family. Then there was a whole network of mental health centers that we could refer children to. We had a questionnaire that gave us guidelines. You'd go in. You'd take a look at the house. You'd watch the interaction and you'd do an evaluation based on that. A lot of it was intuitive. A lot of it was rapport...You're seeing people at a vulnerable time. So what I would do—in order to make sure they kept the appointment—I'd mail a coloring book and remind them that, okay. We have an appointment. Then I'd call in the morning. You really had to be dogged in tracking down people. You're dealing with people who weren't sophisticated, in some cases, in terms of making and keeping appointments, writing them down...You had to make it where they really saw the value in what you were doing. So that was the challenge.

In time, the unit fell apart. "It was decimated," Jacobs said. "Now I think they're down to 80 Fire Marshals, or less, from 300, so nobody is doing it.

Toward the end of her career, she failed the hearing test, and was placed on "light duty." "They don't want you running around with a gun if you don't hear stuff," she said. "So I worked in the EEO Unit for a while, which was a pleasant experience up until one point. I actually left the unit because it was a choice between leaving the unit or filing a complaint against it. Typical Fire Department—puts in one of the biggest harassers going. It was either: leave the unit, shoot this guy, or go somewhere else. So I chose to go somewhere else. I worked in the Medical Unit. I knew the chief...that captain in the Fire Academy who tore up my deficiency...At that point he was the chief in charge of the medical unit. They give the annual physical."

Jacobs retired in November 2000. "I achieved my goals," she said. "I was 49 when I retired. I managed to never actually have arrested anybody! I would always give up the arrest. It wasn't a notch that I wanted." Looking back, she fondly recalled her years in the Fire Department, experiences that included, "sitting around a dinner table with a group of men and then occasionally a woman firefighter...We talked about our day; our days off; our vacations; what we were going to do for the holidays. We talked about politics. We argued. We'd laugh. We'd fight and the day would pass and you'd look forward to going to work the next day. I didn't go to work thinking about United Women Firefighters or the union. I went to work thinking: I wonder if Brian's wife had the baby...For most intents and purposes, it's a typical work place."

> We would have Thanksgiving dinners together. We'd have Christmas dinners together. We'd share New Year's Eve. Those were special times...and we made it special because we were stuck there. We had to be together. I've had firefighters invite me to their homes for Thanksgiving. So it's been very special. It was 20 of the best years of my life.

A Lasting Legacy: An Open Door Policy

For 24 years, Brenda Berkman's career was fueled by a fierce competitiveness, a desire to excel *and* to prove her point—that women were capable of having careers in these coveted jobs where they got to perform a valuable public service. Just as she had served as a lighting rod for criticism and vilification, she has also been the most visible public face of the female firefighters in the FDNY. She has spent a lot of time in the spotlight as a spokesperson and advocate for women in the fire service.

On the day she was promoted to captain at the Brooklyn headquarters of the FDNY, Metrotech Plaza was abuzz with satellite trucks and media outlets from New York City to Japan. In March 2006, a documentary movie about the experiences of women in the FDNY aired on public television.[20] Throughout her career, Brenda received many accolades and awards. On the night she received the John Commerford Award from the New York Labor History Association, she spoke about the role of history:

> One of the most important lessons that studying history taught me was an appreciation for how hard it is and how long it takes to achieve meaningful social change...I knew that any change worth accomplishing usually doesn't happen overnight. Because I knew about the history of women's struggles in the New York Police Department and black male firefighters' struggles in the FDNY, as well as the much larger civil rights and social justice struggles in American history, when I began the struggle in 1977 to have women hired as New York City firefighters, I expected resistance to the idea that women could be firefighters. Maybe not the rabid hatred and physical threats that occurred—but certainly I expected animosity. Studying history gave me the perspective to know that the process of integrating women into the FDNY would be a marathon and not a sprint.[21]

In 1983, when Cyndi Lauper's song, "Girls Just Want to Have Fun" was at the top of the pop charts, Brenda Berkman recorded what it was like to be on duty in the firehouse. She kept a daily record of her activities, later to become an exhibit in the ongoing court case. On August 3, 1983, she wrote in her journal, "Several runs, no fires. Read The Idiot. Someone had put 'Caution AIDS' sticker on my ladder. Bed was all messed up. *Playboy* cartoon on bulletin board. Written out on room bulletin board: 'The missing link between man and woman: Roll up your sleeves bearded lady.' BB erased. 2nd watch: 12–4:30 a.m. Did floor and dishes."[22]

A lot has changed since women first signed on and began their journey out at Randall's Island. One big change lies within young women who have grown up in a different world. Title IX, which has provided girls with access to publicly funded sports programs in the schools, has made a significant contribution to the physical abilities and mental conditioning of young women. "Women are much more demanding and are a lot stronger than I was 20 years ago," Jacobs pointed out. "The young women today believe they can do anything. Enough of them do that they are challenging the powers that be. As long as there are ways that they can get their foot in the door, then it will continue."[23]

"It just thrills me to hear my male co-worker firefighters talking about how they want their daughters to get a lacrosse scholarship or a tennis scholarship, or some kind of scholarship, and they're planning on this," Berkman said.[24]

Recruitment campaigns are essential to attract the next generation of FDNY firefighters. But the kind of campaign—what the message is and how it's being delivered—is critical. "The [public relations] firm the department hired…came up with this slogan: 'Heroes Wanted,' which we felt was not really a good outreach to historically excluded groups," Berkman said. "After 9/11, all these people who had had no contact with the Fire Department—in their minds, was [the image] of firefighters being killed by buildings falling down on top of them. So we really felt that that was counterproductive in terms of recruiting people of color…Heroes wanted! We got people applying from Japan and California and Australia and yet they were not able to significantly increase the number of people of color and women applying."

As an advocate for women's rights, Maureen McFadden sees the recruitment piece as a key part of the effort to improve the department's record of diversity:

> You can see it in the cities that are doing well. Someone at the top either said, "This is the right thing to do," or, "We don't want to get sued!"…They've put into place the mechanisms that do the right things. They've made sure that the testing is job-related and that it was fair. They've done a great deal of work on recruitment. When you have a department that has actively discriminated against a group as long as the FDNY has, it doesn't work to just slap a woman's picture on a recruitment poster. You have to make active outreach to a group that you have rejected. You have to make a tacit admission that you have rejected this group; that you have a long history of rejecting them, and then you have to have expertise in reaching out to these people. Recruitment and letting women know that these jobs are available; that they're good jobs…that they can raise their families; they can have lots of time off.…If you present them intelligently and you give them the facts about salaries and benefits, watch how fast women are going to flock to these jobs.

Ultimately, women have to see other women in the job. "The experts say that until women see women on the rigs, they're not going to go for those jobs," McFadden said. "They're not going to think that they're open to them and they're not going to think: 'Hey, I can do that!'"

As Brenda Berkman put in the papers for her retirement on September 14, 2006, she was still slender, fit, and strong. But the tensions and stress she's absorbed over decades shows in her face. She spoke about the legacy that she and the other pioneers left for other women to follow:

> I think things are changing slowly—very slowly—not as fast as I would like to have them change. I'm very impatient about all this...Sometimes when I get depressed about things...I look at what women went through in the suffrage movement...We are better off than our foremothers were because we have more opportunities available to us. On the other hand, women had a lot of opportunities during World War II and all of a sudden, they were yanked right out from under them. So I know that nothing is ever written in stone in terms of opportunities for minorities and women...Things could revert, but they'll never revert back to where they were...I really think that we have made a difference.[25]

Ever since 1977, people have accused Brenda Berkman of having an agenda. "I should *hope* I have an agenda," she said. "I'm not ashamed of the fact that I'm interested in issues that are larger than my own individual concerns. My agenda is that I don't want any more little girls growing up and having somebody say to them: 'You can't do that because you're a little girl.' Not because you're not smart enough or not strong enough or you don't have the training to do it. But just the fact that you're a girl [means] you can't do that. That, I think, is idiotic. So I'm not going to change that in my lifetime, but certainly I think, things are a little bit better than they were in the 1950s. Hopefully it'll never go back to the fifties. *That's* my agenda."[26]

PART FOUR

Technology

From Economics to Electronics:
The Making of an Activist

Lois Ross, a tall, slender blonde, grew up in a blue-collar union household. Her strong trade union sympathies and allegiance to working-class values went with her when she made the trip from her home in Bloomfield to the Rutgers College campus in New Brunswick, New Jersey. After graduating in 1977, Ross went to work for the Women in Apprenticeship Program (WAP). She spent the next seven years as an advocate on behalf of women breaking into skilled blue-collar jobs in New York City.

In 1986, she made the transition to a second career in electronics. The move didn't present any built-in barriers that often confront females: Ross had good math skills. She was familiar with the field and was able to see herself in it. She was interested in science and technology and knew she had an aptitude for it. She also possessed a great deal of determination—one of the key predictors of success amongst women entering nontraditional fields. As opportunities opened up, she was able to take advantage of them.

The difference between the welcome she received in her new career and the barriers women still face in the skilled blue-collar jobs serves to highlight the ongoing problem of sex segregation in the workplace. Within the last few decades, women have made both lateral and vertical moves into science and technology, whereas in skilled blue-collar jobs there's been very little movement in either direction. Today, there are 10 times the number of women working in the field of engineering than are employed in construction jobs.

Although great advances have been made in a whole host of occupations, the majority of women are still employed within a narrow range of traditional "female" jobs. Contrasting occupations in which females have made progress, such as science and technology, with those blue-collar jobs in which women have made little, highlights some of the reasons why there is a discrepancy between the outcomes. They in turn shed light on the enduring factors that prevail—in the workplace, educational institutions, employment offices, and in the home—and together, continue to undermine women and confine them to the female job ghetto.

From Economics to Activism

Nearly 200 years after Rutgers College was founded in 1776, the prestigious state school went coed. Lois Ross was a member of that first class of women in 1972. "There were 500 women and about 7 or 8 thousand men," she said.[1] Using a technique made popular by the women's movement, some of the female students started to meet to discuss issues they faced on campus and in the classroom. As Ross recalled, "We had a women's consciousness raising group on campus *because* we were the first class of women and there were some problems dealing with that. So women got together in my dorm and we had a weekly meeting, just a regular CR group."

Ross came from a blue-collar, working-class family and grew up in Bloomfield, New Jersey. Both of her parents worked in factories. Both were members of trade unions. "My father was an aerospace machinist," she recalled. "He worked in a plane factory making parts...for the Curtis Wright Corporation. He worked in a factory all his life, for about 40 years. He graduated from tech school and was someone who could fix a lot of things. I remember when I was a kid, if the vacuum cleaner was broken, he'd have it sitting on the table. And he'd do some magic on it and 10 minutes later, the thing would work. I thought he was magic! So that was my father.

> My mother worked in a factory most of her life, in Westinghouse. Then she stayed home for about 10 years when my sister and I were born, and then soon went back to work cleaning peoples' houses. My father was in the Machinists' union....They were both very vocal union supporters. They always told me unions are essential to working peoples' lives—without unions, working people would be nowhere.

In 1954—the year that Ross was born—her father's income as a skilled worker employed in a unionized manufacturing plant was sufficient to enable her mother to stay at home and care for their young children. This salary was the desirable "family wage" that trade unions had traditionally argued was the necessary prerequisite to support men in the workforce and their wives and children in the home.[2]

Although during the 1950s, there was little encouragement for women to seek professional careers, as always, some exceptional women did gain entrance to occupations and professions then off-limits. The year that Ross was born, the Treasurer of the United States was a woman. Decades before the American Express commercial aired on television, a signature served to prove the identity of the woman who wielded one of the nation's most powerful pens. In New York City in May 1954, "Mrs. Ivy Baker Priest had trouble getting a check cashed by a cautious hotel clerk. She asked him to compare her signature with one on a dollar bill. Her signature had appeared on all currency since January 1953, when she became treasurer of the United States."[3]

By the 1970s, momentum was on the side of women who were making the argument for gender equality in all areas. Throughout the decade, the cause of feminism continued to attract converts who challenged the notion of separate spheres for men and women. On August 26, 1970, the 50th anniversary of women's suffrage—the date when women finally won the long struggle to cast their votes—50,000 women in New York City and 100,000 nationwide marched in support of the first annual "Women's Strike for Equality." "Don't iron while the strike is hot," was a popular slogan of the day.[4]

At Rutgers, Ross got active in the feminist movement. She enlisted in the efforts to preserve safe and legal abortions for women. As she recalled, "There was a group called Committee for Abortion Rights and Against Sterilization Abuse, an abortion rights group, and my roommate and I ended up starting a New Brunswick chapter. [CARASA was a grassroots organization that supported women's right to obtain legal abortions.][5] We did a lot of work around that issue for a couple of years. We marched on Washington and did stuff like that."

Despite her fascination with her father's "magical" mechanical ability, Ross entered Rutgers University thinking she would eventually study law. Despite the message contained in the popular TV series of the day, starring "Perry Mason," as the lead attorney and "Della Street," as his able female assistant, she aspired to a career as an attorney.

But a big discovery awaited her in the classroom. In the eighteenth century, economics was dubbed the "dismal science." Yet after enrolling in an economics course, far from dismal, Ross found it liberating:

> I ended up getting some fairly radical professors who just happened to be at Rutgers and taught political economy. They didn't just teach plain old economics. They taught about power and how power is held, and how power is related to wealth. I had some sort of intuitive understanding of that. But when I actually started really studying it, it really fascinated me. So I decided to major in it after my very first course. It was with a radical economist, so it got me started.

Another economics class pointed her toward her future career. As she described it, "Just as I was leaving school, I took some labor economics courses. Women and the economy and occupational segregation—segregation by sex and race—was also a pretty hot topic. So I did some research papers on women and the economy, looking at why women made so much less than men and what was going on for women economically. There again, the big factor that stood out above everything was occupational segregation—women confined to certain jobs and excluded from others. I was really very, very interested in that." Although she received several offers for scholarships to pursue a Ph.D. in economics, she set out on a different path.

The Economics of Sex Discrimination

For decades, Paul Samuelson's "Economics" has been the standard textbook in college classrooms. The Ninth Edition was published in 1973 when Lois began studying the subject. In a chapter on discrimination, Samuelson reviewed the reasons why women operated at an economic disadvantage. At the time, women's full-time earnings averaged less than 60 percent of men's earnings. He employed some vivid demonstrations of the differences awaiting female college graduates when they finally entered the workplace:

> Female college graduates of the past enjoyed earning opportunities, over a lifetime, fully as unfavorable as male high school graduates...How can it be that there are relatively more honors graduates among the Radcliff fraction of Harvard students than among the males and yet, when the twenty-fifth reunion of the class compiles frequency distributions of full-time earnings, the men *begin* where the women *leave*

off in the salary scale? Little wonder, then, that school teaching and library jobs are considered to be high-paying for a woman and quite low-paying for a similarly qualified man. If you examine the organization charts of large corporations, banks, insurance companies, how is it that there are so many male mediocrities among the vice-presidents, and so few women with rank above that of assistant vice-president (and then usually for female personnel administration)? There is no need to belabor these facts, which are all too well known by everyone.[6]

Samuelson outlined some of what he called the "bad" reasons commonly offered by employers for excluding women. Though written more than 30 years ago, some still have a familiar ring: "Women are built by nature to tend babies in the home. They are emotional. They have monthly ups and downs. They cannot carry heavy weights. They lack self-confidence. Men will not work under a woman. Man-to-man talk will be inhibited by the presence of women.... If you mix men and women on the job, they will carry on to the detriment of efficiency and good morals.... If a woman does turn out to be a superlative economic performer, she's not feminine; she's harsh and aggressive, with a chip on her shoulder against men and the world.... Women workers, seeking pin money, take bread from the mouths of family breadwinners."[7]

As the Nobel Prize-winning professor pointed out, in an ideal, competitive world, irrational bigotry would be removed, and women would no longer be lumped into the female job ghetto, but would work alongside men, "each getting and deserving equal pay." But even then, certain obstacles would still get in the way of perfect equality: "One should not leave this subject with the notion that all differentials between racial, ethnic, or sexual groups are based upon discrimination. If that were so, the outlook for equality would be a more cheery one."[8]

Economists' use of the term "rational," refers to the assumption that employers will choose to maximize their profits by maximizing their prices and minimizing their costs. So, in making the decision to hire one of two workers, a rational employer will choose the one who is the most productive and costs the least. But, as Samuelson pointed out, even after irrational economic discrimination is removed, inequality will remain. "No mere banishing of prejudice and bigotry will be able to provide miraculous uniformity of opportunity and incomes." Due to differences, such as "human capital," meaning education, and "drive," meaning the individual's will to succeed, inequality will always exist.[9] He left out other sources of discrimination, such as institutional control of access to jobs by unions, yet another case of decision making based on "nonrational" considerations resulting in discrimination.

Yet Samuelson held out hope for change and concluded his assessment of discrimination on a positive note: "Economic analysis demonstrates that great gains can be expected from removal of irrational discrimination."[10]

Throughout the 1970s, economic evidence accumulated and underscored the point that concentrating 85 percent of women into a narrow range of employment categories—Samuelson's "female job ghetto"—led to a dampening effect on their wages. The academic work that made occupational segregation a "hot topic" while Ross was studying at Rutgers was done by economists Heidi Hartmann, Barbara Bergmann, and Barbara Reskin, among others. Their research on the significance of sex segregation in the workplace described the many factors—cultural, social, and institutional—that together add-up to preserve the female job ghetto. During the 1970s, "59 cents, to every man's dollar," became a common refrain.[11]

In the early 1980s, the National Research Council set up a Committee on Women's Employment and Related Social Issues to study the ongoing wage gap and other employment disparities between the sexes. The project concluded its work in 1986 with publication of a two-volume study, edited by Hartmann and Reskin. Together, Volume I, *Women's Work, Men's Work: Sex Segregation on the Job*, and Volume II, *Computer Chips and Paper Clips: Technology and Women's Employment*, provided a blueprint that clearly laid out the dynamics of discrimination. The scholars who contributed to the project also included a set of policy recommendations for, "ameliorating the waste to the economy, the financial loss to women and their families, and the demeaning of the human spirit that comes from the rigidities inherent in segregating jobs by sex."[12]

The goldmine of data, analysis, and recommendations contained in these studies are still invaluable, since the factors they identified more than 20 years ago continue to prevail—despite the passage of time. Like any set of blueprints, they can only be of value if they're put to use.

Equal Blue-Collar Employment Opportunity

After graduating from college in January 1977, Ross veered off the academic track. As she recalled, "I decided that I didn't want to stay in academia. I wanted to do something very practical. I wanted to be an activist. I wanted to make a difference and not just hide out in academia." She decided to fight discrimination and not just study it.

While working for a community group in New Jersey, Ross learned about Mary Garvin's efforts to recruit women for the skilled blue-collar jobs then opening up for women. She set aside her own plan to develop a program that would focus on occupational segregation: "I had actually written a proposal to get women into nontraditional jobs. I was maybe a quarter of the way through writing it and I was going to apply [for funding] to the New Jersey Department of Education, which was doing some work around that area."

The WAP starting up in New York City sounded like an ideal opportunity and Ross explored the option. "It was exactly what I was trying to do in New Jersey. So I went to talk with her and she hired me...My job was recruitment, counseling, and job development. Our first job was to get the word out that we were there."

Due to changes in the law and organized pressure from the women's movement, new occupational opportunities were opening up for females in the highly paid skilled trades. This provided a practical experiment. Would women seize the chance to enter occupational fields that were traditionally male-dominated? WAP provided one door for willing women to walk through, and Ross was now on the other side waiting to help.

At this point, WAP was functioning as an informal organization with a bottom-up perspective. Ross described how the group operated in the beginning: "We were very much a grassroots group at that point. All the women who were doing the counseling were pretty grassroots. And Mary was herself a carpenter."[13]

The initial efforts at recruitment by the fledgling organization were wildly successful: "We did a lot of radio and I think some TV," Ross recalled. "Mary Garvin was the spokesperson. And phone calls just started pouring in. I'll never forget the first time she went on the radio—the phone rang off the hook the entire day....But we didn't know if 20 people would call [or] nobody would call. We had no idea. I think, by the [end of] the first week, we had a hundred people signed up."[14]

> We went out and spoke at different women's groups. We went anywhere we were requested to go and spoke everywhere. Then women would come in and we'd have an interview process. We would talk to them about their background.

The counselors helped to prepare the recruits for what they were about to face. According to Ross, "We tried to present the picture as real as we could, so we wouldn't get people being discouraged and dropping out.... We were orienting women, [and] trying to give them a sense of what the jobs were like; what kind of skills were needed for the jobs; what they would be up against in terms of discrimination and hostility. We helped them to fill out applications for the electricians' union, and the plumbers' union, 'cause you had to go through that whole process with the apprenticeship program[s]. So there was a lot of prep work that had to be done with the women. We probably talked to hundreds, maybe thousands of women initially."

The women who learned about WAP and were willing to try a new trade came from a variety of backgrounds. Some welfare recipients were enrolled in the Work Incentive Program (WIN). Well before President Clinton's much maligned "welfare reform" in the mid-'90s, work requirements were being imposed on women dependent on welfare. Beginning in 1968, the WIN program provided training and job placement services to recipients of AFDC, for both unemployed fathers and female heads of households. "The Work Incentive Program was notified of our program, so we received a lot of women from what was called 'WIN' at that time," Ross recalled.

The screening process at WAP, in addition to identifying basic qualifications such as age and education set out by the union apprenticeship programs, tried to identify other, often intangible qualities in the recruits. As Ross explained, "I think an understanding that they had to be willing to really stick this out and they had to really want to do this kind of work." She recalled that the interviewers also tried to identify experiences the potential recruits had doing manual labor or working with tools. They wanted to learn about, "any exposure of any kind to construction work. Anything they had done in their own home, like build a cabinet. Any informal type of work, we looked at very closely. One woman had done painting. She was an artist. We got her a job painting boats in a boat yard. They wanted someone who could paint. So she ended up doing that for a long time."

After seven years as an advocate, Ross found that her enthusiasm for WAP was waning. Originally in 1979, when she began working with Mary Garvin, their mutual goal was to empower the women who were willing to enter skilled, nontraditional jobs. Everybody was "starting from scratch."[15] This required a tremendous amount of determination on the part of the recruits, and the experiences at WAP were designed to shore up a sense of common struggle.

> The first group of women who came through were aggressive, assertive. They knew what they wanted and they were determined to get it. With some, it was political and with some it was just the force of personality. The first women, it was not an issue.... It was understood that, "Hey, I'm going to have to get out there and bust balls to get this job."[16]

But as things changed, Lois decided to bail out: "I left because I saw the whole original, grassroots organizing type of atmosphere, where we organized women to do for themselves, as opposed to social work stuff, you know: 'We'll get you a job.'"

Lois felt that the change in emphasis had the effect of undermining the women who enrolled in the program. Their sense of self-determination and willingness to stay the difficult course ahead of them was weakened if, "they didn't have a sense of the struggle, of what it took to even get to the point where they could be in a position to get a job."

At WAP, Ross worked to develop placements for women in skilled trades' jobs and in apprenticeship and training programs. After a few years and the initial receptiveness, she found that contractors and employers in general were developing a resistance to hiring women.

"It got more and more difficult to get women jobs," she said. "It really did, after the initial burst, the first couple of years."[17] Ross described her experiences as a job developer, a task that required constant care and attention. Mary Garvin, Ross, and the other staff at WAP met with the unions and other employers. As she recalled, "We met with everybody who would meet with us—all the apprenticeship programs. We sent letters and had meetings. Any pull, any connection we had, we would use to get an 'in.' It was really difficult. I remember, I met with Con Edison and AT&T. You know, it wasn't AT&T—it was New York Tel at that point...and Brooklyn Union Gas."

We met with all the big employers who might have federal contracts. We were especially focusing on people with federal or state contracts because they were more likely to be responsive to us. Usually you'd have to follow-up for maybe a year before you even got a promise of a job. And they would give you one or two jobs here and there. It was like: "Okay. Now we've got our token woman. Now don't bother us anymore." It wasn't that difficult to get the first few jobs, but to get a steady stream of jobs after that was very difficult, once they got their token women. She perceived a shift in the mission of the organization, as it developed closer ties to its funding sources. "Women in Apprenticeship—it was really kind of a bureaucracy and their hands were partly tied by being state-funded."

"Women in Apprenticeship changed its name to Nontraditional Employment for Women—NEW—when it became a training organization for women going into the trades and other skilled jobs." From her perspective, this was the point that WAP changed from being part of a social movement to becoming a typical, bureaucratic, top-down nonprofit organization. Although its mission remained worthy, its behavior and basis for decision making changed. The days when WAP would organize women to take to the streets with pots and pans in pursuit of their goal of construction jobs were over.

With a new executive director on board, Ross found herself disagreeing with many of the changes being implemented: "She was very tight-fisted as to how she wanted the place run. She brought in social workers who were apolitical and inexperienced with tradeswomen. She deliberately eased out people who were political, who were young and ready to get out there and make some noise. And that's an example of what can happen in a women's organization when it's taken over by a larger organization with other political agendas. So I never really related to NEW very well after she eased out the more grassroots people and put in the social worker types."[18]

Shortly before leaving the organization, Ross had an experience that underscored the shift in the mission: "I remember actually, before I left, I did a workshop for women. I used to do a lot of workshops to introduce women to what we do. And I said, 'We're not here to get you a job. We're here to assist you and give you the skills and the knowledge that you need to get out there and get yourself a job.' Well that caused a big uproar! I heard about it later: 'What do you mean? You're telling women that we're not here to get them jobs?' 'Well,' I said. 'We're here to assist women, not to hand out jobs.'"

The training NEW provided for women did prove to be very successful. Lois developed an appreciation for the program and for the skill it took to keep it funded: "The executive director was able to keep the funding coming through her connections. It was a very good program. And she was particularly good for the program in that she really kept the money flowing and expanded into training. It was good because it was very specific training for women, instead of just throwing [them] into the other programs. I think it was a good move to make. But again, the organization had changed. It became more and more bureaucratic and less grassroots, less activist-oriented, more into social work, which I didn't feel very comfortable in, so I left."[19]

Ross realized she was experiencing a classic case of burnout. As she described it, "I was totally burnt to a crisp."[20] She decided it was time to take on a new, albeit related, challenge.

A "Trade" of Her Own

Ross's experience at WAP contributed to the choice of her new career: "I decided to go to electronics school. I had placed a number of women in electronics jobs and they seemed to really enjoy it. It looked like an interesting job. And they were getting paid very well. And I'd always liked math and physics. I said, 'Let me just try this out!' So I took an electrical wiring course for free at Brooklyn Tech and I loved it. I did very well at it. I said, 'Well, this is something maybe I could do.' Then I enrolled in New York City Tech."[21]

Another factor in her decision to study electronics was the length of the program being offered at the school: "It took me a year and a half," she explained. "That was another thing, 'cause I could get in and get out pretty quickly."

She felt the need to try a different type of work, something that didn't require nurturing:

To be perfectly honest, I was totally burnt out working with people! I was. It was just emotionally draining, at that point. I wanted to do something that did not involve taking care of people. So actually, it was a very deliberate decision to move away from a care-taking type of thing. See, I'm not a social worker. I am really an organizer. And when the job moved more and more from organizing to [a] social work type of thing, it just became less suitable for me. I was too burnt out to keep organizing, at that point. I said, "Let me go back to school and do something that I can make a little money too. So I really liked it. I just found that I had an aptitude for it."

Once in school, her activist nature kicked into gear. "We started a group at school called Technicians for Social Responsibility. We talked about technology and critiqued ways that technology was being used that were not so hot. So it was really fun!"

Studying electronics, Ross was still on a "nontraditional" employment track. The number of women enrolled in her program was well below the 25 percent it would take to classify electronics as a "traditional" field of employment for females. As she recalled, "There were four women out of hundreds of guys."

Nearing the end of her training, she attended a career fair to learn about the opportunities in her field. Here she discovered what was to become her new career: biomedical engineering. At the departmental career day sponsored by her school, she heard presentations about different job opportunities:

> My co-worker now was the person I heard speaking at New York City Tech about biomedical engineering. He was so eloquent, really. As soon as I heard him speak, I knew that was what I wanted to do—immediately! He cast it as a very responsible job for someone who cared about people. The work you were doing was directly related to saving peoples' lives. It required a sense of responsibility because...you could hurt someone if you didn't do a good job on the equipment. So I guess that's what I liked. Also, it wasn't nuclear war and it wasn't the military.

Ross was looking for a place to use her skills that would contribute to her vision of a just world. The niche she found called on her new technical skills and was in harmony with her sense of social responsibility. "If you're going to be in electronics, it's a great place to be because you're very aware of the human consequences of what you do," she said.

Even before completing her program, Ross landed a job working part-time in biomedical engineering. Then, in 1984, she went to work in Jersey City and Hoboken, New Jersey, after graduating from the program. "I worked at two different hospitals at the same time," she explained. "I learned a lot there because there were just two of us on the job and I had to learn everything fast! So I learned a tremendous amount. On my job, I have to know a lot about physiology and clinical practice, and how the equipment is used in surgery. I have to know not just the equipment, but the whole procedure and what's going on. So it's very interesting. I get to know a lot."

In 1986, she joined the biomedical engineering department at St. Luke's-Roosevelt Hospital in New York City. The demands of the larger department opened up new challenges. One part of the job required that she develop in-service training courses for the staff. As she explained in 1996: "In fact, I organized most of them. We [just] did a video for a course on pacemakers. We did a course on external pacemakers. Instead of implanting wires in the body, they can pace someone from the surface of the body. And that's a very different kind of technology, so you have to learn about that, and other technologies, as they develop. Laser technology is now increasing in use, and I have to learn about lasers, which I've been doing. I'm in charge of the whole laser program here now. So as things move along, it's interesting. It's not always interesting, but it's often interesting," she offered with a laugh.

Teaching became an increasingly important part of her job. As she noted, "I've trained most of the technicians here and written a lot of the procedures for training. I've organized a lot of technical seminars. My passion, really, is teaching."

The field of biomedical engineering is dependent upon on-the-job training. As Ross described the process, "You study electronics generally. Then you are actually trained on the job, because no one can know what a pacemaker is like. I mean, where are you going to work on a pacemaker except in a hospital? Or laser [technology]? So it really is on-the-job training here."

In 1992, another opportunity for advancement opened up when the hospital expanded. Ross explained how her promotion came about: "We were actually building two new hospitals and we were going to get completely new equipment for both. They needed someone to supervise that whole process and make sure the installment went well and the equipment was checked out properly and installed. And we hired seven new people to do that, and we needed someone to run the team. I was the logical person because I know the equipment really well and I'm rated well to work with the staff."

Once again, training medical personnel was an important part of her job: "When we installed the new hospital with all the new equipment, nobody knew [how to use] any of this equipment. That was one of our biggest jobs, to be on hand so people could learn from us. We would train people and stand by the first few days to make sure that they were okay with it."

Ross also taught in other venues. She shared her enthusiasm for engineering when she taught an introductory class for blue-collar employees at the Port Authority.[22] Next, she taught a similar class for railroad workers:

> I taught at New York City Tech. I was an assistant teacher there for the electronics lab. My favorite thing was a pre-engineering course for Metro North workers. We had a great time learning about what engineering is, sort of critiques of engineering: what are the different aspects of engineering; safety issues; ethical issues; math; computers. Metro North wanted to upgrade their staff and have their people become more technically proficient. They're trying to encourage people to go to engineering school. Their technology is changing very rapidly and people are going to be out of work if they don't update their skills.[23]

She enjoyed her role in bolstering the students' confidence in their own abilities. "It was exciting to give the [students] a sense that they would be able to survive school and to learn and move on," she said. "I think people came out of that with a great sense of self-esteem."

Her own feelings of competency and assuredness on the job grew as she accumulated some experience. "I feel very confident on this job," Ross said. "I really do." That was not always the case. As she explained, "I think it took me about five years. I used to be afraid, sometimes, if I got a new piece of equipment in and I didn't know it. I was like: 'Oh my gosh! How am I going to repair this?' Now, I'm just like; 'Give me anything.' After about five years, I felt very, very confident. I just feel like I can pretty much do anything. It's sort of like learning music. Once you've learned the music and you've kind of gotten over the hurdle of being able to read music, people can give you almost anything and you can play. You might fumble along for a while, but..." the critical component of the job is the ability to absorb information and to use it to analyze a technical problem.

As a supervisor, Ross was instrumental in bringing other women into the biomedical engineering department at St. Luke's-Roosevelt Hospital. She described the sense of personal satisfaction involved: "I was able to help get two women hired, which is phenomenal. There are three women on my job, which is almost unheard of. Most departments in the city have *no* women. And that was on my own, really, pushing very hard for that. I felt good about it. I was able to do that and [to] give them a lot of support on the job. And we support each other. It's real nice."

The small number of women in her field has always been a concern. By 1996, she still felt that women were not making enough headway in electronics. "In my field, it hasn't changed in 20 years," she said.[24] "There's still approximately four percent in engineering. I'm a technician. I'm not an engineer. [There are] just very, very few women. There's still a long way to go. It would be nice if there was a program for women in technical jobs."[25]

Ross' recognition of the ongoing need for programs to recruit and mentor women in technical fields was confirmed when she ventured out to explore her own career options. As she described her experience, "I went on an interview [in 1996] for a biomedical job. It was a supervisory position, actually, it was [for] a department head, but the guy didn't want to pay the person for a department head, so he called it a supervisor. I am highly, highly qualified. I already do the job here at a much bigger hospital. This was a very small hospital. I supervise 10 people now. This was [to be supervising] about three people."

> I'm very concerned about how the men will react to you. I don't think they're going to like having a woman here. He actually said this in an interview. I was surprised he said it. I was very, very angry. I just said, "I work with all men, mostly. I have no problem being respected." So, I mean, the fact that he could ask that question in 1996 of someone who is, beyond doubt, highly over-qualified even, for the job, and to bring up the fact that I'm a woman, I just thought was abominable. It just shows that this issue is very real. It's very much alive. It's out there on all levels of society— all levels of society. So it makes me angry!

Expert Allies for the Next Generation

While Lois Ross encountered resistance from unions and employers when she worked for WAP, trying to bring women on board as skilled blue-collar workers, she had a different kind of experience in her new field as a technician. She was able to enter the training program without difficulty. She was able to learn both in the classroom and on-the-job. The skills and knowledge she needed to do the work were not withheld from her. She received mentoring, support, and encouragement. She received promotions. She received the respect of her supervisors and peers. All of the things that permit people to succeed at their work and are taken for granted in most fields. Despite the attitude expressed by the man who interviewed her in 1996 for a supervisory position, in general, she found a high-level of acceptance within her field.

Statistics show that women's participation in technical and scientific fields stands in striking contrast to the early 1960s. In 1962, the astronaut John Glenn, the first American to orbit the earth, spoke before the U.S. Congress. His message was that there was no place for women in the nation's space program. "It is just a fact. The men go off and fight the wars and fly the airplanes and come back and help design and build and test them. The fact that women are not in this field is a fact of our social order," he said. The first female pilots who had prepared themselves to enter the space program and dubbed themselves the "Mercury 12" were denied that opportunity. It took several decades for female pilots and scientists to finally prove that they had "the right stuff" to be included in NASA's space program.[26]

Despite the slow start, tremendous headway in these historically male fields has been made. Currently, women make up 20 percent of the workforce in science, engineering, and technology development.[27] Although obstacles remain, many programs are now in place to introduce young women to fields such as computer science, engineering, and robotics. Mentoring programs and professional associations for women in science abound.

Yet choices and opportunities are much bleaker for young women who are *not* college-bound. A report by the National Women's Law Center in 2002 documented "the startling degree" to which gender-based assumptions still flourish in one of the most important educational venues for blue-collar youth. The study, based on data from 12 states, including New York and California, showed that in much of the country, high school vocational and technical courses remain nearly as segregated by sex as they were 30 years ago.[28]

Although girls make up 96 percent of the students enrolled in cosmetology courses, 86 percent in home health aide courses, and 87 percent in child care courses, more than 90 percent of students enrolled in automotive, carpentry, and plumbing courses are boys. A review of New York City's vocational education programs in 2001 showed that they remain highly segregated by sex. The predominantly female schools offered almost no advanced math or science courses. On the other hand, the predominantly male vocational schools were able to offer special programs providing entry into computer technology jobs.

Programs funded by state and federal dollars—vocational schools, job training programs, and state employment agencies—demonstrate either a widespread bias or an almost total lack of awareness that many women may be interested in other kinds of careers in "nontraditional" employment. Meanwhile, case managers and vocational counselors continue to steer females into programs that prepare them for "women's work"—low-wage work such as child care, cosmetology, hospitality, and general clerical work.

Meanwhile, the Institute for Women's Policy Research, headed by Heidi Hartmann, continues to chart the disparities and their consequences in all their depressing detail. The Institute's report, "Still a Man's Labor Market: The Long Term Earnings Gap," issued in 2004, documents the ongoing sex segregation in the workplace and the economic consequences for female wage earners:

> Within each of the six major occupational categories in the labor market, at least 75 percent of the workers are of one gender, and "women's jobs" pay less. Perhaps because of the generally low pay scales in the female career occupations, only 8 percent of men work in them. In contrast, 15 percent of continuously employed women, apparently more eager to seek higher-paying male jobs, work consistently in male occupations. These women, however, earn one-third less than their male counterparts in male elite and less-skilled jobs. Among the few women who make it into the middle-tier of good male jobs (the skilled blue-collar jobs), the more formal wage structures (due to unions and civil service regulations) mean that their pay lags men's by only one-fifth. Increasing women's entry into this tier of male good jobs would thus increase their earnings substantially. For the preponderance of women who remain in the female sector of each tier, earnings are strikingly low.[29]

Tremendous possibilities are open in a wide array of technological fields, including electronics. Young women need to understand the full range of options—receive encouragement to explore these options—and made to feel welcome when they show up to take advantage of them.[30]

To get out of the female job ghetto, women need some essential skills, a certain mindset, and opportunities to develop these building blocks, including math skills. The Access for Women program in Brooklyn offers an opportunity to overcome the fear of math and to take basic, hands-on courses in electronics and building maintenance. The same program that extended this opportunity to Lois Ross back in 1986 is still offering a chance to young girls and women to sharpen and gain mastery over a new set of skills. Director Nona Smith finds ways to instill confidence and overcome inner resistance to learning basic competencies in math and science. She succeeded in convincing the Metropolitan Transportation

Authority to become a partner with her in providing an electronics course beginning in the fall of 2007.[31]

Building on her interest in making the burgeoning field of electronics accessible to others and her passion for teaching, Lois Ross pursued a Master's degree in communications, computing, and technology. Since her graduation from Teachers' College at Columbia University in 2001, she has been designing curriculum and teaching innovative courses on computers, engineering, and electronics.

Ross is determined to develop better—more successful—methods to introduce the wonders of technology to young women. Toward this goal, she is preparing a grant proposal for the National Science Foundation with an emphasis on changing the way that engineering education takes place in the classroom. Meanwhile, she's designed courses for employees of the city's transit and rail systems that explore both the basics and the creative aspects of electronic engineering. Chances are that she will once again be back in Brooklyn, this time at the head of the class, teaching the MTA course in electronics at Access for Women.[32]

TEN

That's Just the Way It Was: AT&T and the Struggle for Equal Opportunity

Certain stories of working-class women in America gain currency—usually with the help of Hollywood. One is that of Crystal Lee Jordan, whose life story was fictionalized in the popular film of the 1970s, *Norma Rae*. The movie depicts an organizing drive to bring a union into a cotton mill. The real story was based on the long battle to organize a union at the J.P. Stevens mill in Roanoke Rapids, North Carolina.[1] The character Norma Rae represents the latest generation employed by the mill where she works alongside her mother and father. Although they hesitate out of fear to embrace the cause of unionization, Norma Rae becomes a firebrand. The photo of Sally Fields as Norma Rae, standing on the table to hold aloft her message to her workmates—"UNION"—moments before being dragged from the plant by police, has assumed an iconic status.

The movie concludes on a high note, as election ballots are counted and the union wins the right to represent the workers. As anybody who has participated in a union organizing drive knows, this victorious ending is premature. The struggle to get a contract and to keep union supporters on the job accelerates *after* the vote count. A powerful sequel to Norma Rae could show that next stage—when the battle is really joined.

Likewise, the stories about the combatants in the battle for affirmative action often stop at the plant gates. Women and minorities win the right to the job. But turns out, this is just the beginning of what frequently proves to be an even tougher struggle to get to the next stage: acceptance.

In 1970, American Telegraph & Telephone (AT&T) was the largest private corporation in the United States and the single largest employer of women. The communications monopoly enjoyed a reputation for progressive, forward-looking employment policies. The reality was that jobs were allocated along sex- and race-segregated lines. The Equal Employment Opportunity Commission (EEOC), created by the Civil Rights Act of 1964, with no enforcement powers, was still trying to figure out how to accomplish its mission regarding sex discrimination in the workplace. The National Organization for Women (NOW), was in its prime. Promoting employment equality for white- and blue-collar women was a high priority on its ambitious agenda. The paths of all three—the company, the agency, and the advocates—converged in 1970 when AT&T was selected as the ideal vehicle for the EEOC to challenge the employment practices of American corporations.[2]

In 1966, NOW came into existence largely out of a real concern over employment discrimination and the reluctance of the EEOC to address the issue. The telephone company was one of its first targets. The campaign orchestrated and carried out by NOW activists set an ambitious agenda for itself. Blue-collar women were included in its mission. A national task force and activist chapters compiled data documenting discriminatory patterns that violated the Title VII provisions of the Civil Rights Act. The case against the phone company was presented to the EEOC, as the agency charged with investigating employment discrimination. The case put together by NOW gained momentum in December 1970, when the EEOC took on the task of examining employment practices at the huge telecommunications monopoly.[3]

The government and the company came to an agreement in 1973. At that point, new career paths opened up for phone company employees. Job possibilities broadened for men and women—males were now encouraged to enter the female preserves of telephone operators and clerks and women became eligible for the skilled craft jobs and professional positions formerly off-limits for females.[4]

After the first consent decree was signed, the focus amongst middle-class women in management and professional positions stayed firmly on career advancement.[5] However, the objective was much more diffuse when it came to working-class women inside the system. Although white-collar women received support and even official sanction for their organizing efforts within the company, women who went to work in the skilled craft jobs traditionally done by men met up with a hostile environment in the workplace and stonewalling from their elected union officials. And union activists were caught up in responding to a climate of ever-greater management control in the workplace.

Although women working in the skilled blue-collar jobs did make gains, they had a tough time doing so. Their numbers remained more negligible than necessary, and their individual roads more difficult, whereas professional women throughout the system scored major improvements. And race ended up taking a back seat to gender in the implementation of the EEOC consent decrees within the communications monopoly.[6]

This story offers a rich stew, with many players and great promise. But ultimately, it underscores the opportunities lost in the long struggle to build a more vibrant model for meaningful affirmative action for blue-collar women in the American workplace.

"One Ring-y Dingy:" The Phone Company, Paternalism, and Women's Place

Lilly Tomlin's comedic genius created a popular character who greeted the nation every week on NBC's *Rowan and Martin's Laugh-In*—Ernestine, the overly curious, energetic, always opinionated, telephone operator with the distinctive snort. From December 1969 until *Laugh-In* went off the air in 1973, Tomlin's irascible operator always began conversations with her callers with the words: "One Ring-y Dingy." Her "signature headset and plug board that made listening in on everybody's conversation easy" made Ernestine a familiar figure.[7] Meanwhile, the actual conditions for the real, live operators were no laughing matter.

In earlier decades, the Bell System popularized other phrases to identify the ubiquitous operators and to convey the desired decorum prescribed for these employees. The person behind "The Voice with a Smile" was trained to project courtesy, in a clearly enunciated, pleasing tone.[8] With few exceptions, until the late 1960s, the voice belonged to a white female. For generation after generation, the phone company was a family affair, a patriarchal arrangement that reflected a strict adherence to gender and racial stereotypes. White males performed the technical jobs and ruled from the upper reaches of management; white females performed the routine, repetitive jobs that required a nurturing nature to accommodate the customer and manage the clerks and operators in the front ranks.[9]

In 1942, Catherine Conroy went to work as an operator for the phone company in Wisconsin. The job bored her so much that she soon moved on to another job as a trainer. She then took part in the campaign to organize a union for phone workers, eventually becoming a full-time union representative. Her background, both on the job and as a union advocate for Bell System employees, schooled her in the realities of sex and race discrimination. She gained experience in combating systemic hiring and promotion practices that held women back—especially minority women—and this fueled her participation in the feminist movement.

Conroy described just how dull and programmed was the position of operator at the phone company: "We still had a number of offices where the operator all day long said, 'Number please. Thank you,' and plugged into a current connecting one customer to another...If I hadn't had the opportunity to get away from that board, I think I would have quit because I couldn't stand it...The system had it down to such a time and motion study routine. Where you put your hands and how you put your feet on the floor and how you sat—everything was programmed...The paternalism was just so bad. It was kind of the Mother Bell family. Everyone was expected to conform. They told us how to look. They told us how to act...There was no tolerance for any misbehaving or breaking of the rules...They didn't fire you so fast, but they nagged you to death, and that interference in every move you made and everything you did really turned me off."[10]

As Conroy assumed greater levels of responsibility within the Communications Workers of America, she was able to see the overall pattern that prevailed within the company: "The whole history of the Bell System has demonstrated...that men went in one door to one office and women went in the other. And women got just so far in the system on any kind of job. All the best jobs, all the top jobs, all second level, third level, fourth level, fifth level [jobs], were always male—always."[11]

Even as women moved into a broader range of positions in the late 1960s, limits based on gender were still firmly in place. The strict code of conduct and decorum extended even to clothing: pantsuits, an item enjoying popularity in the sixties, were prohibited according to the company's dress code. Skirts and dresses were required. But change was coming, as restrictions based on gender biases began to grate on female employees. Women throughout the system were beginning to recognize the prevalence of sex discrimination. Soon they were backed up, not only by the law, but by a women's movement that understood the importance of organizing, and an agency that finally began to use the power it did have to enforce the law.[12]

Dial "0" for Oppression

The inclusion of sex as a category in the provisions of the civil rights bill was first proposed as a joke by segregationist Rep. Howard D. Smith—as a reduction ad *absurdum* to derail the debate taking place in the U.S. House of Representatives. But the proposal gained adherents who successfully argued on its behalf. Rep. Katherine St. George, a Democrat from New York, put it succinctly: "Women are entitled to this little crumb of equality. The addition of the little, terrifying word—SEX—will not hurt this legislation in any way." But the addition of that three-letter word to the Civil Rights Act of 1964 with its Title VII provisions for equal employment, suddenly guaranteed a new legal basis for economic rights for all Americans.[13] The trick was to turn the legal presumption into a reality borne out in the lives of real women. At first, it was slow-going.

That Title VII had the potential to bring about huge changes in the lives of working women was immediately apparent to some. Betty Friedan, still in the limelight from the success of her 1963 book, *The Feminine Mystique*, was certainly in the forefront of those who were paying attention. As Friedan recalled, she spotted a story in *The New York Times* about a Yale Law School professor named Pauli Murray, who had observed that, "Unless women were prepared to march on Washington as the black people had done, the sex discrimination provisions in Title VII would never get enforced and women would lose their historic chance."[14]

Murray, an African-American, an attorney, and a scholar, was a pioneer in her own right. She was one of the women who served as a bridge between two generations of female activists and two movements—the Women's Movement and the Civil Rights Movement. Soon after the EEOC set up to do business, Pauli Murray was on the inside. Working at the agency, she was able to witness firsthand the lassitude when it came to enforcing provisions of Title VII related to sex. She was only one of the powerful women with a direct link to the agency who understood that most of the EEOC Commissioners would have to be educated about the definition of sex discrimination and then prodded into playing an active role to dismantle it.[15]

At the EEOC, the addition of sex discrimination seemed frivolous. Although confusion prevailed at the agency about the definition of what actually constituted sex discrimination, women knew it when they saw it. Fully one-quarter of the complaints filed with the EEOC within the first year came from working women. They were ready to contest inequities when they encountered them, now that they had a vehicle to do so. The lever that was soon to be wedged under the world as women knew it was employment.[16]

Telephone worker Lorena Weeks was one of those women who didn't have trouble figuring out when she was being discriminated against on the job. In 1966, the Southern Bell employee from Wadley, Georgia, a single mother of two, applied for a better paying job that was closer to her home. The company turned down the 19-year employee's application for the job of "switchman." They based the denial on state labor law enacted decades earlier to protect women from onerous conditions, such as night work and heavy lifting requirements. Southern Bell argued that there were bona fide occupational qualifications for the job that precluded females from filling them. Weeks filed a complaint with the EEOC. From her initial push to move into this job, throughout the five years it took to win her case, and even after getting into the plant doing the job she sought, Weeks was harassed. She described the constant level of opposition she faced at work as, "almost unbearable at times."[17]

She stood up alone. As her case slowly wound its way through the system, she eventually ended up in federal court. But she wasn't alone in the pursuit of her single-minded objective. Shortly after she began her journey through the EEOC system, her cause was taken up by NOW. The Weeks case became a cause for thousands of women across the country who championed her right to work in the job of her choice. It was part of the huge campaign launched by NOW to address the systemic discrimination within the company.[18] Ultimately, the EEOC embraced a different approach to eliminating discrimination—away from the pursuit of individual, case-by-case complaints—to a broader, institutional strategy for achieving appropriate relief from discrimination at AT&T. Weeks—after losing in the lower court—got support from NOW that enabled her to appeal the case.[19]

In March 1969, Judge Griffin Bell, a future attorney general, ruled that Southern Bell had to put Weeks to work as a switchman. She got the job, along with a back pay settlement. Harassment was still a part of her life in the plant. But through her endurance and determination, her court case established a legal precedent.

In *Weeks v. Southern Bell Telephone & Telegraph Co.*, the Fifth Circuit Court of Appeals ruled that "an employer could rely on the bona fide occupational qualification exception only by proving that he had ... a factual basis for believing that all or substantially all women would be unable to perform safely and efficiently the duties of the job involved." In his opinion, Judge Bell wrote that, "Title VII vests individual women with the power to decide whether or not to take on unromantic tasks—an autonomy that men have always had."[20]

In 1970, the EEOC took on the whole Bell System and its discriminatory treatment of minorities and women. In effect, the huge scope of the case offered the agency a perfect platform to showcase what compliance with Title VII required from American corporations. After completing a complex and painstaking investigation, the EEOC issued its findings in 1971. Voluminous in size and comprehensive in detail, the official report—"An Unusual Competence"—labeled Ma Bell "the largest oppressor of women." At this point, one out of every 56 working women in the United States was employed by the system. Lorena Weeks was one of the individuals who testified before the EEOC/Federal Communications Commission hearings on AT&T and thus helped to pry open the doors to the skilled craft jobs for other women. As she did so, she had a whole movement behind her.[21]

As NOW set out to challenge this sexist edifice complex, a battle plan evolved. Activists in chapters across the country poured their passion into putting Ma Bell's practices in violation of Title VII in the spotlight. Frustrated by the limits they faced as Bell System employees, members of NOW working for the company set out to organize in-house Women's Rights Committees. They then channeled their issues and insider's knowledge into outside agitation. This combination produced reams of credible evidence that NOW activists then took into the streets, corporate boardrooms, and presented before regulatory bodies.[22]

Sociologist Sally Hacker was one of the many professional/activist women who lent her expertise to building the case against the company in damning detail. The dynamic nature of the campaign and its broad scope are evident in documents sent out to share the strategies designed to hold the corporation accountable and to call attention to its practices. The robust and humanistic nature of feminism as practiced by NOW at that early stage is manifest in the breadth of the demands and the inclusive vision for reforming corporate practices that were oppressing the workforce.[23]

In June 1972, Hacker prepared a memo on a national action plan for AT&T. The broad range of issues of concern to NOW activists included Bell system practices that, "exploit and dehumanize its workers—particularly women ... We might begin to think about adding to our usual list of affirmative action demands, the demand that *nobody* be asked to do jobs in the way Bell sets up some of theirs—e.g., operators. These jobs should be reorganized more humanely, and workers at all levels should have more control over their working conditions. If we are truly working toward a feminist-humanist society, let's begin to *change*—not merely *get into*—some of these powerful and oppressive institutions."[24]

Tool Belts of Their Own

Venus Green and Ilene Winkler were among the ranks of women attracted by the high pay of the telecommunications jobs that now opened up to women. After getting hired, both women attended the training school run by the local phone company, New York Telephone, and went to work in a job with a title—switchman—that left no doubt about who had filled it before the terms of the consent agreement. It took some time before the company changed the name of the job to switching equipment technician. In time, both women served as shop stewards for Local 1101 of the Communications Workers of America (CWA), the union that went into court to try to short-circuit the agreement signed by the company.

Both women began their careers in 1974. Green used her paycheck to pursue an expensive, elite education at Columbia University. Her dissertation was turned into a book: *Race on the Line: Gender, Labor and Technology in the Bell System*. Winkler stuck to the path of rank-and-file activist throughout her career. For years, she participated in a caucus of her fellow workers that put out a newsletter—*The Bell Wringer*—and eventually ran oppositional slates for elected office in the local. After 28 years as a skilled technician, Winkler retired.

Venus Green and Ilene Winkler were each activists, feminists, and politically conscious women. Yet neither was drawn to the job by consciousness but rather by the lure of a man-sized paycheck. Green, a graduate of Hunter College, was in one of the first groups that included women. She described her motivation for taking the job:

> I had been working in publishing, getting no money, and I was [an] assistant to [a] managing editor at Random House. No pay, no possibility of moving forward. I went back to school one day and a friend of mine was at school and she had on a tool belt and the whole deal. She worked for AT&T and made loads of money compared to what I was making in this publishing job. She suggested that I go [apply] because they were hiring women at the telephone company. That's how I became a switching equipment technician...I was looking at it from the perspective that I wouldn't have to type and I would have a skill...It's funny because I knew about the [EEOC] case, but I didn't connect the case to the job at that very moment.[25]

Ilene Winkler, a college graduate, was also employed in the low-paid precincts of publishing when she heard that the phone company was hiring: "It wasn't anything that I was interested in at all. It just seemed like a good paying job. The starting pay for the job was the top pay for the [work] I was doing before, a low-level publishing company job. It just seemed like an interesting place and I don't think I gave it that much thought."[26]

The company's training program consisted of lectures on technical topics—the principles of electricity, the basics of computers—esoteric subjects for the women as well as for many of the men. Early on, Winkler and the other women going through the classes made common cause. She attributed her ability to survive in a strange and predominantly male environment to this support:

> I think the solidarity and having other women to talk to about what it was you were going through was just so important...This whole bunch of us used to have lunch together. I don't think I ever would have survived it if I had to do it by myself. I think it was invaluable.[27]

After six months of training, the women joined the men on the job—working in the "switch room" or on the "frame." Each had devised her own strategies to make it through the school, which had a high dropout rate for both genders. As Green explained, she was good at absorbing a lot of written information and regurgitating it on tests. Once they were on the job, figuring out how to perform the given tasks, get the work done, deal with new co-workers, and survive proved to be a much greater challenge.

Collision: Equal Opportunity
Meets Up with Obstacles

Litigation got women the jobs. AT&T provided the training. But women still faced enormous obstacles once on the job. The EEOC agreement fell short on a number of counts. One was the failure on the part of management and the unions to prepare for the entrance of the new-comers and to respond to their issues once they were on the job.

Certain clashes were inevitable as the terms of the settlement were being carried out. It stands to reason that the white men occupying these skilled positions would feel threatened by the wave of arriving newcomers—and that charges of special privileges and government interference would surface. According to one source, a white male who started as a switch-man with New York Telephone in 1971, the men working in these positions quickly coined numerous expressions to capture these sentiments. One popular pejorative substituted other words to complete the acronym EEOC—"the Eventual Elimination of Caucasians." "Switch Bitches" and "Frame Dames" were two more appellations the men came up with for their new co-workers. Blue-collar humor was used as a way to convey the not-so-latent hostility.

A tense tango followed as issues of race and gender dominated the workplace. Both the company and the union played up the fear factor. Two unions represented the skilled craft workers at the phone company: the CWA and the International Brotherhood of Electrical Workers (IBEW). Most of the operators and clerks were represented by a patchwork quilt of "independent" unions loosely joined together within the National Federation of Telephone Workers. While the IBEW chose to participate in discussions with the EEOC and the company on issues covered by the terms of the collective bargaining agreement for New England Bell, the CWA declined to do so. Despite repeated attempts to involve the union in discussions, the union played no active role until entering into litigation to head off the agreement.[28]

In *Communications Workers of America: The Story of a Union*, an official history of the CWA published in 1977, there is no discussion of the EEOC case, the consent decree, and very little regarding race and gender. One passing reference is made to "women's liberation" and a few sentences dispatch with the subject of women in craft jobs. The decision to go into court is side-stepped.[29] But for the women coming onto the job, the CWA's action conveyed a strong message. As Winkler described:

> The union went to court to stop the plan, on the grounds that it overrode seniority. But, as I learned more about it, I found out that there had never really been a senior-ity system for promotions in the first place. So it felt to us like they had gone to court to keep women out of the job. The only way you could get promoted within the Plant Department, at that point, was if you were already *in* the Plant Department. There was no way, if you were an operator or a clerical in another department, that you could get any of these jobs—until the consent decree was signed. So the union was in court, basically trying to stop women from getting into these jobs.[30]

Both management and the unions failed to extend the golden opportunities to the women already employed in blue-collar jobs within the system. Theoretically, the openings in the skilled craft jobs were supposed to result in new opportunities for the clericals and operators. But this path to advancement for Bell System women happened only on a small scale, as Winkler described it:

> That was part of the consent decree, but...They mostly filled the female slots by [outside] hiring, which, when we got into the jobs, we discovered was a real problem. A lot of people really resented the fact that we'd been hired, quote "off the streets" for the top-paying job in the local.[31]

Local 1101 continued to play a negative role by pitting worker against worker. Green described how this occurred: "The union was one of the greatest obstacles because, first of all, they constantly filed those reverse discrimination suits...We had to pay union dues whether they represented us or not...Women and blacks were a large segment of union membership who were not represented in this period. I'm talking about '74 probably even up 'til '80, '81. The union did not participate in planning for the implementation of the first consent decree. They refused to. Then they went to court, and they challenged the consent decree for years until they finally lost. CWA was totally obstructionist in this period."[32]

Although fear understandably figured into the mindset of the established workforce, it might have been addressed in a number of constructive ways. Instead, both management and the union exacerbated it. Green describes the symbiotic relationship between management attitudes and those held by the union:

> I think many of those guys felt threatened. I think the company did a very good job of introducing fear into white men, fear that their jobs were going to be taken, fear that they were going to be displaced. And of course, a part of that fear is real...If you've been able to get people in your family—whole families—if you've been able to get your family a job in this company and now these jobs are going to have to be competed for, that is a threat. That is a real threat.[33]

As Green and Winkler took on the role of shop stewards for Local 1101, their activism helped them understand the issues facing all workers at the phone company. But the easy solidarity between women in the company training program was harder to come by on the job.

Blue-Collar Activism and "Corporate Feminism"

The contrast between the two environments—white- and blue-collar—was exceedingly stark. Even as white-collar women within the Bell System organized, agitated, and challenged the prevalent, discriminatory practices of their employer—such as differences in benefit packages based on gender—they were also able to take advantage of the corporate structure and its perks. White-collar women could also benefit from policies that allowed them to communicate their message and win adherents to their point of view with ease. They were able to post meeting notices on company bulletin boards. They organized official committees and thus were able to meet on company time. Their in-house activism took different forms; setting up consciousness-raising tables in the cafeteria; sponsoring movie nights and outside speakers; protests against corporate stag parties.[34]

This is not meant to denigrate their significant accomplishments. It is all to their credit that the activist feminists amongst the white-collar women within the Bell System took on a huge challenge and achieved so many of their goals. But the conditions were very different from those of the women who challenged gender prerogatives in the harsher, blue-collar sphere.

In the streets, trade union feminists and civil rights activists were always notable additions to the rallies and marches in support of women's rights—alongside the Bell System advocates.[35] But this cross-fertilization never took place within the company. The dividing line between the white-collar and blue-collar feminists was never breached. Class realities and corporate identities precluded this particular brand of sisterhood.

As the blue-collar pioneers walked into the workplace, they faced a much tougher set of circumstances. When Venus Green showed up for her first assignment at 140 West Street, she was one of only four or five women on the job:

> I can remember working on the installation of those switching systems into the World Trade Center, so it was fairly new at that time. [There were] thousands of men…switching equipment technicians…cable splicers, frame people…all the [telephone] trades came into West Street. This is the financial district, so there are hundreds of thousands of phones. Millions of phone lines—loads of men.
>
> For that first crew of us—there weren't even women's bathrooms. Those kinds of things had to be changed when we first went on the job…As I stayed on the job, more and more classes graduated and so more and more women came through.

As Green explained, her job, though nontraditional, didn't put her into intensely, all-male, locker-room environments decorated with pornography that some phone company women in certain job titles encountered. This was especially the case for those women working in the "outside" craft jobs. But Green described several incidents that, in her words, were "really vicious:"

> One time, for this young woman's birthday, they gave her a party and bought a big birthday cake and put a dildo in it. Women who would not let them touch them were marked, either as gay or [as] a problem…So once you have an attitude problem, then you get put into the ugly bin. You know? "She's just ugly." Sometimes the racism [and sexism] would be so explicit. Like, for example, if some woman from another part of the company came down on the floor for whatever reason, with high heels and a dress, they would carry on about, "Oh, it's so wonderful to have something beautiful come in here, given what we have to see every day"…That kind of comment.

Venus Green was working on tasks she described as repetitive and reminiscent of "all the things you can say about women's work applied, albeit in a skilled trade." She came to see this segmentation of work as part of the deskilling process taking place throughout the system.

Ilene Winkler had a different experience. She worked in a small crew: "Maybe 15, 20 people who were responsible for two big million dollar computers. There was a lot of responsibility and a lot of autonomy. It was really fun. You got to figure out really interesting things and people were really into the job. The systems were new. They were just introducing electronic systems and the management didn't know all that much. So it was like you were running the place yourself and people were conscientious. That went on for about five years and it was really enjoyable."

But she also got to witness the difficulties women faced who were in the position of being dependent upon co-workers to share their knowledge. "Sometimes they'd tell you to work with somebody who would train you," said Winkler. "It would be the men who knew what they were doing. Basically, if they were nice, they would train you. If they weren't—then they wouldn't train you."

Both Green and Winkler viewed the union as a vehicle with the potential to address workplace problems. Management kept the union on the defensive, attuned to their own agenda, as Green explained, "You have to spend so much time fighting things that management throws out to you that you don't have the time to actually propose new propositions."

One of the things Green wanted to see happen fell into this category—an unrealized ambition—was to organize amongst the women working in the skilled jobs. "See, when I was working as a switching equipment technician, [we made] no attempt…to organize as women—as craftswomen."

Why women never made any attempt to support each other in this way is a subject for speculation. According to Green, "It may have been because things were so bad in those years that the women—to try and identify with each other—could have been catastrophic, in the sense that already, you're in this man's job, and to try and organize can always be given the spin that you're looking for special consideration—something special. I think that had a very, very neutralizing force on the impetus to organize in terms of our own identity. Like, you're separating yourself out. You're not one of us."

Looking backward, Ilene Winkler is harsh on herself for the missteps she made—youthful errors—such as impatience and adopting a confrontational attitude. But, like Venus Green, she also chose to put her energy into representing her co-workers. She served as a union steward.

She also took on the more difficult, outsider role of reformer within her union. Here she had more success. Women's issues were getting "swallowed up" within the local's agenda, according to Winkler. Agitation was necessary to gain the attention of both the membership and their union leadership.

But overall, the fact that women's issues got lost was just one more lament in a sad litany of the local's decline. In 1974, the women came into the union three years after a militant, lengthy strike had gone down to defeat. Local 1101, with 11,000 members in several hundred worksites in Manhattan and the Bronx, had a history of militancy within the ranks of the membership and active rank-and-file opposition groups to challenge both their union hierarchy and workplace conditions. One tradition was the use of direct actions, including frequent walkouts at various locations. All of this militancy got squashed after the strike.[36]

Still, Winkler was able to play a central role in concerted efforts by other leftist, progressive activists to challenge the union leadership's standard method of operating and to rekindle a sense of trade unionism within the dispirited ranks of Local 1101. As she described it, by the time she got active, there was a very low level of participation and a high level of apathy within the union: "Nobody had any real level of involvement," she explained. This had to be built building by building, which, as she described, was a "do-it-yourself project" for activists.

The caucus set out to build awareness and a sense of involvement by putting out a newspaper, *The Bell Wringer*. For decades, the paper consistently included women's issues as part of their program, always alongside numerous other concerns. However, the constant drum beat for issues such as child care, the need for flextime in the face of long and inflexible shifts, pregnancy disability, promotions, upgrades and tutoring, family leave, and discrimination paid at times, as some of these items made their way into the bargaining demands put forward by the CWA. And some issues, such as safety and health, carpal tunnel syndrome, child care, harassment on the job, and the stress resulting from it, affected all of the union members. "The union doesn't have a handle on the level of stress and harassment," said Winkler. "There is a whole lot of alcoholism. So the stewards are trying to protect people who are falling apart on the job." Automation has always been a huge issue facing CWA members, one that continually erodes both conditions on the job and job security. Health care premiums also assumed an ever-greater importance. Effective union representation on a whole host of critical issues was on the plate of the caucus. Eleven years after putting out the first issue of the paper, the group put together a slate to run in opposition to the union leadership.

As Winkler wrote in 1989, for *The Troublemaker's Handbook*, "The local has an entrenched, very bureaucratic leadership... It is very distant from the membership. Virtually all of the officers have been full-time union officials for over 15 years. They are very conservative politically and socially, and they are all white with one exception. The workforce, on the other hand, is very mixed. The clericals are mostly black women, with a very small Hispanic and Asian membership. The top crafts are mostly white men, although some sections are better integrated than that. There's a very sizable black membership, but the structure of the union is very white, very male." The caucus prescription for change was based on accountability and democratic representation.³⁷ Winkler ran for Treasurer on *The Bell Wringer* slate.

"People are disgusted," said Winkler in 1990. "We had a 17-week strike in 1989 and there was no meeting during the strike. We really need a union," she said. But Winkler's assessment, coming after a lifetime spent in the struggle, is that the type of unionism currently being offered to the membership is not up to the challenges facing the membership: "The point of a union is supposed to be to pull the strengths of people together and to unify people. You can't do that unless you're willing and really committed to training new people and involving them and not seeing them as a threat to whatever little status and perks you've managed to achieve for yourself. It's [a question of] whether you're rising with everybody or whether you're rising by stepping on other people, in a sense."

Winkler's activism took yet another form within Local 1101. Despite a healthy degree of skepticism, she did get involved in several attempts to set up a women's committee within the local. Eventually, she was part of a group that set an agenda acceptable to the leadership and accomplished some interesting work on behalf of the women in Local 1101. But throughout its fractured history, the Women's Committee had its bruising encounters with the officialdom. One startling example resulted from efforts to take up the issue of the extreme sexual harassment faced by some women in the craft jobs and led to the local disbanding the committee.

"We tried to deal with this but we got stymied by the union," said Winkler. "It was one of the things that led to the committee being dissolved. To be fair, I think there's a commitment from the union that everybody should be treated properly. But when it comes down to fighting the grievances, they haven't done it. And they haven't done it in some of these garages. This is a problem that's really most acute with the splicing garages and the places where there are a tiny number of women."³⁸

Winkler described one particular garage where this problem went unabated for years: "There was one situation that kept coming up over and over and over again of a third level manager—that's a high-level manager—who just ran the place like a tyrant. He would drive out every single woman who managed to get an upgrade into that garage. We couldn't do anything about it. The union would not confront him because he was so vicious that, at one point, when people tried to confront him about something—I don't even remember what it was—he went and got the LM-2 showing how much money the chief shop steward and a bunch of guys were making. And he put it out in the craft lounge. I mean, he made it very clear that he was going to retaliate viciously if anybody challenged his power. This was a company guy."

That's why you get to all these private settlements, because somebody will end up out on disability—having a nervous breakdown. Then somehow, she'll get a lawyer or the company will settle it. But nobody would discipline these people. This is what would happen. When we would try to do something public about it, we would be told, Don't do that. You'll jeopardize the settlement. And the women would be out having nervous breakdowns, so they couldn't do anything. It was terrible!! It was really a bad situation.

After her retirement, Winkler speculated that the situation probably has not changed: "I would be really surprised. It was awful. Now, in the inside crafts, I don't think it was as bad a situation.... But the real serious sexual harassment, we didn't get as bad... There were more women. And the lights were on."

To the everlasting ignominy of Local 1101, this topic proved to be taboo throughout the entire time Winkler spent at the phone company. Women being harassed were forced to fight their battles by themselves. These individual episodes of gross harassment led to settlements, each with its stipulation for secrecy. The terms of these cases within New York Telephone and its successor companies are bound by confidential agreements.[39]

Venus Green theorized from her own experience, as to why women would consent to a vow of silence: "While I don't have any specific knowledge [about this], I can imagine that a blue-collar woman is going to settle and keep her mouth shut. She really needs that job and she has few resources for getting another job like this one. I made more as a switching equipment technician than I made as a college professor. And [even] now, if I were a switching equipment technician, I would probably be making more money than I make as a college professor. So you're not going to lightly challenge this whole big monopoly corporation and cut off your life, as such."

An "Unfinished Agenda"

Despite its limitations, the EEOC agreement did result in real gains. "That settlement was a victory for women. I'm not ever going to deny that. It was a victory for black people," said Green. "I think that white women got the most out of it. But it was a victory for women and for black people. Its implementation was unfair based on class and race... Upper management women did well. Those women that were poised because of years of experience and education were able to make some major leaps. That does not discount the fact that working-class women [also made gains]. If you move from being an operator to a switching equipment technician or even a frame person, your reality changed. Economically, your reality changed immensely, so it *was* a victory."

Just look at what women have been able to do for themselves with these blue-collar jobs. Do you think I would have been able to have this house [a brownstone in Harlem] without having worked at the telephone company? I mean—without having had a job that paid a man's salary. Don't get me wrong. I don't think a man's salary is adequate. But [look at] the difference between that and secretarial or clerical work.

These jobs can be life altering! Look at what they do for men. Men can support families, even keep women at home... This particular highly skilled segment of the primary labor market where it's unionized, those jobs made a difference in women's lives, especially blue-collar women, because not only were you getting that paycheck, you were getting those benefits. And to some extent, you had job security. You could leave an abusive husband. You were empowered.

Research conducted by Herbert R. Northrup and John A. Larsen of the Wharton School of Business took a comprehensive look at the impact of the AT&T-EEOC consent decree. Their 1979 study documented the inroads women had made into the skilled jobs:[40]

Outside crafts, once the bulwark of the male, was 4.7 percent female. The inside craft and service worker groups saw significant percentage gains for females, resulting in a one-third increase in the overall share of blue-collar jobs for females. Thus, females gained in nontraditional jobs and lost in traditional ones...The upgrading of females in the Bell System is undoubtedly a source of great satisfaction, as well as financially rewarding, both to the persons involved, and to all who support equal opportunity.[41]

Venus Green, like other women who benefited from doors being opened by affirmative action programs, champions the need to preserve them:

Affirmative action is about giving people who are qualified, the opportunity to compete for the job. I had to compete for that job as a switching equipment technician. I had to take all those tests...and I had to go through that six months of training and make it. And I was in a class with people who had switching experience. So, affirmative action didn't give me anything. It gave me an opportunity to compete—to *compete*.... I think that's very important that there should be an opportunity to compete, because black people in the country have telephones. We pay taxes. I should have that opportunity because I'm an American.

The legal debate over affirmative action is simmering in the background, waiting for that day when the U.S. Supreme Court justices—a majority of whom are conservative and in the anti-affirmative action camp—decide to take up a case involving employment rights. So far, the court's record on affirmative action in education provides a dismal signal as to which direction they might take when they wade into this territory.

Another part of the unfinished agenda is to repair the break between working-class women and the official Women's Movement. NOW was born out of an alliance that brought women together from the ranks of academia, the professions, government, and labor union women. The inroads the organization nurtured with women on the professional and management career paths were sustained. But since it never succeeded in planting roots within the ranks of blue-collar women, eventually, working-class women lost an important ally and source of outside support that was available to white-collar women.

The trade union feminists who joined forces with Betty Friedan and other trailblazing activists to launch the Women's Movement continued to advocate for a feminist agenda. But they were unable to move their organizations in this direction. What would seem to be working women's natural ally—the unions—got stuck in a defensive posture—and thus were able to offer only limited support for goals that worked toward placing women on an equal footing.

Catherine Conroy's career was a rare model for a successful marriage between feminism and official unionism. She was one of those trade union feminists present in 1966 at the birth of NOW. Then, in 1968, while working in Chicago for the CWA, Conroy set up a chapter of NOW and served as its first president. In 1970, she organized the Chicago activities that took place on August 26 as part of the national Women's Strike for Equality. In 1974, she was at the founding meeting of the Coalition of Labor Union Women (CLUW). She set up CLUW's Milwaukee chapter and served as its first president. Her strong commitment to feminism within the trade union movement was always at the core of her activism. In 1978, Conroy was honored as Milwaukee NOW's "Woman of the Year."[42]

Yet, despite the presence of women like Conroy and other committed feminists at different levels of leadership throughout the CWA, the structure of unions basically ensures that the local leadership—overwhelmingly male—prevails. And by and large, they remain indifferent at best to an agenda that addresses gender equity. Even, in those exceedingly rare occasions, when the local leadership happens to be female, the fear of fighting for something that could constitute a source of division and dissension, keeps a serious commitment to gender equality off the agenda.[43]

PART FIVE

Transportation

ELEVEN

Woman on the Move

Typically, men who drive trucks grew up playing with them. "Hot Wheels," "Big Wheels," Tonka Toys, and miniature conveyances of every description easily capture a male child's heart. Eileen Sullivan had no childhood trucks; she had five children, and had fourteen years service as a waitress before she decided to step into a big rig. Teamster women were not welcome, in the summer of 1978, when she showed up for her first day on the job. An apprentice with a Class 1 commercial driver's license in her future, she was determined to succeed:

> Ten minutes after I arrived on the job site, I was assigned to a huge 10-wheel dump truck. The foreman wanted to "see what I could do." So my formal training began with...get in the truck! Even with limited instructions from the foreman and the assigned driver, I took to the job like a duck to water. This seemed to infuriate them, and they repeatedly assured me that I would not be able to handle this job.
>
> The rest of the week didn't go as well as the first day. I was assigned to different drivers every day as their "helper." The pace of the day depended on the disposition of the driver. Not a single day passed without me being told that I wasn't going to make it here, and not to make a fool of myself by thinking I could. One driver removed the passenger seat in his truck and replaced it with his tool box. That day, I sat on the tool box for more than eight hours, never stopping for bathroom breaks or lunch. He relieved himself on the side of the road or between the tires (which was the most common place for drivers to urinate) and he had his lunch with him.
>
> At the land fill in Roslyn where we offloaded the excavation in a very remote area, one driver turned to me and said, "I could knock you out, put you behind the truck, and dump this load on you, and no one would ever know. You could scream as loud as you want and no one would hear."[1]

Among all the women whose stories make up *Sisters*, Eileen Sullivan's achievement is unique. Each had to overcome fear, doubt, and harassment to sustain a life in the blue-collar world, but Sullivan, who negotiated similar obstacles, not only survived, she alone, actually wound up as a union official in one of New York City's most powerful blue-collar institutions—the 40,000 member Local 100 of the Transport Workers Union (TWU). Sullivan's resume includes an uncommon range of experience on the road to her current position with Local 100.

Although the numbers of women working in blue-collar "nontraditional" jobs are low, the numbers of women in top union leadership positions are—shockingly—lower. Even here, in unions, organizations charged with the mission of advancing the cause of all workers, the road to the leadership still presents daunting political obstacles for women. And the union record in representing the interests of women working in nontraditional jobs is worse than blemished. Evidently for blue-collar women to thrive, there need to be more Eileen Sullivans. But is the answer to changing life at the bottom for women in the trades simply to increase the number of women at the top of the union hierarchy? That's a question we ask Lois Gray of Cornell's ILR School, who has devoted a lifetime to understanding the relationship between unions and their women members. Sullivan's experience and insights—along with those of expert allies like Gray—explain why the promise of equal rights remains unfulfilled and what must be done to fulfill it.

An Uncommon Carrier

In his book about the men who drive big transport machines—locomotives, ships, trains—author John McPhee made reference to the small number—approximately 5 percent—of female drivers in the trucking industry.[2] Despite the low numbers, women have been at the helm of huge machines for more than 30 years. In the span of a generation, women have climbed on board to haul freight, drive locomotives, subway trains, street sweepers, sanitation trucks, ships, emergency vehicles, and "earth movers"—the trucks essential to mining operations. In 2005, the movie *North Country* depicted some of the first women to sit in the driver's seat of these earthmoving machines. Eileen Sullivan was one of the first women on Long Island to step into this new role and to experience the thrill and power of being at the controls.

How "women's liberation," the National Organization for Women (NOW), and Teamster Local 282 got hooked together is the first part of Eileen Sullivan's story. The notorious local that monopolizes the deliveries of concrete and building supplies to construction sites in the New York Metropolitan area was labeled the "candy store for the mob" by federal prosecutors. Feminist organizations out fighting for the rights of females would seemingly be poles apart from the mobbed-up local. Yet in Sullivan's case, the road from one led directly to the other.

In the mid-1970s, Eileen Sullivan was the coordinator for a group called the Women's Liberation Center. The blue-collar women were interested in changing their lives and improving their economic fortunes. "We had women of color. We had African-American women. We had Native American women...Hispanic women," Sullivan said. Their meetings consisted of wide-ranging discussions called consciousness-raising sessions:

> It was just wonderful...We had never talked about these things before and how it affected us as women. We talked about everything from makeup to sex...Fear was a major topic. It wasn't just a one-night topic. We talked about it for a long time. So we just started networking on that level and then we decided that we needed to get a powerful name behind us.[3]

That "powerful name" was NOW. In the late seventies, NOW had clout. The Long Island women wanted to enlist NOW's visibility, power, and ability to open doors behind their own efforts. They started a campaign to get their own chapter. Sullivan described the events that led to the South Nassau Chapter of NOW being chartered and her short, two-year tenure as its president:

It wasn't Nassau NOW or NOW New York, or any biggie-biggie group. It was a very small group of women who were looking to break into the male jobs. That was our motivation. We knew that if we got the name behind us, it would help us a lot. There was a tremendous fight to get a charter. We had to go to Albany. NOW didn't want any part of it. Unfortunately, for a period of time, NOW was kind of an elitist group. A lot of women who didn't share the same ideas we had about this being a place for women to get work and to get blue-collar jobs—good jobs!

But we finally convinced NOW that we needed this chapter and they put their name behind us. We used that as a networking tool to get women jobs. One of the things we did was to get the first 13 women into construction on Long Island. What I learned from that was that there was a tremendous need for women to get better jobs and to do well. There was a lot we had to learn. We uncovered through NOW that a woman could not own her own home improvement business. It had to be owned 51 percent by a man. Nassau County law—ordinance—whatever it was at the time. But this group allowed women to get together that wanted to make a change and wanted to do things differently.

We knew we wanted jobs. We had been speaking to unions and companies for years and nothing was coming until the day we shut down a job site. That's when we got work. That's when it all happened.

Direct action is the thread that runs through all of the organizing Sullivan has done throughout her life in labor. Years later, she wrote a description of the job action in 1978 that led to the first jobs for Long Island women on construction sites:

After years of unsuccessful negotiations with contractors and union officials to hire women, the day came when a small group of women on Long Island took matters into their own hands. We climbed atop a mound of dirt at a construction site with signs saying this (job) was federally funded and was not following the guidelines for hiring women. After some threats of violence from the male workers, the job site came to a complete stop. Shortly after that, the job foreman, local police, and media representatives arrived to discuss our demands. Within one week, we were given 13 positions on other federally funded construction sites as Teamster truck drivers.[4]

By organizing, confronting her fear, and climbing into the cab, Sullivan got a sevenfold increase in salary, plus benefits. As the mother of five children and a husband with a diagnosis of terminal cancer, she needed it. Her career inside IBT Local 282 trucks came to an abrupt end when she was laid off. But with a total of two years under her belt, she was able to qualify for a job as a tractor-trailer driver for Pan American Airlines at JFK Airport. Here again, she was the first female trucker for the airline. But, in contrast to her prior experiences, she readily became one of the crew. Despite the fact that on her first day, her first attempt to back the trailer into the loading dock, took 94 tries!

She faced instant notoriety on the job—1 female and 45 men. But out of the 45, only 2 resented her working there. They took turns harassing her by throwing away her lunch, pissing into her window-washing bottle, and putting up dirty pictures on her locker. Like many women in similar situations, she used her own brand of blue-collar humor to defuse the tension and downplay the insulting behavior. Eventually this worked. And she also made friends and found allies. Three men became as close to her as brothers. "We hit it off from the first. They knew I was serious about the job and that I was not there as a token," she said.

Comparing her two paths to earning a paycheck—serving food and delivering freight—trucking won out as the better deal: "Being a waitress was definitely more difficult and heavier than trucking. Only one or two functions are difficult as a trucker. It was scary," she recalled. "I cried, but not often."[5] Starting out as a truck driver, not a day went by that the men didn't tell Sullivan she'd never make it. She went from internalizing that message—waking up every morning thinking, Is this the day I'll fail?—to a sense of confidence earned by doing the job.

The union representing employees in the Motor Pool at Pan Am was Local 504, Air Transport Division, of the Transport Workers Union of America. The local represented 4,000 workers in 14 separate divisions. Shortly after going to work for the airline, Sullivan found cause to start agitating.

Pan Am Playbook

Persistence is a key character trait for a union activist since most internal organizing efforts come down to a type of trench warfare that requires tenacity and long-term commitment. Eileen Sullivan possessed these qualities in abundance. For 11 years, she represented the members in her local—taking the route from unofficial activist to a top leadership position. Each time she encountered the union's reluctance to act, she countered it with a campaign of her own devising. As is often the case with activists, she first got involved in representing her own grievance after the union declined to pursue it. Success here led her to run for shop steward. Finally, she was asked to take on the role of chief steward. Reluctant to represent the mechanics, she put aside doubts and did it. (Out of 2,000 mechanics, 3 were female.) As chief steward, one issue that loomed large was jurisdictional—Teamster members were doing the work of TWU members. Sullivan started taking photos for the grievances that numbered in the hundreds. Her candid shots of Teamsters at work earned her a nickname: "Miss Kodak."

Asked to run on a diversity slate, she was elected recording secretary of Section 1. The union then removed her from office—illegally—in an effort to, as she described it: "Get the Broad." She and her supporters put together a petition campaign and collected more than 2,000 signatures to challenge the removal. She had to go into federal court to defeat the union's challenge to the validity of the petition. Sullivan experienced a newfound sense of confidence and belief in her judgment after being restored to union office. "I started believing in myself," she said. She was then recruited to run for localwide office. In this election, she ran against four men for the position and beat the highest vote-getter by a margin of more than two to one. As vice president, Sullivan became the first woman to hold a top union office in Local 504.

In her new role, she experienced the difficulties of trying to represent the needs of the women, a distinct minority of the total membership. As she described, "It was a tightrope...walking between the union, the job, and women's issues." Some of the issues affecting the female members included changing rooms, locker rooms, maternity benefits, and sexual harassment that included physical touching. She led a successful campaign to have *Stern Magazine* taken off Pan Am. As she explained, "It had a sticker on it: 'From Pan Am for your reading pleasure.'" But the German glossy featured gross nudity that Sullivan and the other women working there found offensive.

In 1991, Pan Am went into bankruptcy and then out of business. It sank like a stone, taking thousands of jobs down with it. The union's position was that "there was nothing much they could do." Sullivan and other union members organized a group, Severed Employees Legal Fund (SELF) to fight the bankruptcy and its terms. Then they formed another group and went to court to fight for their pensions. She enrolled in Career Connections, a program for displaced workers, and studied at Adelphi University to become a paralegal.

Later, Sullivan described Pan Am as, "an incredible learning experience. It took me though the first third of the alphabet in learning about labor relations and the National Labor Relations Board and...dealing with people."[6]

Dealing directly with sexual harassment taught her that confronting offensive behavior was more effective than absorbing it. Pursuing a grievance yielded a bigger payoff by bringing in co-workers' complaints. Acting as if she knew what she was doing and going with her gut feelings led to new, unscripted, and unorthodox directions to get an immediate remedy—ending the behavior.

She also sought out additional education beyond the shop floor. Sullivan was one of the recipients of a scholarship established by electrician Cynthia Long—tradeswomen's advocate and pioneering electrician in Local 3, International Brotherhood of Electrical Workers (IBEW)—that allowed her to attend the Cornell Labor Studies Program for Trade Union Women. She latched on to every opportunity that came her way to enhance her knowledge.

The plight of Pan Am workers faced with losing their livelihoods—and so much more—led to a television appearance. The *McNeil/Lehrer News Hour* featured two segments on Career Connections, the program for these displaced workers. The first spot aired in 1992 and the second in 1994, as a follow-up on the participants.

Sullivan saw a distinct difference between the male and the female experience. While the women successfully completed the goals they set during the program, the men didn't seem to fare so well:

> More often than not, [the men] became stuck and unwilling somehow to really accept that this was over. I think that they went forward with it as maybe rote, but not really believing that this was over. I saw much more flexibility [with the women], much more acceptance of the situation, and taking stock of what they wanted to do with their lives now and making a decision that it was time to move on. There just wasn't that reluctance.
>
> Why? I think I can speak for myself, personally. There have been so many things in my life that have made me evaluate my position and decide which way to move. I was always progressing and moving in a different direction. I never got into a career or a job and then just stayed there. There was always room for advancement and a need for change for me personally. And I think a lot of women experience this kind of thing. We're challenged every day with some new item. There's always something that challenges us and I think we're always in a forward mode.

Her paralegal studies through Career Connections and the appearances on television were a prelude to the next stage—public advocate for women workers.

Still "Alone in a Crowd:"
Union Women in Nontraditional Jobs

After 20 years in existence, the Brooklyn-based Association for Union Democracy (AUD), a national civil liberties organization for union members, created a special Women's Project. Since the inception of the Women's Project, union women working in nontraditional jobs had become a strong focus. Sullivan brought great expertise and personal experience to the job. Still, Sullivan almost balked when offered the position of Women's Project director, due to the low pay. But the job held an appeal for her beyond the salary. Eileen Sullivan saw the offer as another opportunity to learn:

> I knew Susan Jennik, the executive director of the AUD. She called me to say that the Women's Project needed somebody and would I be interested. I was somewhat reluctant because the money was so bad. But I had just gotten out of paralegal school and I knew working with her, I could learn more about the law, since she's a fantastic attorney and I would learn about civil rights law... It was such a great opportunity for me to be able to talk to women all over the country about problems at work and how to resolve them. It was really very challenging and it validated what I had learned as a struggling worker at Pan Am and from being the first woman there.

At the AUD, she worked with tradeswomen and their organizations in New York City and from across the country, offering advice on how to push union grievances forward, how to get jobs, and how to develop support. She perceived differences in other places to the presence of women in the building trades. Pointing to the work of the Boston Tradeswomen's Network and similar organizations from Oregon to California to Cleveland, she observed,

> There seemed to be an acceptance that this was something that was going to happen and we'd better work with it, whereas in New York, there was such a tremendous reaction against it. The women [in New York] were really very much on their own.

Like so many other women working in construction, Sullivan had experienced sexual harassment. Yet it wasn't until she had to speak out on the topic publicly that she recognized the validity of her own experiences. As she recalled:

> The first time I ever spoke about sexual harassment was after I got employed by the AUD. I was asked to speak at a Solidarity [Network] meeting in New York City. One of the very first things I said was, "I don't know if I can really speak about sexual harassment. I've never been raped." Then, the more I talked, the more I realized that every day on the job, I was experiencing sexual harassment, but I never called it that. To me, it was everyday survival, because it wasn't just at work. It was at the supermarket. It was at the library and it was wherever you went, if you were a woman. It was on my jobs... and I just never realized what I had been fighting all those years until I started to speak about it.
>   Then I really got very excited about the whole topic... It helped me identify how I survived—the things that I did—that were really very much direct action.

She offered two anecdotes from her days as a truck driver to illustrate her method:

When I worked for the airline, I would go to other airlines and deliver freight and there was a table that I would have to write my papers on. The receiver, who was always a guy, would take my papers and sign off on them, and I'd leave. The table had a glass top in many of these places. It's called a highboy, and under the glass top were all these pornographic pictures. I mean, disgusting pictures of women. I would put my papers down, and as he would go to sign it, I'd move it, exposing these pictures. I'd say "Gee, are these members of your family? Is this your wife? Is this your daughter? Is this your aunt? Obviously, this is someone's daughter, perhaps someone's mother. How proud you must be of your family!" They would get all shades of red and not know what to say or do. So, in a situation like that, I would make them uncomfortable. I was angry about what I saw and knew it was inappropriate.

Another example: There was this guy named Tom. I didn't know his name at the time. But every time he would look at me or another woman at work, he would lick his lips in this disgusting manner. One day I said to him, "Why do you do that?" He said, "Well, isn't that what you like?" I said, "No. It's not what we like. This is what we like." And I reached out my hand and I said, "My name's Eileen. I work here. What's your name?" And he told me his name. Then I said, "What do you do here?" He really thought that this was what we wanted to see. It was grotesque. It was awful. So I could do those kinds of things.

Eventually, Sullivan provided expert testimony at public hearings on sexual harassment. She worked the topic into the educational programs she designed for trade unionists. One of these courses was offered on a recurring basis for members of the Marine Engineers Benevolent Association (MEBA). As she recalled:

I would go to Maryland every two or three months when they would have a review. It was a very interesting group. A lot of the men voiced objections to having their little domain changed because there were women [on the ships] now. Some men felt that this benefited both males and females. But the majority [of men] were very concerned that things had to change. I saw a lot of nervousness on the part of the men, not knowing how to speak to the women and what to say.

Sullivan described one conversation with a female officer in Maryland:

She gave me a few horror stories, but she said, for the most part, every ship she's been on, she's been respected. The horror stories were about verbal behavior. Nobody touched her or did any of that kind of violation. People would say things to her as she was coming on board [like], 'We don't want women here.' It was that kind of stuff that she experienced. But for the most part, it had been a positive experience for her, and she was in there for about four or five years.

Sullivan felt that she had achieved some degree of success in breaking down the male resistance to having women on board:

We all seemed to part friends and to have a genuine respect for each other. There was a high-level officer in the room one day. He was talking about, "I know how to motivate one of the guys. I tell them, Hey '...' He used a dirty word, part of the male anatomy. Pick up those tools and get going. But I don't know what to say to a woman to get her motivated the same way. What curse can I call her that's accepted?"

So I asked the class: "How do you feel about that?" Two fellows said they resented being called a name, part of their male anatomy. "How dare he do that!" He was absolutely floored and realized that he had to evaluate his own behavior as a senior officer. I found it very beneficial for myself as well as them.

For Sullivan, the sessions underscored the importance of communication—of listening to people and giving them an opportunity to speak—not stereotyping or classifying others as a group that can never learn. "They did get it," she said. "By the time the day was over, they did get it. It was a very good experience."

The AUD conducted another training program for members of Teamster Local 295. If any union needed training, it was certainly the JFK Airport local, which had just been placed in trusteeship and might have been even more notorious than Local 282. Alleged by federal prosecutors to be under the control of the Lucchese crime family, Local 295 served as Martin Scorsese's model for the truck drivers' union portrayed in the classic 1990 Hollywood movie, *GoodFellas*. Both Susan Jennik and Eileen Sullivan taught the sessions aimed at giving participants some sense of entitlement as union members after years of mob control. The administrator of the trusteeship, Mike Moroney, was impressed by Sullivan's abilities and her background as a truck driver. He approached Jennik to ask if he might offer Sullivan a job. Reluctantly, she consented.

Sullivan's next move was to Local 295. Most of the membership held jobs as employees of Airborne Express, a company that delivered freight from the airlines to customers.

In her new role as a business agent, Sullivan not only worked on behalf of the entire membership but was also able to lend strong support to the women. Out of Local 295's total membership of 2,700, only 88—approximately 3 percent—were female.

In the Driver's Seat

The importance of having the female perspective present at the negotiating table and in union leadership circles is underscored by the experience of Eileen Sullivan. At Local 295, Sullivan found other ways to encourage the women to step up, improve their skills, and exert leadership. Through a combination of education and encouragement, she pressed women to develop their potential and play a role in the union. She also employed old-fashioned hectoring:

What's needed is the ability and desire to make a change. A lot of women, you'll hear them say over and over again: "I'm not ready for this. I can't do this." And I tell them, "Do you think these guys know what they're doing when they first come in? They pretend they know what they're doing. Do you think I knew what I was doing when I first came in? You're going to learn with the job." Certainly they're capable of learning. But I want to see that they're willing to learn and willing to take on a challenge.

She described her goals as a mentor for the women:

It's been very frustrating from the point of view of being a woman. Aside from my goal of training and educating the entire membership, my other main goal is getting another woman to take my place when I leave. I won't be here forever. This is a Trusteeship and it's eventually going to end and the membership will get back their local. There needs to be at least one woman who will do the work that I'm doing. Some one who feels as though she can…If I can identify one or two women who want to go further and get these leadership skills, this is what we need to do.

Inclusion wasn't just a matter of "diversity" insisted Sullivan. "Without a woman's voice involved in the negotiations and arbitrations," [it] would be a travesty…There has to be at least one woman because there are issues that are important to women that get negated when the guys get together…Most women's issues are worker's issues. They're not just women's issues. But, they're the items that the men leave out. You have the day care issues and health and safety. Absolutely! They just leave that out."

From Local 295, Sullivan was appointed Trustee of Teamster Local 851, its similarly twisted sister local at JFK. She was the first female to hold the position of trustee with responsibility for cleaning-up a mob-ridden union. "We set the bar for trusteeships," she said. "Three and a half years to weed out the old guard, educate the rank-and-file, and turn over the local to new officers ready to do the job."[7]

Once again, she mentored the women in Local 851, recalling, "I spent a lot of time encouraging women and getting them involved in the union. Many women went from the rank and file to [being] representatives of their units. Ultimately, the new president was a woman—not my choice—she was not ready—but she won!"

Currently, Sullivan directs the Grievance and Discipline Department for New York City's 40,000-member bus and subway workers' union—Local 100 of the TWU. She is responsible for supervising the union representatives, attorneys, and arbitrators hired jointly by the union and management to represent members who are brought up on disciplinary charges by management or who have grievances against management. She is also intricately involved in representing the women of Local 100:[8]

We now send 10 to 15 women to the Union Summer School every year. Women were a major part in the negotiations in 2002 and 2005 that led to a $6.2 million child care program, maternity leave, and New York state disability coverage. I was the chief negotiator in 2002 on the [new] Child Care/Family Issues Committee. The Child Care Fund was created from those 2002 negotiations. We have increased the numbers of women in leadership roles—on the executive board, as shop stewards and one vice president. We have an annual women's conference and quarterly meetings of the women's committee. We are working hard to get more women to think about upgrading their skills. We got a $7 million skills upgrade and training program in the 2002 contract negotiations.[9]

Of the 40,000 members in Local 100, a little more than 6,000 are female. Women work as bus drivers, along with a few train operators, many token clerks, cleaners, and some who hold clerical positions. "Only three or four are real trades' workers," said Sullivan. "But the fact that women are still well below 25 percent of each title, all of them can be called—'nontraditional.' Women are still struggling with issues of respect on the job, sanitary facilities, more maternity leave, paid time-off through the Family and Medical Leave Act, and joint labor-management sponsored child care centers."

Having spent years as a worker in nontraditional jobs and a labor activist in unions where women are in the minority, Eileen Sullivan has participated at every level in the struggle for female representation within trade unions. Given such a broad perspective, she finds that the message to women is universally the same: Stay back. What it comes down to is that women should, "Get involved, but not too involved."

> Women need to be supported and encouraged. They need to be informed and included in decision making. The male mentality is the dominant mode in union leadership.[10]

Ultimately, the actions that encourage the growth of women's participation in their unions initiated by Eileen Sullivan are dependent on the good graces of male leadership. Despite some singular success stories, the subservient position of women in the labor movement has been both a source of frustration and reflection for Lois Gray throughout her career.

Recipe for Change

Lois Gray is the Jean McKelvey—Alice Grant Professor of Labor Management Relations Emeritus at the New York State School of Industrial and Labor Relations, where she was an associate dean. Gray inaugurated the Cornell Institute for Women and Work. Not only has she spent her life studying and teaching about women in unions and producing scholarship on the subject, but she also served for 25 years as the chair of the New York State Apprenticeship Council. Gray also contributed her expertise to the board of directors for Nontraditional Employment for Women (NEW). Only in recent years did she give that up so as to provide space for "new blood" on the board and some fresh approaches.

For decades, Gray has been a staunch ally of women in the trades. Her explanation of why women in the skilled blue-collar unions still experience difficulties in getting the representation they deserve and require from their unions starts with a simple reality. It begins with the fact that the topic never made it onto the agenda of the unions that represent them. "It was never an emphasis," Gray said. "Women have made headway in doing these jobs, but I don't think that the unions deliberately tried to make that possible."[11]

Gray draws a distinction between the "Rosie the Riveters" and the next generation of pioneers. Whereas the first group had broad government support behind them and a brand of trade union feminism already in place that lent some support to their entrance into nontraditional jobs, the second set of pioneers lacked these advantages:

> In World War II, women went into those jobs because the men were gone. Then, women were represented in a wider range of jobs... The women [during that era] were rebellious and were themselves demanding equal pay and greater opportunities. That probably helped.

Old attitudes prevail and continue to cause interference for women on the job and in their unions. Males in union leadership—for psychological, social, and economic reasons—continue to resist the fact that females are ready, willing, and able to do these jobs:

> Today, tradition and machismo endure, with men seeing themselves as the breadwinners, and view women coming into the jobs as undermining their prestige. While it has changed more at the professional level, these traditional views about the roles for females and males still endure in the blue-collar

world. I see some progress within the building trades unions, but unfortunately, it's very slow.

It's hardly surprising that union women in nontraditional jobs still confront resistance within their unions to getting the representation to which they are entitled to as dues-paying members. Yet there is a certain similarity between the resistance women in nontraditional jobs face and the barriers that block the paths of trade union women throughout the U.S. labor movement.

These barriers are built into the nature of the trade union movement. For example, in an essay on women in union leadership and the barriers to their participation and progress, Gray pointed out that something as basic as a conference for female members can still raise hackles. "Holding conferences of female activists is still controversial." This was written in 2001. As she explained in 2006:

It's considered politically threatening. This is why this problem (exists) in the unions. It doesn't exist to that extent in other organizations like government or corporations or universities. Since unions are political, the officers are elected and they tend to see caucus-forming or any separate organization as politically threatening to the leadership. That's why they are still controversial. The leaders think: If these women get together, what are they going to do? Put up candidates to run against us? Many unions do have separate women's conferences. But where it's a new idea, if someone's trying to start it, (it's threatening). I actually know a person who got fired from her job in a union because she wanted to start one of these conferences.

The problems impeding women's progress begin at the top. As evidence of this, Gray pointed to the recent record of the American Federation of Labor (AFL):

After the Women's Department was abolished by the AFL-CIO (Congress of Industrial Organization), but before the Change To Win breakup occurred in 2005, a committee of the Executive Council of the AFL, called the Committee on Working Women, put out a report in which they outlined the barriers and the lack of progress on getting women into leadership positions in unions. They made a series of recommendations about what should be done. As far as I know, nothing has come from that, at least in a policy statement. [Out of the approximately 60 affiliates in the AFL-CIO and Change to Win federations] there are only *two* presidents of national unions who are female.

This is approximately 3 percent. Women make up 16 percent of the U.S. Congress and 14 percent of the Senate. There is actually a higher percent of women CEO's in the Fortune 500 than women leaders of American labor unions.

"Although there's been some progress at the lower local union levels, and some intermediate levels, at the top, it's still an all-white, male crew," said Gray.

"The Committee's report went to the council. Certainly it wasn't officially released. Other things are seen as a priority, like organizing. Women are subsumed into organizing. They know that most of the workforce that's ripe for organizing is female, since they're in the service and low-wage sectors and most of those employees are women."

The list of reasons why obstacles to women's participation continue to exist within the labor movement is long and familiar. But what is novel is a recipe that could result in change.

With her knowledge of historical models and how women have managed to organize in the past, in combination with her familiarity with the complex conundrums plaguing women in both nontraditional and traditional union settings, Lois Gray has a lot to offer in answer to the question: What would it take to bring about real change?

The pressure for change has to come from both inside and outside the ranks of labor. "I think it has to start from the rank-and-file—from the bottom up," said Gray. Rather than waiting for "the rare, enlightened union leader"—the Eileen Sullivans—"it's up to the membership to press their concerns in a forceful way that leads to positive results. Women need to become more demanding," said Gray.

Other sources have the potential to contribute support, resources, and energy to a campaign for change. As Lois Gray pointed out, both CLUW and NOW have demonstrated serious limitations that have kept them from playing the roles they might have played. "A more independent organization, self-supported, would have been more viable than CLUW in the long run," said Gray. "The lack of independence was a limitation."

> NOW is an organization that has disappointed me a great deal. For years, all their emphasis has been on the professional woman and the members of NOW are professional women. I was a charter member of NOW, but I lost interest in being really active because I didn't feel it was really meeting the priority need—which was working women in low-paid jobs—white- and blue-collar workers. Occasionally, they'll take on a project doing something with women in nontraditional jobs. But it's not an emphasis. Yet as the national organization concerned about the status of women, presumably in all walks of life, NOW would be the ideal organization to do the kind of things that need to be done to provide support for working women.

Models for this type of collaboration can be pulled from the past. The Women's Trade Union League (WTUL), organized back in 1903, is one example of a successful collaboration between activists from inside and outside the ranks of labor. As Gray has written, "The WTUL was an organization specifically designed to fight for women's rights in the labor movement and workers' rights in the women's movement."[12]

The mission of the WTUL was to help working-class women organize. To that end, they lent support to their strikes, enlisted allies for their causes, raised money, and pressed for the rights of working women within their unions. In 1909, activists from WTUL played a huge support role in the "Revolt of the 20,000" that won union recognition for the International Ladies' Garment Workers Union (ILGWU) in New York City and Philadelphia. WTUL consistently supported women rank-and-filers who challenged the ILGWU's male-dominated leadership.[13]

Gray argues that the American labor movement needs to adopt a set of best practices. She points to the model offered by European unions that have implemented comprehensive affirmative action policies within their own institutions. "Change can come about through the adoption of *real* affirmative action programs for women in unions along the lines offered by the European model."

"Unions are still not 'women-friendly' and the inclusion of gender perspectives in all trade union policies is far from being achieved." This statement was part of the "Conclusions and Recommendations" adopted at the 7th World Women's Conference of the International Confederation of Free Trade Unions (ICFTU) in 1999. The ICFTU and its affiliated unions are developing—and implementing—a complete range of programs to make equality more than a slogan.[14]

Gender equality isn't a mystery. But to achieve it, it has to be a goal. The possibilities are limitless. "All women need is the political will to act—to demand change—and to organize," said Gray.

PART SIX

Moving Forward

TWELVE

Against the Grain

Baby Shower in a Shanty

In mid-April 2006, Djar Horn, a third-year journeyman carpenter and member of Local 157 of the New York District Council of Carpenters, went to work for Metropolitan—a subcontractor "rehabbing" an old Wall Street hotel. At the time, she told her foreman she was three-and-a-half-months pregnant. Installing doors, bathrooms, and trim for the windows, Horn wore a respirator as protection from the formaldehyde in the MDS, the "wood-like" product she was installing. Working with a crew of 30 men, some of whom she knew from prior jobs, Horn was the only female carpenter.

By late June, Djar felt she was slowing down and in consultation with her doctor, decided it was time to leave. Learning of her pregnancy, her co-workers were instantly congratulatory, offering advice, and sharing stories about the joys of being a parent. Two days before her departure, the morning coffee break in the carpenters' shanty turned into a baby shower of sorts. The men gave her a card signed by all and a collection of $400. Gifts from carpenters included a classic Pooh memorabilia book and some baby outfits.

"It was really nice," said Horn. "There are times that you have to deal with a lot of jerks on the job. You have to decide what to confront and what not to and have to prove yourself every time you go on a new job. But this was men being open and honest about themselves as fathers. It was really great. I felt they were giving me a lot of respect as a carpenter and also as a co-worker and a friend." Djar's daughter, a baby girl named Nina, was born in October.[1]

This story of quite probably the only baby shower ever organized by men on a New York City construction site provides an optic for a contemporary examination of women in the District Council of Carpenters. Alongside the story of activist Veronica Session, who began her career as a union carpenter in 1989, they provide a measure of the distance women have traveled since they first took up the trade—back when females were seen as interlopers who had no business learning to do a man's job.

Ever since women entered the union in 1978, they've been part of an ongoing effort to make the carpenters' union responsive to their presence. Females have traveled many different routes to gain a level of competency in this trade and gainful employment in the industry. More women have earned membership in the carpenters' union than in any other skilled trade. Over time, female carpenters slowly carved a niche for themselves in the macho world within the union brotherhood. A backward look at three pioneers illustrates the contributions made by that first generation to create a more hospitable environment for the women who followed in their footsteps.

Veronica's Story

Veronica Session speaks with a trace of a drawl imported from her native Wilmington, North Carolina, where she was born in 1958. Both her parents were members of the United Automobile Workers. In New York, her father worked at the GM plant in Tarrytown and her mother in an auto parts assembly plant. At Brooklyn Tech High School, Session set her sites on a career as an industrial designer. While that didn't materialize, she acquired a strong background in math and an interest in the shop classes. Session knew that she wanted to work at something challenging. Two jobs as a bookkeeper, and almost 10 frustrating years at the Bank of Boston left her feeling dissatisfied. "It was a lot of responsibility...for not much money...a lot of friction and it wasn't satisfying," she explained.[2]

"So when I got the notion that I wanted to be a carpenter, I just searched for work around the city...and eventually I got lucky. Somebody said they'd take me on." It took her a year and a half to land this opportunity at a construction job at Downstate Medical Center in Brooklyn. "The foreman said, 'Let's see what you do in a week—see if you're serious.' Then that week passed and he said I was doing 'good.' So I went back and quit my job...He told me I had to contact the union and the Apprenticeship Program. So I contacted them and got in. I was very fortunate. I was on that job for about a year...Of course, that was my first year and my very first job and he said I was doing as good as any third-year apprentice. I appreciated him saying that."

Her aptitude for the work along with the excellent pay, good benefits, and the quality of the instruction she received on the job added up to a positive experience. After completing her four-year apprenticeship, Session was able to make a smooth transition to working as a full mechanic, something that is often an issue for women in the trades:

> I didn't have too much of a problem in that way. I know a lot of women do and even some guys do, especially if they're not company guys. Some companies have apprentices who only work for them, and usually when they turn mechanics, they're pretty decent and they are kept on. But women are always at the bottom rung of everything so they get less of a chance to use their tools and skills as they're building up in their years. That definitely is an issue. Fortunately for me, I made that transition pretty well.

Despite the challenges that women still face within the industry, 18 years later, Session is highly satisfied with her career choice:

> I like using my hands. I like making things. You get to build...And you can see what you've done at the end of the day. You can visually see it, from beginning to

end, whether it's a small project or a big project...You can always see the accomplishment at the end and I like seeing that...I thought it would all come together well for me and it pretty much has.

In addition to her daily labors as a carpenter, Session is a union activist both on the job and after hours. She serves as a shop steward for Local 926 and is an active participant in the District Council's Women's Committee. She ran for the position of local delegate to the council, losing by only five votes. She intends to run again.

Through her union, she also works with Habitat for Humanity. On the day before Mother's Day in 2005, Session worked alongside 36 other women on the reconstruction of a 5-story apartment house in Harlem. She was hopeful that the sight of women working with tools might provide some inspiration for others. "It plants a seed that could grow," she said.[3]

As a shop steward, Session is a conscientious trade unionist—willing to stand up to the boss and also to confront the union when need be: "In our contracts, we're giving up actual rights that will be hard to get back," she explained. As she pointed out, corruption can take many forms—like cronyism—and favoritism. "Certain contractors are known to be bad. And even the good ones push the limit. So on the job, the shop steward needs backup from the union."[4]

At one point, Session needed backup for herself. After a co-worker, a persistent sexual harasser who wouldn't take "No" for an answer, attacked her on the job, she filed a grievance. "The union investigated. My reputation was good and my co-workers supported my story. He was thrown out of the local. I did what I had to do. He was a grown man and should have known better. That's progress. The union did support me. If they hadn't, I would have been furious!"

As for her own willingness to stand up and fight for others, she traces it back to her childhood: "Ever since I was young, I had a sense that, whatever the situation was, that the bad things were going on [because] individual people decided that they were going to do the wrong thing, or they weren't going to do the right thing, or they were going to turn their heads....All these individual people have a decision to make....So I always said, at least in my life I was going to do the right thing and would try to influence people in a positive way. I knew the one person I had control over was me."

In June 2005, *The New York Times* featured Session in a story, "Doing Nails for a Living, With a Hammer," about her role in ongoing efforts by advocates to increase job opportunities for women in construction. The opening paragraph described an incident in the daily life of a female construction worker:

When Veronica Session was leaving work on a recent afternoon, she noticed a picture of a naked woman freshly penciled on the wall. Ms. Session, a carpenter who was finishing an interiors job in Manhattan, said it was common practice for construction workers to scribble suggestive drawings on unprimed walls they know will soon be painted. As she has done many times before, rather than wait for the paint job, Ms. Session decided to grab a brush and paint over the image herself.[5]

This propensity for direct action and a conscious awareness of the need to counter sexist depictions of women on construction sites places Veronica Session firmly within the tradition of the first women who entered these jobs, back when it was an all-male industry. That long line stretches back to Connie Reyes.

"A Rowdy Gang of Girls"

Consuelo Reyes was the very first woman to join the carpenters' union in New York City. In 1978, Reyes was working with Harlem Fight Back, Asian-Americans, Puerto Ricans, and other groups to get construction jobs for minority males. She decided to go for the gold herself: "I'd been going around with these groups as a liaison person and demonstrating with them, getting arrested with them, and beaten—the whole nine yards. I was looking for work. I'd lost my job working in a day care center...and I thought—I'm a damn good carpenter...So I thought, why don't I go for a job. Everybody was against it. I was told things like, 'You're taking a man's job away'...Here I am, a single mother with two kids, and you're telling me I'm taking a man's job away?"[6]

Persistence and a lucky break got her a placement on a 19-story, pre-fabricated building going up on Cherry Street. The foreman, reluctant to put her to work when she showed up with all her tools, offered her a broom to sweep up the shanty. But Reyes had grown up wielding a hammer. As the oldest child, she'd helped her dad on home construction projects. She quickly complied with every "silly assignment" he thought up for her. Finally, he said, "'I guess you really want to work!' He put me to work with the assistant foreman, George Rapp, a wonderful, wonderful man." After that, it took her six months to gain entrance to the union's apprenticeship program.

Stories from Reyes's days as a pioneering tradeswoman and activist are part of the folklore among the women who spent their early years together as members of United Tradeswomen (UT). UT activist Janine Blackwelder recalled:

> The one who has the absolute best story is Connie Reyes. Connie Reyes was this hundred-pound Puerto Rican gal...and she was one tough cookie. She was on a job site where the guys had porno up in the shanty and being a Catholic herself, or being from the Catholic culture, she knew exactly what to do. She brought in little cards with photos of the Blessed Virgin Mary and Jesus on the Crucifix and she posted them in her little area. That porno—it was gross—and it came down immediately. Those men treated her with respect from then on.[7]

The carpenter Irene Soloway described another dimension: "The reason that Connie was able to not only do really well and thrive—not just survive—and actually have fun and make money was because she had six different personas that she could bring out based on who she was dealing with...she could be a mother, a lover, a sister, an innocent, or a sex goddess...she never took any shit, and she wasn't afraid of men. She wasn't intimidated by them, and she had an understanding of what men responded to and could use that to her advantage."[8]

Reyes and Soloway, among the first women to be accepted into the carpenters' union, initiated the tradition of tradeswomen activism in the union. Both were part of the core group that founded and provided leadership for UT. In time, the women carpenters became the most active committee in UT.

Throughout their years in the trade, they took part in reform activities. Reyes played a big role in the small group of activists who called themselves, "Carpenters for a Stronger Union," (CSU) coming forward to publicly oppose the corrupt leadership holding sway over the membership. Soloway participated in a variety of reform efforts. She helped to put out the rank-and-file newspaper, *Hard Hat News*, using a number of clever pseudonyms, such as

"Brick Shields," to disguise her identity. She worked with other civil service carpenters in a long and ultimately successful campaign to get their own union representation within the district council. As a shop steward, she played a major role in the campaign to fight for safety standards for trades' people working on jobs at the city's public hospitals—especially in cases where asbestos was a factor.

In 1994, Soloway summed up some of the distance traveled by the pioneers in the intervening 15 years:

> We tried to inform the carpenters' union what we thought they needed to do to make the union receptive to women and to be inclusive. And over a period of time, we became aware that the carpenters' union was not interested in fresh, new ideas coming from the rank-and-file. We came in with ideas about having sexual harassment [training] for the men in construction. We came in with ideas about having a women's committee that would address the issues of women in construction. We actually came in with ideas about how the apprenticeship school could be more in touch with the apprentices around issues of ethnicity and race.
>
> And what we were always told was, We're all one union. We're all brothers and there's no need to point out these differences because we're all carpenters. So the specific issues for women were never addressed... Now, almost 15 years later, they actually are being addressed. There is actually a women's committee now. It's not an official committee of the carpenters' union, but it's sanctioned to meet within the Carpenters' school and it's advertised in the carpenters' [news]paper that there is such a committee.
>
> There is specific sexual harassment training for men, and it's being done by women who are carpenters. Women who are graduates of our school are now teaching at the school and it's an important part of the program. Another one of our ideas was about teaching labor history in the Carpenters' school, which was then ignored, and now history's being taught in the Carpenters' school.
>
> Although the union and the apprenticeship in the carpenters' union was not what I would consider sexist—we were never discriminated against within the school—but the specific issues that were barriers to women were never addressed specifically. Now those issues are being addressed. We have women who are journey-level carpenters, who are now part of the school and the training and who have sought to take [on] the role of teaching younger apprentices, which is very significant really... So I have to admit that, from coming in as a rowdy gang of girls with big mouths and ideas, not knowing very much about this industry at all, to having people in the union and the school who are very savvy and are acknowledged for their skills... I'm not trying to paint a rosy picture, but that actually exists and that did not exist 15 years ago. So there's encouragement there.[9]

The Troubles

Sexism and harassment weren't the only obstacles. The District Council of Carpenters and its parent union, the United Brotherhood of Carpenters, have appeared repeatedly as the subject of tabloid stories about bribery, stolen funds, sold-out union jobs, mysterious real estate deals, murder, and other mayhem. The history of mob control of New York City's District Council has been on view in state and federal courtrooms. The Carpenters' headquarters, first on 23rd Street and then on Hudson, has been home to a series of corrupt officials.

Looking back to the days when Reyes and Soloway were earning their stripes as apprentices, the lineage begins with Ted Maritas. His term as president of the district council ran from 1977 to 1982, when he disappeared. That Maritas was also a Genovese crime family associate became known in time. Maritas was succeeded by Paschal McGuinness (1982–1991), followed by Fred Devine (1991–1996). Michael Forde currently inhabits the office. Another name of note is Vincent DiNapoli, a capo in the crime family, who was a major figure in New York City's drywall industry.[10]

The mob was able to maintain its control over the district council through its control of union jobs. The complicated calculus of the job referral system can easily be reduced to an old maxim: reward your friends and punish your enemies. Troublemakers found it hard to get a referral. Loyal supporters of the status quo had better luck. Of course, there were many other schemes to funnel money into the coffers of the Genovese family.

The drywall cartel and bid-rigging that went with it was one standard method. In March 1982, Ted Maritas, caught up in the continuation of court proceedings on the drywall case, dropped out of sight—permanently. Rumor had it that he was cooperating with federal investigators, thus causing a severe case of agita for the head of the Genovese family. The common assumption—to use a well-worn Sopranos' cliché—was that Maritas was "swimming with the fishes."

The fallout of all this corruption for the 30,000 members of the union, one of the largest in New York City, was significant.[11] CSU took it upon themselves to convince their fellow dues-paying brothers, as well as the small number of sisters in their ranks, that they paid a price—a mob tax—through this stranglehold on their union.

CSU activists employed a whole arsenal of tools. They posted "Silent Agitators"— stickers to make their case anonymously on job sites; they spoke—often at their own peril—from the floor of boisterous union meetings; ran for union office in some of the locals where they had gained a toehold among the membership; wrote open letters to their leadership; filed cases with the National Labor Relations Board that dragged on for years; and put out publications that sought to sort out the shady deals of their union representatives.

The *Rusty Nail* and *On the Level* were the main weapons of CSU, along with broadsides, dissecting subjects such as mysterious assessments; scab jobs in which payoffs occurred; missing pension funds; nonpayment of benefit funds; unposted job lists; and collective bargaining contracts. In this way, rank-and-file carpenters were able to learn where some of their dues money was going and how their leadership was discrediting the union.[12]

Considering her pedigree, it's not surprising that Consuelo Reyes would enlist in this cause. "I come from a very long line of dominant women. I know that people have a certain view of Latina women...but it's not true. It's a patriarchal society but it's equally matriarchal. I was very happily surprised to find out that one of my ancestors was Ana Roque, the founder of the Women's Suffrage Movement [in Puerto Rico]. She was also the first woman to publish a women's political magazine for suffragettes. She bought her own printing press."[13]

Reyes pointed out that she was born in New York City in 1948—"the same year that Truman de-segregated the military." Both of her parents were political activists. Her father was a printer and an anarcho-syndicalist from Spain, and her mother was a Puerto Rican nationalist. "She basically worked in garment factories in New York City," said Reyes. "But my dad was a really good carpenter and he could fix anything."

After meeting the leader of CSU, Frank McMurray, a member of Carpenter's Local 608, at a tradeswomen's event, Reyes took on the work of union reformer. "It was pretty clear that the union was mob-dominated and that the mob was moving into different locals. . . . Then they wanted to come into my local [Local 531], which was a Queens local, mostly German. . . Our business agent, Robert Waller, moved to align himself with them. He actually threatened me once. . . One of these guys that has never done a fucking day's work! I mean, if you want, take a look at my hands. Those are permanent calluses. No matter what I do, I can't get rid of them. This guy: manicured nails, the $300 shoes."

"So he was sent into our local and I was fighting against that. We were actually demonstrating. We were agitating against the Mafia. We were doing research. We were finding out that they were stealing from our pension funds. . . that they sold the carpenters' home in Florida with all this land for millions of dollars. Poof! The money was just gone. There were no checks and balances. In our union, the union leadership could just dip into any accounts that they wanted. We were doing research, finding out all this information, writing leaflets, and handing the leaflets out on the mob. . . . We would always slip copies of *On the Level* under the door or through the mail slot of the district council every time it came out." Reyes wrote articles for *On the Level*, drew cartoons, operated the mimeograph machine, and helped to distribute the paper. "It was a lot of fun," she recalled.

One event stands out in her long history—lasting up until she left New York City—of oppositional politics in the union. "We were threatened. . . I didn't get beaten up but I did bring a case against my business agent, which I won. I was working on the 59th Street Bridge. I had been handing out leaflets, just the normal stuff I had always done. This one was questioning where the money was disappearing to. . . He came up to the job site and brought my shop steward over. My shop steward was also kind of a bent-nose criminal type person. The business agent, Robert Waller, asked me if I had been handing my stuff out. He told the steward, 'If she keeps fucking around, you throw her off the bridge. You hear me? You throw her off the bridge.' So lunch was called, I got off the job, went down off the bridge, went to the pay phone, called my labor lawyer. Right there and then, he did a deposition."

"Burton Hall took the deposition, we brought the case, went to court, and we won. They thought I wanted money. Fuck! I was making good money. I didn't want any money. The union's lawyer said, 'Well how much do you want?' I said, 'I want an apology from my business agent from the union floor, and a statement by the union that we are allowed free speech—allowed to give out leaflets. We are allowed to print our newspaper and hand it out on any job site."

Reyes recounted the story with glee: "You should have seen when he had to apologize to me. It was so wonderful. That was at a union meeting. It was packed—packed!. . . Oh, the guys loved it. We got a really good response. The whole point of that was for people not to be so afraid. I mean, so many of the men were so intimidated by the fear of goons, by the fear of being beaten up, by the fear of being killed, which is the bottom line. What you're being threatened with is death. I remember when the Mafia killed two guys. . . They were taking scrap metal from big job sites and they could get a lot of money. Two construction workers were taking some of the scrap metal for themselves, and the mob threw them off the building."

Another CSU activist was attacked with a lead pipe, but he fought back—successfully. This story made the tabloids. As Reyes described, "They tried to hurt Gaetano [Macaluso], but he beat the crap out of the guy, which was fabulous. . . You know, it's not a good idea to attack people who are very strong and who've got tools!"

B.A. Robert Waller did issue his apology from the union floor and then, on January 10, 1984, in writing. Later, Waller's letter was printed in *On the Level*: He wrote:

> Dear Sister Reyes and Brother Macaluso: I am writing this letter to you to clarify any misunderstanding we may have had and to promote labor harmony within the union...I want to assure you that I will not threaten you or other members of the union...or inflict you with bodily harm or threaten you with any reprisals if you distribute leaflets critical of various union leadership policies or because you engage in any other protected concerted activities.[14] And so forth.

Reyes's assessment of CSU's role is shared by other knowledgeable observers of the District Council of Carpenters: "We never got really big. We never got to the point of being a mass movement within the carpenters' union...We were a part of what helped put the [District Council into] receivership 'cause we were doing some pretty damned good research."

More chapters—including an infamous shooting of union official John O'Connor—unfolded before 1990, when the Racketeer Influenced and Corrupt Organizations Act (RICO) complaint was filed against the district council. One result of this was the first direct election within the carpenters' union in more than 100 years. The members got to cast their votes in July 1995. By then, Reyes had left town. But a slate of union reformers ran for office in that election. In honor of their predecessors, they took the name Carpenters for a Stronger Union. And a strong woman did play a prominent role as part of that slate.[15]

If I Had a Hammer

Reyes made a pitch to women carpenters to join with their union brothers in reform efforts. In the spring 1985 issue of *On the Level*, she appealed to the sisters: "Some women members are afraid to get involved with NY CSU because they fear they will be black listed. On the contrary, if the women carpenters were organized together with the men, they could get what they want, a fair hiring hall system, an honest union and respect. Right now, the B.A. are not getting you work, so you have nothing to lose! There is an old saying: 'the squeaky wheel gets the oil.' If you remain a nice girl who says nothing on the job and sits quietly in the union hall week after week while the BA sends all his 'good buddies' out to work, you will get nothing!"[16]

But CSU activism wasn't for everyone—female *or* male. A much more successful attempt to organize female carpenters took place under the auspices of UT. The UT committee members started out as novices—green and idealistic—but adapted. Their campaign to set up an official committee within the union started in October 1980 with a petition to demonstrate support for the idea to their union leadership.

The UT petition described the benefits that could flow from such a committee: "We realize that, in order to stay in construction, we must deal with the conditions that force us out. By ensuring that the numbers of women in the union increase, we strengthen our voice and protect our jobs."[17] The organizers saw the committee as a place to deal with sexual harassment, recruitment of women into the union, and ensuring that women received adequate training to become mechanics. They also proposed that, "an optional new course be taught at the apprentice school about the history of the labor movement."[18]

After collecting signatures, the UT organizers sent the head of the District Council a letter, inviting him to meet: "Dear Mr. Maritas: We invite you, as our guest, to meet a small delegation of women for dinner at Gallagher's...to talk about some things that are very important to the women members." Both Reyes and Soloway signed the letter, along with others.[19] Needless to say, Ted Maritas never did accept their invitation. Less than two years later, he disappeared.[20]

In February 1981, an incident outside the carpenters' labor school made headlines. A line—eventually numbering 1,800 men and women—formed to pick up applications for the apprenticeship program. Some women camped out for four days to get their hands on the valuable form. *The New York Times* ran a front page photo of applicant Denise Edwards, smiling and holding aloft her application form.

However, the line turned into what was described in reports as, "a terrifying stampede" and women became the targets of abuse. A UT organizer tried to account for the melee: "This happened because the union and the school officials don't give a damn about women, or men. This wasn't the way to hand out applications and they knew it. They're just trying to get us to fight over a few jobs. In this case, women became the scapegoats for the men's anger and frustration."[21]

> Although the union had announced 2,000 applications would be given out, only 400 positions were supposedly open...Women especially wanted to get into the trade school since construction jobs are the best paying of blue-collar work. The women at the front of the line had come the night before. Members from United Tradeswomen, a rank and file caucus, had been there to cheer them on, offering advice on the program. By morning, the quiet vigil turned into an angry crowd. The men began taunting the women, shouting insults laced with sexual ridicule. The women were frightened but refused to move. Union officials watched the scene from open windows but refused to take action. When they finally opened the doors, people were literally thrown through the glass plates, injuring many more.[22]

One of the officials watching from the window was Charles Fanning, director of the Carpenters' apprenticeship program. Afterward, UT organizers, including Reyes and Soloway, sent their unsolicited suggestions to Fanning: "We are union members who are concerned after the events which occurred on February 23, 1981. We believe that the tension and disruption...could have been avoided. We would like to suggest some measures [to] be taken to secure applicants' safety during further recruitments."[23]

Carpenters active in UT continued to pitch ideas to the union leadership on how to smooth the path for female carpenters and bolster their retention rates—to no avail. Yet, outside the official union channels, they still found numerous ways to support women carpenters on their own—acting on the ideas that the union rejected. They held workshops to orient women to the union—its bylaws, benefits, history, and contracts; and on strategies to get steady work. They sent out surveys to find out what was happening out on the job sites; they met with women to collect information on what companies were hiring—or not, in an effort to document discrimination; and they participated in the campaign UT launched to get women hired onto construction jobs at the Javits Convention Center.[24]

Years later, Charles Fanning and Irene Soloway appeared before the New York City Commission on Human Rights to offer testimony about gender and race relations in the New York City District Council of Carpenters. On April 26, 1990, Charles Fanning delivered a smooth, deliberate presentation of facts as he interpreted them: "To the best of my knowledge, we don't have a formal program—other than myself—urging everybody at the monthly

District Council meetings to support women and minorities on the job. We haven't [formed a women's committee or people of color committee within the District Council to foster retention and advancement opportunities]. But it's not a bad idea," he admitted.[25]

Asked about sexual harassment, Fanning gave a pat answer: "Nobody has ever come to me in the 22 years that I've been Director of Training and said [someone exposed himself to me, or there's pornography on my site]. If they did, I would pursue it until I resolved the situation," he assured the commissioners.[26]

His statements were in response to riveting testimony delivered by the journeywoman carpenter Shirley Hemmings. The day after describing some of her experiences as a black woman working in the carpenters' trade, Hemmings woke up to find her photograph on the front page of *The New York Times*. She clearly had captured Fanning's attention.

In her guise as "Brick Shields," Soloway described the commission hearings for the *Hard Hat News*: "Shirley Hemmings is a journey-level carpenter in Local 608. She says that women are treated like trash on the job. 'Not even second class citizens any more ...' she talked about discrimination by the union in hiring (the shape up list is ignored...), being laid off first. Consistently (she was told by her foreman, 'we can't lay off men and keep women'), being grabbed on the job, flashed, cursed as a 'nigger,' cursed as a woman, used as a laborer, asked for sexual favors—'that's how the other women kept their jobs,' and always laid off first."[27]

After completing the union's apprenticeship program, Shirley Hemmings believed that she stood a chance to earn a decent living: As she said in her testimony: "After reaching journey-level status, I was often commended by the big bosses. Nevertheless, when there was a layoff, men with less seniority were kept while I was constantly laid off." In answer to why she kept going back, Hemmings added, "This is how I feed my family. It isn't fun, but it's a way of making a living. And I'm qualified."[28]

Other carpenters—male and female—also testified before the commission. As Soloway described, "Many women, anonymously or not, talked about sexual harassment in the form of rape threats, porno, and graffiti (often with their name on it), and direct physical threats."[29]

Michael Murphy, a member of Bronx Local 17, and a longtime activist with CSU, provided his own commentary on corruption and its relationship to race in the carpenters' union at the hearings:

> The construction trade is a cesspool. The Hispanics and blacks of New York City are the largest manpower pool of non-union labor in the city. There has been a concerted effort by the unions and contractors to prevent the tradesmen of the minority groups from becoming organized. A colleague was gunned down in front of his house for trying to organize minorities.[30] Discrimination prevails in job referrals.[31]

Murphy was asked why he was testifying about discrimination in his union, since he is not a minority. He replied, "If you want to maintain a strong union and union control on the job, you have to bring minorities in...it's the right thing to do."[32]

The road to representation, inclusion, and doing "the right thing" has been long and rocky for members of the carpenters' union. But throughout its history, there have always been brave, bold souls, both male and female, who, like Hemmings, Murphy, McMurray, and other members, stood up to challenge the status quo. Soloway was always an agitator—and an effective one.

Rebel with a Cause

Offering her public testimony before the Human Rights Commission, Soloway included an issue close to her heart—the barriers that cut down on the number of women working in the civil service trades' jobs. Under Section 61 of the state Civil Service Law, commonly called the "1-in-3" rule, city agencies can choose from among the three highest-scoring individuals who are eligible for the job. Once considered, the agency can then remove them from further consideration.[33] Soloway testified about the impact of this system on women:

> You need five years of experience as a journey person to take the [civil service] test…My experience was that I was fairly high on the list and I was rejected by each agency. I was a qualified applicant, so I assumed it was something to do with my gender…I think the city should *not* have the opportunity to discriminate in this way.[34]

Eventually, Soloway did get hired as a carpenter by the city's Health and Hospitals Corporation (HHC). Her activism on that job got its start around asbestos—and a campaign to prevent routine exposure on the job. Asbestos, once called the "magic mineral," and later found to cause crippling breathing disorders, mesothelioma, and other cancers, is a serious problem for all trades' people doing maintenance work on older buildings. The Board of Education is one city agency among many with a long, problematic history of ignoring the problem of exposure to employees in its asbestos-ridden facilities.[35] So, despite the fact that HHC buildings include the city's public hospitals, asbestos was a source of contention for those construction workers concerned about health and safety practices—and willing to speak up.

Certainly Irene Soloway was in that camp. In 1994, she spoke about the progress that resulted from putting up a fight, rather than submitting silently to working with the deadly microscopic fibers. "When this first started, I was doing fire code violation work in the hospital system—opening up ceilings and having asbestos fall down on your head. [While] I can't say my shop is perfect now, there's a much more informed and alert way of dealing with asbestos. Now, nobody works with asbestos. If it's perceived, the job stops. A crew comes in [and], cleans it up. They don't always clean it up the way that you'd want them to, but there is no more just pushing people to do it. People are pretty aware about asbestos and the shop has, with some exceptions, a standard, which is: You don't endanger yourself with asbestos."[36]

It wasn't always like that. Soloway took on the issue as a crusade. As she described, asbestos was "the one issue that could make me act like a lunatic. It was knowledge I couldn't put on the side," she recalled. After her vocal opposition and willingness to stick her neck out became apparent, some co-workers came to her and asked her to take on the role as their shop steward. She insisted on an election, rather than being appointed by the union, feeling that this would enhance her legitimacy among the members. She recalled her first meeting: "After I got elected, one guy told me to fuck myself and walked out. The other carpenters laughed and said, 'How do you like being steward?'"[37]

But Soloway used her position to good advantage. She contacted the White Lung Association (WLA) for information to educate herself and her co-workers. She brought samples from the job site to the WLA to have them properly tested. And she encouraged direct action at the many separate work sites:

> We've stopped so many jobs. And [now] we go into hospitals sometimes, where people [do] work with asbestos. They don't say anything. We go in, and we say: Do a test and *then* we'll work here. They have to do it. So I feel like the work we

did around that has paid off, to a certain extent. We got training and we still get it regularly. As those things go, it was good. It made it official—put the official stamp on the fact that you don't work with certain things—chemicals. You only work with respirators. I think it made a difference. I feel like we got pretty far on that.[38]

Another long-term project also yielded a positive outcome. Soloway, along with hundreds of other civil service carpenters, campaigned for over a decade to achieve direct representation within the district council. "We've been fighting for so many years to simply be able to have regular meetings of civil service carpenters on a schedule," she said. As Soloway described it in 1994, that decade-long drive was about to pay off: "Now we're going to have our own person. He has a commitment to having regular meetings, to having stewards training, to give us access to union lawyers, to things like getting our union work cards on time. Things that are important to people, that are indirectly a result of the [overall] reform process [in the union]."[39]

Soloway, writing under the pseudonym "Harry McBone" for the *Hard Hat News*, shared the steps taken by the organizers to reverse the history of poor representation. To accomplish this goal, the organizers retained their own legal counsel. They organized meetings. They lobbied the International union in Washington, D.C. They contested the results of the mail-in poll conducted by the parent union in D.C. and took the matter up with the Independent Counsel appointed by the court to oversee affairs in the district council.[40] This campaign paid off in 1994, with the appointment of Mike Power to the district council, as business agent for all carpenters throughout the civil service system in all of the agencies. He took up their grievances, negotiated contracts, and dealt with workplace issues, including health and safety.

Soloway's organizational savvy made a huge contribution to the success of this effort. Mike Power worked closely with her throughout this entire chapter and described some of her contributions:

> I met her very early, long before I ever got appointed to the district council. She was a great supporter of mine in trying to bring about change. Without her, and some other people, I never would have been able to accomplish that. But the thing I most admire about Irene was the high esteem she was held in by her fellow workers. I think that's a great thing to say about anybody in construction, but particularly a woman... She was greatly admired and she had a great sense of fairness about what was right. Health and safety was a huge thing for her and she was highly involved in exposing the issue. Irene was probably one of the most dedicated people that I have met in the last 34 years.[41]

The Circle Game

On a cold Friday evening, December 1, 2006, hundreds of women carpenters and their children filed into a large room at the union headquarters for the annual holiday party. Sponsored by the Women's Committee, the event offered an opportunity to get a sense of the dynamic presence of women in the union and to view the give-and-take between two generations: the pioneers and the young women who are struggling to learn, to get work, and to support their families. A joyful hubbub filled the room as friends connected with each other and children sought out new acquaintances.

Before the holiday party—the food, festivities, Toys for Tots, and raffle—the Committee put together a panel discussion. It featured women carpenters with more than 20 years working in their trade. They spoke about what it was like to survive as a pioneer and provided some advice for the younger women. Comments included stories like, "I had two sons and I was very motivated to make money! I decided that the ultimate thing for me would be to get a man's salary!" Or, "In my experience, discrimination is much more covert now." Another woman offered this anecdote: "You hear that you're 'taking a man's job.' I've been on the job for 25 years. Yet they see us walk on the job and they say: 'Why is *she* here?'"...Or tips, such as: "If you let them push you into a corner, they will." Or—"I carry a box of band aids on the job to cover up porn."[42]

Panelist Rebecca Lurie joined the staff of the carpenters' school back in 1992 as a counselor—a pioneer now paving the way for women from inside the union. Lurie traces her history back to the early days when women were like strangers in a strange land—struggling for equilibrium and acceptance. Her own story started in upstate New York. A self-described hippie, she got involved in construction through working on alternative types of building projects.

In the face of daunting obstacles, women had to be creative in developing coping strategies. Early in her career, Rebecca Lurie faced a problem on a project: "It was a motel that had very cheap plastic laminated wall covering: I put the hole in the wrong place for the pipe, and that's the kind of thing you can't patch. And someone had got me a book during this time, *Against the Grain*, and there was an expression in it: 'a good carpenter knows how to fix her mistakes.' So I was all by myself, and there was this mantra that I just started chanting: A good carpenter knows how to fix her mistakes. And that was for me, an experience, because I figured out a way to fix my mistakes."[43]

Against the Grain became Lurie's bible. Written and illustrated by pioneering carpenter Dale McCormick, it offered a common sense approach to gaining competency. Along with learning how to fix mistakes, the author counseled patience in learning the craft: "Do not get frustrated at yourself; look to your method," McCormick wrote. The manual also punctured the mystique of male ownership of skill. "Men have learned it slowly over the years and if they did not learn the mechanical skills well enough, they learned how to bullshit."[44]

Lurie kept on finding a way to learn. She went to the library to read about fasteners. She went to the hardware store. "I asked more questions than they could tolerate," she recalled. "And I remember being very, very demoralized when I got laid off—that they never had me do anything beside move materials. I was very disappointed that they laid me off, 'cause I was the *best* damn materials handler around. How could they lay me off?...And it turned out to be a really good opportunity. I learned that when one door closes, you can have better opportunities...So one of my strategies was to just keep on working."[45]

Eventually, patience and persistence pays off, Lurie said. "You start feeling comfortable handling your tools. They start to feel like your own. You take pride in your tool box and in ownership of your tools. It's something you can really gauge."

She recalled other aspects of the struggle to survive in an alien workplace culture. "I remember during my apprenticeship, being appalled at the level of sexism....A woman carpenter apprentice's husband came on the job and beat her up in the morning, before work started. And by the time I arrived, it had already occurred. I was appalled and I was having a conversation with everybody. They were like, 'You don't get involved with that. That's his wife and you don't touch that.' It was all about noninvolvement and condoning it because you don't know what their business is...he could be right in doing it. And I was appalled for days."

"But in terms of how I tolerated the crew—how I handled everybody's response—I took everybody so seriously and I ended up angry at everybody...If I had stayed dogmatic in my responses, I couldn't have survived. You have to walk out. And I have walked out. In different instances, I've changed jobs. I have had instances where I walked into the bathroom and cried. I have had horrible days when I went home. But my own sense of tolerance of these people, and their opinions had to adjust. I've figured out ways to maneuver—different ways to have conversations or to change to things that are humorous—to turn things around."

Lurie was able to share her skills and coping strategies with others after she became a counselor for the union's apprenticeship program. In 1994, both Lurie and carpenter Deborah Starr Reed were hired to address the issues of retention and recruitment from the inside. Lurie taught the first sexual harassment course given at the carpenters' school. As she described, the program was an attempt to train shop stewards in the fundamentals of sexual harassment.[46]

Lurie also began going out to speak about the opportunities for women in the trades. "At the Carpenters' school, we get calls all the time for Career Day speakers," she said. "And I said to my supervisor, 'I think you should send the women.' I think that's who needs to go to these things. Any one of us could tell them what a carpenter does, but it's the women who can influence other women.... So it was kind of an interesting place to be. You see that, from this official capacity, you could have some impact."

In 2000, Lurie was hired by the Consortium for Worker Education to direct a program for high school students, male and female, which provides instruction as a route from vocational school into the union's apprenticeship program. A profile of the program prepared by the Fiscal Policy Institute pointed to the "lengthy and difficult history of efforts to open up entry into the unionized segment of the trades' labor market." But the fact that the unions have bought into this program has led to more positive results. Largely because of this labor-backing, the program, called Construction Skills 2000 (CS2K), "has enjoyed consistent success and support at providing pre-apprenticeship training for teenagers, mostly black and Latino, from New York City public schools. The program currently trains about 150 participants per year. Upon completion of the program, participants apply for the union-based apprenticeship program of their choice."[47]

Lurie maintains her union book and is an active contributor to the—now official as of 2002—Women Carpenters' Committee. On March 31, 2007, she took part in another panel discussion about organizing and tradeswomen and described the role of the Carpenters' Women's Committee in trying to address the needs of women in the union. Sounding very much like the women from UT, she said, "We wanted to create a space where it was safe for women to ask their questions and to get information."[48]

The number of women in the carpenters union in New York City has grown from 200 to 450—just less than 2 percent. Yet the number of women within the ranks of the apprenticeship program has doubled within the past few years.[49] Women currently comprise 13 percent of the apprenticeship program. Despite the huge amount of progress—and the many special programs set up by activists on the Women's Committee of the New York City District Council—issues remain that complicate the lives of female carpenters.

One is the persistent bias against the presence of women on the job. Women are still seen as a novelty act—under pressure to prove their worth—repeatedly. As Rebecca Lurie pointed out, "We work ourselves out of a job every day we go to work. And the fact is, that there's a tremendous bias against women, no matter how good you are."[50]

Out on job sites, Veronica Session sees this attitude cropping up in various ways. Asked which presents a bigger problem for her—race or gender—she laughs and says, "It depends on the day." But in general, she sees gender as the bigger issue: "There are minor things that aren't minor for women.... I think the bathroom thing is an issue, 'cause you're made to feel kind of like, less than. Even though it's construction, it's a job for us and we shouldn't be treated as less because we don't work in an office. So we should have an accessible bathroom. We should not have to go through changes to get it. . . . I think that also sends a message to the men—kind of like: We're just not worthy or something."[51]

Aside from the pornography, comments about displacing a man from the job, and the lack of bathroom facilities for women, there are subtle and not-so-subtle messages for women to pick up on. Walking past a construction site at the corner of 42nd Street and Sixth Avenue, Session points to the huge photos that cover the fences surrounding the site, noting that all of them feature males. She produces a copy of an advertisement that is more than an oversight, one example of the lingering sexism in the industry: "Stanley Tools selling their FAT/Max XTREME Tape Measure" with the slogan, "You Could Use A Regular Tape. YOU COULD ALSO RIDE A GIRL'S BIKE TO WORK."[52]

But for every negative, there are off-setting positives—including the paychecks—for women. Irene Soloway can clearly see the change in the landscape from her vantage point as a pioneer:

> The women who are coming in now . . . say that men are friendlier—that some of the barriers are down. The difficulty of maintaining a livelihood in the industry is probably still harder for women than men. But these younger women that I've met feel a certain kind of confidence about it. And I think the men have gotten used to us being a part of the industry. Many problems [still] exist, but the real pioneering days, in terms of social barriers to women in construction—that big, monolithic kind of thing we experienced in the 70s, has changed.[53]

Soloway sets her life in the trades into a broader framework: "There's a certain amount of job satisfaction in being a carpenter. That's been part of my staying power—being part of a large, important industry in New York City—and knowing hundreds and hundreds of people in the industry. This may seem really corny, but there's still a concept of, quote-unquote 'brotherhood.' You go on the subway and you see these guys who have sheet rock dust on their shoes and their *Daily News*, and a cooler, and you just know each other. They're you and you're them . . . you don't have to know each other's names. I don't feel isolated. . . . You know what their lives are like and they know what your life is like. [Well] to a certain degree, as a woman, they're not sure, but *you* know what their lives are like. And you know it's dangerous, but it's an exciting occupation. That's what I like about it. It could be better, but I have to say, I admire a lot of things about the people whom I work with. I've learned a lot being in construction, and my community is enormous!"[54]

THIRTEEN

Getting Past Pioneering

As young women set out to enter skilled blue-collar jobs in the early twenty-first century, some of their experiences will echo those of their predecessors. Happily though, some won't. Changes are taking place, albeit slowly. Margarita Suarez and Angela Olszewski speak for a younger generation of women working in the construction trades. Both project a sense of calm self-possession. One has an effervescent personality; the other is low-keyed. But the two young women have very different backgrounds and motives: blue-collar Angela was attracted by the trade; Margarita, a product of the middle class, was attracted by the challenge.

Angela Olszewski worked at any number of unskilled jobs before learning about the training program at Nontraditional Employment for Women (NEW). After graduating from the 12-week pre-apprenticeship program, she went from a clerical position for the New York City Parks and Recreation Department to learning how to set tile. She brought the trade union principles she learned from her father to her new world. It would prove to be a valuable asset.

Margarita Suarez studied computer science in college and then went to work in the field. As she advanced in her career, she witnessed a steady progression of women in science and technology. In 2000, she left a high paid, comfortable position at Columbia University to go to work at NEW. Eventually she decided to take up a trade and applied to become an apprentice elevator mechanic.

Following their entrance into the skilled trades, their experiences on the job and in their unions, their achievements, the obstacles they face, and the organizing they undertake on behalf of other women add up to a contemporary, activist perspective on what remains a frontier for females.

A Circuitous Road to Elevator Mechanic

Margarita Suarez was born in Manila, Philippines, in 1967. When she was six months old, her parents migrated to Rochester, New York. At age 11, her family moved to Jacksonville,

Florida. After graduating from high school, she attended Columbia University, where she majored in computer science. In 1989, she went to work for Columbia:

> Just as I was about to graduate [in 1989], I landed a full-time job as a systems programmer...That was a very nurturing environment. I had to learn everything. In fact, it was like an apprenticeship, except it wasn't formal. It was on-the-job train-ing. You're basically thrown into some situations and you're working with someone who is more experienced. You pick up tips and tricks and they instruct you. And you figure it out on your own.[1]

One year later, Suarez took advantage of the tuition exemption offered to Columbia University employees and enrolled in a master's program in computer science through the School of Engineering. She had to supplement her liberal arts background with courses in statistics, probability, and mathematics. Even after completing this degree in 1994, she kept taking courses, studying Spanish and then earning a second B.A. in Women's Studies. Soon after completing this program in 1998, her life took a different turn.

While working for Columbia University, Suarez used her vacation time to travel to other countries. Visiting Nicaragua as a tourist, she happened upon the small town of Cunedega. Here she learned that 10 years before, tradeswomen had set up a women's construction cooperative. This group included women from New York City. She spent a few days in town as a volunteer: "They taught me how to lay blocks, how to tie iron reinforcements together. It's called metal lathing in New York City. I learned how to pour concrete, all in just three days."

After returning home, Suarez found opportunities to work on other construction proj-ects. She went to the Catskills to help build a wood-fired kiln at a pottery school. As she described, "I've always had an interest in building things. This was all tying together, because when I was young, my dad, who is an architect, used to have a carpentry shop in the garage. I remember, at the age of five and six, being in there with him while he was building something. He would let me finish pounding the nail, or I would hold the wood together while he drove the nail."

In 1998, Hurricane Mitch tore through Central America. Margarita Suarez volunteered to raise funds to help rebuild houses in Nicaragua. It was then that she met some of the trades-women who once again worked with the construction cooperative they'd set up back in 1986, to help rebuild the small town. She got to know electrician Evan Ruderman and carpenter Rebecca Lurie on this project. Suarez had her own reasons for helping out:

> I actually had a selfish reason for getting involved with their fundraising project. I wanted to be one of the women to go on the building brigade...They welcomed anyone who wanted to help. There's always a powerful exchange when women are helping each other from different countries. There's something that each side gets from the other...We went down in February 1999. There were six of us. Only one was a professional builder, from Wales. There were three or four women from New York City and one from Boston. We were there for a month and we started the first house of that project. Eventually, there were 30 houses built, so that was really great to be the inaugural brigade to start it all off.

This experience had a profound impact on her. As she recalled, "I had kind of been tak-ing life as it comes. Then, at that point, I was realizing that I'd had this incredible experience of going to Nicaragua, helping out these people who lost their entire house, and working with these women who had third-grade educations, but were learning a trade to make a living. We were building something that someone could live in and actually making something out of nothing—and also, just being around a different way of life, a different tempo, different values, and different levels of wealth or poverty. After going to Nicaragua a couple of times...the main conclusion I arrived at was that there are many types of crisis in the world. There's losing your e-mail and there's losing your house. I found it harder and harder to reconcile the amount of stress and pressure that I was putting upon myself or people were putting on me to get that e-mail back up at four o'clock in the morning, when I had just returned from helping someone get their house back up."

"So it was a really hard decision to make. It took me about a year to come to the decision. Part of it was fear of change, I'm sure, and the insecurity of the unknown. But part of it was also that I had a mint position. I was making lots of money, [working] for a nonprofit, without the pressures of being on Wall Street...I had a lot of education. There were a lot of smart people everywhere, lectures to attend, movie screenings and classes to take, access to the gym, and to the 22 libraries." All this she left behind in 2000.

As a first step, she called NEW to volunteer her services: "I was about to get my resume together and I was looking on Idealist.org and found out that NEW actually had a position that was open. It was three days a week, coordinating the federal WANTO grant. WANTO stands for Women in Apprenticeships in Nontraditional Occupations."[2]

> I knew nothing about labor unions, really. I mean nothing about construction unions in New York City. I hadn't really focused on labor...in college. So I almost felt that I wasn't qualified for the job. But it did really interest me, so I interviewed for it and ended up landing it. That started the career change.

At NEW, Suarez immersed herself in the world of the skilled trades. As she worked with the directors of apprenticeship programs, she developed an appreciation for their receptivity or resistance to women in their trades. She began to teach and developed a curriculum for high school students preparing to enter the construction trades. She also became an advocate on behalf of tradeswomen. Then, while working on a pilot project to recruit women into an apprenticeship program, Suarez made the leap herself. She applied to take the test for the elevator service and repair division of Local 3, the electricians' union.

Definitely Her Father's Daughter

Growing up in Green Point Brooklyn, Angela Olszewski was part of a bustling blue-collar neighborhood. Her roots in the working class are deep. "The folks in the family who came to Ellis Island basically went to Green Point and stayed there for 100 years," she said. Her grandfather worked for Taylor's Iron Foundry and was a union shop steward. "It was such heavy, hard work. He also was a bartender on the weekends and when he was a kid he delivered ice with his father in a horse and wagon."[3]

Olszewski's mother, an Italian-American, worked at a machine embroidery sweatshop. "My cousins and I used to go to the factory. It was just a little shop. I have all these memories. Before there was a 'take your daughters to work day,' I was going to work with my parents." Her father, a Polish-American, jumped at the chance to apply for a civil service job with the

Sanitation Department. "He had taken the test in his 20s and there was a freeze on hiring so he didn't get called until he was in his 30s," she recalled. For the last 10 of his 20 years on the job, Olszewski's father began to agitate within his union and in this he had an apt assistant:

> My dad did quite a bit of his own rabble rousing. When he started the job, there was a three-man truck picking up garbage. During his time, it was reduced to two men, one driving and one lifting....My dad would try to talk to the men and say, "You're going to throw your back out. You're going to mess up your elbows."...I began to help him with his grievance letters....My dad would give me a synopsis or some notes and I would compose his letters. From 16 on I was doing that for him and that really started to educate me about the process of grievance and fairness and justice in the union.

She helped out at home in other ways: "My parents were always working so much, so they took a big chance in the 70s and purchased two properties in Brooklyn. My father knew he could fix them up. Over the years, as I got older, I began to help him with renovations. I still do to this day. I recently renovated two bathrooms in the buildings and it blew them both away. I tiled them up and grouted them. He was just floored about how quickly I did it and turned it around. They were beaming with pride, I could tell."

Before she learned this skill, she worked at a series of odd, colorful jobs—everything from selling cigars at the famous Mom's Cigars at Fifth Avenue and 20th Street, to doing market research. "I called it an electronic sweatshop," she recalled. Then she worked for the Brinks Armored Car Company in the money room. "I counted millions and millions of dollars in cash, night after night."

On the job, Olszewski learned about the union-busting campaign carried out years before by Brinks:

> It happened well before I got there. I realized while I was there that something was strange. All the management was white and all the workers were mostly people of color. There was a white guy on the day shift and I was the white girl on the night shift. Right there, the picture felt weird. I brought it up to management: how come there's not a nighttime differential? Every three months, we'd have a meeting and they'd explain to us how it would not be good if we had a union. They said, "If anybody ever asks you to sign cards...you're going to spoil what we have here." I heard about NEW while I was at Brinks. I filed it in the back of my head.

Her next job was selling tennis permits as a Seasonal Clerical Associate for the Parks Department. "I worked in a very high-profile location called The Arsenal, where former Parks Commissioner Henry Stern worked." After she spoke up to management about a couple of unfair practices that were prevalent at the job location, her days were numbered. "My season was up, it truly was. I just ran right to NEW."

Looking back, Olszewski concedes that she had "mythologized" the construction trades' unions: "I just figured: skilled construction trades? I bet those unions are good. I bet there's solidarity there." Looking to select a trade, she knew what she wanted: "I definitely wanted to go into a skilled finishing trade where my work would show, 'cause I was going after it with a lot of pride. I wanted to really get involved in something and be proud of it...I came through the door at NEW saying I wanted to be a bricklayer:"

> Again, I was looking at it very romantically. I wanted to do arches and I was thinking what I could do with landscaping, like what you see in beautiful old brick

buildings. But really, brickwork nowadays in new construction is façade and it's very plain. So the director discouraged me. It was good that she did, because as time went by and I learned more about that union, I'm glad I didn't go in that direction. It would have broken my heart.

So I went to the library and I took out a bunch of books on tile. I started leafing through the pages and I just fell in love with it because it's such a finishing trade. This one thing stuck in my head: these tiles that were inside a canal that was around a palace [that was built] in the fourteenth century. I thought, wow! That's what I want. I want to put something up and I want it to last longer than me.

Completion of the 12-week program at NEW is a milestone for the women who are hopeful about the new possibilities awaiting them. The graduation at NEW is a recognition of the special meaning the ceremony holds for both the students and their families. Angela Olszewski spoke about the significance it held for herself and her classmates:

I kept my [graduation] program from that day. It was great. Two people dropped out of our class, but the rest of us really hung in there. We got very close during the 12 weeks. If you saw somebody sinking, you picked them up. We were tight like that. I wrote and read a poem at the ceremony and it was tied to the context of the experience that we all had. But what was amazing to me was—when I looked out at the audience—they were applauding like crazy. So many people had tears in their eyes. I couldn't believe it.

A Is for Access

In gaining entrance to their respective union apprenticeship programs, both women had the benefit of a boost from an attentive, experienced training organization—NEW. While working as the WANTO coordinator for NEW, Suarez could see one problem—information about applying to union apprenticeship programs was not widely disseminated. At the same time, the building trades unions were reluctant to take extra measures that might bring in more female applicants. This was one of the stumbling blocks that NEW worked to address. Meanwhile, some unions did work closely with NEW in an attempt to recruit female applicants through innovative programs.

As part of her job, Suarez was heading up a pilot program to recruit women for the Elevator Division of Local 3, International Brotherhood of Electrical Workers (IBEW).[4] "We were able to collect 120 completed applications, out of thousands and thousands of requests for information," she explained. "Out of that 120, only 15 or so actually finished and went to the testing and the interview. Out of those, 7 passed the test. Four were admitted after the interview and showed up."

During this process, Suarez decided to test herself. "I knew it would be a good trade for me because two of my mentors...are in the International Union of Elevator Constructors.[5] So getting feedback from them, they knew I would be happy in this trade—probably more than happy! The reason for that is that, in my trade, although there are many manual aspects to it, and menial [ones] as well, there is a troubleshooting function that the best mechanics are good at...It's a good trade for me because I think I'm really good at synthesizing information and drawing conclusions about different technologies. Being introduced to new ones, I don't feel threatened or nervous about that."

Another aspect of her decision resulted from her work as an advocate for tradeswomen:

> Actually, [it was] an experience I had in Washington and meeting with the vice-president of the Building and Construction Trades Department[6]...The other activists I was working with are saying, "Hi, I'm Lauren Sugerman, Elevator Constructor." "Hi, I'm Beth Youhne, Operating Engineer." Then I would introduce myself as Margarita Suarez from Nontraditional Employment for Women. Already, that's placing myself outside this conversation. I am an outsider. I thought: why don't I see what it's like to be on the inside. I'll get some firsthand experience. I'll build some credentials for future work...I knew my WANTO funding was going to run out.[7] So it was either fight for more funding, or actually switching to the other side and advocate for women from the inside.

After getting accepted into the apprenticeship program, Suarez had to pass on her first job placement from the union, to finish up all of the paperwork for the WANTO grant she was administering. Then she was ready to set out on a new career.

B Is for Barrier-Busters

Olszewski had a trade all picked out. But she faced some obstacles as the union kept putting her off. Finally, Olszewski was accepted into the apprenticeship program of Local No. 7. On February 14, she began a 12-week pre-job training program with the Bricklayers Union. "It was for all the trades: bricklayers, marble, terrazzo, and tile."

Both in the classroom and on the job, she excelled. "It was really fine," she said. "The instructor was a jolly good guy. The class was so small that we had his attention. Basically, I could ask him anything I wanted—he was always right there...I was the only woman at that facility except for the secretary [in the office]. She was pleasant—very pleasant: 'Hi Angie, how you doing?'"

But as she got closer to going onto a job site, a bit of subtle sexism became apparent. There was an agreement in place between the union and the company that was worked out by NEW. As Olszewski described it, "The agreement went something like this: The company said to the union, 'If you take her, we'll try her,' while the union said to the company, 'If you train her, we'll take her.' I'm training and I want to get to work at this company. Then my apprenticeship coordinator started to say, 'That's a tough shop, Angela. It's heavy work.'"

> But I was up for it. This is what I wanted to do. I knew I wanted to get my hands on this material...to touch marble and to actually set every piece of marble is a wonderful experience. It really is and it totally vibrates with me, that I know I should be doing this. This is the trade I want...My first job with that company was the Bridge Tower apartments on First Avenue right by the 59th Street Bridge. That's where the Roosevelt Tram is, right? And we did white Carrara marble.[8] Oh, that was so beautiful!

After working on that job for two months and meeting all of the production standards set for her, Olszewski got an invitation from her International union to attend its Masonry Camp. The one-week camp is held every summer on Swan Island in Maine. "Basically, it's a public relations type of event, where they bring together what they consider outstanding apprentices from all over the country from all the different trades: brick, stone, terrazzo, and tile. I was the only one from my local and there were two other women apprentices. One was a bricklayer from Detroit and the other was a stone mason from Philadelphia...It was really incredible. What they want to facilitate is that the architects and the stone masons understand each other."

Upon returning to her former job, Angela soon ran into difficulties with a co-worker. A pattern of harassment began to build. At first, she chose to avoid his shenanigans. She sensed that he was trying to provoke her into a response. He had a habit of climbing onto a pallet in the changing room and stripping. One day, he sat down beside Olszewski and brushed up against her. She told him off in no uncertain terms. Then out on the street, he continued to exhibit inappropriate behavior. One day, he reached into his pants and pulled out his penis. As she described the incident, "I turned my head away. I caught sight of one guy looking over in his direction and he's like appalled...like he's just being so embarrassing to all of us. Despite that, nobody said anything...It's disrespectful. I'm not a prude. I'm not going to be a Puritan about these things. As I tell women, this is not the choir of angels that you're joining. But I just felt he was daring me to say: 'Please don't take your penis out.' I'm not going to play into his hands."

> So in less than a week's time, we're all on the street again and there's a pretty woman walking by. I felt so bad for her...On a hot summer day, she turned the corner and all the construction workers were sitting on the ground eating their food. So they all start catcalling. And this guy is like the master of ceremonies. He's screaming to her: "Are those real?" "Are those real?" And she's trying to be digni-fied and just walk. But finally she turns around and she grabs both her breasts and she shakes them at him and she goes: "They're real!" "They're real!" Is *that* real?' He says: "You want to know if it's real?" And he starts unzipping his pants to take his penis out again.
>
> I was just so fed up. So I got up and I walked away. I went to a pay phone. I called my apprentice coordinator. I was so disappointed ... Somebody could just say: "Listen. Don't do that." Nobody steps up. So I called and I said, "I just want somebody to talk to him, I don't want to do it because that's what he wants me to do. He wants me to come to him and say 'Please don't. And psychologically, I'm not playing that game with him.'" So I return to work and one of the other mechanics says, "You know, that wasn't right what he did out there." I said, "If it was me and a hundred other women, it wouldn't be the same as if you said something...Just you. It would mean everything." He said, "You're right."

The union representative did show up on the job. He told the man to take his tools—that he was off the job. At this point, things turned dramatic, as Olszewski described it: "He came running up the stairs. Someone jumped between us. He was screaming and crying, tears in his eyes. He was really upset that he was getting kicked off that job...It's a shame that it had to come to that stage, but that just seems to be the way it always goes." But she appreciated the fact that the union responded so quickly and took a severe action.

One year later, Olszewski was at a union meeting. "He walked right up to me and said, 'I'm very sorry. I was an ass. I had to go to a union hearing. I had to pay a fine.' Not only that! I heard a story through the grapevine. He went to another job with a woman tile setter—her name is Rita—and the foreman on that job was giving Rita a hard time. This was after the incident with me. This man stuck up for her. So maybe he learned a big lesson. Maybe he's an ally now—so it could be great!"

On her next big job, she worked on the Ritz-Carlton Hotel at Battery Park. "There were a lot of great opportunities there for training, and I was very, very diligent about keeping track of the skills I needed to acquire," she explained. "After a while, the foreman complimented me quite a bit: he told me I had hands of gold. I was really good at marble setting. But he kind of pigeonholed me into this one particular project—doing backsplashes right behind the sink. That's not uncommon when you work on a big job... But as an apprentice, I need to try everything."

This has been an ongoing problem for women—not receiving the full range of training needed to survive as a journeyperson. Olszewski broached the subject of moving on to a different task repeatedly with her foreman. As she put it, "My apprenticeship is going to be over one of these years and if I don't have these skills, they're going to be like, kid, we don't have anymore backsplashes for you. I asked him once. I asked him twice."

Once again, Olszewski was selected by the International union to participate in an exhibition of her new skills. She participated in the International union's exhibit at the Smithsonian Folk Life Festival. The exhibit was called Masters of the Building Arts. "I was there installing tile and people would walk through the exhibit and ask you questions," she recalled. "It was a wonderful experience."

There were two other women and some men of color. As Olszweski said, "We really looked very politically correct on up this stage in the nation's capitol. And that's when I realized that there are a lot of façades and they're not just on the buildings. So I did that and I was very proud to do that and I was paid handsomely to do that. While I was at the Folk Life Festival, I spoke to the president of my local. He asked me, 'How's it going?' I said, 'Things are going good, but I want to move on to doing walls.' He said, 'If things don't change, let me know.'"

"I returned back to the Ritz-Carlton with an agenda—that I was moving on from the back splashes! The [new] apprenticeship coordinator showed up, but he said to me, 'You know Angela, I don't want you to burn your bridges.' And right there I lost complete faith in him. I thought: You know, I've been doing this better on my own and I will continue to do it. So I let him walk away that day and I went home. I looked at all the paperwork and I wrote down all the different tasks that I've been doing." She sent the information to all interested parties including her International union, local union, and the company. When Olszewski showed up at work, her foreman said, "You're upset. Lady, there's nothing to be upset about!" Not that day but the next day, they moved her on to the job she had requested. She won a victory and it happened at the end of August 2001. Then September 11th dawned.

A year and a half after Olszewski completed her three-year apprenticeship program she received her certificate. "I got it in the mail. It says: 'This is to certify that Brother Angela Olszewski has completed the training and required hours to be a Journeyman Tile Setter.' The date on the document is May 12, 2003."

Girl Helper

Margarita Suarez experienced a smooth path throughout her apprenticeship. Her first assignment was, as she described it, a "mint placement." She consistently received support and also got to see some of the more tender aspects of her fellow mechanics. Only "a handful" of women were in the apprenticeship program. She knew of at least one female mechanic working in her division. When Suarez was sent out on her first referral, the company didn't give her work. She went back to the Joint Employment Office maintained by the union and employers. There she learned that, "That wasn't supposed to happen."

But after that inauspicious beginning, she got a good placement at Nouveau Elevator Industries, a large, privately held company run by a family of mother, father, and their four sons. She started on a Thursday and by Monday, was assigned to sit with the resident mechanic. "I didn't know it at the time, but afterward, he told me that that was my test: that the boss said, 'Take this girl helper and she what she's made of—see if we're going to keep her or not.' He said that I passed the test and they were going to keep me. That was kind of nice in hindsight, since I didn't even know so I wasn't nervous and I was just being myself."

About two months after starting, a resident job opened up at the NYU Medical Center on 30th Street and First Avenue. The university pays to have two mechanics and two helpers on this job. Even before she arrived on the scene, the stage was set for her entrance.

> Unbeknownst to me, my boss had put out the word that if anyone screwed up in front of me, there would be hell to pay. Meaning, take down the porn; be nice to her; I don't want to hear any bullshit kind of thing. Her first conversation with her boss, her future supervisor, was also an eye-opener. He said, "I'll talk to you frankly. You're the first woman I've ever had in my department. I'm not really sure some of the guys are going to be good and I don't know about the rest of them. So if anything should happen, whatsoever, this is my cell phone number. I want you to call me right away." I took that as a good faith effort for him to support my success.

Suarez's supervisor provided another piece of welcome information that was encouraging to the new Nouveau employee: "He also said that he would like to say when he retires that he had a couple of women mechanics under him. So that felt really good, especially after being turned down for that first job." Nobody was overtly unwelcoming, with the exception of one mechanic. But then, he was uniformly out of sorts with everyone.

The two mechanics Suarez worked with turned out to be positive experiences in different ways. She described the first mechanic, "He's a really smart guy, kind of nerdy and quirky. He's got a very obsessive personality, so when he's talking about something, he'll just talk and talk and give you a lot of information. I like it and I get along with him. After the first day, he said to me, 'When they told me you were going to come down here, I didn't know what to think. I was a little bit nervous; a little bit anxious. I didn't know what was going to happen. But we're okay, right? It's working out, right?' It was really earnest and sweet of him to even admit to me that he was feeling anxious. It just felt really nice and close. So I had a pretty good idea that it would work out well."

The second mechanic was even more nervous at the start: "Now that I know his personality a little better, he tends to assume the worst. So I think he was probably thinking: 'Oh, they're sticking the girl helper here. I don't know if that's going to mean more work for me.' But I've been pulling my weight and learning and I think they've been happy with how I've been doing. The different comments and overall behavior of her co-workers led her to the belief that they have a positive attitude toward her." She points to the fact that these men are young as a plus.

> They're in their early 30s. Although they've been in the field for 15 and 10 years respectively, they're young enough to imagine a girl doing this, even though they've never seen one before.

After working at the Medical Center for almost a year, she had to cover the hospital by herself. "I actually worked on three elevators and didn't break anything, didn't hurt myself, I didn't hurt anyone else, so it feels kind of good. I'll get paid as a B Mechanic...for a day of overtime. My mechanic was joking with me that this is more money than I pretty much make in a week. It's not true, but it's close."

Suarez experienced an act of acceptance from her union brothers soon after she started in the apprenticeship program. As she described it: "The shop steward at my company is actually the chairman of the elevator division, so he knows me. The interesting thing is that before they knew I had quit [my job] at NEW, the Office of Apprenticeship Training and Employer Labor Services, OATELS, with whom I had done some work on a pilot project to offer technical assistance to employers and unions...asked me to speak about these recruitment practices."

> This was for the Eastern States Apprenticeship Conference in Maine. All the apprenticeship directors go and I know a bunch of them from my work at NEW...So I arranged to get time off with my boss. In Portland, I went to register and the first person that I saw was my shop steward, the chairman of my division. My division has 1,600 people out of 33,000 in Local 3, so I wasn't thinking that we would be there in force. So he said, "What are you doing here?" I said, "Oh, I'm speaking."

All of the Local 3 representatives attended her talk. "It was really nerve-wracking," she recalled. "There's always a bit of distance that they put between me and them." But after her talk, they were standing nearby. "My shop steward came up to me. He just said, 'Do you have a lapel pin?' I said, 'No, I don't.' Then he said, 'Here. Take one. You need one of these. It's an Elevator Division, IBEW, Local 3 lapel pin.' So I took that as a sign that I did good ... That gesture of handing me a pin, I think, was like, 'Okay, you can kind of be one of us, 'cause we're the delegates who go to the conferences kind of thing.'"

Getting Beyond the Gender Divide

As she took her place in the apprenticeship program, Suarez didn't see herself as a pioneer. "I didn't consider myself a pioneer when I entered this field 'cause two of my mentors have been in this field for 25 years. Women have been going into the trades for so many years. Then when I arrived and found out that I was the first one in the company and one of four in the [apprenticeship] school, it made me feel a little bit like a pioneer. On the other hand, I really feel that because of the work that was done before me, I'm in a good position."

> Also, it may have something to do with [the fact that] the best mechanics, the hot shots in my trade are not the brawniest ones but the brainiest ones—the ones who can fix elevators that no one else can fix. So maybe they're able to appreciate that in somebody—whether they're a man or a woman—more than looking at the size of a woman and saying: she can't pull her weight.

For Suarez and other women in the trades, the ability to figure out a solution to problems that require sheer strength is one problem that an intelligent approach can resolve. "If you're smart enough, you can use a tool," she explained. "If you need a four-foot lever and you only have a two-foot lever, you work with the two-foot lever and you don't hurt yourself. You figure out how to get the best advantage out of what you've got. You use two two-foot levers. Or you use two people."

I think it's harder in the physical realm than it is in the intellectual realm. PhD programs are getting more and more women and you see more women seeming to make it in government settings and in higher office. Now, it doesn't mean that they're not experiencing hardship or discrimination. But it seems so much more visceral on this level. It's much more obvious. They'll tell you to your face what they're really thinking in this field. They won't mask it.

Out on the blue-collar frontier, Suarez maintains a sense of delight at the lifestyle differences she perceives between herself and her fellow mechanics. "At the moment, I'm putting in my time changing minds on a personal level and I'm finding out really interesting things, like, I wonder how you get the grease stains out of your work pants from the dirty, greasy machines. And not a single mechanic that I've asked has been able to tell me because he doesn't do the laundry. Not only does he not do the laundry, but he doesn't care about the laundry. Then I found out that both my mechanics have never made a grilled-cheese sandwich. They didn't know how they would go about it... Which tells me that they've never ever cooked, not even like macaroni and cheese, or something from a box. So remember, these are guys who can fix a very complicated elevator. It's a very different lifestyle, very different."

But people can learn. Just as Suarez taught her mechanics how to make a grilled-cheese sandwich, women can learn how to wield a hammer, a saw, or how to figure out spatial relationships. Just as people learn public speaking in a classroom, so women can learn new skills. "It's a big project to somehow get the word out when it's been assumed all this time that women can't do this, or don't want to do it, or shouldn't do it. We have to get to the point where women—and girls—just know that they can do it! Cause right now, we're at this awkward stage where the women know they can and they want to but they've missed out on 20 years of experience holding a hammer that the boys have had. So of course they're going to be disadvantaged in the workplace."

Obstacles still abound that together, prevent young women from assuming an equal place in society. "I definitely think the girls of today have it a lot better than I did when I was a girl," Suarez said. "They have Title IX. It's a big factor. Because of Title IX, they have Mia Hamm [the soccer legend] to look up to... they have role models. But on the other hand, the gender roles are passed down by the parents—by the society. So there's a contradiction for these girls. 'I can do anything but I've got to make grilled-cheese for my husband and do the laundry.'... More and more it is changing, but for the most part, we're still struggling against these messages."

The messages start in the bassinette—and the playroom, Suaerz argues. Typically, girls don't grow up playing with certain items that are standard issue for boys—this serves to work against the development of their perception of spatial relations. Suaerz described her sense of the logic behind this thinking:

Girls don't get blocks. I think the problem is that a lot of people would like to say "Girls don't get blocks because they don't want blocks." There's something inherently—biologically—different about girls that makes them bad at blocks so you might as well not give them blocks.

I had to do a lot of thinking about these kinds of issues when I was studying for my gender relations degree. And my personal philosophy is that, yes, there may be biological differences, just like there's tall people and short people and muscular people and flabby people. But even if there is some genetic disposition toward that, maybe correlated with gender or not, I think the realm of societal influences and these forces are so great that it overcomes the biological forces—if they exist.

Her prescription: keep on trying to set an example; continue to make the case for equality. Progress is getting to the point where women enjoy real equality. But progress isn't self-sustaining or linear:

You'll make some progress and times will be good for a while and then people get complacent. Things get taken away and times are bad again. It's a cycle as I see it. Civil rights has been that way. Feminism has been that way. My conclusion is that you just have to keep on plugging. You've got to have people around who are always working toward that ideal...people are going to need that momentum...So you just keep working at it.

"Our Mission: To Boldly Go Where No Woman Has Gone Before."

Women Electricians T-shirt

In the 1970s, thinking out loud about how to design an ideal training program for women in the trades, pioneering carpenter Ronnie Sandler saw the need to address two common myths—that women didn't want these jobs—and that they couldn't do them. Now, more than three decades after the enactment of Title VII, we have enough evidence to know that, "women can do it all."[9]

A familiar quip has it that, "Ginger Rogers did everything Fred Astaire did, but she did it backward and in high heels." Out on the job, the pioneers did everything the men did—but under difficult circumstances. They had to learn while being jeered at, undermined and set-up to fail—but they didn't.

Setting out to enforce equal employment opportunity in New York City in the mid-1970s, Judith Layzer came to see that women had to be in the "pipeline" before they could qualify for skilled blue-collar jobs. Three decades later, what does that lengthy pipeline process look like?

For firefighter JoAnn Jacobs, it's essential that little girls—and boys—see someone who looks like them, to be able to visualize a similar future. Children's storybooks regularly display a full cast of characters—male and female—within their pages. Most books that depict vocational opportunities for young people also include both sexes and different races and ethnicities as a signal that everyone has an opportunity to do the work. A series of books on "Great Jobs" includes one on plumbing.[10] Photos show both young men and women, down on the floor, dressed in dungarees, putting wrench to pipe. But in reality, role models remain scarce.

As women sought to enter the skilled trades in the auto plants and the steel mills, the construction trades, in civil service and other blue-collar jobs, they did so by standing on the shoulders of the men of color who had fought this fight before them. Today, Lower Manhattan is virtually a huge construction site. A journey up and down the streets surrounding the former World Trade Center shows that minority males have made significant headway in securing building trades jobs. Although still underrepresented, a combination of continuing pressure and the demand for labor has won a more equitable share of jobs for minority men. But it is still rare to spot a woman in their midst—on the job sites, at the lunch wagon, or walking up the street to the subway.

Two by two, all God's creatures entered Noah's Ark. That minimalist tradition continues today for women entering skilled blue-collar jobs. Aside from construction, there is still a long list of skilled blue-collar jobs that remain "nontraditional" for females. In 2002, only two women worked in production jobs at the *New York Post*. Getting into Local 2 of the Pressmen's union appears to be an almost impossible dream for women, more than 30 years after female journalists sued to be liberated from the "women's page."[11] The exclusion of women from pressrooms was an issue back in the days when Susan B. Anthony was raising hell. To retire this tradition, access to skilled jobs needs to become a reality rather than a pipedream for far greater numbers of women.

Angela Olszewski argued this point eloquently on June 24, 2004. In testimony before the U.S. Senate Committee on Health, Education, Labor and Pensions, she described the critical need to fund vocational and technical education programs like those at NEW, that successfully open doors to high-paying, skilled jobs for women. Speaking from experience, she illustrated both the benefits and the barriers women face as they seek to enter the blue-collar trades:

> These jobs are very rewarding. My financial rewards from this career are incredible to me. I joke to my friends that I now pay in taxes the amount I used to earn for a living. Let me take you through my annual income for the past four years as a tile setter. First Year Apprentice: $18,000. Second Year Apprentice: $32,000. Third Year Apprentice: $46,000. Journeyworker: $55,000.[12]
>
> NEW has been around for 25 years, but unfortunately the obstacles and conditions, which prevent women from entering and succeeding in these careers, still exist. Many of the men that I work with have family in the construction business, who provide significant assistance to their entry into the trades and allow them to bypass some of the formal requirements. However, few women are able to enter the trades this way—their path is often much more difficult. I have seen men brought right into this industry, and I have seen women fill out an application only to be told to wait and maybe we will get back to you.

"In the summer of 2001, my International union participated in the Smithsonian Folklife Festival here in Washington D.C. We demonstrated our crafts while people stepped forward to ask questions about it. I was so proud to be there, because I showed every little girl who passed by, one more choice in her life."[13]

Shane, a classic of the Old West, depicts the struggle of the farmers—the "sodbusters"—to win their place on the prairie. Tormented by the cattlemen who staked their claim because they got there first, the farmers had to endure the destruction of their crops, the abuse and the escalating tactics designed to drive them out. "Just remember," one homesteader tells a gunfighter, "there's a law in this land." To which the gunfighter says, "The law's three-days ride from here."[14]

Like the homesteaders, women working in blue-collar nontraditional jobs have endured. But unlike the homesteaders, their ranks are still small. The laws that guarantee equal employment opportunity are on the books—but remote—due to lack of enforcement. All too often, it still takes a lawsuit to ensure that an individual woman is able to exercise those rights.[15]

But the experiences of the pioneers have taught us what works. Models and programs exist. There is a storehouse of information available to widen opportunities for young women. To reap the benefits of the contributions that the pioneers made—and continue to make—the gains of the Women's Movement must be extended to working-class women. One strategy to change the dismal face of feminine poverty—where women and children make up the mass of the poor—is to broaden access to skilled blue-collar jobs.

In her powerful memoir, pioneering journalist Lynn Sherr posed a question for today's young women:

> We begged, then demanded, then won, the right to work. We came on the scene as "girls" who were supposed to know their place, which was nowhere. Today, with the privileges we've earned...we know that our place is everywhere. So now what? Will young women of the next decades be so lucky...or so persevering? Will they have to be?[16]

Epilogue: Where Are They Now?

JOI BEARD: "I'm still in business! I'm just trying to run Derby Electric; trying to obtain electrical licenses to branch out in other states/cities; I'm consulting and also teaching in the apprenticeship program for Local Union 3, for Nontraditional Employment for Women, and the Consortium for Workers Education program—Construction Skills 2000."[1]

BRENDA BERKMAN: "After 25 years of service to the FDNY and New York City, I retired in September 2006. Thinking that I would take 6 to 12 months off before finding another job, instead, I have been inordinately busy! This includes volunteering for the Women in the Fire Service Oral History Project (codirector), Meals on Heels (cook), the World Trade Center Tribute Center (volunteer docent), the feminist conference—Freedom on Our Terms—and various other service projects.

I am also working to broaden the distribution of the PBS documentary about the first women firefighters in the FDNY, *Taking the Heat*.

I have also had the pleasure of traveling and speaking in the United States, the United Kingdom, and Australia. But one of my greatest (and guilty) pleasures at present is drawing, painting, and print-making—something I have not done since junior high school."[2]

JANINE BLACKWELDER: After life as an ironworker, Janine segued to working for a nonprofit organization in New England. Then she relocated to Texas and set herself up as a travel agent, specializing in ecotourism. She also taught English as a second language to Mexican immigrants. In 2005, she started a battle with breast cancer and was diagnosed as cancer-free in February 2007. She now lives in Austin, Texas.[3]

BRUNILDA HERNANDEZ: "I am a public health nurse with Arlington County, Virginia, Department of Human Services. I am currently certified as a Childbirth Educator and a Child Care Health Consultant. I have been working as a Registered Nurse for eight years now [June 2007] and have been with Arlington since September 2001."

"I work in the Maternity Clinic, the Family Planning Clinic, Child Health Clinic, and Immunization, and the Newborn/Postpartum Clinic. The other half of my work is spent as a case manager for approximately 20 families. I do home visits, developmental exams on the children, among other things."

"I love my partner Melissa of nine years, my dog Hannah, and my home. My goal is to stay healthy to be able to enjoy my life. My dreams are to travel extensively with Melissa and to have a wonderful circle of friends, neighbors, and community....Also to work for social justice, peace, and to end poverty and homelessness."[4]

JOANN JACOBS: "I work two days per week, on the average, as a mentor/advisor at the FDNY High School for Fire and Life Safety in Brooklyn, New York. Since my retirement in August 2000, I have traveled to Australia (two times), Netherlands, Brazil, Egypt, France, Italy, Guatemala, Greece, Thailand, Vietnam, Cambodia, Canada, Montserrat, Belize, and one cruise to the Caribbean. I have gone on an archeological dig in Thailand with the Earth Watch."

"I work on the house I own in Queens. I garden, read, and play tennis. I am getting over my fear of water by going snorkeling and have even been scuba diving! I don't put pressure on myself by planning *too* far ahead. I'm having a great time not working!"

"I sponsor a woman in Nigeria through the organization Women 4 Women International. She receives funds for a year to help with school fees for her children and business training for herself."[5]

ANN JOCHEMS: "Being 3rd generation civil service and having accumulated so many years—17 and more—toward my pension, after the sad ending at the BOE, I took several city, state, town and county civil service tests. I found my niche in real estate appraisal and am working toward my state license. I have risen rapidly and have been with the commercial division of the county for almost two years."

"Licensure is a threefold requirement combining education, experience, and a state test. I'm about 95 percent there, having completed all required courses, passing the state test, and acquiring 30 months experience. I have to write four appraisals, which I am in the process of doing now and will complete before the end of 2007."

"The body of knowledge for appraisal is vast and interesting. My colleagues have almost all had other careers, so that too is interesting. Because of my construction background, I came in with a high title, having spent a lifetime inspecting buildings. As this, too, is civil service, my pension and seniority rights are preserved."

"I enjoy the combination of field inspections and office work—research, analysis, documentation, valuation, and review. As it is so interesting and varied with much growth potential, I feel my eclectic 12 years of college and dozens of building trades classes are not for naught."

"In August 2006, I got my 15-year coin in AA. I mention that since it was part of my demise at the BOE...I want to work my program of recovery, including recovering from the pitfalls of pioneering as a tradeswoman. My goal is to nurture my spiritual development."[6]

LAURA KELBER: "I live in Brooklyn with my husband, three teen-aged kids, a dog, a cat, and a bird. I got a Master's degree in environmental health and worked in the field for a while. Currently, I'm pursuing a career as a screenwriter."[7]

CYNTHIA A. H. LONG: "I have been a journeywoman for more than 31 years. Currently, I am still working as a rank-and-file union construction electrician. I continue to do grassroots organizing with tradeswomen and am still working for systemic and institutional change through "Operation Punch List" and fighting racism and sexism in America."[8]

REBECCA LURIE: "When I was pregnant with my first son in 1992, I decided it was time to try something new. I loved teaching and had been doing it at the union apprenticeship school on a part-time basis. I went to NEW and quickly moved up to the position of program coordinator. Since then, I have spent eight years at the carpenters' union in a full-time position, managing their pre-apprenticeship program, among other things. This includes developing their sexual harassment policy and training."

"For the past seven years I have been at the Consortium for Worker Education where I run a training center. My title is Director of Workforce Development. We run a pre-apprenticeship program for the building trades. We also have a bakers training program, in partnership with the Bakers' Union. I enjoy working with people and trying to creatively solve problems.

My goals and dreams are to be happy! I enjoy working with people and trying to collectively solve problems. I enjoy it when our work can blend with policy to make more work opportunities for the traditionally underserved."[9]

YVONE MAITIN: "I am now at JFK Airport. I am on a rotating shift. I'm learning a lot about myself and confirming those things I know about my job. My work partner is an asshole, but that is not news. However, what is news is that I have a work partner. I'm used to working alone. I am the mechanic, and he is the engineer. He makes sure I know that. He's a short guy with a big ego and a big complex about that. It seems the more things change the more they stay the same. One last thing about the job is that I seem to have to justify my right to this job even after more than 23 years here."

"One of the good things [in my life] is my granddaughter, who is now 12. I am passing on the strategies to her. I am involved with a group called the Women's Press Collective.... I speak with other women about entering the trades. I take art classes. I look forward to retiring some day. I appreciate what I have learned about myself in the last 20 years and the women I have met."[10]

ANGELA OLSZEWSKI: "I am a union tile layer and a member of the Bricklayers union, Local No. 7 Tile, Marble & Terrazzo of New York and New Jersey. For the last five years, I have been the Job Readiness instructor at Nontraditional Employment for Women for their evening training program. For the last year, I have also been the Program Coordinator of Nontraditional Employment for Women's evening training program, NEW@Night (NAN). This last year (2007) has been incredibly intense, as I have been working full-time construction in the day and then 20 to 30 hours per week in the evenings and on Saturdays at NEW. I love it! But, I will be resigning from NEW soon to work one job—construction—and enjoy the summer."

"I will be restarting law school in mid-August at CUNY School of Law. I can't wait! My dream is to train myself to be a powerful advocate for working people. I also love to meditate and write poetry."[11]

MARTY POTTENGER: "In March 2007, I made the move to Portland Maine, my new home, after living in New York City for almost 30 years. I am now the director of Terra Moto Inc. in Portland Maine. This is an arts and equity initiative that began in January 2005. I was commissioned by the Center for Cultural Exchange to conduct 100 interviews almost 1 year after the Border Patrol Raid on Portland. The interview subjects included ex-governors, religious leaders, State Senate President Edmunds, Mayor Dunson, business leaders, homeless people, Native leaders, Latino/a leaders, custom agents, artists immigration lawyers, policymakers, legislators, bankers, city workers, and leaders from refugee as well as immigrant communities, including Rwanda, Bosnia, Cambodia, Vietnam, Somalia, Sudan, Afghanistan, Israel, French-Canada, and Arcadians. In fall 2005, we held the premier of 'home land security' and had civic dialogues at City Hall. For the winter/spring season in 2006, we presented 'home land security' and began a Portland City/Schools Partnership. In fall 2006, we moved into City Hall and planning, meeting, fundraising continues for the Arts & Equity Initiative."

"One exciting part of the program is the civic artists' pilot project. As part of building a sustainable replicable model, eight artists-in-residence(s) will be identified and paired with eight policymaking civic institutions. Likely institutions include police, fire, finance, sanitation department, school board, teachers' union, mayor and/or city manager's office, water board, public library, local jail, election board, state senate, and possibly the governor's office. The artists will be from different disciplines—painters, photographers, poets, story-tellers, sculptors, and installation artists—chosen out of the weekly classes. To effectively reach our core objectives of increasing equity, as well as staff diversity in all the participating agencies, more than 50 percent of PAIR artists will be people of color. The expectation is that PAIR Portland will serve as a two-year experiment to be followed by a national pilot initiative that expands the program to three more cities."[12]

CONSUELO REYES: "I am in private practice as a psychotherapist. I am trained in Neural Linguist Programming (NLP). I have been working for different service providers, including the Belloni Boys Ranch Treatment facility in Coos Bay, Oregon [2004–2005]. They provide treatment for sex offenders and community offenders, meaning drug and substance abuse. In 2006, I worked at a crisis center that also served as a halfway house for people with extreme bipolar disorders and schizophrenia. We received intensive suicide prevention training."

"I do all kinds of outdoor stuff—including rock climbing, mountain climbing, hiking, camping, and have been since I was 18-years-old. Now I live in the perfect place for it—Southern Oregon. We were wild women…and some of us still are! I've learned that politics has nothing to do with aging."[13]

LOIS ROSS: My NSF grant proposal is aimed at reforming engineering education, which has been stagnant and alienating. I am part of a movement to reform it, and one way is to use the "studio method." I am looking to incorporate this into the Transit Workers' "Intelligent Transit" engineering program, which is being developed now.

"My great love is for *animals* and *wildlife*—being outdoors and preserving land—especially in the semiurban area where I live. We are planting thousands of trees and aquatic plants to create new habitats and preserve the last remaining open spaces in our densely populated area here in Bloomfield, New Jersey. Nothing makes me happier than rescuing animals and returning them to their natural environment."

"I help manage an 'urban oasis' pond and nature preserve, which we adopted and are lovingly restoring. We are also fighting to save land along our rivers and to preserve [them] as greenways."

Ross serves as the president of the Friends of Clark's Pond and Third River, and edits their newsletter. In September 2005, she wrote an article, "What to Do If You Find a Baby Bird." More information about the nature preserve can be found by contacting: turtle34@comcast.net.[14]

EVAN RUDERMAN: Evan learned that she was H.I.V. positive in 1988. She retired with a full pension from the IBEW—after she made a successful appeal. She became an activist in AIDS causes. In 2002, she represented New York area women at the World AIDS Conference in Barcelona, Spain. She continued to participate in organized struggles to make HIV-medications available and used her own experience in a monologue she wrote and then delivered in a televised PBS documentary that aired in 1996. She died on November 18, 2003. Her family and friends held a memorial celebration of her life on Sunday, February 8, 2004. Many of her sister tradeswomen were in attendance.

Evan wrote a description of one aspect of her experience as a representative of women at AIDS conferences:

I was in a job that was traditionally, always a man's job—wages and benefits that were supposed to be for a breadwinner to support a family. If I'd gone into nursing,

I wouldn't have had the same benefits or gotten the same pay, so my Social Security benefit would have been lower. When I went to the national HIV conference, they had a pre-conference with 1,000 women...Looking at all those women—I realized that I was at the top—the highest rank of benefits, privilege, and health care. So even though I had been really sick, I had gotten really good health care. What I saw was that many women were working many jobs, whereas I was working in one, male-oriented job....A lot of women were waitresses. Or they did office work, or factory work that didn't seem long-term, wasn't unionized, and had children. This showed me how housework and childrearing are devalued in our society.[15]

RONNIE SANDLER: "Besides skiing, I am doing some consulting for Compliance USA, Inc. with Northern New England Tradeswomen who are looking at starting a Correctional Industry Training Program with the new Women's Prison (correctional facility) in Windsor Vermont. I am on the Board of Directors for Tradeswomen Now and Tomorrow (TNT). I am also working part-time doing house inspections for insurance companies. Compliance USA, Inc. is now 10-years-old!"[16]

VERONICA SESSION: She continues her activism on all fronts. On August 24, 2007, she took part in the making of a video being produced to promote the interest of young women in the construction industry. She also continues to participate in Career Day events at New York City schools under the auspices of the Women's Carpenters' Committee. "Girls need to see a woman who's doing the job," she said. "For years, the carpenters' union has been sending women out to do these presentations. Women need more career options and they need to see female faces in these roles."

She still participates in the Habitat for Humanity building program in Harlem through her union and is considering a run for office as a delegate from her local to the District Council of Carpenters.[17]

IRENE SOLOWAY: I did pre-med at night while working as a carpenter at Lincoln Hospital. After two years of full-time Physician's Assistant school, I participated in a one-year clinical fellowship in liver disease. I am now working as a physician assistant at Albert Einstein College of Medicine's Division of Substance Abuse. I am doing primary care, including HIV and hepatitis C treatment. Many of our patients are construction workers, who are always surprised when I tell them about my work background. I have found that my nontraditional experience helps them relate to me, as I can relate to them as well.

I work in one of Albert Einstein's nine methadone clinics. Along with the clinic's doctor, we have started a pilot project to treat hepatitis C on-site. We are one of the very few methadone clinics that have done this and are developing a protocol for the treatment of substance abusers in the primary care setting. Our model is that of a partnership between the medical provider and patient in which it is acknowledged that we are learning from each other. With our patients, we have started an education/support and advocacy group dedicated to fighting back against the hepatitis C epidemic in our community. We have started a peer education program where patients demonstrate knowledge of this disease and go to other clinics, harm reduction centers, and forums, to educate both providers and patients.

I'm also working on a grant doing hepatitis C screenings and vaccination at syringe exchange centers and on the street in the South Bronx. And still meeting lots of construction workers in my job! I feel very fortunate that I have found work which combines organizing and clinical medicine: an exciting combination![18]

MARGARITA SUAREZ: "I was promoted to mechanic in March 2006. I am the first woman to apprentice and become a mechanic in this division of my company (midtown and downtown Manhattan—perhaps one of the busiest regions in New York City) and the first woman (of four) to be promoted in my apprenticeship class (the company has the prerogative to compensate a worker above the minimum set by the union). My company now employs three women in the same division (all apprentices. I have worked with all of them). As of June 2006, I knew of six working female apprentices in IBEW Local 3's elevator division (1,600 members) and knew of no working journeywomen. Because of the increased recruitment efforts of the Joint Apprenticeship and Training committee and NEW, 4–6 more either have started or will be starting soon. The 'elevator women' have begun to meet weekly at NEW for informal tutoring and support, and we've started an e-mail list to keep in touch between meetings. Though female participation in our industry is still embarrassingly low, I feel that the men are adjusting well to what many of them have expressed to me was a very frightening prospect (working with a 'girl'). Elevator maintenance, repair and modernization is proving to be a trade that, although uncharted by women, is one in which they have great potential to succeed."

"I continue to serve on the board of TNT [Tradeswomen Now & Tomorrow], though because of work responsibilities, my involvement recently has been limited. I speak regularly at NEW to promote my trade and teach the occasional class there."[19]

EILEEN SULLIVAN: I have been the Director of the Grievance & Discipline Department for six years and the codirector of the Office of Contract Compliance Department, and Long Island Political Action Committee (PAC) for TWU Local 100. As you can see by my "titles," I am very involved in assisting members—from MTA Contract Compliance through preparing their cases for arbitration (the MTA issues 16,000 disciplinary letters a year) and PAC Coordinator for Long Island. I am on the Executive Board of the Long Island Federation of Labor, Long Island Educators Advisory Board, a Committee Woman for the local Democratic Club, and the Nassau County Labor Committee for Nassau County Executive Thomas Suozzi. A lot of my work for Local 100 includes training and education on grievance handling and arbitration.

"Most important!!! 5 kids, 11 grandkids (18 with my husband Bruce's)!!!"[20]

ELAINE WARD: "There's nothing like the good old-fashioned perseverance and persistence. The list is getting longer of 'moments I'll always remember,' like when I got the form letter from the city telling me that I was considered Qualified for the NYC Master Plumber's License ('Pinch Me' I said to myself—this is real!)"

"Isis Plumbing, Inc. opened for business in spring of 2001. However, I think of the date of 'full speed ahead' as the summer of 2003 when I became a protégé in the Mentor-Protégé program of the Queens Women's Business Center. Fall of 2004 I received the Rose Award for Excellence in Entrepreneurship!"

"The jobs I write proposals and price are small residential and/or commercial jobs. They may include any of the following: installation of gas equipment, such as a boiler or hot water heater or both; installation of a new gas meter; violation correction by removing fixture installed without a permit (which requires a permit and inspection); completion of jobs begun by other plumbers (licensed or unlicensed) but not completed properly in the Building Department via the permit and inspection process; installation of water meters (DEP permits required); installation of back flow preventers (more DEP paperwork); consulting to architects and engineers—troubleshooting Building Department computer records for plumbing inspection and sign-off status; preparation and delivery of permit and inspection paperwork for other NYC Licensed Master Plumbers."

"The way I feel about the work I do is that I love being the creator of my success. I have so much gratitude for everything I have learned to get where I am. I feel like I am at the very beginning of such a fantastic life."[21]

KAY WEBSTER: "I am living my dream of putting my weight toward building a better world and pulling off enjoying 'the battle' more and more. I am currently the cochair of an activist (and gorgeous) community garden: The M'Finda Kalunga Community Garden on the Lower East Side. We hold cultural festivals each year: The Chinese Moon Festival, Juneteenth, Cinco de Mayo, Saimhain/Halloween, and Sukkot to bring our vibrant communities together in celebration of each other's holidays. We also organize to retain affordable housing, keep the neighborhood safe, and we organize against the war(s). We have children's and seniors' gardening programs. We'll hold movie nights this summer (2007). It is a good place to build community."

"I am also a copresident of P.S. 130, an elementary school in Chinatown. It is an amazing school with a caring and generous community. We have many projects internal to the school, and we organize a health and family day each year for the entire neighborhood. We partner with many community groups to provide a free dental clinic, asthma and diabetes screening, housing advocacy, Chinese cultural works, and joyful activities for children."

"I continue to teach and lead in Reevaluation Counseling, an international peer-counseling network. Along with my husband Steve (one of the most soulful musicians I know), I am raising my son, Lee, who has been my best teacher on organizing a neighborhood. We have been lucky enough to be joined in the past year by my mom, a feisty octogenarian from whom I got a lot of my 'spit.' I still employ my construction work skills to build walls when I need them as well as doing occasional plumbing work for friends or myself when needed!"[22]

ILENE WINKLER: "I completed a master's degree program at New York University in May 2005, studying public history. I hope to document the history of labor activists in New York City! Also, I had breast cancer in 2000, and I now volunteer as a hotline counselor at SHARE [Self-help for Women with Breast or Ovarian Cancer], which is a peer-support group for women and families with breast and ovarian cancer—putting all that shop steward experience to good use."

"I turned 60 and am looking forward to becoming a senior activist. After 28 years, I am now retired from Verizon as a Central Office Technician."[23]

Notes

Preface

1. U.S. Census Bureau, *Statistical Abstract of the United States: 2003* (Washington, DC: Government Printing Office, 2003), 401.
2. Nancy MacLean, "The Hidden History of Affirmative Action: Working Women's Struggle in the 1970s and the Gender of Class." *Feminist Studies* 25 (Spring 1999), 47.
3. Janine Blackwelder, interview with author, tape recording, Chesterfield, MA, December 17, 1994.
4. David Witner, "Labor and the New Millennium: Class, Vision, and Change. The Twenty-Second North American Labor History Conference." *International Labor and Working-Class History* 60 (Fall 2001) 216.
5. Jane Latour, "Live! From New York: Women Construction Workers in Their Own Words." *Labor History*, Vol. 42, No.2 (May 2001) 179–189.
6. Stacy K. Sewell, "Review of State of the Union: A Century of American Labor," New York History (Summer 2004) 284–286. Nelson Lichtenstein, *State of the Union: A Century of American Labor* (Princeton NJ: Princeton University Press, 2002).
7. Conversation with the author, Women Carpenters' Committee Holiday Party and Panel Discussion, December 1, 2006.
8. C-SPAN 2-Book TV interview with Taylor Branch, February 5, 2006.

One   Rosie's Daughters

1. See *The Encyclopedia of American Economic History* and the data of historians, whose estimates vary on the numbers and impact of the women who responded to the demand for their labor. Alice Kessler-Harris, *Women Have Always Worked* (New York: McGraw-Hill, 1981), 142–143; and *Out to Work* (New York: Oxford University Press, 1982), 276–287.
2. Tony Marcano, "Famed Riveter in War Effort, Rose Monroe Dies at 77," *New York Times*, June 2, 1997.
3. Sheila Rowbotham, *A Century of Women: The History of Women in Britain and the United States* (London: Penguin Books, 1997), 249–250.
4. See obituaries for Rose Monroe, posted on www.rootsweb.com/~kypulask/military/ww2/rosie.htm. Accessed on August 30, 2007.
5. Nancy MacLean, *Freedom Is Not Enough: The Opening of the American Workplace* (New York: Russell Sage Foundation, 2006), 298.
6. Alice Kessler-Harris, *In Pursuit of Equity: Women, Men, and the Quest for Economic Citizenship in 20th Century America* (New York: Oxford University Press, 2001), 268–269.
7. MacLean, *Freedom Is Not Enough*, 267.
8. "Between Memory and History: The Women's Movement in New York City, the 1960s and 1970s" (Session 84). Panel Discussion at First Gotham History Festival, City University of New York, October 6, 2001, transcript.
9. Ruth Rosen, *The World Split Open: How the Modern Women's Movement Changed America* (New York: Penguin Group, 2000).

10. Rosalyn Baxandall, "Between Memory and History," October 6, 2001.

11. "Fact Sheet On: Why and How to Organize," *Women Office Workers*, March 1976. Author's copy. As a union organizer for District 65, I got to witness Margie Alpert's forceful presence at the delegate meetings at the Astor Place union headquarters in New York City.

12. Claudia Dreifus, "Don't Compromise, Organize," in "The Gazette, News from All Over," *Ms.*, June 1974. Dreifus, described the participants at the conference, which was held at the Martin Luther King Center in New York City: "The next time an antifeminist barks that the women's movement is 'nothing but a bunch of idle middle-class white females with a moderate complaint,' tell him (or her) about the First New York Women's Trade Union Conference. In January, 600 women—young and old, black and white, welders, cab drivers, teachers, union officials, assembly-line workers, and secretaries—met…to share their experiences and learn what they can do to improve the lot of the 33 million women who labor for a living." Approximately 1 percent of New York City's cab drivers—out of 44,000 drivers—are women, 33 years later. See Melissa Plant, *Hack: How I Stopped Worrying About What to Do with My Life and Started Driving a Yellow Cab* (New York: Random House, 2007).

13. Betty Friedan, *Life So Far: A Memoir* (New York: Simon & Schuster, 2000), 184.

14. MacLean, *Freedom Is Not Enough*, 266.

15. Ronnie Sandler, e-mail correspondence with author, May 15, 2007.

16. Ronnie Sandler, interview with Ann Jochems at the 9th Annual Northern New England Tradeswomen's Conference, tape recording, March 26, 1995.

17. Nan Robertson, *The Girls in the Balcony: Women, Men, and The New York Times* (New York: Random House, 1992), 185.

18. See Mary Margaret Fonow, *Union Women Forging Feminism in the United Steelworkers of America* (Minneapolis: University of Minnesota Press, 2003); and Marat Moore, *Women in the Mines: Stories of Life and Work* (New York: Simon & Schuster, 1996). See also United Women Firefighters' Records, Robert F. Wagner Labor Archives, New York University for organizing in both the Uniformed Firefighters Association (UFA) and the Patrolmen's Benevolent Association (PBA), New York City.

19. Susan Eisenberg, *We'll Call You If We Need You: Experiences of Women Working Construction* (Ithaca, NY: Cornell University Press, 1998), 191.

20. MacLean, *Freedom Is Not Enough*, 267.

21. Ibid., 266–267.

22. National Organization for Women-New York City Chapter Records, Robert F. Wagner Labor Archives, New York University.

23. See Judith Layzer Papers, Robert F. Wagner Labor Archives, New York University.

24. Judith Layzer, interview with author, tape recording, New York City, April 2, 2005.

25. An interview with Layzer on August 17, 1981, by Miriam Ourin recounts the range of efforts, supported by archival documents, of this work. Layzer describes one panel discussion in which one of the speakers, the director of an auto sales company, was actually "converted" to hiring women mechanics on the spot. "That's right, at the very same meeting, and we have it on video tape. It was actually quite theatrical…" Layzer also described speaker Joyce Hartwell's comments at this discussion; "She brought out that women haven't had the experience that men typically do as children in fixing things. In fact, it isn't only or chiefly the lack of experience but it's the *expectation* that they are not able to do this kind of thing."

26. United Tradeswomen Records, Robert F. Wagner Labor Archives, New York University. This rich collection includes documentation of WITT, WAP, All-Craft, and numerous other advocacy organizations.

27. Ibid.

28. Ibid.

29. Ibid., Box 1, Folder 10.

30. See Tanya Melich, *The Republican War Against Women: An Insider's Report from Behind the Lines* (New York: Bantam Books, 1996). Donald T. Critchlow, *Phyllis Schlafly and Grassroots Conservatism: A Woman's Crusade* (Princeton, NJ: Princeton University Press, 2005); and Susan Faludi, *Backlash: The Undeclared War Against American Women* (New York: Doubleday, 1992).

31. See Melich, *The Republican War Against Women*, especially Part II—"The Misogynist Reign of Reagan-Bush, 1980–1992"; See also MacLean, *Freedom Is Not Enough*, "The Lonesomeness of

Pioneering" and "The Struggle for Inclusion." Both authors trace, with great clarity and precision, the progression of policies that eroded the national commitment to affirmative action. Together, they provide a road map for tracing the forces and policies that moved the country so far to the right and so far away from compliance with civil rights laws.

32. See Francine Moccio, "Contradicting Male Power and Privilege: Class, Race and Gender Relations in the Building Trades" (Ph.D. diss., New School for Social Research, 1992), 212–214; 236–243. See also Ann Jochems, "A History of Nontraditional Employment for Women (NEW), The First Years. 1978–1992." (M.A. thesis, Baruch College, The City University of New York, 2003).

33. For decades, members of the New York City Council, under the auspices of the Women's Committee (with several name changes—Women's Issues Committee, The Committee on Women, etc.), have provided a mechanism for public scrutiny of gender issues in the workplace. See United Women Firefighters Records, Box 4, Folder 1, for example. See also Moccio, "Contradicting Male Power and Privilege," for Eleanor Holmes Norton, age-discrimination suit against Local 3 apprenticeship programs, 239–240.

34. See "Tradeswomen Protest Attack on Affirmative Action, 'more sisterhood in the brotherhoods!'" *Labor Notes*, June 29, 1983. Members of the Chicago CLUW demonstrated at the Federal Building in the Loop, along with members of Chicago Women in the Trades. Chicago CLUW members from the carpenters union and from the skilled trades in the auto plants were on the picket line to protest proposed revision in Executive Order 11246 that would exempt 75 percent of federal government contractors.

35. The author had numerous conversations with committee members, including steelworkers, carpenters, and so on, while serving as director of the Women's Project, Association for Union Democracy, 2000–2002. In March 2002, many committee members attended the founding convention of Tradeswomen Now and Tomorrow, TNT, in New York City. See www.tradeswomennowandtomorrow.org.

36. See United Tradeswomen Records, Box 2, for documentation of legal advocates for tradeswomen. See also, www.equalrights.org and www.legalmomentum.org.

37. Ronnie Sandler, interview, March 26, 1995.

38. See United Tradeswomen Records, Box 2. *Tradeswomen*, the quarterly journal, grew out of *Trade Trax*, a newsletter published by Tradeswomen, Inc. See www. tradeswomen.org.

39. Sandler, interview, March 26, 1995.

40. See Anne Lawrence, "Six Hundred Attend Conference of Women in Blue Collar Trades," *Labor Notes*, June 29, 1983. See also United Tradeswomen Records, Box 2, Folder 7, for documentation on the conference.

41. Lynn Sherr, *Susan B. Anthony in Her Own Words* (New York: Random House, 1995), 324. She spoke these words at her last public appearance—her final birthday celebration in Washington, D.C. on February 15, 1906.

Two   United Tradeswomen: Organizing for the Guaranteed Right to Work in Any Job

1. United Tradeswomen Records, Box 1, Folder 1, Robert F. Wagner Labor Archives, New York University.

2. Evan Ruderman, interview with author, tape recording, New York City, March 6, 1996.

3. Lois Ross, interview with author, New York City, March 6, 1996.

4. United Tradeswomen Records, Box 1, Folder 3.

5. Association for Union Democracy—Women's Project Records, Box 3, "United Tradeswomen," Folder, December 3, 1989; Robert F. Wagner Labor Archives, New York University.

6. Yvone Maitin, interview with author, tape recording, New York City, April 19, 2005.

7. Marty Pottenger, interview with author, tape recording, New York City, September 27, 1994.

8. Kay Webster, interview with author, tape recording, New York City, November 19, 2004.

9. Irene Soloway, interview with author, tape recording, New York City, March 6, 1996. Evan Ruderman, Lois Ross, and Irene Soloway were interviewed as a group to discuss United Tradeswomen at the Robert F. Wagner Labor Archives, New York University.

10. Consuelo Reyes, interview with author, tape recording, North Bend, OR, August 4, 2005.

11. Ross, interview with author, tape recording, New York City, July 29, 1996.

12. Cynthia Long, interview with author, tape recording, New York City, September 26, 2004.

13. Ross, interview, March 6, 1996.

14. Maitin, interview, April 19, 2005.

15. "In *Meritor Savings Bank v. Vinson* the Supreme Court ruled that sexual harassment on the job is a form of gender discrimination and thus in violation of Title VII of the Civil Rights Act." *The Feminist Movement*, edited by Nick Treanor (San Diego, CA: Greenhaven Press, 2002), 222. For a discussion of the case, see J. Ralph Lindgrew and Nadine Taub, *The Law of Sex Discrimination* (St. Paul: West Publishing Company, 1988), 181–183.

16. United Tradeswomen Records, Box 1, Folder 2.

17. Suzanne C. Carothers and Peggy Crull, "Contrasting Sexual Harassment in Female- and Male-dominated Occupations," in *My Troubles Are Going to Have Trouble with Me* edited by Karen Brodkin Sacks and Dorothy Remy (New Brunswick, NJ: Rutgers University Press, 1989), 219–228.

18. Ibid., 220.

19. United Tradeswomen Records, Box 1, Folder 1.

20. Janine Blackwelder, interview with author, tape recording, New York City, August 1, 1990.

21. United Tradeswomen Records, Box 1, Folder 1.

22. Ilene Winkler, interview with author, tape recording, New York City, December 16, 2004.

23. Ross, interview, July 29, 1996.

24. United Tradeswomen Records, Box 1, Folder 3.

25. Ibid., Box 1, Folder 2.

26. Frank McMurray, interview with author, tape recording, San Rafael, CA, August 19, 2005.

27. James Haughton, interview with author, tape recording, New York City, November 11, 2004.

28. Ross, interview, March 6, 1996.

29. United Tradeswomen Records, Box 1, Folder 7.

30. Ibid.

31. Ibid., Box 1, Folder 8.

32. Ibid.

33. Ibid.

34. James McNamara, interview with author, tape recording, New York City, December 27, 2004.

35. See "Corruption and Racketeering in the New York City Construction Industry," Final Report to Governor Mario M. Cuomo, New York State Organized Crime Task Force; Ronald Goldstock, Director, December 1989, 17. Four members of United Tremont Trades were indicted in February 1989 for extorting money from contractors; one example of many similar rackets.

36. United Tradeswomen Records, Box 1, Folder 3.

37. Ross, interview, July 29, 1996.

38. Ibid., March 6, 1996.

39. Nancy MacLean, *Freedom Is Not Enough: The Opening of the American Workplace* (New York: Russell Sage Foundation, 2006), see Chapter on "the Lonesomeness of Pioneering."

40. See Susan Brownmiller, *In Our Time: Memoir of a Revolution* (New York: Dial Press, 1999), 60; and Phyllis Chesler, *Woman's Inhumanity to Woman* (New York: Thunder Mouth Press/Nation Books, 2001), see Chapter Nine, "Women in Groups."

41. United Tradeswomen Records, Box 1, Folder 2.

42. Ibid., Box 1, Folder 4.

43. Ibid., Box 1, Folder 2.

44. Ibid.

45. Ibid.

46. Ibid.

47. Miriam Frank, interview with author, tape recording, New York City, December 5, 2004.

48. Maitin, interview, June 22, 1995.

49. Maitin, interview, April 19, 2005.

50. Irene Soloway, interview, March 6, 1996. Her reference is to the Young Lords, who occupied administration offices at Lincoln Hospital in 1970. See Miguel Melendez, *We Took the Streets: Fighting for Latino Rights with the Young Lords* (New York: St. Martin's Press, 2003); see Chapter 8, "The Butcher Shop"—Lincoln Hospital.

Three   Learning to Labor on High Steel

1. Mike Cherry, *On High Steel: The Education of an Ironworker* (New York: Quadrangle/The New York Times Book Co., 1974), "A Note to the Reader."
2. Gay Talese, "The Bridge," in *Fame and Obscurity* (New York: The World Publishing Company, 1970), and Joseph Mitchell, "The Mohawks in High Steel," in *Up in the Old Hotel* (New York: Pantheon Books, 1992).
3. See "Fran Krauss: Ironworker." Interview by Nancy Powell, in *Hard-Hatted Women: Life on the Job*, edited by Molly Martin (Seattle: Seal Press, 1997), 104.
4. See Ruben Rusario and Jerry Capeci, "Mob Takes a Big Hit Over City Contracts," *Daily News*, May 31, 1990; Peter Bowles and Chapin Wright, "Windows Case' Mistrial Bid," *New York Newsday*, August 12, 1991; and Serge F. Kovaleski, "Autopsy Slated for Mob Corpse," *New York Newsday*, August 12, 1991, story on John Morrissey.
5. Janine Blackwelder, interview by author, tape recording, Chesterfield, MA, December 17, 1994.
6. Janine Blackwelder, interview by author, tape recording, Brooklyn, August 1, 1990.
7. Janine Blackwelder, interview, December 17, 1994.
8. Ibid., August 1, 1990.
9. Ibid., December 17, 1994.
10. Ornamental Iron Workers Local 580 Records, Unprocessed, Box 19, Union Dues, 1979–1987, Robert F. Wagner Labor Archives, New York University.
11. Janine Blackwelder, interview, August 1, 1990.
12. Janine Blackwelder, conversation with the author, February 7, 2004.
13. Roger Waldinger and Thomas Bailey, "The Continuing Significance of Race: Racial Conflict and Racial Discrimination in Construction," Paper presented at the 1990 meeting of the American Sociological Association, January 1991, 28.
14. Ibid., 15.
15. Blackwelder, interview, December 17, 1994.
16. Ibid., August 1, 1990.
17. Local 580 Records, Box 10, "Summary of the June 18, 1991 Settlement Conference before Judge [Robert L.] Carter."
18. Ibid., Box 9, "Plaintiff's Post-Hearing Brief," July 1987.
19. Ibid., "EEOC Against Local 580, Opinion," April 15, 1988.
20. Ibid., Box 10, "Summary of the June 18, 1991 Settlement Conference."
21. Blackwelder, interview, December 17, 1994.
22. "Discrimination in Ironworkers Local 580," *Union Democracy Review*, No. 110, January 1997, edited by Herman Benson, 7.
23. Ibid.
24. Robert Fitch, Interview by author, hand-written notes, New York, December 10, 2005.
25. Stacy Kinlock Sewell, "Left on the Bench: The New York Construction Trades and Racial Integration, 1960–1972," *New York History*, Spring 2002, 203–216. See also James Haughton interview with author, November 11, 2004.
26. Robert Fitch, "Affirmative Action," remarks delivered at The Brecht Forum, New York City, October 13, 1995.
27. Janine Blackwelder, interview, August 1, 1990.
28. Ibid., December 17, 1994.
29. Ibid., August 1, 1990.
30. Ibid., December 17, 1994.
31. Ibid., August 1, 1990.

32. Ibid., December 17, 1994.
33. *Building Barriers: Discrimination in New York City's Construction Trades,* A Report by the New York City Commission on Human Rights, December 1993, 269–274.
34. Blackwelder, interview, August 1, 1990.
35. James B. Jacobs, *Gotham Unbound: How New York City was Liberated from the Grip of Organized Crime* (New York: New York University Press, 1999), 111–112; 212–213.
36. Blackwelder, interview, December 17, 1994.
37. *Union Democracy Review*, No. 110, January 1997, 7.
38. Jacobs, *Gotham Unbound*, 112.
39. Arnold H. Lubasch, "Mafia Captain Is Prosecution Witness," *New York Times*, September 12, 1991.
40. Blackwelder, conversation with author, February 7, 2004.
41. Blackwelder, interview, August 1, 1990.

Four   When Worlds Collide:
The First Women in Electricians' Local 3

1. Richard Price, *Bloodbrothers* (New York: First Mariner Books, 1999).
2. Murray Kempton, "Well, Go Ahead—Think," *New York Post*, October 24, 1957.
3. Martha S. LoMonaco, "International Brotherhood of Electrical Workers," in *The Encyclopedia of New York City*, edited by Kenneth T. Jackson (New York: Yale University Press, 1995), 593; and Francine Moccio, "Contradicting Male Power and Privilege: Class, Race and Gender Relations in the Building Trades" (Ph.D. diss., New School for Social Research, 1992), 75.
4. Price, *Bloodbrothers*, 5.
5. Ibid., 227.
6. See Moccio, "Contradicting Male Power and Privilege," 68–69; 126; 127.
7. Ibid., 128–129.
8. Ibid., 132; and LoMonaco, *The Encyclopedia of New York City*, 593.
9. See Moccio, "Contradicting Male Power and Privilege," 148; see also Grace Palladino, "Irreconcilable Differences: Issues of Class, Race and Gender," in *Dreams of Dignity, Workers of Vision: A History of the IBEW,* Grace Palladino (Washington, DC: IBEW, 1991).
10. Gene Ruffini, *Harry Van Arsdale, Jr.: Labor's Champion* (Armonk, NY: M.E. Sharpe, 2003).
11. See "Susan Eisenberg: Electrician," in *Hard-Hatted Women: Life on the Job*, edited by Molly Martin (Seattle: Seal Press, 1997), 216–217.
12. See Moccio, "Contradicting Male Power and Privilege," 209–210.
13. Ibid., 59–60.
14. Evan Ruderman, interview with author, tape recording, New York City, March 6, 1996.
15. Cynthia Long, interview with author, tape recording, New York City, September 26, 2004.
16. See Moccio, "Contradicting Male Power and Privilege," 140.
17. Brunilda Hernandez, interview with author, tape recording, Alexandria, VA, March 19, 2005.
18. Both All-Craft and NOW-NYC were active in the effort to get women hired on the docks. On February 12, 1979, *The Jersey Journal* and *Jersey Observer* ran a photo of Audrey Neal, the first woman to become a "longshoreman" on the eastern seaboard.
19. Joi Beard, interview with author, tape recording, New York City, December 21, 2004.
20. See Ruffini, *Harry Van Arsdale, Jr.*, 175, for the IBEW-Urban League connection in New York City.
21. Early on, this became a common practice—to count a minority woman as filling two slots—gender and race.
22. Kelber, interview with author, tape recording, New York City, July 7, 2005.
23. See Ruffini, *Harry Van Arsdale, Jr.*, 114–117. Also, Harry Kelber, *From the Great Depression to the New Century: My 60 Years as a Labor Activist* (Townsend, MA: A.G. Press, 1996).
24. *Electricity: Science* Service, United States of America: Nelson Doubleday and OD Ham Books, 1969), 30.

25. See Moccio, "Contradicting Male Power and Privilege," 330.
26. See *Building Barriers: Discrimination in New York City's Construction Trades,* A Report by the New York City Commission on Human Rights, December 1993, 195.
27. See Elliott J. Gorn, *Mother Jones: The Most Dangerous Woman in America* (New York: Hill and Wang, 2001).
28. Long, interview, September 26, 2004.
29. See Moccio, "Contradicting Male Power and Privilege," 212; 239–240; 304.
30. Herman Benson, *Rebels, Reformers, and Racketeers: How Insurgents Transformed the Labor Movement* (Bloomington, IN: 1stBooks, 2005), Chapter Nine, "Rescuing Democracy in the International Brotherhood of Electrical Workers."
31. See Moccio, "Contradicting Male Power and Privilege," Chapter Three.
32. Ruderman, interview, March 6, 1996.
33. Long, interview, September 26, 2004.
34. Kelber, interview, July 7, 2005.
35. Hernandez, interview, March 19, 2005.
36. See Moccio, "Contradicting Male Power and Privilege," 154–156.
37. Ibid., 216, "notion of 'biological destiny' and a 'woman's place,' which rested on socially constructed definitions of masculine and feminine," 278, on " 'manliness'—as a complex process of dominance and exclusion—on overestimation of men's ability and underestimation of women's, and the painful contradiction when women enter men's work: either acknowledge they're less 'manly' or that women are as 'skilled' as men" 284, 303–304,—"the labeling had to do with accommodation or resistance to the status quo, wherein femininity is associated with conformity. Active women who tried to change their work environment were considered gay, no matter what their sexual orientation actually was."
38. Ana Medina joined the IBEW at the age of 34. She writes: "I began my apprenticeship on July 1, 1985. Joining the electrical trade propelled my family out of minimum wage poverty into a livable wage. Although my poem is a sad one, I also want to express that my career has been a *great* experience. I was the first woman instructor in my Joint Apprenticeship Training Council." June 30, 2006, hand written correspondence with author. This poem first appeared in *Pride and a Paycheck*, Vol. 8, No. 2, March/April 2006, 3.
39. See Moccio, "Contradicting Male Power and Privilege," 225.
40. Ibid., 226.
41. Ruderman, interview, March 6, 1996; James B. Jacobs, *Gotham Unbound: How New York City was Liberated from the Grip of Organized Crime* (New York: New York University Press, 1999), See Chapter 5, "Exhibiting Corruption: The Javits Convention Center."
42. See Moccio, "Contradicting Male Power and Privilege," 101.
43. Ibid., 44.
44. Association for Union Democracy, Women's Project Records, Box 11, Robert F. Wagner Labor Archives, New York University.
45. Ibid.
46. Kelber, interview, July 7, 2005.
47. Beard, interview, December 21, 2004.
48. Hernandez, interview, March 19, 2005.
49. The 2000–2001 graduating class of Local 3 electricians from the Harry Van Arsdale Labor College was a little over 85 percent male, and almost 15 percent female.

Five   "Ticket to Ride"

1. Kay Webster, interview with author, tape recording, New York, November 19, 2004.
2. Elaine Ward, interview with author, tape recording, New York, March 29, 1997.
3. "Sal Magundie," "Plumbers Election," *Hard Hat News*, New York, No. 8, Spring, 1991, 4. James Jacobs, *Gotham Unbound: How New York City was Liberated from the Grip of Organized Crime* (New York: New York University Press, 1999). See *Union Democracy Review* for continuing coverage of Local 2, Local 1 and UA tribulations.

4. Laura Koss-Feder, "Women-Owned Hard-Hat Companies Are Booming," WE News, March 31, 2003. See todaysnews@womensenews.org.

5. James McNamara, interview with author, tape recording, New York, December 27, 2004.

6. "Galvanized steel pipes are used for supply lines...and is strong—a nail has a hard time piercing it—but its useful life is only 50 years or so," *Stanley Basic Plumbing: Pro Tips and Simple Steps*, edited by Ken Sidey (Des Moines, IA: Stanley Books, 2002), 16–17.

7. In her interview, Elaine Ward described several attempts to establish a connection to the very few women in her union local. One, Maureen Brown, was "the first woman to become a member of Local 2. In 1996, she was elected to local-wide office as a Trustee. Although she was a pioneer and a trailblazer, Maureen prided herself on being, 'one of the guys.'" She died in January 2001 of ovarian cancer. *Union Democracy Review*, No. 134, February/March 2001, 9.

8. *Building Barriers: Discrimination in New York City's Construction Trades*, A Report by the New York City Commission on Human Rights, December 1993, 117–118.

9. Gay Talese, *Fame and Obscurity* (New York: World Publishing Company, 1970), 183.

10. Elaine Ward, "Booming," in *Hard Hat News*, No. 12, Fall 1997, 6.

11. Susan Eisenberg, *We'll Call You If We Need You: Experiences of Women Working Construction*. (Ithaca, NY: Cornell University Press, 1998), 22.

12. Ibid., 19–20.

13. Joseph P. Fried, "One Degree in Fine Arts, and One in Plumbing," *New York Times*, December 24, 2006.

14. Ibid.

Six   "Sticking to the Union"

1. Herman Benson, "A Rising Tide of Union Democracy," in *The Transformation of U.S. Unions: Voices, Visions and Strategies from the Grassroots*, edited by Ray M. Tillman and Michael S. Cummings (Boulder, CO: Lynne Rienner Publishers, 1999). As John Sweeney assumed leadership of the AFL-CIO, Benson wrote: "But in Sweeney's program...the means of unleashing the principal mass of labor power is missing. The army of labor, still in reserve, is the great untapped resource with the potential for changing the United States....A thousand organizers can perhaps win a few thousand new recruits to their unions. But millions of union members, if imbued with pride in their unions, if convinced that this movement is truly theirs, if persuaded that it defends people against narrow private interests, can become the social force that shapes public opinion and creates a new mood in the country. The key to releasing that power is to rekindle the spirit of union democracy."

2. Yvone Maitin, interview by author, tape recording, Brooklyn, April 19, 2005.

3. Ibid., June 22, 1995.

4. "In Operating Engineers Local 14, New York," in *Union Democracy Review*, No. 161, March/April 2006, 5.

5. See www.thelaborers.net//operating_engineers/iuoe_mcguire_guilty.html. 5/6/2005.

6. "How to Suppress Democracy in Operating Engineers L. 30," in *Union Democracy Review*, No. 130, June 2000, 11.

7. Yvone Maitin, correspondence with author, December 9, 2002.

8. Ibid., July 12, 1990.

9. Ibid., April 19, 2005.

10. Ibid., July 12, 1990.

11. Maitin, correspondence, December 9, 2002.

12. Maitin, interview, April 19, 2005.

13. Ibid., July 12, 1990.

14. *The Builders: The Seventy-Five Year History of the Building & Construction Trades Department, AFL-CIO* (Washington, DC: Building and Construction Trades Dept., 1983), 143–144.

15. Maitin, interview, June 22, 1995.

16. Ibid., July 12, 1990.

17. Ibid., April 19, 2005.

18. Ibid., July 12, 1990.
19. Ibid., June 22, 1995.
20. Ibid., July 12, 1990.
21. Maitin, correspondence, December 9, 2002.
22. Maitin, interview, July 12, 1990.
23. Ibid., June 22, 1995.
24. Ibid., April 19, 2005.
25. Ibid., June 22, 1995.
26. Ibid., April 19, 2005.
27. Ibid., June 22, 1995.
28. Ibid., April 19, 2005.
29. Ibid., June 22, 1995.
30. Ibid., April 19, 2005.

Seven   Uncivil Service at the Board of Education

1. Ann Jochems, interview with author, tape recording, New York, July 26, 1990.
2. Ann Jochems, "A History of Nontraditional Employment for Women (NEW), The First Years, 1978–1992" (New York: Master's Thesis, Baruch College, The City University of New York, School of Public Affairs, 2003).
3. Jochems, interview with author, tape recording, Freeport, NY, December 16, 2004.
4. Ibid., July 26, 1990.
5. Ibid., December 16, 2004.
6. Ibid., July 26, 1990.
7. Ibid., December 16, 2004.
8. Ibid., July 26, 1990.
9. Ibid., December 16, 2004.
10. Jack Schierenbeck, "Against the Grain: Pioneer Female Board Carpenter Fights for Job—Again," *New York Teacher*, February 27, 2002.
11. Miriam Frank, "Hard Hats and Homophobia: Lesbians in the Building Trades," in the "Labor Comes Out" issue of *New Labor Forum*, guest edited by Miriam Frank and Desma Holcomb, Spring/Summer 2001.
12. Miriam Frank, interview with author, tape recording, December 5, 2004.
13. AUD Women's Project Records, Box 1, Folder, "Lesbian Tradeswoman," 1990–1991. Robert F. Wagner Labor Archives, New York University.
14. Jochems, interview, July 26, 1990.
15. Ibid., September 20, 1994.
16. Ibid., December 16, 2004.
17. Ibid., July 26, 1990.
18. Ibid., September 20, 1994.
19. Ibid., December 16, 2004.
20. Schierenbeck, "Against the Grain," February 27, 2002.
21. Anita Hill, *Speaking Truth to Power* (New York: Doubleday, 1997). Senator Alan Cranston of California summed up the dismissive assessment of [Anita Hill's] claims: "I am appalled at statements being made that these are not serious charges because they involve verbal, not physical, abuse. I am appalled at the stunning admissions of a lack of sensitivity to the problem of sexual harassment. What has a majority of this body been saying to all the women who are subjected to sexual harassment? Who have been, are now, or will be subjected to sexual harassment?," 140.
22. Jochems, interview, September 20, 1994.
23. Ibid., July 26, 1990.
24. Ibid., December 16, 2004.
25. Carl Campanile, "School's Out for Loafers," *New York Post*, June 26, 2003; Campanile, "Klein to Clean Up Corrupt Janitors," *New York Post*, July 2, 2003; Alison Gendar, "Read It and Sweep," *Daily*

News, May 19, 2003; David M. Herszenhorn, "Council Panel Holds Inquiry on Custodians in the Schools," *New York Times*, November 13, 2003; Herszenhorn, "16 Custodians in City Schools are Accused of Corruption," *New York Times*, May 6, 2005.

26. Eric Pooley, "Swept Away," *New York Magazine*, May 30, 1994, 28–33. Before Pooley's expose tied in to Susan D'Alessandro's trial, other reports of corruption had surfaced over the years. See Joseph Berger, "A Report Cites Custodians for Misconduct on the Job," *New York Times*, November 12, 1992. Berger also points to the "system that is virtually one of a kind in the United States…operating as semi-independent contractors, with their own budgets and purchasing and hiring authority," Liz Willen, "School Clean Up," *New York Newsday*, November 13, 1992. This probe of custodian fraud was carried out by Edward Stancik, the school's special commissioner of investigation, who, years later, investigated Ann Jochems.

27. Jochems, interview, July 26, 1990.

28. Robert Feliz, Esq., interview, New York, December 20, 2004.

29. *Building Barriers: Discrimination in New York City's Construction Trades*, A Report by the New York City Commission on Human Rights, December 1993, 143–145. Ann Jochems, in line for a promotion at the time, testified anonymously, as did many other tradespeople, rightfully fearing retaliation.

30. Ibid.

31. *New York Magazine*, Ibid., 30.

32. Jochems, interview, December 16, 2004.

33. *New York Magazine*, Ibid.

34. "In Memorium: Susan D'Alessandro," *Union Democracy Review*, No. 134, February/March 2001, 9. In 1996, Susan received NOW-NYC's Susan B. Anthony Award, honoring "individuals whose selfless efforts at the grassroots level have furthered the cause of women's equality." Susan was 49 at the time of her death.

35. Jochems, telephone interview with the author, January 8, 2005.

36. Michael Power, interview with the author, tape recording, New York, March 23, 2005.

37. Jessica DuLong, "Carpenter Building Bias Case against City," *New York Newsday*, February 3, 2002.

38. FOIA correspondence from the New York City Department of Education, Reference No. 2006–45; August 4, 2006.

Eight   Double Vision: Breaking Down Doors at the FDNY

1. Brenda Berkman, interview with author, tape recording, New York City, March 1, 1995.

2. Nancy MacLean, "The Hidden History of Affirmative Action: Working Women's Struggles in the 1970s and the Gender of Class," *Feminist Studies*, 25, No.1, Spring 1999. 43–44.

3. Berkman, interview, August 7, 1996.

4. Ibid., December 7, 2004.

5. JoAnn Jacobs, interview with author, tape recording, New York City, November 3, 2004.

6. Sam Roberts, "New York City Losing Blacks, Census Shows," *New York Times*, April 3, 2006; "Relief for More Lady Bravest," *New York Daily News*, May 17, 2007.

7. Michael Gannon, "Still Few Women in New York City Fire Department," *Journal News*, March 31, 2006; Kevin James, "Myths about FDNY and Race," *The Chief-Leader*, August 11, 2006; Ari Paul, "UFA, Vulcans at Odds on Bias Suit," *The Chief-Leader*, July 20, 2007; and "Vulcans: UFA Out of Line in Opposing Suit," August 31, 2007.

8. Maureen McFadden, interview with author, tape recording, New York City, May 5, 2005.

9. "Affirmative Action Update: After 25 Years of Court Battles SFFD Consent Decree is Ended," *Tradeswomen*, Winter, 1998–1999, 18.

10. Jacobs, interview, November 3, 2004.

11. Berkman, interview, March 1, 1995.

12. "Angry Firemen," *Daily News*, March 13, 1986.

13. "Firefighters Defend Standards: Court Stays Sifton Ruling," *Fire Lines,* Vol. 22, April 1986.
14. Nicholas Mancuso, president of the Uniformed Firefighters Association, observed that "Judge Sifton's order shows a complete disregard for what it takes to be a firefighter." Ibid.
15. Editorial, *The Chief-Leader,* U.D. (March 1986); An editorial in *New York Newsday,* "Light Dawns in Firehouses: The Judge Saw Red," said in part: "OK, fellas, the day of the fire house fraternity party is over. Come join the 20th Century," June 18, 1986.
16. Brenda Berkman, Association for Union Democracy 30th Anniversary Conference, New York City, April 8, 2000; "Brenda Berkman: Pioneer Firefighter at the AUD Conference," *$75 + Club News,* No. 74, Association for Union Democracy, July 2000, 1–3.
17. Vulcan Society, 45th Anniversary Issue, *Journal,* "Battalion Chief Wesley Williams, 1897–1984," Founder, Vulcan Society. FDNY.
18. Berkman, interview, March 1, 1995.
19. Jeanne Russell, "Reward for Job Well Done," *New York Newsday,* January 4, 1996. Jacobs was quoted in the piece: "When I'm going out and doing recruitment, there's more of a chance that those that look like me—little black girls—will want to be firefighters."
20. "Taking the Heat" aired on March 28, 2006 on the PBS series, *POV.* Writing in *The Chief-Leader,* Ginger Adams Otis noted, "It's not the kind of Fire Department history that's taught to rookies at the Randall's Island training academy, but [it] spotlights one of the most riveting, and uncomfortable chapters in the history of 'The Bravest,' " March 17, 2006.
21. Remarks of Captain Brenda Berkman on accepting the John Commerford Award, NY Labor History Association, November 10, 2005.
22. United Women Firefighters Records, Series II, Legal Files, Brenda Berkman Journal, Entry for August 3, 1983.
23. Jacobs, interview, November 3, 2004.
24. Berkman, interview, December 7, 2004.
25. Berkman, interview, March 1, 1995.
26. Ibid., December 7, 2004.

Nine From Economics to Electronics: The Making of an Activist

1. Lois Ross, interview with author, tape recording, New York, July 29, 1996.
2. See Alice Kessler-Harris, *In Pursuit of Equity: Women, Men, and the Quest for Economic Citizenship in 20th Century America* (New York: Oxford University Press, 2001), 40, 42, 69.
3. *The Unicorn Book of 1954,* edited by Joseph Laffan Morse (New York: Unicorn Books, 1955), 432.
4. See Rowbotham, *A Century of Women,* 436–437; *The Decade of Women: A Ms. History of the Seventies* (New York: Paragon Books, 1980), 6.
5. Changing the Face of Medicine: Dr. Helen Rodriguez-Trias, www.nlm.nih. gov/changing the face of medicine/physicians/biography_273.html. Dr. Helen Rodriguez-Trias was a founding member of the Committee for Abortion Rights and Against Sterilization Abuse. Accessed on June 23, 2005.
6. Paul A. Samuelson, *Economics* (New York: McGraw-Hill Book Company, 1973), 796.
7. Ibid.
8. Ibid., 797–799.
9. Ibid., 799.
10. Ibid.
11. Brooklyn singer/songwriter Bev Grant sang the lyrics, "59 cents to every woman's dollar," at union events.
12. *Women's Work, Men's Work: Sex Segregation on the Job,* edited by Barbara F. Reskin and Heidi I. Hartmann (Washington, DC: National Academy Press, 1986), x.
13. Lois Ross, group interview with author on United Tradeswomen, New York, tape recording, March 6, 1996.
14. Ross, interview, July 29, 1996.

15. Ibid., March 6, 1996.
16. Ibid.
17. Ibid., July 29, 1996.
18. Ibid., March 6, 1996.
19. Ibid., July 29, 1996.
20. Ibid., March 6, 1996.
21. Ibid., July 29, 1996.
22. Ibid., March 6, 1996.
23. Ibid., July 29,1996.
24. Ibid., March 6, 1996.
25. Ibid., July 29, 1996.
26. Martha Ackmann, *The Mercury 13: The Untold Story of Thirteen American Women and the Dream of Space Flight* (New York: Random House, 2003). See Tom Wolfe, *The Right Stuff* (New York: Bantam Books, 1983), 206–207 for a description of "the Right Stuff" in males.
27. W. Michael Cox and Richard Alm, "Scientists Are Made, Not Born," *New York Times,* February 28, 2005.
28. "Title IX—An Educational Opportunity in Vocational Technical Education: A Promise Still Owed to the Nation's Young Women," June 2002. See also "Invisible Again: The Impact of Changes in Federal Funding on Vocational Programs for Women and Girls," National Women's Law Center, Washington, D.C., October 2001.
29. Stephen J. Rose and Heidi I. Hartmann, "Still a Man's Labor Market: The Long-Term Earnings Gap," Institute for Women's Policy Research, 2004.
30. Dorothy Samuels, "Finally, Let's Train a Generation of Women Electricians," *New York Times,* July 27, 2002.
31. Meredith Kolodner, "Making Advancement Add Up," *The Chief-Leader,* August 17, 2007.
32. Lois Ross, correspondence with author, July 14, 2006.

Ten   That's Just the Way It Was:
AT&T and the Struggle for Equal Opportunity

1. Henry P. Leifermann, *Crystal Lee: A Woman of Inheritance* (New York: Palgrave Macmillan, 1975); Mimi Conway, *Rise Gonna Rise: A Portrait of Southern Textile Workers* (New York: Anchor Press/ Doubleday, 1979).
2. Venus Green, *Race on the Line: Gender, Labor, and Technology in the Bell System, 1880–1980* (Durham, NC: Duke University Press, 2001); Lois Kathryn Herr, *Women, Power and AT&T: Winning Rights in the Workplace* (Boston: Northeastern University Press, 2003), 2, "No One Objected: That Is Just the Way It Was." Alice Kessler-Harris, *In Pursuit of Equity: Women, Men, and the Quest for Economic Citizenship in 20th Century America* (New York/Oxford: Oxford University Press, 2001); Nancy MacLean, *Freedom Is Not Enough: The Opening of the American Workplace* (New York: Russell Sage Foundation, 2006), 124, "just the way things were."
3. Betty Friedan, *Life So Far: A Memoir* (New York: Simon & Schuster, 2000); Herr, *Women, Power and AT&T.*
4. Kessler-Harris, *In Pursuit of Equity,* 250; Herr, *Women, Power and AT&T,* 37.
5. Herr, *Women, Power and AT&T.*
6. Green, *Race on the Line;* See Chapter 8, "Black Operators in the Computer Age."
7. See www.lilytomlin.com; "Ernestine: 'I gave the best years of my life to Ma Bell and what did it get me? When she went to pieces, so did I. I've got operator's hump from plugging and unplugging. I've got carpal tunnel from all those years dialing.'"
8. Green, *Race on the Line,* see Chapter 2, "'Hello Girls': The Making of the Voice with a Smile."
9. Ibid. See Chapter 7, "Racial Integration and the Demise of the 'White Lady' Image."
10. Jamakaya, *Like Our Sisters before Us: Women of Wisconsin Labor* (Milwaukee: The Wisconsin Labor History Society, 1998), 25–26.

11. Ibid., 29.
12. Herr, *Women, Power and AT&T*, see Chapter 1, "Testing the Rules."
13. Friedan, *Life So Far*, 170; Jo Freeman, "How 'Sex' Got Into Title VII: Persistent Opportunism as a Maker of Public Policy," *Law and Inequality: A Journal of Theory and Practice*, Vol. 9, No. 2, March 1991, 163–184. "Dial 0 for Oppression" was a slogan on a sign carried by NOW activists in New Orleans, see Lois Herr, *Women, Power and AT&T*, 98; and MacLean, *Freedom Is Not Enough*, 139.
14. Friedan, *Life So Far*, 162–163.
15. Pauli Murray, *The Autobiography of a Black Activist, Feminist, Lawyer, Priest, and Poet* (Knoxville: University of Tennessee Press, 1989), see Chapter 29, "Civil Wrongs and Rights," and Chapter 30, "The Birth of NOW."
16. See Kessler-Harris, *In Pursuit of Equity*, 249–250; 280; 293–294; and MacLean, *Freedom Is Not Enough*, 123–124; 132.
17. See Herr, *Women, Power and AT&T*, 43–46; and MacLean, *Freedom Is Not Enough*, 123–125.
18. Ibid.
19. Herr, *Women, Power and AT&T*, 18–19; MacLean, *Freedom Is Not Enough*, 131–133; 139.
20. Leslie Friedman Goldstein, *The Constitutional Rights of Women: Cases in Law and Social Change* (Madison: University of Wisconsin Press, 1988), 507; MacLean, *Freedom Is Not Enough*, 125.
21. Herr, *Women, Power and AT&T*; MacLean, *Freedom Is Not Enough*.
22. Ibid.
23. See Green, *Race on the Line*, 239–240; and Herr, *Women, Power and AT&T*.
24. NOW-New York City Chapter Records, Box 6, Folder 9. Robert F. Wagner Labor Archives, New York University. The AT&T documents in the collection provide an excellent counterpoint to the contention that working-class women were not part of NOW's agenda. See Box 12 in particular for AT&T documents.
25. Venus Green, interview with author, tape recording, New York City, July 2, 2005.
26. Ilene Winkler, interview with author, tape recording, New York City, July 13, 1990.
27. Ibid., December 16, 2004.
28. See Green, "CWA opposes Consent Decrees," in *Race on the Line*, 242–248; and Herr, *Women, Power and AT&T*, which shows the degree to which the EEOC sought to involve the CWA, 22, 24–25, 57, 114, 143–144.
29. Thomas R. Brooks, *Communications Workers of America: The Story of a Union* (New York: Mason/Charter, 1977), 238–239.
30. Ilene Winkler, interview, July 13, 1990.
31. Ibid.
32. Green, interview, July 2, 2005.
33. Ibid.
34. See Herr, *Women, Power and AT&T*, "As a corporate feminist, I had room to explore and air my concerns. I didn't have to be subversive," Herr writes in her preface.
35. Ibid., 7–8.
36. Dan LaBotz, *A Troublemaker's Handbook: How to Fight Back Where You Work—And Win!* (Detroit, MI: Labor Notes, 1991), 202; and Aaron Brenner, "Rank-and-File Struggles at the Telephone Company," Chapter Four, in "Rank-and-File Rebellion, 1966–1975," (Ph.D. diss., Columbia University, 1996).
37. See Ilene Winkler in *A Troublemaker's Handbook*, 202.
38. Ilene Winkler, interview, December 16, 2004.
39. As director of the Women's Project, Association for Union Democracy, the author worked with individual and committee women from Local 1101. See Women's Project, AUD Records, Box 1, Folder, "Communications Workers of America (CWA): Local 1101, 1999–2000:" Robert F. Wagner Labor Archives, New York University.
40. Green, *Race on the Line*, 238–239.
41. Herbert R. Northrup and John A. Larson, "The Impact of the AT&T-EEO Consent Decree," Labor Relations and Public Policy Series, No. 20 (Industrial Research Unit, the Wharton School, University of Pennsylvania, Philadelphia, 1979), 45.
42. See Jamakaya, *Like Our Sisters Before Us*, 31–32.
43. In 2003, Cornell University held a conference in honor of Alice H. Cook's hundredth birthday. In "Women and Unions: Still the Most Difficult Revolution?" on November 21–22, at the School

of Industrial and Labor Relations, Ithaca, NY, participants addressed this question. See www.ilr. cornell.edu/alicecook100th/ for papers.

Eleven   Woman on the Move

1. AUD Women's Project Records, Box 16, Folder "Women in Nontraditional Jobs: Stories," Robert F. Wagner Labor Archives, New York University. Eileen Sullivan's story was collected for the *Manual for Survival for Women in Nontraditional Employment* (New York: NOW LDEF and AUD Women's Project, 1993).
2. John McPhee. *Uncommon Carriers* (New York: Farrar, Straus and Giroux, 2006), 33.
3. Eileen Sullivan, interview by author and Brenda Bishop, hand-written notes, JFK Airport. August 17, 1990.
4. Eileen Sullivan. "Stories," AUD Women's Project Records.
5. Sullivan, interview, August 17, 1990.
6. Eileen Sullivan, interview by author, tape recording, New York City, March 5, 1996.
7. Eileen Sullivan, correspondence to author, September 11, 2006.
8. *Local 100 Express*, Transport Workers' Union, May 23, 2003, 9.
9. Sullivan, correspondence, September 11, 2006.
10. Ibid.
11. Lois Gray, interview by author, tape recording, New York City, July 24, 2006.
12. Lois Gray. "Women in Union Leadership," in *The American Woman 2001–2002: Getting to the Top*, edited by Cynthia B. Costello and Anne J. Stone (New York: W.W. Norton, 2001), 110–111.
13. Annelise Orleck. *Common Sense and a Little Fire: Women and Working-Class Politics in the United States, 1900–1965* (Chapel Hill: University of North Carolina Press, 1995), 43.
14. "Giving Women A Voice," *Booklet 6: Gender Equality: A Guide to Collective Bargaining* (Geneva: International Labour Organization, 2002).

Twelve   Against the Grain

1. Djar Horn, telephone interview by author, handwritten notes. May 2, 2007.
2. Veronica Session, interview by author, tape recording, New York City, July 26, 2006.
3. Damien Cave, "In Harlem, 37 Women Unite to Build a Mother's Dream," *New York Times*, May 8, 2005.
4. Session, interview, July 26, 2006.
5. Louise Kramer, "Doing Nails for a Living, with a Hammer," *New York Times*, June 12, 2005.
6. Consuelo Reyes, interview by author, tape recording, North Bend, OR, August 4, 2005.
7. Janine Blackwelder, interview with author, handwritten notes, New York City, February 7, 2004.
8. Irene Soloway, interview with author, handwritten notes, New York City, February 7, 2004.
9. Irene Soloway, interview with author, tape recording, New York City, August 31, 1994.
10. James B. Jacobs, *Mobsters, Unions, and Feds: The Mafia and the American Labor Movement* (New York: New York University Press, 2006), 184.
11. Ibid., 183–184; 200–201. For the (pending) trial of Michael Forde, see Barbara Ross and Michael McAuliff, *New York Daily News*, "Construction Union Facing Bribery Trial Backs Hillary," October 26, 2007.
12. Carpenters for a Stronger Union Records, Robert F. Wagner Labor Archives, New York University.
13. Reyes, interview, August 4, 2005.
14. *On the Level*, Spring 1985, Vol. 5, No. 1, 2.
15. Henry Zieger, "NYC Carpenters Still Married to Mob?" *Hard Hat News*, Fall 1995, 8; Jack Newfield, "Sleazy Does It in Vote for Carpenters' Prez," *New York Post*, June 13, 1995. Palm cards distributed to carpenters coming to cast their ballot at the Borough of Manhattan Community

College, July 20–24, 1995, included those from the CSU slate—John Greany, president; Barbara Trees, second vice president; Jack Durcan, chair of the District Council Trustees. Michael Bilello, running on the American Dream slate, was the highest vote getter among the reformers. He was given a job by the administration, but was later fired after he persisted in pursuing contractors who were cheating the Benefits Fund, through nonpayment.

16. Connie Reyes, "Women Carpenters' Thoughts: A Fair Hiring Hall," *On the Level*, Vol. 5, No. 1, Spring 1985, 5–6.
17. United Tradeswomen Records, Box 1, Folder 7; Petition and Letter, October 9, 1980. Robert F. Wagner Labor Archives, New York University.
18. Ibid.
19. Ibid. Letter to Ted Maritas, October 13, 1980.
20. Jacobs, *Mobsters, Unions, and Feds*, 184.
21. United Tradeswomen Records, Box 1, Folder 7, *Workers View Point*, February 23, 1981.
22. Ibid.
23. United Tradeswomen Records, Box 1, Folder 7. Letter to Charles Fanning. March 9, 1981.
24. Ibid., Box 1 Folder 8.
25. See *Building Barriers: Discrimination in New York City's Construction Trades*, A Report by the New York City Commission on Human Rights, December 1993, 185.
26. Ibid., 186.
27. "Brick Shields" "Hard Hats Talk at Human Rights Hearing," *Hard Hat News*, No. 6, Summer 1990, 3; 8.
28. See *Building Barriers*, 82.
29. See *Hard Hat News*, No. 6, Summer 1990, 3; 8.
30. The "colleague" was Willie Nordstrum, who was shot to death in 1978. He first ran as an insurgent candidate for business manager of Local 488 in 1975. See *Union Democracy Review*, June/July 2004, 4.
31. See *Building Barriers*, 81.
32. Ibid.
33. See Reuven Blau, "Say 1-in-3 Rule Is Abused by Agencies," *The Chief-Leader*, May 14, 2004.
34. See *Building Barriers*, 84–85.
35. See Ann Jochems interviews for asbestos-related neglect. See Meredith Kolodner, "Sues DOE, Union Custodian: Demoted for Asbestos Claim," *The Chief-Leader*, September 7, 2007.
36. Soloway, interview, August 31, 1994.
37. Ibid., July 5, 1990.
38. Ibid., August 31, 1990.
39. Ibid.
40. See "Harry McBone," "City Carpenters Seek a New Local," *Hard Hat News*, No. 10, U.D. (August 1993), 8.
41. Michael Power, interview with author, tape recording, New York City, March 23, 2005.
42. Author attended the Holiday Party at the District Council of Carpenters; handwritten notes.
43. Rebecca Lurie, interview with Ann Jochems, tape recording, New York City, February 28, 1995.
44. Dale McCormick, *Against the Grain: A Carpentry Manual for Women* (Iowa City: Iowa City Women's Press, 1977), 3.
45. Lurie, interview, February 28, 1995.
46. Ibid., See Greg Butler, "Hostile Work Environment: Inside the New York District Council of Carpenters' Sexual Harassment Training Program," January 30, 2001. *gangbox@excite.com* (The Infamous Vinnie Gangbox).
47. See "The New York City Construction Labor Market Trends and Issues: A Labor Market Profile," Fiscal Policy Institute, June 2003, 1–5.
48. "Sisters on the Frontline," Cornell Conference; Panel moderated by author; handwritten notes.
49. "Sisters in the UBC: Press Kit," distributed at the Tradeswomen Organizing Panel, "Sisters on the Frontline" conference, March 31, 2007.
50. Lurie, interview, February 28, 1995.
51. Session, interview, July 26, 2006.
52. Tour of the 42nd Street site after interview on July 26, 2006. Session mailed a copy of the Stanley ad to the author.

53. Soloway, interview, August 31, 1994.
54. Ibid.

Thirteen   Getting Past Pioneering

1. Margarita Suarez, interview with author, tape recording, New York City, December 22, 2004.
2. Since the U.S. Congress passed the WANTO Act in 1992, it's been part of the national system to develop the workforce. The WANTO grants provide technical assistance to employers and labor unions to encourage employment of women in nontraditional occupations and, once enrolled, to improve their retention rates. The grants also go to community-based organizations such as NEW and Chicago Women in Trades.
3. Angela Olszewski, interview with author, tape recording, New York City, December 18, 2004.
4. The pitch to put in an application for the Elevator Servicer and Repairer Apprenticeship Program asked, "Want a career that will enable you to reach new heights?" Recruitment was done through NEW, and NYCHA—the New York City Housing Authority, for participants of the Housing Authority's Resident Services Program.
5. Reference to Lauren Sugerman, president of Chicago Women in Trades and Connie Ashbrook, executive director of Oregon Tradeswomen. See the Portland, Oregon Plan of Action, Western Regional Summit. Youth of Color and Women in the Highway Construction Trades, September 21–23, 2004; and "Collection of Best Practice Summaries," by the Federal Highway Administration, Oregon Department of Transportation, and Oregon Tradeswomen, Inc.
6. Both Margarita Suarez and Angela Olszewski were elected to the Board of Directors of TNT—Tradeswomen Now and Tomorrow. The organization helped to launch the first national women's committee of the AFL-CIO's Building and Construction Trades Department in 2005. After presenting their case at the Legislative Conference of BCTD, the department established a Committee of Women in the Trades. After 27 years, the Building Trades' unions put their official stamp on women working in the construction trades.
7. TNT and member organizations continually have to lobby for funding for WANTO. Despite its proven success, funding was held steady at approximately $1million per year since its enactment in 1992.
8. From Italy—one of the historically important marbles—named after the locations of their quarries.
9. Chicago Women in Trades recruitment flier.
10. Katherine Frew, *Plumber* (New York: Children's Press/A Division of Scholastic, 2004)
11. Jane Latour, "Women's Project Report: Breaking Down Blue-Collar Barriers," *Union Democracy Review*. Association for Union Democracy, No. 140, February/March 2002, 11.
12. Angela Olszewski, witness, Nontraditional Employment for Women, New York, Journeywoman and Instructor, Testimony June 24, 2004.
13. Ibid.
14. Shane, Paramount Pictures, George Stevens, producer and director, screenplay by W.B. Guthrie, 1953.
15. See *Pollard v. E.I. DuPont de Nemours & Co.*, 2001, hostile work environment of former DuPont employee Sharon Pollard; Linda Greenhouse, "Justices Weigh Whether Railroad Retaliated against Worker," *New York Times*, April 18, 2006; "History of Tradeswomen Litigation," www.equalrights. org/publications; "In the Courts," www.legalmomentum/inthecourts; "Timeline of Major Supreme Court Decisions on Women's Rights," ACLU Women's Rights Project.
16. Lynn Sherr, *Outside the Box: A Memoir* (Emmaus, PA: Rodale, 2006), 341.

Epilogue: Where Are They Now?

1. Joi Beard, e-mail, September 2, 2006.
2. Brenda Berkman, e-mail, September 14, 2007. Revson Fellowship Newsletter, December 2006, p. 3.

3. Janine Blackwelder, correspondence, February 7, 2005. Telephone conversation with Blackwelder's brother, February 18, 2007.
4. Brunilda Hernandez, correspondence, November 22, 2004, May 22, 2007.
5. JoAnn Jacobs, correspondence, May 25, 2007.
6. Ann Jochems, correspondence, December 30, 2003, May 16, 2007; e-mail, August 30, 2006.
7. Laura Kelber, correspondence, May 21, 2007.
8. Cynthia Long, correspondence, November 22, 2004.
9. Rebecca Lurie, correspondence, December 30, 2003.
10. Yvone Maitin, correspondence, December 31, 2003; e-mail, September 3, 2006.
11. Angela Olszewski, correspondence, May 21, 2007.
12. Marty Pottenger, e-mail, March 22, 2007.
13. Consuelo Reyes, telephone conversation, July 7, 2007.
14. Lois Ross, correspondence, July 14, 2006.
15. Douglas, Martin. "Evan Ruderman, 44, Activist for Many Causes," *New York Times*, November 21, 2003. Document from Marty Pottenger with Evan Ruderman remarks in reference to Pottenger's play, *Abundance*, November 18, 2005.
16. Ronnie Sandler, e-mail, August 26, 2007.
17. Veronica Session, telephone conversation, August 26, 2007.
18. Irene Soloway, correspondence, January 12, 2004; e-mail August 31, 2006.
19. Margarita Suarez, e-mail, August 31, 2006.
20. Eileen Sullivan, correspondence, January 24, 2004.
21. Elaine Ward, e-mail, September 11, 2006.
22. Kay Webster, correspondence, May 30, 2007.
23. Ilene Winkler, correspondence, December 30, 2003.

Select Bibliography and Sources

Interviews

All interviews were tape recorded in person by the author in New York City, unless otherwise indicated. The oral history collection for *Sisters in the Brotherhoods* will be housed at the Robert F. Wagner Labor Archives, New York University.

Pioneers

Ann Jochems, July 26, 1990; September 20, 1994; December 16, 2004; January 8, 2005 (telephone, handwritten notes).
Brenda Berkman, March 1, 1995; August 7, 1996; December 7, 2004.
Brunilda Hernandez, March 19, 2005, Alexandria, VA.
Consuelo Reyes Tyrrell, August 4, 2005, North Bend, OR.
Cynthia A. H. Long, September 26, 2004.
Eileen Sullivan, August 17, 1990; March 5, 1996.
Elaine Ward, March 29, 1997.
Evan Ruderman, March 6, 1996.
Ilene Winkler, July 13, 1990; December 16, 2004.
Irene Soloway, July 5, 1990; August 31, 1994; March 6, 1996; February 7, 2004 (handwritten notes).
Janine Blackwelder, August 1, 1990; December 17, 1994, Chesterfield, MA; February 7, 2004 (handwritten notes).
JoAnn Jacobs, November 3, 2004.
Joi Beard, December 21, 2004.
Kay Webster, November 19, 2004.
Laura Kelber, July 7, 2005.
Lois Ross, March 6, 1996; July 29, 1996.
Marty Pottenger, September 27, 1994.
Rebecca Lurie, February 28, 1995 (Interview by Ann Jochems).
Ronnie Sandler, March 26, 1995 (Interview by Ann Jochems at the 9th Annual Northern New England Tradeswomen Conference).
Veronica Session, July 26, 2006.
Yvone Maitin, July 12, 1990; June 22, 1995; April 19, 2005.

"Next Wave"

Angela Olszewski, December 18, 2004.
Djar Horn, May 2, 2007 (handwritten notes).
Margarita Suarez, December 26, 2004.

Expert Allies

David Raff, November 30, 2004 (telephone; handwritten notes).
Franklin McMurray, August 19, 2005.
James Haughton, November 11, 2004.
James McNamara, December 27, 2004.
Judith Layzer, April 2, 2005.
Lois Gray, July 24, 2006.
Maureen McFadden, May 5, 2005.
Michael Power, March 23, 2005.
Miriam Frank, December 5, 2004.
Robert Felix, December 20, 2004 (handwritten notes).
Robert Fitch, December 10, 2005 (handwritten notes).
Venus Green, July 2, 2005.

Collections, Robert F. Wagner Labor Archives, New York University

Carpenters for a Stronger Union
Communications Workers of America, Local 1101
James McNamara Papers
Judith Layzer Papers
Local 580, Ornamental Iron Workers Records
National Organization for Women-New York City Chapter Records
United Tradeswomen Records
Women's Project, Association for Union Democracy Records

Books and Articles

Ackmann, Martha. *The Mercury 13: The Untold Story of Thirteen American Women and the Dream of Space Flight.* New York: Random House, 2003.

Antilla, Susan. *Tales from the Boom-Boom Room: Women vs. Wall Street.* Princeton, NJ: Bloomberg Press, 2002.

Barry, Kathleen M. *Femininity in Flight: A History of Flight Attendants.* Durham, NC: Duke University Press, 2007.

Baxandall, Rosalyn, Linda Gordon, and Susan Reverby, eds. *America's Working Women: A Documentary History-1600 to Present.* New York: Vintage Books, 1976.

Beddoe, Deirdre. *Women Between the Wars, 1918–1939: Back to Home and Duty.* London: Pandora, 1989.

Benson, Herman. *Democratic Rights for Union Members: A Guide to Internal Union Democracy.* New York: Association for Union Democracy, 1979.

———. *How to Get an Honest Union Election.* New York: Association for Union Democracy, 1987.

———. *Rebels, Reformers, and Racketeers: How Insurgents Transformed the Labor Movement.* Bloomington, IN: 1stBooks, 2005.

Bernhardt, Debra E. "Life Under a Hard Hat: A Question of Skill." *New Yorkers at Work: Oral Histories of Life, Labor and Industry.* Robert F. Wagner Labor Archives, New York University, 1985.

Bowman, Constance and Clara Marie Allen. *Slacks and Calluses: Our Summer in a Bomber Factory.* Washington, D.C.: Smithsonian Institution Press, 1999.

Braid, Kate. *Covering Rough Ground.* Vancouver: Raincoast Books, 1991.

Bravo, Ellen. *Taking on the Big Boys: Or Why Feminism Is Good for Families, Business, and the Nation.* New York: Feminist Press at the City University of New York, 2007.

Brenner, Aaron. *Rank-and-File Rebellion, 1966–1975.* PhD. Dissertation, Columbia University, 1996.

Breslin, Jimmy. *Table Money.* New York: Penguin Books, 1987.

Brodkin, Karen and Dorothy Remy, eds. *My Troubles Are Going to Have Trouble with Me: Everyday Trials and Triumphs of Women Workers.* New Brunswick, NJ: Rutgers University Press, 1984.

Brooks, Thomas R. *Communications Workers of America: The Story of a Union.* New York: Mason/Charter, 1977.

Brownmiller, Susan. *In Our Time: Memoir of a Revolution.* New York: Dial Press, 1999.

Building and Construction Trades Department. *The Builders: The Seventy-Five Year History of the Building & Construction Trades Department, AFL-CIO.* Washington, DC, 1983.

Byrd, Barbara. Women in Carpentry Apprenticeship: A Case Study. *Labor Studies Journal* 24 (Fall, 1999).

Carlson, Peggie. *The Girls Are Coming.* St. Paul: Minnesota Historical Press, 1999.

Cherry, Mike. *On High Steel: The Education of an Ironworker.* New York: Quadrangle/New York Times Book, 1974.

Chesler, Phyllis. *Woman's Inhumanity to Woman.* New York: Thunder Mouth Press/Nation Books, 2001.

Chetkovich, Carol. *Real Heat: Gender and Race in the Urban Fire Service.* New Brunswick, NJ: Rutgers University Press, 1997.

Cobble, Dorothy Sue. *The Other Women's Movement: Workplace Justice and Social Rights in Modern America.* Princeton, NJ: Princeton University Press, 2004.

Colatosti, Camille and Elissa Karg. *Stopping Sexual Harassment: A Handbook for Union and Workplace Activists.* Detroit, MI: Labor Education and Research Project, 1992.

Coleman, Penny. *Rosie the Riveter: Women Working on the Home Front in World War II* New York: Crown Publishers, 1995.

Conway, Mimi. *Rise Gonna Rise: A Portrait of Southern Textile Workers.* New York: Anchor Press/Doubleday, 1979.

Costello, Cynthia B. and Stone, Anne J. eds. *The American Woman 2001–2002: Getting to the Top.* New York: W.W. Norton, 2001.

Critchlow, Donald T. *Phyllis Schlafly and Grassroots Conservatism: A Woman's Crusade.* Princeton, NJ: Princeton University Press, 2005.

Crittenden, Ann. *The Price of Motherhood: Why the Most Important Job in the World Is Still the Least Valued.* New York: An Owl Book, Henry Holt, 2001.

Deaux, Kay and Joseph Ullman. *Women of Steel.* New York: Praeger, 1983.

Deslippe, Dennis A. *Rights, Not Roses: Unions and the Rise of Working-Class Feminism, 1945–1980.* Chicago: University of Illinois Press, 2000.

Dollinger, Sol and Genora Johnson Dollinger. *Not Automatic: Women and the Left in the Forging of the Auto Workers' Union.* New York: Monthly Review Press, 2000.

Donohue, Lynn. *Brick by Brick: A Woman's Journey.* New Bedford: Spinner Publications, 2006.

Doro, Sue. *Heart, Home, and Hard Hats.* Minneapolis, MN: Midwest Villages and Voices, 1986.

———. *Blue Collar Goodbyes.* Watsonville, CA: Papier-Mache Press, 1992.

Eisenberg, Susan. *It's a Good Thing I'm Not Macho: A Cycle of Poems.* Boston: Whetstone, 1984.

———. *Pioneering: Poems from the Construction Site.* Ithaca, NY: ILR Press, an Imprint of Cornell University Press, 1998.

———. *We'll Call You If We Need You: Experiences of Women Working Construction.* Ithaca, NY: Cornell University Press, 1998.

Faludi, Susan. *Backlash: The Undeclared War Against American Women.* New York: Doubleday, 1992.

———. *Stiffed: The Betrayal of the American Male. New York:* Perennial Imprint, Harper Collins, 1999.

Fiscal Policy Institute. *The New York City Construction Labor Market: Trends and Issues. A Labor Market Profile.* New York: 2003.

Fitch, Robert. *Solidarity for Sale: How Corruption Destroyed the Labor Movement and Undermined America's Promise.* New York: Public Affairs, 2006.

Fletcher, Arthur. *The Silent Sell-Out: Government Betrayal of Blacks to the Craft Unions.* New York: Third Press, 1974.

Fonow, Mary Margaret. *Union Women: Forging Feminism in the United Steelworkers of America.* Minneapolis: University of Minnesota Press, 2003.

Frank. Miriam. "Hard Hats and Homophobia: Lesbians in the Building Trades," *New Labor Forum*, No. 8 (Spring/Summer 2001).

Frank, Miriam and Harriet Tanzman. "Climbing That Ladder: Jobs and Opportunity." *New Yorkers at Work: Oral Histories of Life, Labor and Industry*. Robert F. Wagner Labor Archives, New York University, 1985.

Frank, Miriam, Marilyn Ziebarth, and Connie Field. *The Life and Times of Rosie the Riveter: The Story of Three Million Working Women during World War II*. Emeryville, CA: Clarity Educational Productions, 1982.

Freeman, Jo. "How 'Sex' Got Into Title VII: Persistent Opportunism as a Maker of Public Policy." *Law and Inequality. A Journal of Theory and Practice*. Vol. 9, No. 2 (March 1991).

Frew, Katherine. *Plumber*. New York: Children's Press/A Division of Scholastic, 2004.

Friedan, Betty. *Life So Far: A Memoir*. New York: Simon & Schuster, 2000.

Goldstein, Leslie Friedman. *The Constitutional Rights of Women: Cases in Law and Social Change*. Madison: University of Wisconsin Press, 1988.

Gorn, Elliott J. *Mother Jones: The Most Dangerous Woman in America*. New York: Hill and Wang, 2001.

Green, Venus. *Race on the Line: Gender, Labor, and Technology in the Bell System, 1880–1980*. Durham, NC: Duke University Press, 2001.

Greenwald, Maurine Weiner. *Women, War, and Work: The Impact of World War I on Women Workers in the United States*. Ithaca, NY: Cornell University Press, 1980.

Griffin-Cohen, Marjorie and Kate Braid. "Training and Equity Initiatives on the British Columbia Vancouver Island Highway Project: A Model for Large-Scale Construction Projects." *Labor Studies Journal* 25 (Fall 2000).

Hagen, Susan and Mary Carouba. *Women at Ground Zero: Stories of Courage and Compassion*. Indianapolis, IN: Alpha Books, 2002.

Herera, Sue. *Women of the Street: Making It on Wall Street—The World's Toughest Business*. New York: John Wiley & Sons, 1997.

Herr, Lois Kathryn. *Women, Power and AT&T: Winning Rights in the Workplace*. Boston: Northeastern University Press, 2003.

Hill, Anita. *Speaking Truth to Power*. New York: Doubleday, 1997.

Hill, Herbert. *Black Labor and the American Legal System: Race, Work, and the Law*. Washington, DC: The Bureau of National Affairs, 1977.

Holmstedt, Kirsten. *Band of Sisters: American Women at War in Iraq*. Mechanicsburg, PA: Stackpole Books, 2007.

Hutchinson, John. *The Imperfect Union: A History of Corruption in American Trade Unions*. New York: E.P. Dutton & Co., 1972.

International Association of Bridge, Structural and Ornamental Iron Workers, AFL-CIO. *Ironworkers 100th Anniversary: 1896–1996. A History of the Iron Workers Union*. Washington, DC, 1996.

International Labour Organization. *Giving Women a Voice. Booklet 6. Gender Equality: A Guide to Collective Bargaining*. Geneva: Labour Law and Labour Relations Branch, Bureau for Workers' Activities, 2007.

Jackson, Kenneth, ed. *The Encyclopedia of New York City*. New York: Yale University Press, 1995.

Jacobs, James B. *Gotham Unbound: How New York City Was Liberated from the Grip of Organized Crime*. New York: New York University Press, 1999.

———. *Mobsters, Unions, and Feds: The Mafia and the American Labor Movement*. New York: New York University Press, 2006.

Jamakaya. *Like our Sisters before Us: Women of Wisconsin Labor*. Milwaukee, WI: The Wisconsin Labor History Society, 1998.

Jochems, Ann. "A History of Nontraditional Employment for Women (NEW), The First Years, 1978–1992." Master's Thesis, Baruch College, The City University of New York, 2003.

Kelber, Harry. *From the Great Depression to the New Century: My 60 Years as a Labor Activist*. Townsend, MA: AG Press, 1996.

Kessler-Harris, Alice. *Women Have Always Worked. A Historical Overview*. Old Westbury: Feminist Press, 1981.

———. *Out to Work: A History of Wage-Earning Women in the United States*. New York: Oxford University Press, 1982.

———. *In Pursuit of Equity. Women, Men, And the Quest For Economic Citizenship In 20th-Century America*. New York: Oxford University Press, 2001.

La Botz, Dan. *A Troublemaker's Handbook: How to Fight Back Where You Work—And Win!* Detroit, MI: Labor Notes, 1991.

Laffan, Joseph, ed. *The Unicorn Book of 1954.* New York: Unicorn Books, 1955.

Latour, Jane. "Live! From New York: Women Construction Workers in Their Own Words." *Labor History,* Vol. 42, No. 2 (May 2001).

Leifermann, Henry P. *Crystal Lee: A Woman of Inheritance.* New York: Palgrave Macmillan, 1975.

Levine, Suzanne and Harriet Lyons, eds. *The Decade of Women: A Ms. History of the Seventies in Words and Pictures.* New York: G.P. Putnam & Sons, 1980.

Lichtenstein, Nelson. *State of the Union: A Century of American Labor.* Princeton, NJ: Princeton University Press, 2002.

Lindgren, J.Ralph and Nadine Taub. *The Law of Sex Discrimination.* St. Paul, MN: West Publishing, 1988.

MacLean, Nancy. "The Hidden History of Affirmative Action: Working Women's Struggles in the 1970's and the Gender of Class." *Feminist Studies,* 25 (Spring 1999).

———. *Freedom Is Not Enough. The Opening of the American Workplace.* New York: Russell Sage Foundation; Cambridge, MA: Harvard University Press, 2006.

Margolis, Jane and Allan Fisher. *Unlocking the Clubhouse: Women in Computing.* Cambridge, MA: MIT Press, 2003.

Martin, Molly, ed. *Hard-Hatted Women: Life on the Job.* Seattle: Seal Press, 1997.

Martz, Sandra, ed. *If I Had a Hammer: Women's Work in Poetry, Fiction, and Photographs.* Watsonville, CA: Papier-Mache Press, 1990.

McCormick, Dale. *Against the Grain: A Carpentry Manual for Women.* Iowa City: Iowa City Women's Press, 1977.

McPhee, John. *Uncommon Carriers.* New York: Farrar, Straus and Giroux, 2006.

Medina, Ana M. "On the Day I Finally Cried at Work," *Pride and a Paycheck.* Vol. 8, No. 2 (March/April 2006).

Melendez, Miguel. *We Took the Streets: Fighting for Latino Rights with the Young Lords.* New York: St. Martin's Press, 2003.

Melich, Tanya. *The Republican War against Women: An Insider's Report from behind the Lines.* New York: Bantam Books, 1996.

Michelson, Maureen and Michael Dressler. *Women and Work: Photographs and Personal Writings.* Japan: New Sage Press, 1986.

Mitchell, Joseph. *Up in the Old Hotel.* New York: Pantheon Books, 1992.

Moccio, Francine. *Contradicting Male Power and Privilege: Class, Race and Gender in the Building Trades.* PhD. Dissertation, New School for Social Research, 1992.

Moore, Marat. *Women in the Mines: Stories of Life and Work.* New York: Twayne Publishers, 1996.

Moses, Claire Goldberg, and Heidi Hartmann, eds. *U.S. Women in Struggle: A Feminist Studies Anthology.* Urbana: University of Illinois Press, 1995.

Murray, Pauli. *The Autobiography of a Black Activist, Feminist, Lawyer, Priest, and Poet.* Knoxville: The University of Tennessee Press, 1989.

National Women's Law Center. Washington, DC. *Invisible Again: The Impact of Changes in Federal Funding in Vocational Programs for Women and Girls.* 2002.

———. *Title IX: An Educational Opportunity in Vocational Education: A Promise Still Owed to the Nation's Young Women.* 2002.

Needleman, Ruth. *Black Freedom Fighters in Steel: The Struggle for Democratic Unionism.* Ithaca, NY: Cornell University Press, 2003.

New York City Commission on Human Rights. *Building Barriers: Discrimination in New York City's Construction Trades (Executive Summary).* New York: 1993.

New York State Organized Crime Task Force. *Corruption and Racketeering in the New York City Construction Industry: Final Report to Governor Mario M. Cuomo.* New York: 1989.

Niemann, Linda Grant. *Railroad Voices.* Palo Alto, CA: Stanford University Press, 1990.

———. *On the Rails: A Woman's Journey.* San Francisco: Cleis Press, 1997.

Northrup, Herbert R. and John A. Larson. *The Impact of the AT&T—EEOC Consent Decree.* Labor Relations and Public Policy Series, No. 20. Philadelphia: Industrial Research Unit, The Wharton School, University of Pennsylvania, 1979.

NOW Legal Defense and Education Fund and Association for Union Democracy. *Manual for Survival: For Women in Nontraditional Employment*. New York: Association for Union Democracy and NOW Legal Defense Education Fund, 1993; Revised edition, 1999.

O'Farrell, Brigid and Sharon L. Harland. "Craftworkers and Clerks: The Effect of Male Co-worker Hostility on Women's Satisfaction with Non-traditional Jobs." Social Problems, 29 (February 1982).

———. "Women in Blue-Collar Occupations, Traditional and Non-traditional," in Ann Helton Stromberg and Shirley Harkess, eds. *Women Working: Theories and Facts in Perspective*. Mountain View, CA: Mayfield, 1988.

Orleck, Annelise. *Common Sense and a Little Fire: Women and Working-Class Politics in the United States, 1900–1965*. Chapel Hill: The University of North Carolina Press, 1995.

Paap, Kirsten. *Masculinities under Construction: Gender, Class and Race in a Man's Man's World*. PhD. Dissertation. University of Wisconsin, 1999.

Palladino, Grace. *Dreams of Dignity, Workers of Vision: A History of the IBEW*. Washington, DC: International Brotherhood of Electrical Workers, 1991.

Plant, Melissa. *Hack: How I Stopped Worrying about What to Do with My Life and Started Driving a Yellow Cab*. New York: Random House, 2007.

Price, Richard. *Bloodbrothers*. New York: First Mariner Books, 1999.

Price, Vivian. *Hammering It Out: Community Pressure and Affirmative Action in U.S. Highway Construction Employment*. PhD. Dissertation, University of California, Irvine, 2000.

Reskin, Barbara and Heidi Hartmann. *Women's Work, Men's Work, Sex Segregation on the Job*. Washington, DC: National Academy Press, 1986.

Robertson, Nan. *The Girls in the Balcony: Women, Men, and The New York Times*. New York: Random House, 1992.

Rose, Stephen J. and Heidi I. Hartmann. *Still a Man's Labor Market: The Long-Term Earning's Gap*. Institute for Women's Policy Research, Washington DC, 2004.

Rosen, Ruth. *The World Split Open: How the Modern Women's Movement Changed America*. New York: Penguin Group, 2000.

Rowbotham, Sheila. *A Century of Women: The History of Women in Britain and the United States*. London: Penguin Books, 1997.

Ruffini, Gene. *Harry Van Arsdale Jr.: Labor's Champion*. Armonk, NY: M.E. Sharpe, 2003.

Samuelson, Paul A. *Economics*. New York: McGraw-Hill Book, 1973.

Schroedel, Jean Reith. *Alone in a Crowd: Women in the Trades Tell Their Stories*. Philadelphia, PA: Temple University Press, 1985.

Seely, Megan. *Fight Like a Girl: How to Be a Fearless Feminist*. New York: New York University Press, 2007.

Sewell, Stacy Kinlock. "Left on the Bench: The New York Construction Trades and Racial Integration, 1960–1972." *New York History* (Spring, 2002).

———. "Review, State of the Union. A Century of American Labor." *New York History* (Summer 2004).

Shaw, Lynn J. *Diverse Working Class Women in the Skilled Trades: An Apprenticeship Model for Success*. PhD. Dissertation, Claremont Graduate University and San Diego State University, 2001.

Sherr, Lynn. *Susan B. Anthony in Her Own Words*. New York: Random House, 1995.

———. *Outside the Box. A Memoir*. Emmaus, Pa.: Rodale Press, 2006.

Sidey, Ken, ed. *Stanley Basic Plumbing: Pro Tips and Simple Steps*. Des Moines, Iowa: Stanley Books, 2002.

Siegel, Deborah. *Sisterhood Interrupted: From Radical Women To Grrls Gone Wild*. New York: Palgrave Macmillan, 2007.

Sjoholm, Barbara, ed. *Steady As She Goes: Women's Adventures at Sea*. Seattle: Seal Press, 2003.

Summerfield, Penny. *Women Workers in the Second World War: Production and Patriarchy in Conflict*. 2nd edition. London: Routledge, 1989.

Swerdlow, Marian. *Underground Woman: My Four Years as a New York City Subway Conductor*. Philadelphia, PA: Temple University Press, 1998.

Talese, Gay. *Fame and Obscurity*. New York: World Publishing, 1970.

Tillman, Ray M. and Michael S. Cummings. *The Transformation of U. S. Unions: Voices, Visions, and Strategies from the Grassroots*. Boulder, Co: Lynne Rienner Publishers, 1999.

Treanor, Nick. *The Feminist Movement*. San Diego: Greenhaven Press, 2002.

Union Women's Alliance to Gain Equality. *Organize: A Working Women's Handbook.* Revised edition. California: Union Women's Alliance to Gain Equality, 1981.

U.S. Census Bureau. *Statistical Abstract of the United States: 2003.* Washington, DC: Government Printing Office, 2003.

Waldinger, Roger. *Still the Promised City? African-Americans and New Immigrants in Postindustrial New York.* Cambridge, MA: Harvard University Press, 1996.

Waldinger, Roger and Thomas Bailey. "The Continuing Significance of Race: Racial Conflict and Racial Discrimination in Construction." *American Sociological Association,* 1991.

Wertheimer, Barbara Mayer. *We Were There: The Story of Working Women in America.* New York: Pantheon Books, 1977.

Witwer, David, "Labor and the New Millennium: Class, Vision, and Change. The Twenty-second North American Labor History Conference." *International Labor and Working Class History,* 60 (Fall 2001).

Wolfe, Tom. *The Right Stuff.* New York: Bantam Books, 1979.

Newspapers and Magazines

The Chief-Leader
Fire Lines
Hard Hat
Hard Hat News
In Brief (Legal Momentum Newsletter)
The Journal News
The Journal (Vulcan Society)
Labor Notes
Local 100 Express (Transport Workers Union)
Ms. Magazine
The New York Daily News
New York Magazine
New York Newsday
New York Post
New York Teacher
The New York Times
Pride and a Paycheck
Tradeswomen
Union Democracy Review
$75+ Club News

Web Sites

info@tradeswomennow.org
nycdcwomencarps@yahoogroups.com
nyctradeswomen@yahoogroups.com
operationpunchlist@yahoogroups.com
womeninoveralls@yahoogroups.com
Womensenewstoday@womensenews.org
www.cluw.org/
www.equalrights.org
www.gangbox@excite.com
www.herownwords.com
www.ilr.cornell.edu/AliceCook100th/

www.legalmomentum.org
www.lilytomlin.com
www.nlm.nih.gov/changingthefaceofmedicine/physicians/biography_273.html
www.RootsWeb.com/~kypulask/Military/WW2/Rosie.htm
www.sistersinthebuildingtrades.com
www.thelaborers.net/operating_engineers/iuoe_mcguire_guilty.htm
www.tradeswomen.org
www.tradeswomennowandtomorrow.org

Acknowledgments

Early on in this project, I started to think of the book as making a quilt. Many people have made contributions along the way. Some sent snippets of material for the project: countless news clippings have arrived in the mail and over the Internet. Others shared stories, suggestions, support, and offered encouragement in countless ways: Skip Drumm and Alan Gross; Sharon Kirtley; Bruce Kayton; Nancy Greenberg; Mimi and Abby Diamond; Bette Craig; Elaine Harger; Tami J. Friedman; Susan Wilson; Miriam Frank; Donn Mitchell; BJ Kowalski; Jack DuMars; Jeff Mar; Alex Ness; Philip Steinfeld; and especially Susan Lippman, Harry Berberian, and Herbert Hill.

For many years, Patricia Logan has been tirelessly transcribing these interviews. I appreciate her expert service, willingness to respond to the pressure of time, as well as the encouragement she has provided throughout this project.

The tradeswomen who have trusted me to tell their stories are always a source of inspiration—exemplars of undaunted courage. Needless to say, I am in their debt. The many "expert allies" who participated in this project and who, through their work—and some through their archival records—have made major contributions to the struggle to bring about a more just world, are owed my thanks...As are the many other advocates who contribute their mighty labors toward the goal of achieving equality—in our lifetimes.

In the summer of 2005, the Mesa Refuge did indeed provide a welcome respite from the world at an incredibly difficult time in my life—and an oasis to concentrate on my manuscript. My writer/companions, Mary Dickson and Barbara Gates, made the experience a safe and fruitful harbor.

I am indebted to my employer, District Council 37, American Federation of State, County, and Municipal Employees. My position on the *Public Employee Press* has provided a means to improve my writing and editorial skills. But more than that, many people at DC 37 have provided a constant source of encouragement over the last four years. I appreciate all of their good wishes.

I am also indebted to my workmates on the *PEP*—especially to Greg Heires, who told me to read my contract; to EJ Dobson, my "coach" who offered tough love to get me moving; to Molly Charboneau for her enthusiastic exhortations; and to my editor, Bill Schleicher—a Dutch uncle, Jewish mother and mentor—rolled into one source of invaluable support. The incomparable, calm and competent Rose Rizzo has made an important contribution to this project and I am in her debt.

I am especially grateful to my Inwood family in New York City—Russell Smith, Jessie Smith, and Diana French, for their countless acts of patience, support, and love. And to my sisters, Mary Butler, Betsy Walters, and Susie Morin, who, as always, have been a fount of love and encouragement. I am especially indebted to Susie and my brother-in-law, Philip Morin—a master craftsman—for reading almost the entire manuscript and their many helpful suggestions. Also to my brother-in-law David Walters, master boat builder—for sharing the image of concentrating on the "cabinet." And to my newest brother-in-law, Danny Hebert, for his enthusiasm as he waits to read the book! My New Orleans family is a constant source of support. Their love has infused every aspect of this work.

I am indebted to a number of historians who welcomed me into their circle. Stacy Kinlock Sewell generously made time in her very busy life to read eight chapters and to offer an invaluable critique. Nancy MacLean provided helpful editorial comments and encouragement at difficult moments. Her own work is a source of constant inspiration for me. My participation in the North American Labor History Conference gave birth to the idea for the book. I am indebted to David Witwer for inviting me to present my first academic paper at the conference. Many historians at the NALHC have provided encouragement and have offered helpful suggestions: Nancy Gabin, Elizabeth Faue, Alice Kessler-Harris, Janine Lanza, Lisa Phillips, and Marc Stern, among others.

Debra Berhhardt always said, "Archives are forever." Thanks to her, the Robert F. Wagner Labor Archives is the repository for collections that document women in the labor movement: the "movers and shakers" as well as other rebels, reformers and "troublemakers," without which—as she wisely recognized—the history of the labor movement is incomplete. I am greatly indebted to Gail Malmgreen, archivist extraordinaire, for her many thoughtful acts and her willingness to be of assistance.

My editor at Palgrave Macmillan, Chris Chappell, has my sincere gratitude for forcing me, in his firm yet gentle fashion, to get to the finish line. Early on, my editors for the Palgrave Oral History Series—Linda Shopes and Bruce M. Stave—believed in this project. They have consistently been encouraging and supportive, while trying to urge me onward!

There is one person without whom this book would not exist: my friend and colleague, Robert Fitch. I thank him for all of his editorial assistance, his countless readings of these chapters, his many valuable suggestions, insights, and patience. He never tired of the conversation. For that and all else, I am in his debt.

Index